Wissenschaftliche Untersuchungen zum Neuen Testament · 2. Reihe

Herausgeber / Editor
Jörg Frey (München)

Mitherausgeber / Associate Editors
Friedrich Avemarie (Marburg)
Judith Gundry-Volf (New Haven, CT)
Hans-Josef Klauck (Chicago, IL)

257

Joel Kennedy

The Recapitulation of Israel

Use of Israel's History in Matthew 1:1–4:11

Mohr Siebeck

JOEL KENNEDY, born 1970; 2008 PhD at the University of Aberdeen; presently involved with independent research and teaching.

ISBN 978-3-16-149825-1
ISSN 0340-9570 (Wissenschaftliche Untersuchungen zum Neuen Testament, 2. Reihe)

The Deutsche Nationalbibliothek lists this publication in the Deutsche Nationalbibliographie; detailed bibliographic data is available in the Internet at *http://dnb.d-nb.de*.

The book was printed by Laupp & Göbel in Nehren on non-aging paper and bound by Buchbinderei Nädele in Nehren.

Printed in Germany.

Acknowledgements

This book is a revised version of my doctoral thesis submitted to the University of Aberdeen in February 2008. The research and composition of the thesis could only have been possible through the support of many kind persons. Moving to Aberdeen was a tremendous undertaking, and yet a remarkable amount of details all providentially came together to make it a reality. Many family members as well as numerous friends helped in a diversity of thoughtful ways. A generous financial scholarship from the Saint Andrews Society of North Carolina assisted with expenses. The loving congregation at Gilcomston South Church of Scotland warmly embraced and helped my family immensely throughout our time in Aberdeen. I am especially grateful to my supervisor, Professor Francis Watson, for his excellent oversight and generous patience throughout the entire process of this thesis. The examiners of my thesis, Tomas Bokedal and Michael Bird, made numerous valuable suggestions that I utilized. Many thanks to several critical readers who offered various helpful comments: Dale Allison, Stanley Porter, Jason Hood, Robyn Kennedy, Elaine Wainwright, and Eugene Boring. I very much appreciate Jörg Frey's recommendation of this work for publication, as well as the help of Henning Ziebritzki and the staff at Mohr Siebeck. The interest, patience, and loyal support of my children, Elisabeth, Victoria, and Benjamin, I gladly acknowledge. While much of my time was dominated with this work, there were those valued moments that I happily left it to hang out with them. Finally, with the utmost gratitude and recognition, my wife Robyn is to be enormously thanked for the myriad of ways she lovingly supported, accommodated, and encouraged me. Therefore, to her this work is affectionately and appreciatively dedicated. *Avise La Fin*.

November 2008   Joel Kennedy

Table of Contents

Chapter 1

Introduction

1.1 Approaching the Gospel of Matthew

In his work on the early church, Ernest Renan encapsulated the conviction of many throughout church history regarding the Gospel of Matthew when he wrote,

Cela était plus important que l'exactitude biographique, et l'Évangile de Matthieu, tout bien pesé, est le livre le plus important du christianisme, le livre le plus important qui ait jamais été écrit. Ce n'est pas sans raison que, dans la classification des écrits de la nouvelle Bible, on lui a donné la première place. La biographie d'un grand homme est une partie de son œuvre.[1]

For almost two millennia, the Gospel of Matthew has functioned within the Christian community as an authoritative and dominant canonical writing, as well as being a respected and influential text among numerous individuals and groups outside of Christianity. The Gospel of Matthew has served a pervasive and substantial role in the growth and expansion of Christianity throughout history. In the patristic period,[2] Matthew was the most dominant Gospel, being most frequently utilized in the ancient church.[3] Matthew's dominance continued during the medieval era, throughout the Reformation period and the subsequent Enlightenment age, and on into the modern period.[4] While approaches to the text and teaching of Matthew have changed and developed over the centuries, it has nevertheless maintained a prominent and influential position throughout these centuries. Scholarly study of the Gospel of Matthew has been practiced throughout the centuries, and each successive generation of scholars is indebted to

---

[1] Renan, *Les Évangiles et la seconde génération Chrétienne*, 212–213.

[2] Well exhibited in the volumes by Simonetti, *Matthew 1–13* and *Matthew 14–28*. Full documentation can be found in E. Massaux, *Influence de l'évangile de saint Matthien sur la littérature chrétienne avant saint Irénée*.

[3] van der Horst, *Jews and Christians in Their Graeco-Roman Context*, 208.

[4] For overview of the history of the interpretation of Matthew, see Luz's *Wirkungsgeschichte* in his commentaries on Matthew and *Matthew in History*; Kealy, *Matthew's Gospel and the History of Biblical Interpretation*; and Clarke, *The Gospel of Matthew and Its Readers*.

those previous for furthering the knowledge and understanding of this gospel. Current scholarly study of Matthew certainly shows no sign of abating, as witnessed by the explosion of commentaries on this gospel in the last twenty years. Proliferation in scholarly methods of research has contributed greatly toward this increase of writing about Matthew as varying perspectives are brought to the text.

While the text and teaching of Matthew has been subjected to much scholarly attention throughout the centuries, beginning in the eighteenth and nineteenth centuries scholars who were greatly influenced by the surrounding philosophical environment of the Enlightenment pursued study of the biblical texts utilizing a more vigorous historical criticism than had generally been practiced in the past. This led to an expansion of critical methods for ascertaining the history of early Christianity. Following a period in the nineteenth and early twentieth centuries of closer attention to the earliest Christian sources, particularly Mark and Q, which was especially spurred on by a critical examination of the historical origins of Christianity, Matthew then began to be studied with renewed vigor. This renewal of interest in Matthew principally resulted from its being positioned as a work dependent upon Mark, Q, and other possible sources, which has been the dominant view in biblical scholarship.[5] The Gospel of Matthew has continued to be the subject of intense study by a wide variety of scholars that have sought to further advance scholarly study of the text.

Matthew has been studied utilizing various types of critical approaches that have especially dominated the twentieth century: source, form, tradition, redaction, literary, and social-scientific criticism. All of these approaches have contributed insights that have greatly expanded knowledge and understanding of Matthew's Gospel. Utilizing these approaches, numerous subjects and themes have been assessed in Matthew from different perspectives: historical, social, cultural, literary, and theological. The questions, work, and knowledge to be gleaned from Matthew appear to be almost endless given the variety of critical approaches that scholars can now utilize, and further evolution of critical approaches will no doubt continue to expand into the future.

---

[5] This has certainly been the prevailing scholarly viewpoint, with a variety of perspectives within the two-source theory. Beyond the standard critical commentaries, see Streeter, *The Four Gospels*; Kilpatrick, *The Origins of the Gospel according to Matthew*; Stein, *Studying the Synoptic Gospels*; France, *Matthew: Evangelist and Teacher*; Stanton, *A Gospel for a New People*. However, it deserves mention that many scholars have dissented, providing other viewpoints that, although they command less support, nevertheless offer an array of helpful insights. See Goodacre, *The Synoptic Problem: A Way through the Maze* and *The Case Against Q*; Farmer, *The Synoptic Problem*; Dungan, *A History of the Synoptic Problem*; Cope, *Matthew: A Scribe Trained for the Kingdom of Heaven*.

One thematic area within Matthean studies that has long deserved further attention, utilizing a variety of critical approaches, is the christological use of Israel's history in Matthew 1:1–4:11, which is the subject of this book. Due to the substantial amount of data that can be gleaned from Matthew and the word-limitations of a thesis, the present work has necessarily confined itself to these early chapters of Matthew. The primary area of focus for this work is to examine and describe the christological use of Israel's history in Matthew 1:1–4:11 with rigorous attention to every element that demonstrates this usage. The prevailing theme or concept that adequately encapsulates the use of Israel's history maintained in Matthew is that of recapitulation.

Due acknowledgement of Irenaeus' initial contribution of the concept of recapitulation in Jesus' life to the seed-thoughts of this work should be noted. However, his conception of recapitulation is used in connection with Jesus' recapitulation of Adam and humanity rather than Israel.[6] Also beneficial was the work of N. T. Wright, where for example he notes that the evangelists tell "the form of the story of Israel, now reworked in terms of a single human life." Jesus is the climax of Israel's history and thus the gospels give "the story of Jesus told as the history of Israel in miniature."[7] Elsewhere, Wright identifies Jesus as the recapitulation of Israel in his reading of the parable of the sower, which is a programmatic explanation of Jesus' own ministry.[8] In addition, the general use of the concept recapitulation by various scholars to describe parts of Matthew also provided a further impulse. However, the need became clear that this concept in Matthew should be further studied in much greater detail because to date there has been no substantial study of this theme in Matthew.

While appropriation of the concept recapitulation has often been used to characterize portions of Jesus' experience in the early chapters of Matthew, especially on 2:15, recapitulation has not been closely analyzed by scholars. This study has sought to fill this lacuna with meticulous consideration of the utilization within Matthew's Gospel of recapitulation. In Matthew, Israel's history is recapitulated, and the manner in which this recapitulation is communicated is the overarching argument of this work. In brief, the concept of recapitulation that is utilized in this study, which seeks to describe Matthew 1:1–4:11, is primarily focused on the element of repetition. This especially involves how Israel's history is repeated and reenacted in the presentation of Jesus in Matthew 1–4. Also included in the concept of recapitulation that is discussed within this study: the summing

---

[6] See Irenaeus, "Against Heresies," in Roberts and Donaldson (eds.), *The Ante-Nicene Fathers* vol. 1, 454–455, 547–548; cf. Torrance, *Divine Meaning: Studies in Patristic Hermeneutics*, 68–69, 121–122.

[7] Wright, *The New Testament and the People of God*, 401–402.

[8] Wright, *Jesus and the Victory of God*, 235–237.

up of Israel's history in Jesus' early life; Jesus as the corporate representative of his people Israel; and Jesus as the embodiment of Israel in his recapitulation. All of these are aspects and components in the discussion of Jesus as the recapitulation of Israel.

1.2 Christology in Matthew

To fully situate the standpoint and argument of the present work, it is considerably important and would prove beneficial to briefly survey two major areas of scholarly focus in Matthean studies: christology and the use of the Old Testament. As mentioned above, there have been multitudes of themes studied in Matthew, some of which intersect with these two key areas.[9] Many of these themes and topics underlie this work to some degree and are discussed at various points; however, for the purpose of adequately introducing this work, christology and the use of the Old Testament are the two most relevant components in situating a proper focus upon investigating the recapitulation of Israel in Matthew 1:1–4:11. The following section will briefly survey Matthean research on these two topics, the range of scholarly views, the extensive ways that these two topics have been further sub-divided in scholarly research, as well as providing comments upon how the present work fits these viewpoints.[10]

A brief foray into the various critical approaches in light of their interaction, influence, and help with understanding christology in Matthew is important in properly orienting the present work in terms of that ongoing discussion. Study of the christology of Matthew has occupied the attention of scholars from the very beginning[11] due to the obvious orientation of the Gospel itself upon presenting and proclaiming the life and teaching of Jesus Christ. The text and teaching of Matthew has dominated the church's understanding of christology throughout the history of the church. Much of

---

[9] Beyond the standard critical commentaries, there are numerous works on Matthew generally that indicate many of these themes. See Stanton, *The Interpretation of Matthew* and *Gospel for a New People*; France, *Matthew: Evangelist and Teacher*; McKnight, 'Matthew', 527–541; Riches, *Matthew*; Luz, *The Theology of the Gospel of Matthew*; Senior, *What Are They Saying About Matthew?*; Bauer and Powell, *Treasures New and Old*; Carter, *Matthew: Storyteller, Interpreter, Evangelist*; Aune, *Gospel of Matthew in Current Study*; Gurtner and Nolland, *Built Upon the Rock*.

[10] While most of the following survey by necessity must give prominence to works within the last hundred years, this is by no means out of any disrespect for scholars' work in earlier centuries. Indeed, no current scholarly work could be done without their prior work, where all should rightfully acknowledge that we stand on the shoulders of giants. Cf. Allison, *Studies in Matthew*, 117–131.

[11] See Simonetti, *Matthew 1–13* and *Matthew 14–28*.

this understanding in the patristic and medieval periods was dominated by various kinds of historical and dogmatic questions that faced the church. During and following the period of the Enlightenment, further types of historical questions were pursued, and this led toward the expansion of critical approaches that now underlie modern scholarly biblical research. Each of these approaches has been utilized in ascertaining the christological teaching of Matthew and will be further dealt with below. While additional research on the history of the church's interpretation of Matthew in regard to its christology is valuable and worthwhile,[12] the work of this thesis must primarily remain centered upon the text.

The dominant focus for the discussion of Matthew's christology has especially centered on the use of various titles/desriptions: Messiah/Christ,[13] Son of God/divine sonship,[14] Son of Man,[15] Kyrios, Son of David,[16] Son of Abraham, Teacher/Preacher, Healer,[17] Prophet,[18] the Coming One, Servant, Emmanuel,[19] Shepherd,[20] and Wisdom.[21] Many scholars have undertaken efforts to outline the use and meaning of these titles in Matthew through general surveys. Others have offered more specialized studies that have focused exclusively upon one title in Matthew, utilizing various critical approaches. Nevertheless, efforts to understand and define the christology of Matthew with sole attention to the titles in Matthew has met ample disapproval by various scholars of late, which is further dealt with below.

Within the work on titles in Matthew, further attempts have been undertaken by some scholars to determine the most important title for this Gos-

---

[12] Well exhibited in the commentaries on Matthew by Luz.

[13] Verseput, *The Rejection of the Humble Messianic King: A Study of the Composition of Matthew 11–12.*

[14] Head, *Christology and the Synoptic Problem*, 200–214.

[15] Luz, "The Son of Man in Matthew: Heavenly Judge or Human Christ," 3–21.

[16] Gibbs, "Purpose and Pattern in Matthew's Use of the Title 'Son of David'," 446–464; Suhl, "Der Davidssohn im Matthäusevangelium," 67–81; Burger, *Jesus als Davidssohn*, 72–106; Kingsbury, "The Title 'Son of David' in Matthew's Gospel," 591–602; Head, *Christology and the Synoptic Problem*, 180–186; van Aarde, "ΙΗΣΟΥΣ, The Davidic Messiah, As Political Saviour in Matthew's History," 7–31. Arguing for a royal, davidic christology in Matthew, see Nolan, *The Royal Son of God: The Christology of Matthew 1–2 in the Setting of the Gospel.*

[17] Duling, "The Therapeutic Son of David: An Element in Matthew's Christology," 392–410.

[18] Knowles, *Jeremiah in Matthew's Gospel: The Rejected Prophetic Motif in Matthean Redaction.*

[19] Kupp, *Matthew's Emmanuel: Divine Presence and God's People in the First Gospel.*

[20] Garbe, *Der Hirte Israels*; Willetts, *Matthew's Messianic Shepherd-King.*

[21] Suggs, *Wisdom, Christology, and Law in Matthew's Gospel*; Johnson, "Reflections on a Wisdom Approach to Matthew's Christology," 44–64; Deutsch, *Lady Wisdom, Jesus, and the Sages: Metaphor and Social Context in Matthew's Gospel.*

pel. One of the most common positions in this regard has been especially led by Jack Dean Kingsbury, who strongly argues that Son of God is the preeminent title for Matthew's story.[22] Understanding the use of Son of God in Matthew is an important component of this work because it plays a significant role in the early chapters and closely relates to the recapitulation theme. The attention given by Kingsbury to the Son of God title in Matthew has proven valuable in describing and understanding Matthew's christology, and this study has sought to build on his insights in many ways. Also important for this work is a correction of some overemphasis in Kingsbury on Son of God as "the unique filial relationship that exists between God and Jesus"[23] which overshadows other significant elements of what is textually communicated about Son of God in the early pericopes of Matthew. The other aspects of what Son of God means in Matthew, while they are occasionally dealt with cursorily by Kingsbury, are often relegated to minor subsidiary aspects, therefore obscuring the overall presentation of Jesus as Son of God in Matthew. When closely studied, Jesus as the Son of God in Matthew reveals further varied meanings beyond his filial relation to God.[24] Israel was called God's son (Exod 4:22–23; Hos 11:1), as was Israel's king (2 Sam 7:14; Ps 89:26–27). Matthew appropriates these elements in his overall christology, and these further christological elements are a large part of the focus of this study on Jesus and the recapitulation of Israel.

James Dunn concurs that Son of God is the "most important christological affirmation for Matthew." However, he rightly recognizes that Jesus' identification with Israel is an important component in Matthew's Son of God christology. Dunn summarizes that "Matthew thinks of Jesus' sonship in terms of a mission that fulfilled the destiny of Israel."[25] Denying the filial viewpoint on Matthew's use of Son of God is obviously unwarranted, as it becomes even more apparent later in the Gospel (cf. 11:25–27). However, this study argues that Matthew's employment of Son of God in these early chapters most directly relates to its prior use in the Old Testament in

---

[22] Kingsbury, *Matthew as Story*, 57, 76, 93, 161–163; cf. *Matthew: Structure, Christology, Kingdom*, 162.

[23] Kingsbury, *Matthew as Story*, 51.

[24] Davies and Allison, *Matthew*, 1.720, state that Son of God in Matthew "is to some extent multivalent ... varies according to context." Luz, *Studies in Matthew*, 93–96, argues that Son of God in Matthew is both a confessional title (vertical dimension) and ethical title (horizontal dimension).

[25] Dunn, *Christology in the Making*, 48–49, 59. Cf. Gibbs, "The Son of God as Torah Incarnate in Matthew," 38–39: "In his unique filial relationship to God, Jesus embodies Israel's calling in the covenant to be the Son of God ... Jesus' sonship is Israel's sonship"; and Dodd, *The Founder of Christianity*, 105–108. The present work has sought to examine the validity of such christological statements by a closer investigation of Matthew's text to a degree not undertaken in these works.

relation to corporate Israel as son of God and to the king as a representative. The use of the Son of God title in the early chapters of Matthew is vitally connected to Matthew's use of Israel's history and the important fulfillment theme that Matthew accentuates, which is where recapitulation is especially prominent.[26] Attention to the wider narrative context and characterization adds vital information for correctly understanding the meaning of Son of God in Matthew 1:1–4:11. In addition, a significant argument of this study is that the use of Son of God is cumulative, in that more and more information is set forth to the hearer and reader, which is true not only in the reading of chapters 1–4 but throughout the rest of the Gospel.[27]

While many have disagreed with Kingsbury on his standpoint that Son of God serves as the key title for Matthew,[28] for the more closely defined purposes of this thesis that discussion must be set aside other than a few brief remarks here. In regard to titles in Matthew, several scholars have argued strongly that this effort to discover the one dominant title is seriously at fault and misrepresents the variegated orientation of the Gospel upon Jesus Christ,[29] with all of the titles serving a role in the theological presentation of Jesus Christ. Those scholars that have argued against picking one title over the others, most notably Davies and Allison,[30] have persuaded many and are most certainly right in their detailed case for properly appropriating all of the titles to apprehend christology in Matthew.[31] The relations between the titles is also an area for further exploration toward determining a fuller understanding of Matthew's christology.[32] As Luz observes, "Each of the titles encompasses particular aspects vis-à-vis the others; each denotes only aspects of Matthean christology."[33]

---

[26] Kingsbury, *Matthew: Structure, Christology, Kingdom,* 15, 51, does very briefly mention Jesus recapitulating Israel.

[27] Nolland, *Matthew,* 42: "As Matthew's story unfolds, the sense of what it might mean to identify Jesus as the Son also unfolds in all its richness and variety."

[28] Cf. Hill, "The Figure of Jesus in Matthew's Story: A Response to Professor Kingsbury's Literary-Critical Probe," 37–52; cf. Allison, "The Son of God as Israel: A Note on Matthean Christology," 74–81; Head, *Christology and the Synoptic Problem,* 186, 201.

[29] Tuckett, *Christology and the New Testament,* 10, 119, 130, aptly describes the christology of Matthew as "a rather variegated picture," and he also emphasizes the importance of discerning the narrative christology of Matthew.

[30] Davies and Allison, *Matthew,* 3.721, aptly note that "christology is more – much more – than titles."

[31] Cf. McKnight, "Matthew," 533, synthesizes and summarizes Matthew's christology: "Jesus is God's Messiah who fulfills OT promise, reveals God's will and inaugurates the kingdom of heaven through his public ministry, passion, and resurrection, and consequently, reigns over the new people of God."

[32] Cf. Head, *Christology and the Synoptic Problem,* 201.

[33] Luz, *Studies in Matthew,* 96.

Further attention beyond the titles is also crucial as other christological actions, attributes, characterization, and themes can be recognized when the whole of Matthew is utilized. As Mogens Müller has recently complained, "little attention has been paid to the so-called indirect christology, the constructing of the theological impact of Jesus in the way of telling his story."[34] This type of approach is well exhibited in a monograph by D. Kupp and a commentary by Ben Witherington. Kupp offers a narratival, christological reading of Matthew 1–4, particularly within his thesis on Emmanuel in arguing for a story of divine presence in Matthew.[35] Witherington provides a sapiential reading of Matthew, highlighting Matthew's wisdom christology, with attention to narratival and biographical elements as well.[36] Also crucial toward understanding Matthean christology is the interweaving of Jesus' teaching and person.[37]

Tending to the other means of communicating christology in Matthew beyond titles is an important argument of this thesis. Narrative insights, thematic portrayals, structural details, use of the Old Testament and other literature and traditions, parallels and correspondence (also called typology), and sociological insights have all contributed to understanding the christology of Matthew.[38] Charting the historical development of christology in comparison with the rest of the New Testament and other early Christian literature is also an important enterprise that brings Matthew's christology into focus.

While understanding the titles in Matthew is obviously an important area of focus, the discussion of titles in reality should serve as a subsidiary area of christology in Matthew and not be the predominant focus of attention. This insight has been convincingly argued, notably by Leander Keck,[39] and thus a fuller pursuit of other aspects in Matthew's christology has been undertaken by some scholars. One little known but immensely helpful study that covers the whole of Matthew is the work by William Kynes, *A Christology of Solidarity*. In this monograph, Kynes highlighted

---

[34] Müller, "The Theological Interpretation of the Figure of Jesus in the Gospel of Matthew: Some Principle Features in Matthean Christology," 157; cf. Luz, *Matthew 21–28*, 637–642.

[35] Kupp, *Matthew's Emmanuel*, 52–66.

[36] Witherington, *Matthew*, 16–21.

[37] Thiselton, *New Horizons in Hermeneutics*, 286–288.

[38] France, *Matthew: Evangelist and Teacher*, 279–317, provides a helpful "portrait of Jesus' that includes a more extensive, multifaceted grasp of christology in Matthew that moves beyond titles alone"; cf. Blair, *Jesus in the Gospel of Matthew*; McKnight, "Matthew," 532–535; Luz, "Eine thetische Skizze der matthäischen Christologie," 221–236; de Jonge, *Christology in Context*, 91–96; Schnackenburg, *Jesus in the Gospels: A Biblical Christology*, 74–130; Matera, *New Testament Christology*, 26–47; Hurtado, *Lord Jesus Christ*, 316–340.

[39] Keck, "Toward the Renewal of New Testament Christology," 362–377.

a significant aspect of Matthew's christology "by focusing on Jesus' representative role ... an appreciation of Jesus' solidarity with his people as
their representative before God."[40] The insights and general methodology
of Kynes' work proved helpful for the work of this thesis. Beyond his
commentary in collaboration with W. D. Davies, Dale Allison has also
contributed an excellent study in *The New Moses* that not only surveys
much of the background literature, but also deeply delves into Matthew's
text for ascertaining the presentation of Jesus as the new Moses.[41] Many of
his insights, as well as his methodology, aided the research for this thesis.

While closer examination to the christological details of Matthew's text
remain to be done, the refinement of approaches to christology in Matthew
will definitely correct some of the deficiencies of the past, and it is a hope
that the present work will enhance a greater understanding of christology
in Matthew. This study seeks to penetrate further into Matthew's christology, in as detailed a manner as possible, by especially seeking to understand the story of Jesus in Matthew's early chapters as a recapitulation of
Israel's history, something that to date has not been undertaken to this degree.

Form criticism and tradition criticism have offered various useful insights toward understanding christology in Matthew, led obviously by the
pioneering work of Bultmann,[42] Dibelius,[43] and Schmidt.[44] While the practice of form criticism was objected to by some, and then later overshad-
owed by other subsequent approaches, it led to many constructive avenues
of thinking that has undergirded all subsequent scholarly work, whether
acknowledged or not. Distinguishing the historical Jesus' life and teaching
from subsequent developments in the early church was an important conception. Acknowledging the changes and developments that took place
over the era that ranged from Jesus' ministry to the final composition of
the Gospels is now commonplace. Certainly varying disagreements have
been expressed as to how it developed, why, and how expansive the developments really were. While these issues continue to occupy scholarly research, the debt to form criticism is nevertheless acknowledged. Seeking to
define the varying episodes that the Gospels utilize in their presentation of
Jesus was also a significant development in christological understanding.
While the ways these episodes and scenes were defined and categorized
have often been disagreed with, the practice of seeking to understand these
smaller units of the Gospels rightfully continues to be examined and discussed.

---

[40] Kynes, *A Christology of Solidarity*, 7.

[41] Allison, *The New Moses*.

[42] Bultmann, *The History of the Synoptic Tradition*.

[43] Dibelius, *From Tradition to Gospel*.

[44] Schmidt, *Der Rahmen der Geschichte Jesu*.

The research work of this thesis has benefited from form critical insights and it has been utilized at various points. It underlies the discussion of Matthew's christology in relation to recapitulation, although it remains for the most part a critical tool utilized in the research and is not directly discussed as such. The present work does not delve into the tradition history of Matthew 1–4, other than to note some of the discussion of that endeavor and highlight components that directly affect interpretation of some of the pericopes. The chapter on the genealogy also was aided by Old Testament scholars that practiced form criticism on the various kinds of literature, especially in regard to classifying genealogies.

Another area of critical focus that directly resulted from both source[45] and form criticism is the work of redaction criticism, which has especially been useful for the work of this thesis in discovering and describing Matthew's christology.[46] Based on the most common synoptic theory that Matthew used and adapted Mark, Q, and probably other traditions, whether written or oral, redaction critics have interpreted Matthew's Gospel on this basis to determine Matthew's own theological perspective. By comparing and contrasting Matthew's use of Mark and Q, scholars have determined key aspects of Matthew's christology that have highlighted many aspects overlooked when the Synoptic Gospels are merely harmonized or when the Gospels are only interpreted with exclusive attention to one Gospel alone.[47] In addition, comparison and contrast with Luke's Gospel has also brought further insights into understanding Matthew's christology. Redaction criticism underlies much of the work of many commentaries, monographs, and articles on Matthew in the last fifty years and therefore has resulted in a profound influence on the discussion of the christological orientation of Matthew.

Unlike form and tradition criticism, which is less utilized in contemporary biblical scholarship,[48] redaction criticism remains a key interpretive viewpoint that underlies most scholars' work in describing Matthew's christology. The use of redaction criticism for understanding Matthew's christology informs and undergirds much of the present work. However, because Matthew 1–2 is unique to Matthew, except where there are some

---

[45] Allen, *Matthew* was an important early work in Matthew on source criticism.

[46] Key works in this regard are Bornkamm, Barth, and Held, *Tradition and Interpretation in Matthew*; Strecker, *Der Weg der Gerichtigkeit*; Rohde, *Rediscovering the Teaching of the Evangelists*; Gundry, *Matthew*; Gnilka, *Das Matthäusevangelium*; and Goppelt, *Theology of the New Testament*, 2.211–235.

[47] A helpful overview of synoptic research in relation to christology can be found in Head, *Christology and the Synoptic Problem*.

[48] Bauckham's, *Jesus and the Eyewitnesses: The Gospel as Eyewitness Testimony*, is a recent work that could possibly reinvigorate further discussion and development.

general common aspects that intersect with the early chapters of Luke,[49] use of redaction criticism in this regard is less useful for these chapters. For Matthew 1–2, the massive and erudite study by Raymond Brown on the infancy narrative in Matthew is a major resource of information, and throughout the discussion of Matthew 1–2 it was utilized.[50] With Matthew 3:1–4:11, this work does utilize many of the helpful insights that redaction criticism can bring to light for further understanding Matthew's christology. While primary attention is given to Matthew's text, comparison with the other Evangelists proves helpful in further understanding Matthew's work, particularly in reference to the christology that is communicated.

The last thirty years has seen an explosion of work by scholars utilizing literary and narrative criticism with considerable attention to Matthew as a unified coherent narrative. Many of the insights that scholars have highlighted using this method have coincided with and corroborated some of the conclusions drawn from redaction criticism. However, many scholars utilizing literary criticism have usually given exclusive focus to Matthew with less or no regard to other comparative historical and literary sources.[51] Kingsbury led the way in the literary approach to Matthew.[52] His earlier work primarily utilized redaction criticism,[53] but it has no doubt influenced his literary critical work on Matthew, which has exclusively focused upon the text of Matthew. Other scholars have furthered the use of literary criticism on Matthew with many helpful insights, such as David Bauer,[54] David Howell,[55] D. J. Weaver,[56] Janice Capel Anderson,[57] Margaret Davies,[58] Warren Carter,[59] Mark Allen Powell,[60] and John A. Barnet.[61] Focus on Jesus as the main character has been especially important. Common to literary criticism on Matthew is attention to plot, characterization, settings, structure, and discourse.

---

[49] There are some commonalities; however, this is not substantial enough to warrant an argument that Matthew used Luke or vice versa.

[50] Brown, *The Birth of the Messiah.*

[51] See Meier, "Gospel of Matthew," 4.623, for a particularly negative view of narrative criticism.

[52] Kingsbury, *Matthew as Story.*

[53] Kingsbury, *Matthew: Structure, Christology, Kingdom.*

[54] Bauer, *The Structure of Matthew's Gospel.*

[55] Howell, *Matthew's Inclusive Story.*

[56] Weaver, *Matthew's Missionary Discourse: A Literary Critical Analysis.*

[57] Anderson, *Matthew's Narrative Web.*

[58] Davies, *Matthew: Readings, A New Biblical Commentary.*

[59] Carter, *Matthew: Storyteller, Interpreter, Evangelist.*

[60] Powell, "The Plot and Subplots of Matthew's Gospel," 187–204; and "Matthew," 868–900.

[61] Barnet, *Not the Righteous but Sinners: M. M. Bakhtin's Theory of Aesthetics and the Problem of Reader-Character Interaction in Matthew's Gospel.*

Further christological insights have been gleaned utilizing other types of literary approaches such as reader-response,[62] deconstruction, feminist, and social criticism.[63] While these approaches frequently illuminate important details in Matthew, they are only dealt with cursorily in this thesis. However, one critical approach that proved instructive for this thesis is feminist criticism, which bridges literary and social-scientific criticism. The specific area in this thesis that this is generally utilized is in regard to the discussion of the five women in Matthew's genealogy.

The most helpful insight from literary critics is the appreciation of the whole of Matthew as story, a coherent narrative in and of itself that should be read and interpreted as a narrative. Eugene Boring duly assesses narrative in Matthew and the relation it has to christology when he writes that Matthew is "fashioned to express in narrative form the christological convictions of early Christianity."[64] Attention to the narratival coherence of Matthew underlies various areas in this work and is crucial to the argument at several points in the thesis, especially in regard to structure and literary unity. Narrative portrayal also plays a part in understanding Matthew's presentation of Jesus, and this is utilized at various points in this work as well.

Another burgeoning industry in Matthean studies is social-scientific criticism. Various scholars have sought to appropriate insights from the field of social-science in understanding Matthew's Gospel, some of which overlap in various ways with literary criticism.[65] At various points in this work, some of the helpful insights from social-scientific criticism are utilized in a general manner. Although much more could have been used, necessities of space demanded that it remain only a small part. In terms of direct implication for christology in Matthew in relation to the recapitulation of Israel, while there are certainly further avenues to be explored, it could not be adequately developed here.

Situating Matthew in the broader environmental milieu of Judaism, early Christianity, and the Greco-Roman world has been an essential area of research.[66] Exclusive focus upon the text of Matthew without compari-

---

[62] Mayordomo-Marín, *Den Anfang hören: Leserorientierte Evangelienexegese am Beispiel von Matthäus 1–2*.

[63] Moore, *Literary Criticism and the Gospels*.

[64] Boring, "Matthew," 109.

[65] Balch, *Social History of the Matthean Community*; Malina and Neyrey, *Calling Jesus Names*; Malina and Rohrbaugh, *Social-Science Commentary on the Synoptic Gospels*; Carter, *Matthew and the Margins*.

[66] Note the plea in this regard by Hengel, "Tasks of New Testament Scholarship," 67–86, which is a slightly abbreviated translation of "Aufgaben der neutestamentlichen Wissenschaft," 321–357. Well exhibited in regard to the Gospels is Cartlidge and Dungan, *Documents for the Study of the Gospels*.

son to other texts and approaches contemporary to it has been one of the dangers with exclusive utilization of literary criticism. The work of scholars in understanding the broader background of the time and environment is indispensable for understanding Matthew and his christology. Expansive growth in specialties of scholarly focus has been both a blessing and a curse in that only a small minority scholars can adequately command even a few of these specialties. However, the insights to be gleaned from this expansion in knowledge cannot be overlooked by scholars. Relying upon the results of others' work has therefore become a requisite in this regard, and collaborative studies that synthesize the knowledge from this wide field should prove increasingly necessary.

One key writer of this period is Josephus, and his works are of prime importance for understanding the history and traditions of the first century. Discussion of Josephus is especially important in chapter two of this thesis as it helps to highlight Matthew's recapitulation of Israel's exodus history in the early life of Jesus. Philo is another important writer for understanding the wider background of the Jewish world, and he is referenced at a several points in this work. Greco-Roman works are an important resource for language, historical, sociological, and cultural issues.[67] Furthermore, there is now some agreement that this Gospel is to be generally classified as a type of ancient biography.[68] The Greco-Roman background to Matthew is difficult to quantify in that specifics about Matthew's audience are not known. Although assumptions about the community of Matthew often proceed upon a Syrian background, this hypothesis, while certainly possible, is not an established fact.[69] Therefore, it appears reasonable based on the Gospel itself to assume for the present work that Matthew's hearers and readers were Jewish and Gentile believers and non-believers.[70] Nevertheless, the influence of the Greco-Roman environment upon Matthew's audience[71] is a complicated endeavor, and it appears best to proceed cau-

---

[67] Well exhibited in Danker, "Matthew: A Patriot's Gospel," 94–115. Also see Riches and Sim, *The Gospel of Matthew in its Roman Imperial Context*.

[68] Aune, *The New Testament in Its Literary Environment*, 46; Cf. Aune, *Greco-Roman Literature and the New Testament*, 107–126; Stanton, *Jesus of Nazareth in New Testament Preaching*, 117–136. Further discussion on the genre of Matthew see Talbert, *What is a Gospel? The Genre of the Canonical Gospels*; Shuler, *A Genre for the Gospels*; and Burridge, *What are the Gospels? A Comparison with Greco-Roman Biography*.

[69] Stanton, *Gospel for A New People*, xii, admits, after much work based on Antioch as Matthew's audience, that he was finally unpersuaded by it. Cf. Bauckham, *The Gospel for All Christians*.

[70] For recent work on Matthew's Gospel in relation to the Gentile mission see Wilk, *Jesus und die Völker in der Sicht der Synoptiker*, 83–153, 240–242; and Lee, *Mission to the Jews and the Gentiles in the Gospel of Matthew*.

[71] France, *Matthew* (NICNT), 26, offers an important reminder that one should take into account the illiteracy rate at that time.

tiously with the assumption that there are undoubtedly some influences in the background,[72] in conjunction with the more evident Jewish background.[73] As an educated, literate person, the Evangelist's own influences from Greco-Roman literature and history would probably be much higher than most of his audience. Again, a cautious assumption that there are elements from that background in the Evangelist's body of knowledge is probable. Frederick W. Danker well summarizes the presentation of christology in Matthew: "to present a book that speaks to Judean and at the same time assists Greco-Romans to use their cultural experience as a stepping stone to appreciate the uniqueness of Jesus Christ, the messiah, the Great Patriot, who includes them in his people."[74] Therefore, there are several places in the present work where Greco-Roman literature and history are discussed as helpful elements, for both comparison and contrast, toward understanding Matthew's text.

Other scriptural texts, especially the Old Testament scriptures, which is dealt with further below, are an indispensable part of determining Matthew's christology in this work. Other translations, such as the Septuagint and the Targums have been invaluable assets, and these prove very important at various points for discussion of Matthew's christology.[75] Discovery of texts such as the Dead Sea Scrolls has led toward a greater understanding of Matthew, the exegetical methodology as a whole as well as its christology.[76] Discussion of the Dead Sea Scrolls takes place at various points in this thesis, especially where applicable to christology. The vast amount of Rabbinic literature is an important resource as well,[77] although this is made considerably problematic with the utilization of literary works that were compiled long after Matthew was written. Obviously, Rabbinic literature like the Mishnah and Talmud were the result of developing oral tradi-

---

[72] The infancy narrative of Matthew is especially rich with motifs (dreams, portents, etc.) that can be connected with a Greco-Roman background, particularly in the biographies of famous individuals. Cf. Bailey and Vanderbroek, *Literary Forms in the New Testament*, 150. Comparative parallels are helpfully listed in Boring, Berger, and Colpe, *Hellenistic Commentary to the New Testament*.

[73] Obviously, the Jewish background and Greco-Roman background are not completely separate worlds, as abundantly demonstrated by Hengel, *Judaism and Hellenism: Studies in Their Encounter in Palestine During the Early Hellenistic Period.* In addition, the antiquity of the Jewish background would certainly appeal to many Gentile readers that respected ancient religions and history.

[74] Danker, "Matthew: A Patriot's Gospel," 115, cites many valuable comparisons toward understanding the background he proposes.

[75] Gundry, *The Use of the Old Testament in St. Matthew's Gospel.*

[76] Stendahl, *The School of Matthew and Its Use of the Old Testament.*

[77] Keener, *A Commentary on the Gospel of Matthew*, provides an extensive amount of references in the footnotes from various Rabbinic sources; however, careless, injudicious, anachronistic use of these references is a potential consequence.

tion, some of which undoubtedly existed in the first century. However, distinguishing and carefully defining this is no small task.[78] While it is a worthwhile endeavor needing much further work and clear methodological precision, due to the constraints of this study, use of Rabbinic material in the following chapters can only be general and limited.

A considerable amount of current scholarly work has rightly sought to appropriate all of the critical approaches: historical, sociological, literary, and theological. Exclusive use of one approach is rightly disapproved, and while increasing specialization limits in many ways the capabilities and competence of scholars, pursuit from as many angles as possible is the only way forward.[79] The encyclopedic commentary of Davies and Allison[80] in appropriating the various critical tools has proven very influential in Matthean studies.[81] Their commentary was a valuable resource in the work of this thesis, and the debt to their efforts is immense, even where there is disagreement. The multifaceted approach that they utilize was also an influence upon the approach of this work, and therefore, the argument of this thesis highlighting Matthew's christology in relation to the recapitulation of Israel is set forth using a variety of critical tools.

1.3 The Use of the Old Testament in Matthew

A second prominent area of focus in Matthean studies has been the use of the Old Testament in Matthew. This subject has received a tremendous amount of concentration, and it is rightly recognized as a key factor in understanding the communicative intention of the text. There are many important areas of research that encompass Matthew's use of the Old Testament.[82] Many have sought to broadly outline Matthew's use of the Old

---

[78] See Neusner, *Rabbinic Literature and the New Testament: What We Cannot Show, We Do Not Know*, for a vehement critique of many scholars' faulty, anachronistic use of Rabbinic literature in this regard.

[79] Cf. Senior, "Directions," in Aune, *Gospel of Matthew in Current Study*, 15, on need for bridges between literary criticism and the classical approach.

[80] Through personal correspondence, Allison affirms that he indeed wrote the whole commentary (cf. 3.ix), with Davies' colloboration diminishing with each successive volume. He also notes that he benefited from many helpful comments by the editor, C. E. B. Cranfield.

[81] Davies and Allison, *Matthew*, 1.1–7, lay out their "principled eclecticism." Mention should also be made of Garland, *Reading Matthew: A Literary and Theological Commentary on the First Gospel*, though a much smaller work for a wider audience also exhibits an excellent utilization of many different critical approaches.

[82] While they are never directly quoted, noncanonical works also play a role in Matthew and they are discussed at numerous points throughout this study.

Testament,[83] which France rightly characterizes as "multi-dimensional."[84] Scores of others have closely analyzed a verse, pericope or larger section toward delineating Matthew's use of the Old Testament. Several key works, beyond the standard critical commentaries, on the early chapters of Matthew were important for the research and writing of this work, many of which cover both the use of the Old Testament and christology.[85] Scholarly attention has also been given to the various textual traditions utilized by Matthew in his use, adaptation, or non-use of Hebrew, Aramaic, and Greek texts.[86] In addition, comparison with texts from the Dead Sea Scrolls has also highlighted Matthew's use of the Old Testament.[87] Matthew's exegetical methodology has occupied some attention, situating it within the broader Jewish and Christian exegetical background of the first century.[88] Attention has been given to Matthew's purposes for utilizing the Old Testament,[89] and there has been a great deal of discussion concerning the important fulfillment quotations and the perspective he has on prophecy being fulfilled in Jesus Christ.[90] Research on the use of typology in Matthew

---

[83] Beyond the standard critical commentaries, see Johnson, "The Biblical Quotations in Matthew," 135–153; Hummel, *Die Auseinandersetzung zwischen Kirche and Judentum im Matthäusevangelium*, 128–135; Stanton, *A Gospel for a New People*, 346–363; France, *Matthew: Evangelist and Teacher*, 166–205; Gundry, *The Use of the Old Testament*; Cope, *Matthew: A Scribe Trained for the Kingdom of Heaven*; Prabhu, *The Formula Quotations in the Infancy Narrative of Matthew*; Hartman, "Scriptural Exegesis in the Gospel of St. Matthew"; McConnell, *Law and Prophecy in Matthew's Gospel*; Smith, "The Use of the Old Testament in the New"; Stendahl, *School of Matthew*; Longenecker, *Biblical Exegesis in the Apostolic Period*, 124–135; Blomberg, "Matthew," *Commentary on the New Testament Use of the Old Testament*.

[84] France, *Matthew: Evangelist and Teacher*, 188.

[85] Brown, *Birth of the Messiah*; Allison, *The New Moses*; Donaldson, *Jesus on the Mountain: A Study in Matthean Theology*; Kynes, *Christology of Solidarity*; Johnson, *The Purpose of Biblical Genealogies*; Nolan, *The Royal Son of God*.

[86] Stendahl, *School of Matthew*; Gundry, *Use of the Old Testament*.

[87] Stendahl, *School of Matthew*, 183–206, led the way in this regard. For critique see Gärtner, "The Habakkuk Commentary (DSH) and the Gospel of Mt," 1–24; and Gundry, *Use of the Old Testament*, 155–159.

[88] Patte, *Early Jewish Hermeneutic in Palestine*; Juel, *Messianic Exegesis*, 31–57; Cope, *Matthew: A Scribe Trained for the Kingdom of Heaven*; Longenecker, *Biblical Exegesis in the Apostolic Period*.

[89] Gundry, *Use of the Old Testament*; Holmgren, *The Old Testament and the Significance of Jesus*.

[90] Strecker, *Der Weg*, 49–85; Pesch, "Der Gottessohn im matthäischen Evangelienprolog (Mt 1–2). Beobachtungen zu den Zitationsformeln der Reflexionszitate," 395–420; Rothfuchs, *Die Erfüllungszitate des Matthäus-Evangelium*; Prabhu, *The Formula Quotations in the Infancy Narrative of Matthew*; Stendahl, *School of St. Matthew*; Moule, "Fulfillment-Words in the New Testament: Use and Abuse," 293–320; Van Segbroeck, "Les citations d'accomplissement dans l'Évangile selon saint Matthieu d'après trios ouvrages récents," 107–130; Beaton, *Isaiah's Christ in Matthew's Gospel*.

has also been undertaken, which is given further attention below. Scholars have also focused research upon the varying kinds of use, such as quotation, allusion, echo, and sought to describe and define these uses.[91] There has been important research on the role these scriptural texts had in the early church as determined by their use in Matthew.[92] Within source and redaction criticism, scholars have compared and contrasted the various uses of the Old Testament in the synoptic gospels,[93] as well as in other early Christian texts.[94]

While many of these areas of research informed much of the work on this thesis and are dealt with at various points, they have remained subservient to a more closely defined area of Matthew's use of the Old Testament. This particular area of study involves a detailed examination of the use of Israel's history in Matthew, especially in regard to how it is recapitulated in Matthew 1:1–4:11. For the most part, scholars have only generally dealt with recapitulation in Matthew through cursory statements that note how Jesus repeats and relives Israel's history.[95] Greater attention to how this is accomplished in Matthew is an area that has deserved more focus. This study has sought to delve much more deeply into explicating the recapitulation of Israel in these early chapters of Matthew.

The primary focus of the present work is examining Israel's history and the recapitulation of it in Matthew. This involves consideration of the use of the Old Testament in regard to Matthew's utilization of Israel's history in his story of Jesus Christ, in addition to other means utilized by Matthew to recapitulate Israel's history. Furthermore, at numerous points this study discusses these various uses of Israel's scriptures because it remains an important area for discussion in refinement of various over-generalized conclusions about Matthew's use of the Old Testament that have proven unsatisfactory. One of the arguments that is subsidiary to the overall argument of this study is that Matthew's appropriation of the Old Testament is more complex, subtle, and variegated than some scholars have maintained.[96] Over-generalizing and too sharply categorizing Matthew's ap-

---

[91] Ellis, *Prophecy and Hermeneutic in Early Christianity*. From a broader standpoint beyond Matthew, see Porter, "The Use of the Old Testament in the New Testament," 94–96.

[92] Dodd, *According to the Scriptures*; Lindars, *New Testament Apologetic*.

[93] Powery, *Jesus Reads Scripture: The Function of Jesus' Use of Scripture in the Synoptic Gospels*.

[94] Ellis, *The Old Testament Canon in Early Christianity*.

[95] Allison, "Son of God as Israel," 74–81, devotes a short insightful article to the topic.

[96] Cf. Sanders, "The Gospels and the Canonical Process," in W. O. Walker (ed.), *The Relationships Among the Gospels*, 223, who duly criticizes the inadequate understanding of McCasland, "Matthew Twists the Scriptures," 143–148, when Sanders states, "Matthew did not twist the Scriptures when he so often reshaped his citations of the Old Tes-

proach to the Old Testament has therefore glossed over this complexity. The present work has sought to re-open and expand this discussion beyond some of these restrictive, inaccurate viewpoints.

The history of Israel is a key sub-category of Matthew's use of the Old Testament that is of primary importance for this study.[97] Matthew is profoundly concerned with Israel.[98] However, to adequately situate the present work, it is exceedingly important to define this "Israel" because there are several ways that Israel can be utilized and is utilized in the text of Matthew. In addition, it is essential to acknowledge that there is a varied complexity in Matthew's use and perspective on Israel that also makes it difficult to rigidly separate these uses of Israel into neatly defined categories.[99] Accepting this complexity, there are three general ways that Israel can be used and is used in the Gospel of Matthew.

1. There is the Israel of the canonical and noncanonical writings, as well as the traditions and viewpoints, which influenced the broader conceptual framework of the Jewish world as well as the early Christian church. This primarily includes Israel's past: Israel as a people, their history, significant events and themes, as well as reference to individuals that contributed to that history. This is significant background for the whole of Matthew where these writings and traditions are variously used and appropriated in the Gospel.[100] Matthew's utilization of this Israel is important theologically for his Gospel and it evidences itself at various points in the Gospel, foremost in the genealogy (1:1–17). Other texts that are significant uses of Israel's past include: 11:2–15; 12:38–42; 17:1–13; 21:33–43; and 23:29–36. This Israel of the distant past is the Israel that receives the most attention

---

tament to suit his overriding theological convictions concerning Christ and the Church ... this was the thing to do."

[97] France, *Matthew: Evangelist and Teacher*, 166–241, deals with various facets of Israel in Matthew.

[98] This intersects with a further important area of Matthean research in terms of answering the difficult questions about anti-Semitism/anti-Judaism. Saldarini, "Reading Matthew without Anti-Semitism," 166–184; McKnight, "A Loyal Critic: Matthew's Polemic with Judaism in Theological Perspective," 55–79; Przybylski, "The Setting of Matthean Anti-Judaism," 181–200; Gaston, "The Messiah of Israel as Teacher of the Gentiles," 78–96; Nolland, "Matthew and Anti-Semitism," 154–169. As with Matthew's broader use of Israel, there is an underappreciated complexity to this issue within the text of Matthew as well as the first-century Jewish and Greco-Roman environment.

[99] Reference to Israel obviously does not necessitate direct mention of the name Israel, as there are other ways to indicate Israel's past, present, and future.

[100] For an attempt to identify use of Old Testament traditions in the Synoptic Gospels see Swartley, *Israel's Scripture Traditions and the Synoptic Gospels: Story Shaping Story*, where he primarily observes these traditions as structural patterns in the Synoptics based on four major traditions, which for Matthew are: Exodus and Sinai (4:12–16:12); Way-Conquest (16:13–20:34); Temple (21–25); Kingship (26–28). Nothing of substance is done for 1:1–4:11.

in this study as it most directly relates to the way that Israel is recapitulated in Matthew 1:1–4:11.

2. There is the Israel of Jesus' day (e.g. 3:1–12), which is a complexity in and of itself given the varieties within Judaism that are now known to have been present during the first century.[101] Matthew evidences this Israel at several points in the Gospel. The work of form criticism as well as social-scientific criticism have brought to light many important aspects where this is evidenced in Matthew. In addition, knowledge from other historical sources, such as Josephus, has also helped identify the Israel of Jesus' day. This conception of Israel receives less attention in this work except when it relates to the overall theme of recapitulation, as well as several brief comments in the footnotes when applicable.

3. There is the Israel of Matthew's own day (e.g. 28:15) that had changed in many ways following the destruction of Jerusalem in 70 C.E and the important developments which that decisive event effected in the subsequent years.[102] Determining the setting of Matthew's Gospel, where the author and community reside, and their characteristics has been a prominent area of focus. Much discussed is the rift between Jewish Christians and those Jews who were opposed to Christian teaching. The degree of separation between these groups has been intensely debated.[103] Attention to Matthew's community has been given much attention in this regard, and there is now a minority persuasively arguing that the Gospels were meant for wider circulation.[104] While these are areas that deserve more research, the constraints of this study have demanded that these areas receive only brief mention in a few footnotes.

The Israel of Jesus' day and the Israel of Matthew's day have obvious continuities with the Israel that Matthew characterizes from the distant past. Again, there is complexity to Matthew's use of Israel, as well as an important mixing of these "Israels" in Matthew's presentation of the story

---

[101] Chilton and Neusner, *Judaism in the New Testament*, xv.

[102] Hummel, *Die Auseinandersetzung*; Trilling, *Das wahre Israel: Studien zur Theologie des Matthäusevangeliums*; France, *Matthew: Evangelist and Teacher*, 206–241.

[103] Saldarini, *Matthew Christian-Jewish Community*; Sim, *The Gospel of Matthew and Christian Judaism*; Overman, *Matthew's Gospel and Formative Judaism* and *Church and Community in Crisis*; Davies, *The Setting of Sermon on the Mount*; Hare, *The Theme of Jewish Persecution of Christians in the Gospel according to St. Matthew*; Levine, *The Social and Ethnic Dimensions of Matthean Salvation History*; Hagner, "Matthew: Apostate, Reformer, Revolutionary?," 193–209; Weren, "The History and Social Setting of the Matthean Community." The most recent work is now Foster, *Community, Law and Mission in Matthew's Gospel*. Cf. Deines, "Not the Law but the Messiah," 53–84; Gurtner, "Matthew's Theology of the Temple and the 'Parting of the Ways'," 128–153.

[104] Bauckham, *The Gospel for All Christians*.

of Jesus.[105] Discussion as to Matthew's conception of salvation history, whether he had a structured viewpoint or not, and what that viewpoint was, is certainly an important element of Matthew's usage of Israel.[106] While this complexity in the use of Israel in Matthew deserves further attention, the limitation of the present work being focused exclusively upon recapitulation has demanded that this remain subservient to the overall concentration upon the way that Israel is recapitulated in Matthew. For certain reasons explained in the following chapters, this study focuses upon the Israel of the distant past, as especially highlighted through the use of the Old Testament, which is theologically interpreted in light of Christ's coming. As Jürgen Moltmann rightly observes, "the synoptics tell the life-story of Jesus in the pattern of the collective remembrance of the history of Israel."[107] By examining Matthew's christological use of the Old Testament, it is argued in this work that Israel's history is recapitulated in several ways in Matthew 1:1–4:11.

Another area that must be given brief attention within the broader use of the Old Testament in Matthew is the use of typology.[108] It is common to characterize Matthew's use of Israel in reference to Jesus as typology. A general definition of typology is offered by Walther Eichrodt as: "persons, institutions, and events of the Old Testament which are regarded as divinely established models or prerepresentations of corresponding realities in the New Testament salvation history."[109] France defines typology in regard to its use in Matthew as "theological reflection in the light of later events which sees the experiences of the people of Israel as an apt parallel

---

[105] See O'Leary, *Matthew's Judaization of Mark*, where she argues for Matthew's rewriting and "torahizing" of Mark.

[106] Meier, "Salvation-History in Matthew: In Search of a Starting Point," 203–215; Walker, *Die Heilsgeschichte im ersten Evangelium*; Strecker, *Der Weg*; Trilling, *Das wahre Israel*; Kingsbury, *Matthew: Structure, Christology, Kingdom*, 25–39; Luomanen, *Entering the Kingdom of Heaven: A Study on the Structure of Matthew's View of Salvation*; Garbe, *Der Hirte Israels: Eine Untersuchung zur Israeltheologie des Matthäusevangeliums*; Eloff, " Ἀπό … ἕως and Salvation History in Matthew's Gospel," 85–107.

[107] Moltmann, *The Way of Jesus Christ*, 148; cf. Wright, *The New Testament and the People of God*, 401–402.

[108] France, *Matthew: Evangelist and Teacher*, 185–191, 207–210; Nepper-Christensen, *Das Matthäusevangelium: Ein judenchristliches Evangelium?*, 163–179.

[109] Eichrodt, "Is Typological Exegesis an Appropriate Method?," 225. Cf. von Rad, *Old Testament Theology*, 329–330, 371–384; Ellis, *Old Testament Canon in Early Christianity*, 62–63, 105–109; Longenecker, *Biblical Exegesis in the Apostolic Period*, 77–78, 125; Goldingay, *Approaches to Old Testament Interpretation*, 98–111; Hurtado, *Lord Jesus Christ*, 569–574. From a broader standpoint see Goppelt, *Typos: The Theological Interpretation of the Old Testament in the New*; Baker, *Two Testaments, One Bible*.

to those of Jesus in the wilderness, and interprets the latter in terms of the former, as an exemplification of the same principles."[110]

A correspondence in history is key to identifying typology, particularly in the use of paradigmatic events. This study would lend varying support for these perspectives on typology as models, analogies, and comparisons, with the paralleling of Jesus and Israel in Matthew. Dale Allison has closely examined Matthew's typology particularly in regard to the new Moses theme and helpfully proposes six devices that are used to construct typologies: explicit statement, inexplicit borrowing, reminiscent circumstances, key words or phrases, structural imitation, and resonant syllabic and/or word pattern.[111]

Robert Gundry furthers the typological conception in Matthew when he states that it involves reiterative recapitulation, in that what happens to the type happens to the antitype.[112] This is an important point that furthers an understanding of Matthew beyond simple parallels, which does not entirely describe what takes place in Matthew. It proves crucial to refine the conception of typology in Matthew more closely, as recapitulation, a repetition of foundational events and aspects of the past that, from the perspective of Matthew, is necessary theologically in communicating the life and work of Jesus Christ. Jesus recapitulates Israel's history, and in concert with Matthew's fulfillment quotations, this outlook upon Jesus marks him as the outcome and climax of that history, a point definitively made at the very beginning in 1:1–17. This reference to recapitulation as a particular subset of typology is the central focus of the present study. As Lampe and Woollcombe state, "that the New Testament writers also recognized the recapitulative nature of prophecy and of the final redemption of mankind is proved by their consistent representation of the acts of God in Christ as a recapitulation of his earlier acts."[113]

Nevertheless, there continues to be active discussion as to how far typology is utilized in Matthew, as well as in the rest of the New Testament, and at this point in the discussion, it appears best to step aside from trying to defend typology as a legitimate label for Matthew's work. The use of Old Testament events, people, themes, and history as model and pattern is undeniable, especially in a work such as Matthew's, saturated as it is with the scriptures of Israel.[114] However, as noted, the typology of Matthew goes beyond simple parallels toward a recapitulation of Israel that is variously portrayed, wherein corporate personality appears to play a role as

---

[110] France, *Jesus and the Old Testament*, 42.

[111] Allison, *New Moses*, 140; further refined in *The Intertextual Jesus*.

[112] Gundry, *Use of the Old Testament*, 209 n. 3.

[113] Lampe and Woollcombe, *Essays on Typology*, 47.

[114] See Watts, *Isaiah's New Exodus in Mark*, 47–52, for hermeneutical considerations that would also apply to Matthew's Gospel.

well.[115] The focus of this work will be on understanding Matthew and in particular, the manner in which Jesus is presented as recapitulating Israel's history. The purpose of this study is not to define or defend typology, something that continues to need further refinement, particularly in comparison with other first century texts. Therefore, this study will avoid the term typology and seek to strictly examine Matthew's text itself in regard to recapitulation.

Christology in Matthew and the use of the Old Testament in Matthew are intertwined within the narratival portrait of Jesus Christ.[116] Matthew's utilization of the Old Testament, in the fulfillment passages as well as in the other uses, is directly related to his christology. While each of these areas can be somewhat isolated from the other for purposes of detailed research, their combination and interpenetration of one another underlies the whole of this work. In Longenecker's analysis of Matthew's use of Scripture, he summarizes that "the Jewish concepts of corporate solidarity and typological correspondences in history coupled with the Christian convictions of eschatological fulfillment and messianic presence come to expression in a distinctly christocentric fashion."[117] Undoubtedly, the entirety of Matthew's Gospel is a work of theological interpretation and presentation of Jesus Christ, and his use of the Old Testament in this regard is a key component in his theology. The christology is saturated with Old Testament scriptures, themes, and traditions; and the use of the Old Testament is vitally connected to the christological perspective Matthew sets forth. To effectively determine the recapitulation of Israel in the early chapters of Matthew will demand constant reference to these two areas of research. As will be further elucidated, recapitulation in Matthew has not received such detailed attention in this regard and the argument of the present work is that it is both relevant and essential that recapitulation be recognized and described.

1.4 Summary of Methodology

This study has directed primary attention to the meaning of Matthew's text in the first century, seeking to best understand it within that context. This focus on the text has been undertaken utilizing various critical tools, one of which is ascertaining theological aspects in the text. Matthew's Gospel is

---

[115] Ellis, *Old Testament Canon in Early Christianity*, 110–112; Longenecker, *Biblical Exegesis*, 77, 126.

[116] Luz, *Matthew 1–7* (2007), 131: Matthew's "entire Christology ... is a reflection on the person and story of Jesus that is determined by the OT."

[117] Longenecker, *Biblical Exegesis*, 134.

an explicitly theological work where the dominant concern is to present the story of Jesus Christ to hearers and readers. For the purpose of the present work, ascertaining Matthew's theological presentation of Jesus Christ is especially undertaken within a broader pursuit of understanding the text within the first century context.

The methodological orientation of this study has been undertaken within the historical critical approach, utilizing the various areas of specialty within this broader science. The meaning of the Gospel within a first-century setting is the fundamental and overarching methodological approach to this study. This attention has been textually centered, with priority to the words and structure of the Greek text. The discussion of what the Evangelist intended for his community/communities must therefore be less of a focus, as it demands a further set of assumptions and approaches that are outside the scope of this study.[118]

This study does utilize some of the helpful insights from literary criticism. The exegetical work for this study was textually oriented, focusing upon the words, structure, motifs, and characterization. Nevertheless, literary criticism is not the only methodology this study has utilized. The one-sided dominance of this approach has been rightly criticized by many, in particular where the world of the text completely dominates the focus in isolation from other historical sources and environment. Therefore, this study has sought to maintain the best use of literary critical tools within the broader historical critical methodology. Attention to the theological components of the text is also of particular importance for this study.

1.5 Scope of the Present Work

The use of Israel's history in the story of Jesus is an important component in Matthew's christology that has deserved substantial attention. The argument of the present work is that Israel's history is utilized within Matthew's christology, serving a key role in the story of Jesus as narrated by Matthew. The term most apt in describing this utilization of Israel's history in Matthew is recapitulation, which includes repetition, summing up, representation, and embodiment. In the first chapter, it is argued that the genealogy (1:1–17) recapitulates Israel's history in a narratological and teleological manner to focus upon Jesus Christ as the fulfillment of Israel's

---

[118] Varying terms will be used to refer to the writer of the Gospel: author, redactor, Matthew, and the Evangelist. The complexities of the authorship issue are beyond the limitations of this study.

history.[119] Primarily the recapitulation element of the genealogy involves repetition, where Israel's history is repeated and summarized, leading up to the climactic fulfillment of that story with the birth of Jesus Christ. In the second chapter, it is argued that in Matthew 2, Jesus passively recapitulates Israel's history, reliving primarily the exodus experience of Israel. The passive element of this recapitulation is due to the fact that Jesus "acts" according to the movements that both God and Joseph produce within the narrative, hence his passivity in repeating, reliving, and embodying Israel's history. In the third chapter, it is argued that in Matthew 3:1–4:11 Jesus actively recapitulates Israel's history, repeating and reliving it as the representative embodiment of Israel. The active element of this recapitulation is due to the fact that Jesus himself initiates the action and reaction within the narrative. Throughout the discussion, the recapitulation of Israel as an element of Matthew's christology is an overarching premise.

Every possible interpretive aspect, acknowledging the necessary limitations noted above, has been utilized to ascertain the use of Israel's history in Matthew's Gospel. This has required an eclectic combination of critical approaches, retaining all their strengths and seeking to overcome the weakness of only using one approach. Methodologically, this primarily involves a textually focused approach, observing literary components, utilizing historical and comparative parallels and environment, and a theological orientation that recognizes the Evangelist's principal focus is christological. Exhaustive analysis of Matthew, such as what some modern commentaries undertake, is not possible given the limitations and focus of this work. Neither is there exhaustive use of primary and secondary literature given similar constraints. What is comprehensively undertaken is the discovery and description of the recapitulation of Israel in Matthew 1:1–4:11 which is the cohesive and distinctive viewpoint throughout this study. The christology of Matthew and the use of the Old Testament in Matthew are essential ingredients toward unfolding the use of recapitulation in Matthew. It is the argument of this work that the recapitulation of Israel is a considerable formative element of Matthew's presentation of Jesus Christ that has warranted further consideration utilizing a variety of critical approaches.

---

[119] Matt. 1:18–25 does not directly contain a clear recapitulation element and thus is not analyzed for the purpose of this study. This pericope especially serves a role in explaining Jesus' divine origin hinted at in the genealogy, his fulfillment of prophecy, his redeeming role, and how he can be a son of David through Joseph's adoption of him.

Chapter 2

Israel's History Recapitulated

2.1 Introduction

The analysis and description of Israel's history in the Gospel of Matthew must start where Matthew itself begins, with the genealogy that serves as an evocative introduction to Matthew's story of Jesus. Israel's history is of vital importance for adequately understanding the Gospel of Matthew, and beginning as it does with a genealogy that recapitulates Israel's history makes this importance especially evident. The recapitulation of Israel in this genealogy involves the repetition and summarizing of that history through a teleological and narratological genealogy. Matthew's genealogy will prove to yield various insights toward understanding the theological interpretation of Israel's history that this Gospel presents and utilizes. It orients the reader to understand both the history of Israel and the story of Jesus, which are fundamentally linked from Matthew's perspective.

For best understanding the form and role of the genealogy in Matthew, detailed attention to and description of Old Testament genealogies must be conducted. The first two sections of this chapter will interact with Old Testament genealogies for better understanding Matthew's genealogy. The first section will seek to classify the forms of genealogies that appear in the Old Testament for help in classifying the form of Matthew's genealogy. The second section will propose an argument for seeing genealogies as compressed narrative summaries. This insight will directly relate toward interpreting Matthew's genealogy as a compressed narrative summary of Israel's history. The final sections will directly deal with the genealogy in Matthew with a thorough exegesis of the pericope, utilizing the insights garnered from the analysis of Old Testament genealogies, and noting how Matthew adapted these for his presentation of Israel's story that climaxes with the coming of Messiah. This investigation of Matthew's genealogy will also direct and provide a secure foundation for analyzing and describing how Israel's history is used in the Gospel of Matthew and the utilization of this theological interpretation in the presentation of Jesus Christ throughout the early chapters of the Gospel (1:1–4:11).

2.2 Classification of Old Testament Genealogies

The study of biblical genealogies has unfortunately languished from lack of focused scholarly attention, especially in comparison to other biblical genres. Genealogies all too frequently are given only a scant general discussion, and they periodically receive no attention at all. Compared to the other genres found in biblical literature, the amount of work on biblical genealogies is minuscule. Narrative, poetry, and apocalyptic attract a large amount of attention, no doubt due to their prominence and importance in biblical literature. Although genealogies get less attention and seemingly bear minor exegetical and theological fruit, they nevertheless were important means of communicating history and purposes by the writers of the various canonical and non-canonical literatures.

Genealogies record the ancestry or descent of individuals, sketching family relations with varying degrees of breadth and depth.[1] As to literary form, genealogies have been classified as a sub-category of list in standard works such as Otto Eissfeldt.[2] George Coats provides a nuanced and helpful definition of genealogy when he states that genealogy "builds on a system of enumeration rather than narration. It is more nearly akin to list, but can incorporate story in its shape. It derives ultimately from tribal circles as a means for the history and validation of tribal units."[3]

To be classified as a genealogy, kinship relations must be expressed or implied.[4] Genealogies can catalogue various amounts of information about successive members of a family line. Some of this information can include birth, age, marriage, offspring, death, and other biographical details. Initially genealogies were used to preserve a family's generational succession, but later they came to be used for the purpose of expressing kinship and social, political, geographical, and religious relationships.[5] Malina and Rohrbaugh summarize

---

[1] Cf. Van Gemeren, "Genealogy in the Old Testament," 654–663. For wider textual and comparative background, see Sparks, *Ancient Texts for the Study of the Hebrew Bible*, 344–360.

[2] Eissfeldt, *The Old Testament: An Introduction*, 11, 25, categorizes, in terms of pre-literary stages, genealogies under *list*, which comes under the broader category of *prose types*. It could be argued that a better way to categorize genealogies is not as a part of some larger literary form, but as a self-contained category itself. More study is needed in this regard.

[3] Coats, *Genesis with an Introduction to Narrative Literature*, 318; therefore, a list would be by comparison merely "a serial document, organizing the items in the serial in a representative, functional order."

[4] Without kinship relations, it is merely a list and not a genealogy. Cf. Wilson, *Genealogy and History*, 10.

[5] Johnson, *Purpose of Biblical Genealogies*, 77–82, presents nine functions of Old Testament genealogies. Cf. Wilson, *Genealogy and History*, 199.

that genealogies can serve a wide range of social functions: preserving tribal homogeneity or cohesion, interrelating diverse traditions, acknowledging marriage contracts between extended families, maintaining ethnic identity, and encoding key social information about a person. Above all, genealogies established claims to social status (honor) or to a particular office (priest, king) or rank, thereby providing a map for proper social interaction.[6]

Genealogies originally developed in the ancient Near East within an oral setting, being committed to memory and passed down from generation to generation, with the addition of new material as family histories grew. Later these genealogies came to be written, solidifying the material and allowing it to be preserved indefinitely.[7] The genealogies that appear within the biblical text are part of this solidifying process and they can be closely examined by scholars to yield a variety of insights and functions.

Genealogies are found in various places throughout the Old Testament, with particular prominence within Genesis and 1 Chronicles. Although close attention to biblical genealogies by scholars has been infrequent, a few significant studies have been conducted within the past forty years that have progressed the comprehension of their form and function. The two most comprehensive and highly influential scholarly works are those by M. D. Johnson and R. R. Wilson.[8]

This section will examine the genealogies in the Old Testament to classify them with the ultimate goal of classifying Matthew's genealogy of Jesus and better understanding the purpose for that genealogy. Genealogies in the Old Testament can be broken down into two broad categories. Most scholars, following Wilson's terminology, use the terms linear and segmented for the two common genealogical forms.[9] Johnson, who preceded Wilson's work, did not designate specific terminology in his study, and used various terms interchangeably.[10] In Johnson's second edition, he discusses in his introduction new developments since his first edition. He calls attention to the greater uniformity of terminology since his study, but he does admit that an even greater precision than this is needed in regard to specific genealogies given the mixing of the two types within Genesis and

---

[6] Malina and Rohrbaugh, *Social Science Commentary on the Synoptic Gospels*, 24–25.

[7] Wilson, "Genealogies," 931.

[8] In addition to these seminal studies by Johnson and Wilson, another could be added by S. Yeiven, who provides the most comprehensive presentation of charts of Israelite tribal genealogies in the appendix of his work, *The Israelite Conquest of Canaan*, 126–233.

[9] Wilson, *Genealogy and History*, 9.

[10] Although Johnson, *Purpose of Biblical Genealogies*, xii, does state in his introduction to the second edition: "The distinction itself was presupposed."

1 Chronicles.[11] Roddy Braun agrees that further distinctions should be utilized in defining the various genealogies, such as breadth, depth, linear, segmented, mixed, ascending and descending.[12] These refined distinctions are particularly useful for classifying specific genealogies, but these precise definitions should ultimately serve as sub-categories beneath the two main divisions that most scholars recognize.

This study will use slightly different terminology for these two basic forms of genealogy. These two categories are unilinear and multilinear. This use of unilinear and multilinear is to be preferred as the most natural and basic division of biblical genealogies, with further sub-categories under each for a more specific identification and definition of individual biblical genealogies. Although within several large genealogies these two basic forms are mixed (e.g. 1 Chr 1–9), an argument can be made that one of the two forms predominates such that each genealogy can be classified under one form or the other. Within the identification of each genealogy under one or the other category, further terminology can be used to define more specifically each genealogy. This will be done below especially in light of best classifying and understanding the genealogy in Matthew.

2.2.1 Multilinear Genealogies

Multilinear genealogies are the most common genealogical form in the Old Testament.[13] This genealogical form follows diverging branches of family divisions from a single ancestor, sketching several family lines together. Most often, this is referred to as segmented genealogy, but given the basic nature and definition of genealogy as a family line, multilinear is to be preferred over segmented.[14] The basic pattern followed is pyramidic, with both vertical and horizontal relationships delineated as multiple lines of descent are sketched.

```
                        A
             B          C          D
          E F G      H I J      K L M
```

Genesis includes several multilinear genealogies (4:1–2; 10:1–32; 11:27–30; 22:20–24; 25:1–4; 12–18; 36:1–43; 46:8–27). It has been observed by

---

[11] *Ibid.,* xii. In Wilson, "Genealogies," 930, admits that the forms can be mixed in written genealogies, such as 1 Chron 6, and thus the distinction between the two forms is not absolute.

[12] Braun, *1 Chronicles,* 1–3.

[13] There are also several lists recorded in the Old Testament, especially in Ezra-Nehemiah. These resemble multi-linear genealogies in that ancestors are mentioned for the various individuals who are listed, but are distinguished from genealogies in their form and function.

[14] Westermann, "Genealogies," 243, also prefers multilinear.

some scholars that "Genesis is fundamentally about one big extended family."[15] Primarily the multilinear genealogies in Genesis are used to trace branches of the family outside of the chosen line and their relations with Israel (e.g. Table of Nations in ch. 10; Ishmael's genealogy 25:12–18; Esau's genealogy ch. 36). Other genealogies within the Pentateuch are Exodus 6:14–25; Numbers 3:1–37; 26:5–62.

1 Chronicles 1–9 is the largest and most complex multilinear genealogy in the Old Testament.[16] Beginning with Adam, the genealogy progresses through Noah and his sons, through Abraham and his sons, through Jacob (Israel) and his twelve sons, and then through the descendants of the twelve sons of Jacob down to the post-exilic community.[17] Within 1 Chronicles 1–9 there are numerous smaller multilinear genealogies listed as well. Elsewhere in 1 Chronicles, genealogies are found in 23:6–24; 24:20–31; 25:1–5; 26:1–11.

There are numerous functions of multilinear genealogies within the Old Testament. They served to express actual kinship relations between individuals through a common ancestor, and particularly served to show the relations of Israel with the neighbors that surrounded her. The link between Israel and those around her, according to the presentation in Genesis, was a common ancestor (Gen 10; 19:36–38; 20:20–24; 25:1–6, 12–16; 36).[18] Braun states, "It is the essential purpose of the genealogy to point to kinship relations between various individuals and groups." All humanity is portrayed by the Genesis narrative as having descended from the three sons of Noah (Gen 10). The various branches within multilinear genealogies, as sketched within the Old Testament, bear elements of commonality as well as divergence.[19] Other functions of these genealogies include tribal relationships, sociological, political, military, status, geographic, and cultic.

The genealogy in 1 Chronicles 1–9 is the most complex and elaborate genealogy, not only in terms of content but also in the various purposes it seems to serve as well. Fundamentally, it serves to present a summary of "all Israel" as an ideal picture of the people of God. It demonstrates "the relations existing between the various components of the people of Israel in the past and relating them in part to those who claimed to be part of Is-

---

[15] Fretheim, "Genesis," 326. Cf. Robinson, "Literary Function of the Genealogies of Genesis," 601.

[16] See Knoppers, *1 Chronicles 1–9*, 245–265, for a detailed discussion.

[17] This large genealogy, although overall clearly a unified multilinear genealogy, does nevertheless contain both of the two main forms. It is a massive and complex genealogy. See Osborne, "Genealogies of 1 Chronicles 1–9," 1979 Dropsie dissertation, cited in Duke, *The Persuasive Appeal of Chronicler: A Rhetorical Analysis*, 52.

[18] Johnson, *Purpose of Biblical Genealogies*, 77.

[19] Braun, *1 Chronicles*, 2.

rael at the time of the writer(s)."[20] Johnson notes the Chronicler's particular concern for the Davidic monarchy and how the author uses this genealogy to focus particularly upon that institution. Another predominant concern is the institution of the temple cultus and the Levitical responsibilities.[21]

2.2.2 Unilinear Genealogies

A unilinear genealogy traces one line of descent through several generations with varying degrees of depth. Family names are given in straight descending progression from the founder to the last or living representative, or in a progression ascending from the last or living representative back to the family head. Unilinear genealogies follow a basic vertical pattern by listing names that connect people to an ancestor, in either descending or ascending directions.

```
A     or     D
B            C
C            B
D            A
```

Genesis contains several unilinear genealogies, especially when dealing with the elect line of descent.[22] The first deals with Seth's genealogy in 4:25–26 and 5:1–32, tracing the line from Adam to Noah in ten generations with a descending unilinear genealogy. The genealogy of Shem appears in 11:10–26, which traces the line from Noah to Abram in ten generations with a descending unilinear genealogy.[23] The genealogy of Isaac appears in 25:19–26, tracing the line from Abraham to Jacob in a descending unilinear genealogy.

There are various short unilinear genealogies throughout the Old Testament. Exodus 31:2 traces Bezalel in three ascending generations to the tribe of Judah. Numbers 16:1 includes a unilinear genealogy for Korah, with three ascending generations as a son of Levi. Numbers 27:1 gives a genealogy for Zelophedad, with four ascending generations as a son of Manasseh. Joshua 7:1 gives a unilinear genealogy for Achan, with four ascending generations as a son of Judah. Ruth 4:18–22 presents a unilinear genealogy for David, with ten descending generations starting with Perez. This genealogy is especially important for understanding Matthew's genealogy and will extensively be dealt with below as a sub-category of unilinear genealogies. 1 Samuel 1:1–2 gives a unilinear genealogy for Elkanah,

---

[20] *Ibid.*, 3.

[21] Johnson, *Purpose of Biblical Genealogies*, 74–76.

[22] Alexander, "Genealogies, Seed and the Compositional Unity of Genesis," 258–259.

[23] The MT and LXX differ here. See Gardner, *The Genesis Calendar: The Synchronistic Tradition in Genesis 1–11*, 244–246.

with five ascending generations. 1 Samuel 9:1–2 lists a genealogy for Kish, father of Saul, with five ascending generations. 1 Samuel 14:3 presents a genealogy for Ahijah, with three ascending generations. Ezra 7:1–5 is a priestly unilinear genealogy for Ezra, with sixteen ascending generations back to Aaron the chief priest. Nehemiah 11:22 includes a unilinear genealogy of Uzzi, with five ascending generations, a descendant of Asaph. Nehemiah 11:24 presents a unilinear genealogy for Pethahiah, with three ascending generations, a descendant of Judah. Esther 2:5 gives a unilinear genealogy for Mordecai, with four generations. Zephaniah 1:1 gives a unilinear genealogy for Zephaniah, with four ascending generations, a descendant of Hezekiah. Zechariah 1:1 gives a short unilinear genealogy for Zechariah, with two ascending generations.[24]

The most commonly given reason for unilinear genealogies is that they seek to legitimize the position or otherwise closely connect the last-named person by relating them to a key ancestor.[25] This practice was especially utilized for certain offices where succession was by heredity, such as the priesthood, Levitical work, and kingship. Wilson claims of unilinear genealogies, that they have only one function, 'to ground a claim to power, status, rank, office, or inheritance in an earlier ancestor'.[26] However, upon closer examination Wilson's claim is unjustified, where it seems that after surveying the many genealogies in the Old Testament a majority of them, especially the shorter genealogies of two, three or four ascending generations, do not in fact legitimize a person.[27] For example, 2 Kings 9:14 presents a unilinear genealogy for Jehu, the son of Jehoshaphat the son of Nimshi. This genealogy does not legitimize Jehu at all, as he is not grounded to a key ancestor for status or office. Therefore, a better way of understanding many of these short genealogies is to see them as extensions of a personal name, or as ancient forms of patronymic for a clearer identification. The longer ascending genealogies, such as Ezra 7:1–5, are no doubt meant to serve as a legitimization by connecting and grounding a particular person to a key ancestor. However, these type genealogies are in fact less common than Wilson and others have supposed.

---

[24] Several non-canonical writings also contain unilinear genealogies: Tobit 1:1–2; Judith 8:1–2; Baruch 1:1; 1 Maccabees 2:1; 1 Esdras 8:1–2 (a genealogy of Ezra that differs somewhat from Ezra 7:1–5); and 2 Esdras 1:1–3 (a genealogy of Ezra that differs somewhat from Ezra 7:1–5 and 1 Esdras).

[25] Braun, *1 Chronicles*, 2, notes that this was a common practice in the ancient near east.

[26] Wilson, "Genealogies," 931: "Writing sometimes helps linear genealogies to function more effectively by permitting them to be longer and therefore more impressive and authoritative."

[27] Legitimization is therefore much over-used by many scholars in this regard, based on Wilson's study, and needs further refinement.

Johnson adds a further purpose, in which purity of descent is defended and used, in particular with the unilinear genealogies of the Levites.[28] This may reasonably be said to be true of both kinds of genealogies, with Ezra-Nehemiah being a particular example in the case of a multilinear genealogy. In Genesis, unilinear genealogies are also particularly used in showing the passing of blessing through the covenant line.[29]

Another aspect of descending unilinear genealogies, especially prominent in Genesis, is to observe the chronological unfolding of generations as a form of history, a kind of narrative retold in a highly compressed fashion. Further extensive discussion of this important kind of narrative will be taken up below. This aspect of unilinear genealogies is particularly useful for identifying the purpose of Matthew's genealogy of Jesus. History can be told in varying ways, through narrative, poetry, or genealogy. Descending unilinear genealogies are a compressed means of retelling history as divinely ordered and theologically structured.

2.2.3 Teleological Genealogies

Unilinear genealogies can have a further sub-category where a particular purpose and structure so dominates the genealogy that they can be further defined as teleological genealogies.[30] The classification teleological has not been used in regard to a genealogy in the Old Testament. However, an analysis of Ruth's genealogy will make it evident that the teleological format is a distinguishable type of unilinear genealogy, and the features of this type of genealogy are strong enough to justify it as a sub-category of unilinear genealogy. Neglect of genealogies in general may have resulted in this failure to appreciate this particular type of genealogy.

This type of unilinear genealogy has a descending structure, starting with an ancestor, who may or may not be important, and descending towards a key individual. Teleological genealogies are descending unilinear genealogies that aim at this key figure and climactically stop with this name. Thus by nature they must be *descending* genealogies as opposed to ascending genealogies, because teleological genealogies follow a family line *toward* a goal. Their aim and *telos* is toward this goal, a key person, at whom they point and with whom they stop. Ascending genealogies seek to ground an individual into the authority and status of a key ancestor, such

---

[28] Johnson, *Purpose of Biblical Genealogies,* 73, attributes this to the midrashic activity of the Chronicler.

[29] Alexander, *From Paradise to the Promised Land*, 9–15.

[30] Teleological genealogy is my term. As a genealogical form, it has not been significantly dealt with by any previous literature. Hagner, *Matthew 1–13,* 9, 12, utilizes it only in regard to Matthew as a general term and not for a classification of the genealogy.

as Aaron for the priesthood,[31] besides those already described as patronymic. Teleological genealogies are a specially intended use of the unilinear genealogical form to communicate a goal and purpose that one key individual embodies. The relevance of teleological genealogies for understanding Matthew's genealogy will become apparent.

Although there is only one example of this genealogy within the Old
Testament, it is nevertheless legitimate to classify this genealogical form.
This one example of a teleological genealogy within the Old Testament is
found at the very end and conclusion of a book, a key purposeful arrangement which will be noted, in Ruth 4:18–22. This unique genealogy starts
with Perez, who although not especially prominent narratively or heroic in
Israel's history, nevertheless was the son of Judah (Ruth 4:12; Gen 38:29).
Starting with a relatively insignificant person such as Perez is in itself important evidence that there is obviously another purpose for this unilinear
genealogy besides the oft-used legitimating of authority, status, or office.
The book of Ruth itself tells a story of individuals, Naomi, Ruth, and Boaz,
who although they bear significant traits worth highlighting in a narrative,
are in themselves easily overlooked characters within the broader sweep of
Israel's history as relayed in the Old Testament. They find prominence
only within the Book of Ruth. Naomi and Ruth are never mentioned in the
rest of the Old Testament. Boaz is only mentioned in the genealogy of 1
Chronicles 2:11–12.[32]

Legitimization of authority, status, or office is simply an inadequate explanation for the genealogy at the end of Ruth, and closer attention to the
genealogy is justified to determine the form and function of this genealogy. None of the names within the genealogy are particularly famous or
significant individuals for Israel's history; all except for one person.
Therein lies the purpose for this genealogy. The story of Israel has been
localized to focus upon a few characters that play an important role in Israel's history because through them comes an all-significant person that
plays a dominant role in Israel. The genealogy ends, as does the entire
book, with the name David. David is the goal, climax, and end of this genealogy.[33] It is a teleologically structured genealogy, emphasizing and aiming at David. The use of numerics within the genealogy also highlights this

---

[31] Cf. Ezra 7:1–5. These types of genealogies should certainly be called "legitimizing genealogies."

[32] The temple pillar is named Boaz in 1 Kings 7:21 and 2 Chronicles 3:17.

[33] Further, it might be argued that the genealogy was understood teleologically by noting that the non-Hebrew versions (LXXa, Peshitta, Old Latin), add after David's name
"the king," as does the Targum of Ruth; see Beattie, *Aramaic Bible: Translation of the
Targum of Ruth*, 32. This possibly influenced Matthew's use as well (1:6), although arguing that Matthew possibly influenced some of these is not unlikely. Josephus also refers
to David as king in his section on the story of Ruth (*Ant.* 5.9.4).

classification. Boaz, who is a hero within the story, stands at the important seventh position within the genealogy. David, a person that needs no elucidation or introduction, stands at the important tenth position.[34] Further analysis of the genealogy within the book of Ruth and its purpose will be dealt later in this chapter.

The fundamental purpose for teleological genealogies is in their aiming toward a goal and by climactically stopping with a key individual. Although Ruth 4:18–22 is the only example present within the Old Testament of a teleological genealogy, the purpose for this genealogical form can still be determined. The author, who either uses a pre-existing genealogical source or crafts one, does so with the intent and purpose of ending with a key individual and using the genealogy to point toward that individual. As opposed to the ascending unilinear genealogies that seek to legitimatize a person by placing them within the family of a key ancestor, teleological genealogies reverse that intent by having its key person placed at the end as the goal.

The classification of the use of a teleological genealogy in the Old Testament book of Ruth yields immediate understanding of what form of genealogy one finds in Matthew 1. This exploration into Old Testament material has been very significant toward understanding Matthew's genealogy as a teleological genealogy. Thus, the classification of Old Testament genealogies has been vitally relevant for understanding Matthew's genealogy. A reciprocal relationship of observing the forms and uses of genealogies in the Old Testament and observing the form and use of the genealogy in Matthew will yield a better understanding of both. Matthew clearly makes use of a teleological genealogy in his first chapter for a variety of reasons that will be outlined below. Fundamental to the use of a teleological genealogy is the goal-oriented emphasis in which the genealogy descends, points toward, and finally climactically concludes. Jesus Christ is the one toward whom the entire genealogy of Matthew points as the goal. According to the teleological genealogy as presented in Matthew, Jesus Christ is the one toward whom the entire history of Israel was pointing as the ultimate end and goal. These points will be explained in extensive detail below.

It is acknowledged that this feature and use of a genealogy as teleological has not previously been utilized. The use of a teleological genealogy is not one that scholarship has recognized or given much attention to. It is an understandable oversight in this regard that might be attributed to a variety of factors. Overemphasis on narrative to the exclusion of genealogy has no

---

[34] Some would say this is why the genealogy starts with Perez, so as to have David at the tenth position. Cf. Sasson, *Ruth*, 181. Note how in Genesis 5 Enoch stands at seventh position and Noah appears at the tenth. In Genesis 11:10–26 Abram appears in the tenth position.

doubt contributed to this neglect. Failure to appreciate entire books literarily, giving due emphasis to the whole text as well as the parts of the text, has also brought about a loss of understanding in the use and purpose of genealogies in the Old Testament. The use of a teleological genealogy in Matthew 1:1–17, which will be thoroughly dealt with below, has been overlooked by some scholars in this regard. Noting the form of genealogy used in Matthew as teleological begs the question, from where was this unique form taken. It will be argued that this form was taken from the Old Testament itself, specifically Ruth, and re-used to make a fundamental assertion beyond what appeared in Ruth.

Further analysis of the teleological genealogy within the book of Ruth as a whole and its purpose will be dealt with in the next section. The relevance of teleological genealogies and classifying Matthew's genealogy as one particular example of this type of genealogy will be further dealt with in section five.

2.3 Genealogy as Narrative: Introduction

Scholarly attention to the use of narrative in the biblical texts has now grown to massive proportions. This study in no way seeks to repeat or expound to any degree this important area of research, except to try to advance the argument for seeing biblical genealogies as compressed narratives. In comparison to the study of biblical narratives, research on biblical genealogies certainly pales.[35] Although obviously less frequent in the Bible, which some might therefore wrongly argue as less important for biblical interpretation, biblical genealogies can yield insight for better understanding a book's intention and theology.[36] For later hearers and readers of these texts, it is important to state the literary impact of the whole, wherein the genealogies are united to narratives such that they are now interlocked

---

[35] Robinson, "Literary Function of the Genealogies of Genesis," 48, 595, notes this lack of attention to genealogy in comparison to narrative, remarking how Alter fails to even mention genealogies at all in his important study of biblical narrative: "The secondary status of genealogies is consistent with a recent tendency in literary theory to raise narrative to a privileged position."

[36] M. Sternberg, *Poetics of Biblical Language*, 133, in speaking of the genealogy in Genesis 22:20–24, notes how this text no doubt seems unpromising for close study, "yet even catalogues bring grist to the Bible's mill, and the lump of history gets assimilated to the art of the personal story. Inserted under the guise of family news, this digression assumes new shape and meaning in context."

literarily.[37] Biblical interpretation must grapple with both narrative and numerative, as they stand interconnected within the biblical texts.

One of the stated goals of Johnson was to study the genealogies in their literary contexts for understanding authorial intent and theological convictions.[38] He persuasively argues that the use of genealogies in the Old Testament is, "broad-based and variegated to such an extent that the genealogical form can be said to have become one of the available forms for writing – and rewriting – history, and thus for expressing the nationalistic and religious hopes and beliefs of the people."[39] Thus, genealogies are far more than a mere list or catalog. They involve convictions and intentions, as do all the other genres employed by the biblical writers. Johnson goes on to state that "the genealogical form could be used as an alternative to narrative or poetic forms of expression, that is, as one of several methods of writing history and of expressing the theological and nationalistic concerns of a people."[40] This insight directly leads into this section's argument for seeing biblical genealogies as compressed narratives or narrative summaries employed by the biblical authors for varying purposes and effects.

Wilson also discusses the relation between genealogy and narrative. He introduces what he calls "genealogical narrative."[41] This is a narrative form that can be distinguished from a list form when the focus of the narrative is on kinship relationships. He goes on to try to distinguish a genealogical narrative from a narrative that contains a genealogy. "In the former the focus of the narrative is the genealogy; in the later the focus of the narrative is not the genealogy."[42]

This section will examine Old Testament genealogies within their contextual and literary environment in order to understand them as compressed narratives or narrative summaries. To proceed in understanding genealogy as narrative, an analysis of the use of genealogies in Old Testament narratives must be presented. Three particular books will be examined, Genesis, Ruth and 1 Chronicles, for better understanding genealogy as narrative. This analysis will directly impact the study of the genealogy

---

[37] Cf. N. Sternberg, *Kinship and Marriage in Genesis*, 136: "In the final formation of the text, genealogy and narrative are inextricable linked." Wilson, "Genealogies," 930, notes that although Old Testament genealogies were once certainly oral, they are now part of a written text: "This fact has important interpretive implications not only because writing has a tendency to modify somewhat the formal characteristics of oral genealogies, but also because the literary context of the Old Testament modifies the purposes that the genealogies can serve."

[38] Johnson, *Purpose of Biblical Genealogies*, ix.

[39] *Ibid.*, 85.

[40] Johnson, *Purpose of Biblical Genealogies*, 82.

[41] Wilson, *Genealogy and History*, 9. Cf. Thompson, *The Origin Tradition of Ancient Israel*, 207, also uses the term similarly.

[42] Wilson, *Genealogy and History*, 9.

in Matthew by identifying it as a compressed narrative or narrative summary.

2.3.1 Genealogy as Narrative in Genesis

The book of Genesis is particularly useful for understanding the relationship of genealogy and narrative.[43] The use and importance of genealogies in Genesis is undeniable.[44] It contains two major forms of literature, narrative and numerative, which are closely woven together.[45] In fact one scholar goes so far as to write, "Genesis is a book whose plot is genealogy."[46] Coats provides a wider narratival perspective on the relation of narrative and genealogy within Genesis when he writes, "The genealogical structure provides connection between the stories, suggesting that the story content in each section is the substance of a genealogical stage."[47]

Westermann notes a particular failure of scholars in dealing adequately with the meaning of the genealogies in Genesis as a whole, although they give much attention to the individual names that appear within the genealogies. He says that the narrative and numerative are "almost equal in extent" and that "this is the only place in the Old Testament where genealogies and narratives are put together in such a way."[48] R. B. Robinson has also commented on this particular failure to deal adequately with the genealogies in Genesis through an article that seeks to redress that imbalance. He sought to analyze the interaction of narrative and genealogy within Genesis, writing that the "genealogies and narrative are orchestrated in a delicate, constantly shifting counterpoint."[49]

---

[43] *Ibid.*, 137.

[44] The compositional history of Genesis must be left aside in this work as the focus is on the final form of the text which is what was read by Matthew and the early church.

[45] Fretheim, "Genesis," 325, says the "genealogies are woven into family stories."

[46] N. Sternberg, "The Genealogical Framework of the Family Stories in Genesis," 41: "Through the interrelation of narratives within a genealogical framework, a chronology is established which recounts the general ancestry of universal history leading to Israel's specific beginnings." By utilizing the French literary critic Tzvetan Todorov, Sternberg analyzes the structure of the narrative plot in the family stories of Genesis. Cf. Alexander, "From Adam to Judah: Significance of the Family Tree in Genesis," 8, also draws attention to this important point, "Almost all the narrative material relates in one way or another to the family tree which underlies the entire book"; Robinson, "Literary Function of the Genealogies of Genesis," 601; Childs, *Introduction to the Old Testament as Scripture*, 158.

[47] Coats, *Genesis*, 31. Cf. Sailhamer, *The Pentateuch as Narrative*, 116.

[48] Westermann, *Genesis: An Introduction*, 3.

[49] Robinson, "Literary Function of the Genealogies of Genesis," 606.

Use of Genealogies to Connect Narratives

One function of the genealogies within Genesis is to connect narratives of preceding events with narrative events that will follow, providing the reader and listener with necessary background for understanding individuals and events that are being narrated within the overall story.[50] Although there are three major sections of Genesis, 1:1–11:9; 11:10–37:1; 37:2–50:26, it can be said that genealogies bind these three sections together making Genesis a unified and complete story.[51]

Broadly, one of the most helpful structural indicators for seeing the integration of genealogy and narrative within Genesis is the use of תולדות to announce new sections within the narrative (2:4; 5:1; 6:9; 10:1; 11:10; 11:27; 25:12, 19; 36:1, 9; 37:2). אלה תולדות is variously translated 'this is the (family) history/story of' or "these are the generations of."[52] B. S. Childs further comments on the use of תולדות when he writes, "The function of the ten *toledoth* formulas is to structure the book of Genesis into a unified composition and to make clear the nature of the unity which is intended."[53] This structural arrangement helps to unite the genealogies to the narratives within Genesis.[54]

Genealogies are used to knit individual accounts of events in Genesis 1–11.[55] The genealogy in Genesis 5 serves as the link between Adam and Noah.[56] Within this genealogy, Noah is placed at the important tenth position. In chapter 11, the genealogy of Abraham is used to connect him to Noah, where Abraham is found in the tenth position from Shem, Noah's son.[57] The link between the genealogy of chapter 10 and the narrative in 11:1–9 has been shown to have several close relations.[58] The genealogy of chapter 10 serves to link the Flood narrative with the patriarchal narratives,

---

[50] Sailhamer, *Pentateuch as Narrative*, 136, cites as an example the genealogy of Terah in 11:27–32 as background for Abraham.

[51] Cf. Alexander, *From Paradise to Promised Land*, 6–15; Fretheim, "Genesis," 325.

[52] Wenham, *Genesis 1–15*, 55, prefers the former, noting that "generations" is misleading because "the generations of X," "are those whom X produces, not the ancestors of X." Wilson, "Genealogies," 930, maintains that the Priestly use of *toledoth* in Genesis gives the book a literary structure.

[53] Childs, *Introduction to Old Testament as Scripture*, 146. Cf. N. Sternberg, "Genealogical Framework," 41: "The generations-formula is a systematizing device which gives structure to narrative traditions." On the symmetry and purpose of *toledoth* in Genesis, see Johnson, *Purpose of Biblical Genealogies*, 26–28.

[54] Cf. Gardner, *Genesis Calendar*, 242–243.

[55] Westermann, *Genesis*, 6: "The genealogies are an essential constitutive part of the primeval story and form the framework of everything that is narrated in Genesis 1–11." Cf. Coats, *Genesis*, 35–39; Fishbane, *Text and Texture*, 28.

[56] Wenham, *Genesis 1–15*, 125.

[57] Cassuto, *A Commentary on the Book of Genesis: Part I* , 250.

[58] Wenham, *Genesis 1–15*, 242. Cf. Sailhamer, *Pentateuch as Narrative*, 130–131.

and 11:10–26 serves to link one of the Flood's survivors, Shem a son of Noah, with Abraham. Consequently, Genesis 11:10–26 is actually the bridge and transition from primeval (1–11) to patriarchal history (12–50).[59]

Genesis 11:10–50:26 is unified with 3 cycles of family stories (11:10–25:11; 25:12–35:29; 36:1–50:26).[60] Chapters 12–50 continue to reveal the link between narrative and genealogy, especially in chapters 12–36.[61] Individual narratives are linked by genealogies to provide an overall flow to the story and the "family history" that is being narrated.

This use of genealogies to connect narratives and as a transition between narratives helps in identifying their function in the text as more extensive than commonly understood. By serving as links within a larger story, they help in unifying the story and the characters that are presented as well as advancing the overall plot. This particular use of genealogy as link and transition helps in ascertaining a closer relationship between narrative and genealogy that has often been neglected in the past. They serve to summarize history, with a rapid pace through a particular era until the narrative pace is slowed down for detailed story-telling.

Integration of Genealogy and Narrative

Use of narratival elements within genealogies in Genesis is somewhat common (4:2; 10:9, 25; 11:30). According to Westermann, "Proximity of genealogy to narrative is demonstrated in the short elaborations within genealogies."[62] Within the unilinear genealogy outlined in Genesis 5, a brief narrative about Enoch appears in verses 22–24. It would be patently inaccurate to assert that this short narrative interrupts the genealogy, because the genealogy continues within the narrative. The short narrative is integrated into the genealogy. The two are woven together in such a way as to hint that the editor saw these two forms not as opposites or contradictory, but complementing one another. Therefore, the relationship between genealogy and narrative is obviously more complex and interrelated than an initial impression might indicate.

---

[59] Wenham. *Genesis 1–15*, 249. N. Sternberg, "Genealogical Framework," 48, argues that the genealogy of Shem should be included in the Patriarchal history because of the structural and thematic unity. She says the separation of 11:10–26 from 27–32 is as arbitrary as is the separation of primeval from the patriarchal. Shem's genealogy starts the history of Israel and concludes the primeval. Cf. Fretheim, "Genesis," 325: "Because genealogies cut across the break between chapters 11 and 12, they witness to the fundamental creational unity of Genesis."

[60] N. Sternberg, "Genealogical Framework," 45. Westermann, *Genesis*, 216, observes that chapters 12–25 are framed by genealogies (11:27–32 and 25:1–18).

[61] Westermann, *Genesis 37–50*, 245.

[62] Westermann, "Genealogy," 244.

Genesis 4:1–26 similarly integrates genealogy and narrative. Here the longer narrative is bracketed by shorter genealogies.[63] Adam's genealogy is given and then narrative information is conveyed in reference to the two sons, Cain and Abel, born to Adam. The chapter closes with another genealogy of Adam that concludes the overall story of Adam's family, introducing a new character, Seth. Within the chapter, a further integration of genealogy and narrative can be observed where Cain's genealogy is given with narrative elements about various individuals in his family. Genesis 4:23–24 also contains a poem that is itself part of and integrated with Cain's genealogy.[64]

Similar to the narrative integration between two genealogies in chapter 4 is the Noah story that appears between the genealogy of 5:32 and 9:28–29.[65] T. L. Thompson comments on 5:28–31,

> This delightful expansion should not be read as secondary to the genealogy or as redactional to it. It is fully at home within the genealogical narrative form, as are the Enoch and Adam expansions. What we have rather is clear evidence that this genealogical tale knows both the garden and the flood narratives and understands itself between the two as a bridge.[66]

The genealogy in chapter 10 contains a number of descriptive and narrative elements (vv. 8–12, 14, 19, 25). Sailhamer perceives that "each of these notes is of special relevance to a particular event yet to be recorded in Genesis."[67] One of Nimrod's kingdoms is said to be Babel, in the land of Shinar (10:9–10), which figures prominently in 11:1–9. This short narrative deals with Nimrod, who was deemed significant and hence given further attention, being called a "mighty hunter before the Lord."

The latter part of Genesis predominately utilizes narrative as the story slows down considerably to focus greater attention upon the sons of Jacob. In regard to Genesis chapters 37–50, Westermann notes how within the Joseph story the genealogy has completely merged with the narrative where the connecting links that are common in chapters 1–36 are missing from these chapters.[68]

The integration of narrative within genealogies as detailed above is further evidence for observing genealogy as a narrative summary. The narra-

---

[63] Cassuto, *Genesis*, 190.

[64] Coats, *Genesis*, 35.

[65] Wenham, *Genesis 1–15*, 96. Cf. Sailhamer, *Pentateuch as Narrative*, 119: "Genealogical list in chapter 5 has been purposefully restructured at its conclusion in order to accommodate the Flood narrative. The Flood narrative has been inserted into the genealogy between the notation of Noah's age at the time he engendered his three sons and the notation of the total length of his life (9:28) and his death (9:29)."

[66] Thompson, *The Origin Tradition of Ancient Israel*, 74.

[67] Sailhamer, *Pentateuch as Narrative*, 130.

[68] Westermann, *Genesis 37–50*, 245.

tive elements that are integrated within genealogies serve to confirm that the genealogy itself can serve as a sort of narrative, though highly abbreviated.

Genealogy as Story

Genesis is a story about an extended family. Observing the whole of the book in this way should help toward understanding the use of so many genealogies within the book. One of the few to do so has been Naomi Sternberg. She writes, "the plot of Genesis 11:10–50:26 unfolds through narratives that are set within a genealogical framework. The narratives and the genealogical framework together organize the plot of generational continuity."[69]

The narrative parts and the genealogical parts are interwoven to create the whole story. The genealogies unify the overall story and provide a continuity and flow throughout Genesis, being "understood as some kind of historical anchor for the larger story."[70] The exclusive use of unilinear genealogies in tracing the elect line or 'seed' has been viewed by some as a royal lineage.[71] The regular practice employed is to first deal with the non-elect line using multilinear genealogies and then going on to delineate with unilinear genealogies the elect line with narrative focus upon that family.[72] Genesis focuses on a unique family line, starting with Adam and continuing down to Jacob's twelve sons, with Judah portrayed with kingly status in 49:8–12.

Another example of genealogy as story can be seen in the genealogies of Shem (11:10–26), Ishmael (25:12–18), and Esau (36:1–43). Narrative information concerning these individuals is scant compared to other characters in Genesis, but their genealogies function as abbreviated narratives by summarizing their histories. "Their histories are provided in their genealogies; their genealogies are their stories."[73]

---

[69] N. Sternberg, *Kinship and Marriage in Genesis*, 35. She states as her thesis, "The narratives unfold until the point where the continuance of the genealogy has been resolved. Only then does narration give way to another block of genealogical material. Narration is another means of determining genealogical direction – that is, establishing heirship." She traces this format through three narrative cycles (11:10–25:11; 25:12–35:29; 36:1–50:26)', 38.

[70] Fretheim, "Genesis," 325.

[71] Alexander, "From Adam to Judah," 18: "Genesis provides a very remarkable and distinctive record of the early ancestry of the royal lines of David."

[72] Cassuto, *Genesis*, 251.

[73] Sternberg, "Genealogical Framework," 44.

Genealogy and Narrative in Tension

Robinson has highlighted another unique aspect of genealogy and narrative
as they interact and create tension. Their reciprocal relationship is a literary strategy that reveals "a very delicate balance between the fixity of
God's purpose in the promise, of which the genealogies are one fit expression, and the freedom and responsibility of the individuals who concretely
bear the promise."[74] This interaction of orderly genealogy and disorderly
narrative can be seen in chapters 10 and 11. Genealogies frame the Tower
narrative. Genesis 10 presents a multilinear genealogy of Noah's family,
starting with the two non-elect lines and finally focusing upon the elect
line of Shem. This genealogy reveals God's commission to be fruitful
(9:1). In between, 11:10–26 presents a unilinear genealogy for Shem. The
narrative disorder of the Tower narrative (11:1–9) is contrasted by the orderly genealogies that bracket it with an ironic word play on the name
Shem, שֵׁם, with וְנַעֲשֶׂה־לָנוּ שֵׁם, "make a name for ourselves." God responds
with judgment in the Tower narrative, and according to Robinson, God's
order sovereignly continues with the line of Shem (11:10–26), making a
name and family for him. This interplay between orderly genealogy and
disorderly narrative takes place throughout the book of Genesis as the elect
line faces obstacles and threats, with God responding by continuing to unfold his promise along the genealogical line.[75] The tension between genealogy and narrative is finally resolved at the conclusion of Genesis when
the genealogy is no longer threatened and the line of promise is secure in
twelve sons.[76]

As can be seen in this analysis, the relation between genealogy and narrative in Genesis is "complex and reciprocal."[77] Although having only
looked at Genesis, a strong case can be made for seeing genealogy as a
narrative summary or as compressed history told through the means of
numerative. The author/editor could select various means of telling and
interpreting that history and did so through the use of both narrative and
genealogy. The varied use of genealogy was a part of the overall telling of
that story. This bears direct influence on the understanding of Matthew's
use of the genealogy within his book. The genealogy in Matthew 1 can
also be seen as a narrative summary, retelling and recapitulating the story
of Israel in a compressed form by the utilization of a teleological geneal-

---

[74] Robinson, "Literary Function of the Genealogies of Genesis," 605.

[75] *Ibid.*, 603.

[76] However even that wider story, as narrated in the Pentateuch, is not fully closed because Exodus opens with a connective waw. There is a transition from the Genesis story,
revealing a new threat from Pharaoh in Egypt, continuing the interplay between genealogy and narrative. Cf. *Ibid.*, 606.

[77] *Ibid.*, 603.

ogy. This type of teleological genealogy compresses the history of Israel into a narrative summary that presents Jesus Christ as the goal of Israel's history.

2.3.2 Genealogy as Narrative in Ruth

Ruth has been classified as a novella, or short story, by various commentators.[78] However, the genealogy at the end of the book has posed interpretive and literary problems in understanding how it fits in with the story. Many scholars in the past simply assigned it to a later hand that found it useful for inclusion to serve as a genealogical appendix. How and why this genealogical appendix fits with the book is not often discussed. The discussion has mostly focused upon whether this appendix was original to the story or not. Scholars in the past have argued the later,[79] but an increasing number of newer studies are arguing the former. In a more recent work by Jack Sasson, he states that the genealogy is tailor made for the story and integral to it.[80] Fred Bush also argues that the genealogy is integral to the story, noting the evidence based on the balancing of the book's chiastic structure (1:1–5 with 4:18–22).[81]

Unfortunately, less attention has been given to the purpose of the genealogy for the story. Admitting the genealogy is integrally related to the story, whether originally or canonically, does not finish the discussion. An analysis of this integration of the genealogy with the narrative and the purposes behind it must be undertaken. This study will proceed on the basis of observing Ruth's genealogy as integral to the story and a proper conclusion to the final form of the text, whatever that compositional history was, because this is the form utilized by Matthew.[82] The unilinear format, specifically a teleological form, of the genealogy also fits with the purpose of the book. This section will seek to briefly analyze the genealogy in Ruth and its relationship to the narrative with the intent of observing genealogy itself as a narrative summary. This will directly impact the understanding

---

[78] Campbell, *Ruth*, 3; Nielsen, *Ruth: A Commentary*, 5.

[79] *Ibid.*, 172. Although Campbell does say the genealogy does not clash with the story. Largely based on form criticism, this older view assumes the genealogy must be distinct from story forms, based on Gunkel's initial work in this area.

[80] Sasson, *Ruth*, 180.

[81] Bush, *Ruth, Esther*, 267. Cf. Larkin, *Ruth and Esther*, 46, also argues for this position: "Work on the nature of ancient genealogy-writing done in the sixties and seventies has shown how purposive and creative an art it was, opening the way to the possibility that it was, after all, always part of the story ... or at least it is in harmony with the rest of the book theologically."

[82] Cf. Nielsen, *Ruth*, 6: "Studies of the book's structure and purpose have demonstrated that the genealogy performs an important function in the story's totality."

of the teleological genealogy in Matthew as a narrative summary integrally related to the entire book.

Genealogy Integrated with Narrative

The use of a chiastic arrangement for the book reveals the integration of the genealogy with the narrative, whether original or not. The book opens, providing the setting for the story, with a family in Bethlehem during the time when judges ruled in Israel (1:1). This period was known as a time characterized as when there was no king in Israel (Judges 17:6; 18:1; 19:1; 21:25). The book closes with a man from Bethlehem, the king of Israel, David. The initial frame of the chiasm introduces the problem and emptiness of Naomi (1:21) who has lost her husband, Elimelech (אלימלך)[83] and two sons (1:1–5). In the wider background is the problem and emptiness of Israel in need of a king during the dark and chaotic time of the judges (1:1). The final frame of the chiasm reveals the solution and fullness of Naomi who has gained a son, Obed, who in turn is the grandfather of King David, the solution and fullness for Israel (4:18–22).[84] The book opens with a family and closes with a family genealogy. Both frames are genealogies containing a list of family names that balance the chiasm.[85]

Genre of Ruth: Similarities to Patriarchal Narratives

Nielsen has insightfully pointed out the resemblance of the book of Ruth to the patriarchal narratives in Genesis.[86] As observed above, the patriarchal narratives contain genealogies that serve as an important part of their structure and story. Like the use in Genesis of אלה תולדות, Ruth 4:18 presents the אלה תולדות of Perez.[87] However, why begin the genealogy with Perez? Why not begin with a more significant name such as Judah? Judah has already been mentioned in 4:12, but that would not rule out repeating his name in a genealogy. Nielsen supposes it is to point to the oddity in Perez's family having Tamar, the daughter-in-law of Judah, as his mother, with Judah as his father. As Tamar saved the family line from extinction,

---

[83] Elimelech's name means "God is king." Cf. Nielsen, *Ruth*, 99: "As the book begins with Elimelech, "God is king," so it ends with David, God's chosen king."

[84] Larkin, *Ruth and Esther*, 46: "It balances 1:1–5, the account of the near extinction of Elimelech's line, with assurance of the continuity of that line; and generally underlines the great themes of the story: Ruth's great reward for her loyalty, and the faithfulness of God's providence through the generations."

[85] *Ibid.*, 46, points out another possible balance of the ten years in 1:4 with the list of ten names in 4:18–22.

[86] Nielsen, *Ruth*, 7. Ruth herself resembles the patriarch Abraham in leaving her pagan nation to serve God.

[87] Johnson, *Purpose of Biblical Genealogies*, 16.

so does Ruth. "What others regard with disapproval becomes a sign of Yahweh's election in Ruth."[88] The use and importance of Tamar in this regard will be substantial for understanding her appearance in Matthew's genealogy.

This genealogy contains ten names, resembling Genesis 5 and 11:10–26, where David is placed in the prominent tenth position.[89] Johnson points out that this תולדות may be used like Genesis 5 and 11:10–26 to establish continuity from the time of the conquest and judges to the period of the Davidic monarchy.[90] This format of bridging gaps also lends support to the argument of seeing genealogies as compressed narratives.

Purpose of a Teleological Genealogy in Ruth

Discussion of the integration of genealogy and narrative must also note the purpose of bringing together these two genres. Whether original to the story or not, something irrelevant for the purpose of this section, the genealogy is affixed to the end of Ruth, which is what the first century hearer and reader would have experienced. Therefore, it is imperative to interpret the entire book with the genealogy textually connected to the whole, as this was the form of the story read by the Evangelist in the first century. Thus, for many literary critics, it becomes necessary that for understanding the whole story at all, one must start with the genealogy as a presupposition for the story.[91] Observing the integration of the genealogy with the narrative only begins the even greater question of why this phenomenon occurs at all.

Wilson briefly discusses and classifies the genealogy in Ruth as a common linear genealogy for supporting the political claims of kings.[92] However, Nielsen perceptively counters: how does a Moabite ancestor serve to legitimate David's right to the throne?[93] Setting aside this significant his-

---

[88] Nielson, *Ruth*, 98. This would provide perhaps another illustration of genealogy and narrative in tension.

[89] *Ibid.*, 43, Five of the names in the genealogy appear in the story, again revealing the tight integration of the genealogy to the story. The hero of the story, Boaz, appears at the seventh place. Cf. Sasson, *Ruth*, 181; Sasson, "A Genealogical Convention in Biblical Chronology," 171–185.

[90] Johnson, *Purpose of Biblical Genealogies*, 78. Unfortunately, other than this general point, and three other brief references, Johnson does not discuss the genealogy in Ruth at all.

[91] Nielsen, *Ruth*, 27: "The genealogy is in fact its basic premise and starting point."

[92] Wilson, *Genealogy and History*, 195. Other than one other brief footnote, Wilson fails to discuss Ruth's genealogy at all.

[93] While the origins of the book of Ruth are uncertain, and the purpose of this section is to examine the book primarily within a first century context, this thesis cannot enter the important discussion of the Davidic history behind Ruth.

torical question, which does not appear to support Wilson's viewpoint,[94] the story itself can be coherently read as a story of David's ancestors that reveals God's providence and the faithfulness of David's ancestors during the time of the judges. A purpose that could then be ascertained from reading the genealogy within the story is to understand the genealogy as teleological. Because the genealogy ends the story, concluding and climaxing the book with David, an argument for classifying the genealogy as teleological is further evidenced.

The story of David's family is told in such a way as to highlight both the heroic and virtuous members of David's family and the providence of God who is at work "behind the scenes" of the story (2:3). The narrative disorders created by the Moabite ancestor, the emptiness of Naomi, the famine in Bethlehem, "the house of bread," and the setting during the time of the judges when Israel needs a king is resolved by the orderly genealogy.[95] The teleological genealogy provides resolution and order, with the providence and election of God in the background, to all of the narrative problems. Sasson has argued that this conclusion properly closes the story and is tailor-made as an ending for the book.[96] The genealogy is teleological, and it serves to close and climax the story with a primary focus upon the overall purpose of the story, to point toward King David. The genealogy serves to emphasize God's election and providence over the family history in a way similar to the unilinear genealogies in Genesis. This history includes not only Ruth and Naomi, but the text also refers to several earlier women in Israel's history, such as Leah and Rachel (4:11), and Tamar (4:12).[97] The use of a teleological genealogy in Ruth serves to focus attention upon the key figure David as well as reveal the underlying providence and election that redeems the disorders that take place within the narrative. This use of a teleological unilinear genealogy further supports the integration of genealogy and narrative in Ruth.

This analysis of genealogy and narrative in the book of Ruth has helped to further see genealogy as narrative in the Old Testament. The integration and connection of Ruth's genealogy with the preceding narrative is much like what was seen earlier in Genesis. This use of a unilinear teleological genealogy combined with narrative in Ruth is significant and beneficial for understanding the teleological genealogy in Matthew. As will be detailed below, Matthew's genealogy can be read as a compressed narrative, that is

---

[94] See Nielsen, *Ruth*, 24.

[95] On the possibility of Ruth's genealogy as a protest against the stricter purity views of Ezra and Nehemiah, see Bailey and Vanderbroek, *Literary Forms in the New Testament*, 184.

[96] Sasson, *Ruth*, 180.

[97] This becomes exceedingly significant for understanding the role of the women in Matthew's genealogy, dealt with below.

itself closely related to and integrated with the entire Gospel narrative and fundamentally intended to focus upon Jesus Christ as the goal of Israel's history.

Both Genesis and Ruth have thus been found to yield particularly useful insights toward understanding genealogies, not in contrast to, but on a continuum with narrative. Various items of evidence have indicated this assertion. Hence, genealogies can be conceived as being narrative summaries or highly compressed narratives. Although this insight has not been especially noted by past scholarship, the observation becomes evident when the parts of a book are read within the whole of the book.[98] This interpretive approach pursues understanding the text as it stands, comprehending the parts, namely the genealogy, and the whole, which constitutes entire books such as Genesis and Ruth.

A final exploration must be made in the book of Chronicles, which also yields further support in understanding the relationship between genealogy and narrative in the Old Testament. Chronicles not only helps in understanding genealogy as narrative, but it also helps in the recognition of the genealogy as a highly compressed historical and theological narrative. In fact, 1 Chronicles 1–9 can best be regarded as a compressed narrative summary presenting a theological interpretation of the history of Israel. This insight leads directly into viewing Matthew's narrative genealogy similarly.

2.3.3 Genealogy as Narrative in Chronicles

The genealogy of 1 Chronicles 1–9 is by far the most complex genealogy in the entire Old Testament, and while thorough analysis of this large genealogy would yield a host of varying details, the following points must be limited to observing its connections with narrative. As seen above, the overall form of the genealogy is multi-linear, with both multi-linear and unilinear genealogies contained within it. While there has been some important discussion among scholars concerning the interpretation of Chronicles on the relation between the genealogy of 1–9 and the rest of the book, many are now insisting that the genealogy is integral to the narrative and therefore inseparable from the entire book.[99] A first-century reading must

---

[98] Old Testament source criticism has a legitimate role that investigates the process and development of each book, but if exclusively utilized it can sometimes have a distorting effect upon exegesis of a book in its final form, a standpoint especially imperative for this thesis' purpose to accept what the first century hearers and readers would have experienced.

[99] Japhet, *The Ideology of the Book of Chronicles and Its Place in Biblical Thought*, 278, seems to be one of the first scholars to do so in the book based on her earlier dissertation; cf. Williamson, *Israel in the Books of Chronicles*, 82; Johnson, *Purpose of Biblical Genealogies*, 55.

regard these two elements as a unified literary work for understanding Matthew.

Two recent studies have especially highlighted this integrative aspect. R. K. Duke argues that the genealogy serves as an introduction to the story of the entire book. He writes, "the genealogical section in Chronicles both leads the audience into the subject and thesis of the narrative and disposes the audience to a favorable reception of the speaker."[100] Gary Knoppers has also recently argued that the genealogy is integral to the entire work of the Chronicler.[101] This newer understanding and appreciation of the genealogy in Chronicles has opened up further insights into the relation between the two. Richard Pratt, who also argues for reading the genealogy as integral to the Chronicler's entire work, adds that it meshes with the overall purpose of the book: to encourage and challenge the post-exilic people of God.[102] As with most introductions to a book, themes within the genealogy of Chronicles are also highlighted in the narrative, especially the emphasis on David and temple worship. Observing this close relationship of the genealogy and narrative is a crucial area deserving further study.

Brief Narratives within the Genealogy

One of the aspects within the genealogy that also points toward understanding it as a compressed narrative is the brief narratival material that appears several times within the large genealogy. Knoppers comments on the appearance of such material: "notes, anecdotes, and comments are not that unusual either in the Chronicler's genealogies or in other genealogies stemming from the ancient Mediterranean world."[103] Four brief narratives occur within the genealogy at 4:9–10; 5:18–22; 5:24–26; 7:21–24. Some element within the genealogy, whether the person's name or an aspect of that person's history, triggered the desire or need on the author/editor's part to include such material. For example, in 4:9–10 the genealogical outline of history slows to narrate information about Jabez, where the Chronicler deems it necessary to include further material about this person within the genealogy. This material was deemed important for inclusion within the genealogy, indicating that genealogy and narrative are not mutually exclusive literary genres. The Chronicler unfolds the genealogical story with brief narratival information between the list of names to communicate information deemed relevant for the purposes of the book. As argued

---

[100] Duke, *Persuasive Appeal of Chronicler* 52. Duke cites Osborne's, "Genealogy of 1 Chronicles 1–9," which also shows the unity of the genealogy with the narrative, 55.

[101] Knoppers, "Intermarriage, Social Complexity, and Ethnic Diversity in the Genealogy of Judah," 15.

[102] Pratt, *1 and 2 Chronicles*, 62–63.

[103] Knoppers, "Intermarriage," 20.

above in regard to Genesis, it would be improper to call this an interruption, which gives a misleading connotation. The Chronicler obviously did not think narrative material within a genealogy to be so dissimilar or dissonant. This use of narrative material within a genealogy is not forced or unnatural, neither should it be regarded as an interruption or suspension of genre, because as has been observed, genealogy stands upon a wide continuum with narrative and can be literarily integrated with it. This inclusion of brief narrative material within what is classified as non-narrative further proves the point that genealogy itself can be seen as a sort of narrative, albeit highly compressed.

Literary Structure of the Genealogy

Another aspect of the genealogy that indicates narrative qualities is the clear literary structure of the genealogy. The portrayal of "all Israel" as the ideal is paramount throughout the genealogy.[104]

The Roots of Israel (1:1–2:2)
The Breadth and Order of Israel (2:3–9:1a)
The Continuation of Israel (9:1b–34)[105]

This structure evidences a symmetrical arrangement, with the first and third section roughly similar in length, with a massive section appearing in the middle.[106] Within the middle section, further symmetrical patterns can be observed.

Introduction to Tribal Lists (2:1–2)
Judah in First Place (2:3–4:23)
Tribes Easily Forgotten (4:24–5:26)
Levi in the Center (6:1–81)
Other Tribes Easily Forgotten (7:1–40)
Benjamin in Honor (8:1–40)
Summation of Tribal Lists (9:1a)[107]

The structural arrangement is not only literary but has clear continuity with the themes emphasized throughout the entire book. The genealogy starts with Adam, narrows down to the 12 sons of Israel, with priority of attention to Judah and the Davidic dynasty, as well as centrality upon the Levi/Aaronic priesthood.[108] The emphasis on David and the Levites is sus-

---

[104] Williamson, *1 and 2 Chronicles*, 24.

[105] Pratt, *1 and 2 Chronicles*, 63.

[106] *Ibid.*, 82, maintains that 9:1a balances 2:1–2.

[107] *Ibid.*, 67, 82: Levi appears in the center, revealing that "this literary arrangement reflected the symbolic arrangement of the tribes of Israel depicted in Numbers 2:1–34." Many other literary aspects can be observed.

[108] North, "Theology of the Chronicler," 376. Cf. Johnson, *Purpose of Biblical Genealogies*, 76, 81–82. Dyck, *The Theocratic Ideology of the Chronicler*, 129.

tained not only through the amount of attention they receive but also through the arrangement of their genealogies within the overall structure of the genealogy. Observing the genealogy as a compressed narrative, one can note how the form and content are brought together in such a way as to communicate the theological intentions of the Chronicler.

Theological Interpretation of History

The Chronicler noticeably communicates with specific theological purposes, and Israel's history is thus characterized in such a way as to communicate those purposes for the hearing/reading audience in the post-exilic period. Narratives inherently portray a perspective, and all historical narratives inherently portray interpretations of that history. Chronicles is a narrative retelling of Israel's history.[109] The genealogy itself is a part of that retelling.[110] A wide span of history is compressed into a genealogical format. Thus, the genealogy can be understood to be a highly compressed historical narrative. This compressed historical narrative in Chronicles unveils a theological interpretation of Israel's history.[111]

Significant efforts to describe the Chronicler's theological viewpoint have only recently been discussed, due to some past misunderstanding and outright neglect of the book.[112] Since the entire book has suffered neglect, this is even truer of the genealogies at the beginning. As seen above, the genealogy in chapters 1–9 serves as an introduction to the entire work.[113] This introduction presents a historical and theological overview of Israel's history through a *"Heilsgeschichte* in a nutshell."[114] As observed above in the case of Genesis and Ruth, the use of genealogies to present and summarize history was not the invention of the Chronicler.[115] This historical overview includes the schematic arrangement of the genealogy. Three blocks of time are outlined: From Adam to Israel (ch. 1); the Pre-exilic pe-

---

[109] Selman, *1 Chronicles*, 26. Cf. Dillard, *2 Chronicles*, xviii, calls it a theological essay or tract.

[110] Japhet, *Ideology of Book of Chronicles*, 508, 516; Solomon, "The Structure of the Chronicler's History," 56.

[111] Johnson, *Purpose of Biblical Genealogies*, 81–82.

[112] Past scholarship maintained that Chronicles was written by the same author as Ezra-Nehemiah. This viewpoint has been refuted by many current scholars, thus opening up a newer exploration into the Chronicler's theology. See Braun, *1 Chronicles*, xx.

[113] Duke, *Persuasive Appeal*, 55, writes, "These chapters serve as the introduction to the total story of the Chronicler. They establish the principle subjects of the narrative, the theological concerns of the narrator, the general time parameters and the laws of reality at work within the story's world-view."

[114] Johnson, *Purpose of Biblical Genealogies*, 73.

[115] Braun, *1 Chronicles*, 13.

riod (2:3–8:40); and the Post-exilic period (ch. 9).[116] Another way of view-ing this material: before, during, and after time of David/Solomon.[117] Commenting on the Chronicler's use of genealogy, Peter Ackroyd writes,

> So too, he has presented in a schematic form the whole history from creation to the post-exilic restoration, summing up the course of events not in narration but in names, names which reflect both the outline of the tradition and the concern with the nature of the community's life which so mark his work.[118]

Consequently, it is through "narration," a compressed genealogical narra-tive, that the Chronicler presents a historical overview of Israel's history. 1 Chronicles 1–9 is a genealogical retelling, or recapitulation, of Israel's his-tory, providing a theological interpretation of that history for the post-exilic audience.[119]

2.3.4 Conclusion

The present section has closely examined Old Testament genealogies, spe-cifically Genesis, Ruth, and Chronicles, and argued at length that when rightly understood, they can be observed to have evident narratival quali-ties. These findings have confirmed that a better understanding and classi-fication of genealogy as a compressed type of narrative is an appropriate literary viewpoint. Genealogies are not to be viewed as an opposite, alien genre from narrative, but on a wide continuum that allows for a greater flexibility of the genres within the context of an entire book in its final form.

As shown in detail above, genealogy and narrative can be mixed within sections, and the two can be integrated at a broader level within entire books. It has also been observed that genealogy can serve as a substitute for narrative, as a summary or a compressed account. The use of a genea-logical narrative is a format utilized to provide a perspective on history, people, and events that the author/editor deemed preferable for the task of communication with an audience that already had a high level of apprecia-tion and fascination for genealogy. The use of genealogical narrative also entails an explicitly theological viewpoint and interpretation of history as divinely ordered and superintended. The presentation of a theological in-terpretation of history is utilized through the use of genealogy, in both its form and content.

Finally, there are three key points in the discussion of the previous sec-tions as it relates to Matthew's genealogy. First, it can now be recognized

---

[116] Dyck, *Theocratic Ideology*, 128.

[117] Selman, *1 Chronicles*, 29.

[118] Ackroyd, *The Chronicler in His Age*, 67.

[119] Japhet, *Ideology of Book of Chronicles*, 516. Cf. Pratt, *1 and 2 Chronicles*, 62.

that a genealogy can serve as a compressed narrative. Matthew's Gospel starts with a genealogy, similar to Chronicles, albeit considerably shorter and unilinear. The genealogy in Matthew is integrated to the narrative that follows, serving a similar purpose to what has been seen in the Old Testament material surveyed above. Furthermore, it will be argued that the genealogy itself serves as a compressed narrative, intentionally retelling and recapitulating the history of Israel in that particular form.

Second, the use of a teleological genealogy has brought to light a significant classification. Matthew's genealogy will be classified as a teleological genealogy, much like the genealogy in Ruth, except that it appears at the beginning of the book. This teleological genealogy is integrated into the following narrative much like what was seen in Ruth, as well as serving as a bridge between the Old Testament story of Israel and the story of Jesus.

Third, it is observed that the genealogy stands as a theological interpretation of history. It will be argued that Matthew's genealogy is a theological interpretation and recapitulation of Israel's history, related to the genealogy in Chronicles. A literary and theological structure is employed, with definite prominence given to David. These three points directly lead into the study of Matthew's genealogy: Viewing Matthew's teleological genealogy as a compressed narrative that serves as a theological interpretation and recapitulation of Israel's history.

2.4 Use of Old Testament Sources in Matthew's Genealogy

Matthew begins the story of Jesus with a genealogy[120] that introduces the reader to Jesus the Christ through a compressed recapitulation of Israel's history. The genealogy of Jesus in Matthew, from Abraham through Zerubbabel, can easily be traced back to literary sources, particularly Genesis, Ruth, and 1 Chronicles. Through the previous analysis and classification of Old Testament genealogies, it is evident that Matthew appropriates, although not exclusively, a unilinear genealogy. The placement of several annotations throughout the genealogy fits within a narratological purpose for a genealogy. Following the temporal unfolding of Israel's his-

---

[120] For books that begin with a genealogy, cf. Zephaniah 1:1; Tobit 1:1; Baruch 1:1. Josephus begins his autobiography with genealogical information, although it differs from the style of Matthew's genealogy (*Vita* 1–6), and comments on the importance of genealogies, especially for priests (*Ag. Ap.* 1.7). Numerous Greco-Roman biographies begin with genealogical material and the use of origins and birth stories is also entirely in line with Greco-Roman works of the period (e.g. Plutarch's *Lives*; Suetonius' *Lives of the Caesars*).

tory, Matthew utilizes a descending format[121] for this unilinear genealogy of Jesus, which will be shown to be teleological.

One of the common reasons given for the use of genealogies is to legitimize the position or closely connect the last-named person by relating them to a key ancestor.[122] As becomes apparent when hearing or reading the genealogy, Jesus is legitimized by the assertion of his familial identity as son of David, son of Abraham, born within the matrix of Israel, and being listed among the royal line of succession.[123] In addition, the genealogy can also be read as a reverse-legitimization, with the use of a teleological genealogy that climaxes the prior story of Israel and completes it. Details for this argument will be presented below.

There has been considerable discussion as to whether the Evangelist constructed this genealogy alone[124] or inherited it from another unknown source. This complex debate as to possible sources beyond the Old Testament material cannot detain the focus of the present section,[125] which will deal with the genealogy as it appears in the text. Theories as to where and how the author accessed this material, while interesting and potentially valuable, cannot be undertaken within the confines of this study. Nevertheless, no direct information exists within the text to alert the reader that a specific source is being used.[126] Whether Matthew inherited all of the genealogy or various parts of it therefore cannot be fully determined.[127]

What can be discovered with reasonable confidence is the use and adaptation of Old Testament material. Although Matthew never directly states where or from whom he got this material, what can be identified is the use

---

[121] Luke's genealogy (3:23–38) is also unilinear, but in an ascending format, which was more common in the Hellenistic period. Cf. Bailey and Vanderbroek, *Literary Forms in the New Testament*, 185. It is also not teleological, and since it ascends, the narrative element inherent in Matthew's genealogy is lacking as well.

[122] It bears repeating that it has been shown that this cannot always be the function in every case because some genealogies are better seen as extensions of a personal name, as argued above.

[123] Mention of royal forefathers was also important for Greco-Roman readers; cf. Mussies, "Parallels to Matthew's Version of the Pedigree of Jesus," 33. On Greco-Roman use and appreciation of genealogy, see Hornblower and Spawforth, "Genealogy," 629.

[124] Davies and Allison, *Matthew*, 1.149, conclude it was the work of the Evangelist; cf. Gaechter, *Das Matthäus-Evangelium*, 25.

[125] For discussion of genre, see Viviano, "The Genres of Matthew 1–2: Light from 1 Timothy 1:4", 31–53.

[126] Luke begins his Gospel (1:1–4) by declaring the knowledge and use of other material in the composition of his Gospel. No such explicit information is given anywhere in the text of Matthew.

[127] Brown, *Birth*, 69–70, speculates that Matthew inherited two Greek genealogies based on the LXX and all Matthew had to do was add the names Joseph and Jesus. However, Davies and Allison, *Matthew*, 1.165–166 are critical of Brown's compositional theory.

of Genesis, Ruth, and Chronicles.[128] Other sources may have been used to some degree, at least as a body of background knowledge of the Old Testament material within the author's mind, but this is difficult to quantify. The specific names that are listed in 1:1–17, some more prominent than others, are found throughout the Old Testament and other literature. Their names are used in various ways in these texts that are also more difficult for determining any direct influence upon Matthew's genealogy.

Matthew utilizes various texts of Old Testament books,[129] as well as other literature that communicated varying information about Israel's history.[130] As Larry Hurtado sums it up, the beginning of this Gospel is "crafted to present Jesus' birth in connection with the biblical story of Israel."[131] The Evangelist's use of the Old Testament scriptures through quotations, allusions, echoes, images, and themes reveals a plentiful and comprehensive knowledge of the Old Testament.[132] Whatever the process of the construction of the genealogy was, analysis of it reveals an evident use of the Old Testament. The redactor, whether the creator of this material or editor, incorporated and integrated the genealogy with the rest of the Gospel. The purpose of this section is to examine the use of the Old Testament genealogical sources for help on understanding Matthew's genealogy.

All of the names listed within the first two sections of the genealogy (vv. 2–13) appear throughout the Old Testament. The third section includes post-exilic names beyond Zerubbabel that are unknown.[133] An analysis of the Old Testament material used and adapted, which involves the use of names, the genealogical formula, and the structure, is an appropriate and necessary endeavor for understanding Matthew's genealogy.

---

[128] In addition, Johnson, *Purpose of Biblical Genealogies*, 190, notes that the use of numbers for periods of time and particularly multiples of seven are possibly an influence.

[129] Arguments as to the extent and exact contents of this body of literature, obviously only later called the Old Testament, cannot be undertaken here. Neither can there be adequate discussion of the amount available to Matthew.

[130] These texts are brought in at relevant points in the following sections.

[131] Hurtado, *Lord Jesus Christ*, 325.

[132] However, precision of terminology in this regard is needed. See Porter, "Use of the Old Testament in the New Testament," 79–96.

[133] Several of these names from Abiud onwards appear variously throughout the Old Testament, but none of them as a part of the Old Testament genealogical sources that Matthew includes. Some have indicated that they see Matthew's hand here in picking various names indiscriminately or for various unknown reasons. Cf. Goulder, *Midrash and Lection*, 229–230, who thinks that Matthew uses symbolic names drawn from various places in the Old Testament for the third section.

2.4.1 The Use of Genesis

The first two words in Matthew, βίβλος γενέσεως, repeat what appears in LXX Genesis 2:4 and 5:1.[134] Use of βίβλος γενέσεως in Genesis 2:4 serves to either conclude the account of creation given in 1:1–2:3 or to introduce the account of the creation of Adam and Eve. Because it is not connected to a genealogy, the direct link this has to Matthew's genealogy is not as apparent. More evident is the use of Genesis 5:1, where it serves to introduce the genealogy of Adam that stretches ten generations to Noah. Genesis 5 is a descending genealogy of Adam, listing the descendants of Adam, who is the first in the list. However, Matthew's genealogy is a descending genealogy that lists the ancestors of Jesus, who is listed last in the temporal order of the genealogy (1:16). Nevertheless, Jesus Christ does appear as the first name in the list (1:1).

In regard to the phrase βίβλος γενέσεως, a major discussion by scholars as to the purpose for this particular phrase has ensued without any clear agreement.[135] The discussion of this phrase involves two related areas. First, what was it meant to evoke, if anything? The gamut of views stretches from it only indicating that a genealogy follows, to it evoking a host of themes, primarily New Creation.[136] Second, to what does it refer to as a heading? This involves what this designation refers to, whether it heads the following pericope from verses 1–17[137], 1:1–25,[138] 1:1–2:23[139], 1:1–4:16[140], or the entire book.[141]

Davies and Allison contend this phrase should not primarily be taken as a quotation or an allusion to a specific text but an echo of the LXX title of the book of Genesis.[142] By the time of Matthew, Genesis served as the title

---

[134] תּוֹלְדוֹת is used in 2:4, with nothing in the Hebrew that corresponds to the Greek βίβλος. ספר תולדת is used in 5:1.

[135] See Allison, *Studies in Matthew*, 157–162, for a helpful brief survey of the views.

[136] Davies and Allison, *Matthew*, 1.149–155.

[137] Hagner, *Matthew 1–13*, 4; McNeile, *Matthew*, 1; Gundry, *Matthew*, 13; Garland, *Matthew*, 15; Sand, *Matthäus*, 40.

[138] Luz, *Matthew 1–7: A Commentary*, 102–104, regards 1:18–25 as an appendix to the genealogy; however in his latest 2007 edition, *Matthew 1–7*, 70, he now regards it as a title for the whole book.

[139] Plummer, *Matthew*, 1; Allen, *Matthew*, 1–2; Johnson, *Purpose of Biblical Genealogies*, 146; Brown, *Birth of the Messiah*, 58–59.

[140] Kingsbury, *Matthew: Structure, Christology, Kingdom*, 11–16; Bauer, *Structure*, 73–77.

[141] Davies and Allison, *Matthew*, 153; Zahn, *Introduction to the New Testament*, 531; Morris, *Matthew*, 19: "the book of the story of Jesus Christ"; Gaechter, *Das Matthäus-Evangelium*, 34–35; Bonnard, *Matthieu*, 15–16; Frankemölle, *Matthäus*, 128–129; Mayordomo-Marín, *Den Anfang hören*, 208–214.

[142] Davies and Allison, *Matthew*, 1.151. For the most part, they have not succeeded in convincing a large majority of scholars of this. Brown, *Birth*, 66 n.7, says it is possible.

of the first book of the LXX and those who heard Matthew 1:1 could have possibly observed the relation or echo created by the use of such a word.[143] As enticing as this view might be from a theological standpoint, it simply cannot be sustained as a primary explanation for this phrase. The indications from both the genealogy and the rest of the Gospel do not add fundamental support for defending this use, particularly the new creation emphasis, which is not a particularly strong theme in Matthew. Had the genealogy started with Adam, this view would have far better exegetical support. Interpreting the phrase as evoking Genesis and the New Creation appears to over-interpret the role of βίβλος γενέσεως in 1:1 due to lack of clearer markers toward reading it this way.

H. C. Waetjen offers a more convincing explanation when he observes that both Genesis 2:4 and 5:1 are an "introduction to historical narration or storytelling."[144] This insight is better grounded and sustained not only by recalling the previous work above on genealogy and narrative, but it also fits the use of genealogy in Matthew's gospel as an introduction to the story of Jesus. The phrase would then immediately refer to the following genealogy, understood as a compressed history in the form of a genealogical narrative. The phrase in tandem with the genealogy serves as the introduction to the entire Gospel and sets the tone for the subsequent hearing/reading of it, although strictly from a literary and structural standpoint it only serves as the heading for the genealogy. The use of תולדות in Genesis is instructive in this regard, serving as a structural device that introduces subsequent history, but within a larger framework of a unified narrative. Hence, Matthew's use of βίβλος γενέσεως can be seen as a bridge or connective element, tying the proceeding genealogical narrative that culminates with Jesus into the previous story that the Old Testament had narrated. Thus, the considerable discussion and argument about how much of the Gospel is meant to be included with the phrase, and whether it is a title or not, appears to be misguided and needs to be rethought. It serves as a heading, akin to the use of תולדות in Genesis, whether one translates it "Book of genealogy," "History of Origin,"[145] or other various options.[146]

This heading certainly looks back, as does the entire genealogy, to the story of Israel as narrated in the Old Testament. The phrase, similar to the uses of תולדות/γενεσεις in Genesis, connects the story of Jesus to the story of Israel as narrated in her scriptural history, revealing the crucially significant point that there is fundamental continuity between the two stories

---

[143] *Ibid.*, 1.151, are content that the hearers would also anticipate a new creation by such an evocative use, "Book of the New Genesis wrought by Jesus Christ."

[144] Waetjen, "The Genealogy as the Key to the Gospel according to Matthew," 214.

[145] BDAG, 193.

[146] The phrase, like תולדות, is one of those expressions difficult to translate into one satisfying phrase that captures the original language.

according to the Evangelist. Jesus' story is Israel's story. Interpreting the phrase in this way, it is therefore not to be taken as a title for the Gospel.[147] From a grammatical standpoint, it must be observed that it is not a sentence, but a nominative absolute.[148] This construction is common throughout Genesis, such as in 11:27, αὗται δὲ αἱ γενέσεις Θαρα Θαρα ἐγέννησεν τὸν Αβραμ (cf. Ruth 4:18). Consequently Matthew 1:1 is best taken as a heading for the following genealogy of Jesus,[149] serving as a narratival connective, adapted from Genesis, which integrates the broadly conceived narrative of Israel's history as told in the Old Testament with the story of Jesus to be told in Matthew's Gospel.[150] The heading, like the genealogy, reaches backward, rooting itself with the prior story of Israel. Through Matthew's portrayal, the two are made into one unified narrative.

The relation and interweaving of genealogy and narrative in Genesis should also impact the further reading of the Gospel of Matthew, where genealogy and narrative are brought together and interrelated. One of the functions of genealogy earlier listed in regard to the discussion of Genesis was to connect narratives, giving background for understanding individuals and events, and thus also to be seen as narratival themselves. Matthew's genealogy serves to link the Evangelist's presentation of the story of Jesus Christ with the Old Testament story of Israel, revealing a fundamental continuity between the two stories that must be underscored for a proper interpretation of the rest Matthew's story of Jesus. Failure to observe this continuity only results in a loss of comprehension of Matthew, and in terms of Matthew's thinking, the entire story of Israel as well.

The final name in verse 1 and the first name to head the genealogy in verse 2 is Abraham (and in v. 17). His name first appears in Genesis within the genealogy of Terah, his father (11:27). Abraham was the forefather of the nation of Israel, having descended from Shem, the son of Noah. Receiving a command from God to move, Abraham left his homeland in Ur of the Caldeans, and migrated to the land of Canaan. He had received the promise from God that he would be the father of a great nation (12:2). Thus, Matthew begins where the entire nation of Israel had begun, with Abraham. Continuity with that prior history should again be underscored. Morna Hooker adds another important point when she states that "the be-

---

[147] Hengel, *The Four Gospels and the One Gospel of Jesus Christ*, 291, does not interpret the phrase as a title of the whole work, but only of the genealogy and birth story. However, it should be noted that he considers ΕΥΑΝΓΕΛΙΟΝ ΚΑΤΑ ΜΑΘΘΑΙΟΝ an ascription attached to the Gospel from a very early period.

[148] Wallace, *Greek Grammar Beyond the Basics*, 50.

[149] Eloff, "Exile, Restoration and Matthew's Genealogy of Jesus Ὁ ΧΡΙΣΤΟΣ," 78.

[150] Wright, *The New Testament and the People of God*, 385, summarizes that "Matthew starts off by deliberately hooking his own plot into the larger plot, the story of the people of Abraham, Isaac, and Jacob."

ginning of the story of Jesus lies in the purpose of God ... in tracing Jesus' line back to Abraham, Matthew is telling us that Jesus has been part of God's plan from the very beginning of the nation."[151] Finishing out the remainder of Genesis are the following names from verses 2–3: Isaac[152] (21:3); Jacob (25:26); Judah (29:35); the brothers of Judah, the twelve sons of Jacob (29:31–30:24; 35:18; 46:8–27; 49:1–28); Tamar (38:6); Perez and Zerah (38:27–30); Hezron (46:12).[153]

Matthew's use of ἐγέννησεν also appears in Genesis within several genealogies (4:18; 5:3–32; 6:10; 10:8–26; 11:10–27; 22:23; 25:3, 19; 46:20–21). The formula that Matthew employs also closely matches some of the genealogical formulas employed in Genesis. In 11:27 the basic formula followed for the genealogy of Terah is Θαρα ἐγέννησεν τὸν Αβραμ. This formula, A ἐγέννησεν τὸν B, is used exclusively, aside from the annotations, within Matthew's genealogy. These textual relations between Matthew and Genesis provide further clues toward the probable use of the LXX by Matthew. The use in 1:1 of βίβλος γενέσεως is the strongest indication of this assertion.

The opening of the Gospel of Matthew with a genealogy resembles the sequence of Genesis 5–9[154], where a genealogy precedes the story of Noah. It also resembles the genealogy of 11:10–32, which opens the story of Abraham.[155] However, Matthew's genealogy slightly alters the descending unilinear format of Genesis, which names the first ancestor and then proceeds to delineate the descendants. Matthew's unilinear genealogy, although clearly a descending genealogy starting in verse 2, specifically names the last descendant first in the heading of verse 1.

Overall, Matthew's use of Genesis is less direct, although some relations exist, in terms of "echoes" of individual stories for each of those named by Matthew, something that is taken up further in a later section of this chapter. There is also similarity in the broader use of genealogy to connect history and present a unified story. The first three annotations within Matthew's genealogy refer to individuals whose stories are told in the narratives of Genesis. The audience of Matthew's Gospel would no doubt have had substantial knowledge of the scriptural narratives of these individuals.

---

[151] Hooker, *Beginnings: Keys That Open the Gospels*, 29.

[152] Ridderbos, *Matthew*, 17, identifies an inclusion between verse 2 and 16, wherein the beginning and end involve miracles; cf. Davies and Allison, *Matthew*, 1.168.

[153] LXX Ασρων; Εσρων in Ruth 4:18. Matthew has Εσρωμ.

[154] Note the use of βίβλος γενέσεως in 5:1 to begin this genealogy and the subsequent narrative.

[155] Cf. Brown, *Birth of the Messiah*, 66–67.

2.4.2 The Use of Ruth

The use and influence of the book of Ruth, and particularly the genealogy, by Matthew for his genealogy, can be shown to be quite extensive.[156] Not only does Matthew repeat all ten of the names used in Ruth's genealogy, but a similar formula, structure, and genealogical form are also used.[157] Thus, it will be demonstrated that Matthew utilized the genealogy in Ruth in two specific ways. The first use involves almost identical verbal agreement between the two genealogies, offering ample justification for classifying this as a quotation. The second use involves an adaptation of the genealogical form and function.

Matthew 1:3b–6a closely follows the Greek text of Ruth 4:18–22. Charted below, there is a side-by-side comparison of these two texts that reveals this close correspondence.

LXX Ruth 4:18–22	Matthew 1:3b–6a
καὶ αὗται αἱ γενέσεις Φαρες	
Φαρες ἐγέννησεν τὸν Εσρων	Φάρες δὲ ἐγέννησεν τὸν Ἐσρώμ,
Εσρων δὲ ἐγέννησεν τὸν Αρραν	Ἐσρὼμ δὲ ἐγέννησεν τὸν Ἀράμ,
καὶ Αρραν ἐγέννησεν τὸν Αμιναδαβ	Ἀρὰμ δὲ ἐγέννησεν τὸν Ἀμιναδάβ,
καὶ Αμιναδαβ ἐγέννησεν τὸν Ναασσων	Ἀμιναδὰβ δὲ ἐγέννησεν τὸν Ναασσών,
καὶ Ναασσων ἐγέννησεν τὸν Σαλμαν	Ναασσὼν δὲ ἐγέννησεν τὸν Σαλμών,
καὶ Σαλμαν ἐγέννησεν τὸν Βοος	Σαλμὼν δὲ ἐγέννησεν τὸν Βόες
	ἐκ τῆς Ῥαχάβ,
καὶ Βοος ἐγέννησεν τὸν Ωβηδ	Βόες δὲ ἐγέννησεν τὸν Ἰωβὴδ
	ἐκ τῆς Ῥούθ,
καὶ Ωβηδ ἐγέννησεν τὸν Ιεσσαι	Ἰωβὴδ δὲ ἐγέννησεν τὸν Ἰεσσαί,
καὶ Ιεσσαι ἐγέννησεν τὸν Δαυιδ	Ἰεσσαὶ δὲ ἐγέννησεν τὸν Δαυὶδ
	τὸν βασιλέα.

The Hebrew text of Ruth 4:18–22 should also be given, as it was possibly utilized to some degree by Matthew, at least explaining some of the orthographic differences between Matthew and the LXX.

וְאֵלֶּה תּוֹלְדוֹת פָּרֶץ פֶּרֶץ הוֹלִיד אֶת־חֶצְרוֹן׃
וְחֶצְרוֹן הוֹלִיד אֶת־רָם וְרָם הוֹלִיד אֶת־עַמִּינָדָב׃
וְעַמִּינָדָב הוֹלִיד אֶת־נַחְשׁוֹן וְנַחְשׁוֹן הוֹלִיד אֶת־שַׂלְמָה׃
וְשַׂלְמוֹן הוֹלִיד אֶת־בֹּעַז וּבֹעַז הוֹלִיד אֶת־עוֹבֵד׃
וְעֹבֵד הוֹלִיד אֶת־יִשַׁי וְיִשַׁי הוֹלִיד אֶת־דָּוִד׃

The correspondence between Matthew and the LXX is sufficiently close enough to justify classifying it as a quotation, even though Matthew does not directly state it as such. Matthew's genealogy repeats all ten names from Ruth 4:18–22 in exactly the same order. Beyond the ten names appearing within the genealogy of 4:18–22, Matthew also refers to three oth-

---

[156] Cf. Scott, "The Birth of the Reader," 86. Cf. Nolland, "The Four (Five) Four Women and Other Annotations in Matthew's Genealogy," 533.

[157] Cf. Brown, *Birth of the Messiah,* 58.

ers that appear in the narrative that precedes the genealogy in Ruth: Judah (4:12), Tamar (4:12), and Ruth (4:13). Thus all but two, Zerah and Rahab, of the fifteen names from Matthew 1:3–6a, appear in Ruth 4:12–22.

There are five minor orthographical differences between these two texts: Ἐσρώμ, Ἀράμ, Σαλμών, Βόες, Ἰωβήδ. In some cases it appears that Matthew possibly followed the spelling of 1 Chronicles instead of Ruth, or it could be that he was using a different Greek text than those presently known, utilizing the Hebrew spelling, offering contemporary traditional spelling, a combination of these reasons, or another reason altogether. In fact, 1 Chronicles 2:1–15 does contain fourteen of the fifteen names that Matthew includes. However, it is multilinear and the genealogical patterns vary here in Chronicles. It is unlike both Ruth and Matthew, and the correspondence between Matthew and Chronicles in this regard is not nearly as close as that between Matthew and Ruth. These orthographical differences reveal an uncertainty as to exactly which text Matthew followed, and whether the Greek, Hebrew, or both were used, as well as wider issues of textual variants. Of the five differences, four can be reasonably explained: Ἐσρώμ appears in other manuscripts of the Septuagint; Ἀράμ appears in 1 Chronicles 2:9, 10; Σαλμών appears in 1 Chronicles 2:11; and Ἰωβήδ appears in 1 Chronicles 2:12 LXX A. In regard to the one remaining orthographical difference involving Βόες, the Nestle-Aland apparatus points out two other variants: Βοοζ and Βοος, the latter of which matches both Ruth and 1 Chronicles 2:11, 12. Matthew closely follows the LXX in most places for these names, although many of these are easily identified as transliterations of the Hebrew. There is certainly a possibility that the Hebrew text was at least consulted.[158] It should be noted that the spelling of certain names was varied and inconsistent throughout this period, thus orthographic analysis is made all the more complex.[159]

All of the names in 1:3–6a, from Judah to David, excluding Zerah and Rahab, appear in Ruth 4. It can reasonably be supposed that Matthew took these ten names from Ruth 4:18–22, added Judah, Perez's father, who had appeared earlier in 4:12. Then the three important patriarchs, Abraham, Isaac, and Jacob were added, causing the list contain fourteen names. Of the four Old Testament women mentioned by Matthew, two are listed in Ruth 4: Tamar in verse 12 and Ruth in verse 13. Neither woman appears within the genealogy itself, but both appear within the narrative that precedes the genealogy, and Ruth appears throughout the book named for her.

---

[158] These differences are part of a complex area of text criticism that investigates which Old Testament text is closer to the original. The LXX in particular instances could certainly contain a more reliable translation of an original Hebrew that the present MT's do not contain. Targums and Dead Sea Scrolls are also not to be overlooked in this regard. This important area of research obviously stands outside the purposes of this study.

[159] Brotzman, *Old Testament Textual Criticism*, 164; cf. Carson, *Matthew 1–12*, 69.

A further crucial observation is that Tamar, who is often viewed negatively by many interpreters both past and present based on negative readings of Genesis 38, receives only a favorable mention in this narrative. She is invoked positively as a part of the blessing that all those at the gate declare following Boaz's public commitment to marry Ruth (4:11–12). The blessing expresses hope that just as Tamar has been the prosperous mother of the house of Perez, so may Ruth be as well. This especially favorable mention of Tamar, not to mention the overwhelmingly positive portrayal of Ruth throughout the entire story, will also be observed as influential upon Matthew's use of them. Consequently, it will be deemed that Matthew's use of these two women should be taken as favorable and positive.[160] Both of these women are childless, in a situation of threat; and the threat appears not only personally devastating but also corporately grim as the entire history of Israel is at stake when the larger story is taken into account. An heir is lacking; threat to the royal line is occurring. However, in both cases, God intervenes with blessing.

Further correspondence between Matthew and the Greek text of Ruth can be offered by observing the employment of the same basic genealogical formula: X ἐγέννησεν τὸν Y.[161] This formula is used nine times in Ruth 4:18–22. Other genealogical formulas were available for use, as seen particularly in 1 Chronicles 1–9, but Matthew chooses to follow Ruth's formula here. This formula is used exclusively in Matthew throughout the genealogy thirty-nine times. The start of the genealogy, Φαρες ἐγέννησεν τὸν Εσρων (Ruth 4:18b) exactly matches the formula that starts the genealogy in Matthew 1:2a, 'Αβραὰμ ἐγέννησεν τὸν 'Ισαάκ. The formula that follows in Ruth 4:19a, Εσρων δὲ ἐγέννησεν τὸν Αρραν, is also matched in Matthew 1:2b, 'Ισαὰκ δὲ ἐγέννησεν τὸν 'Ιακώβ. From here, the formula in Ruth alters to using καὶ between the same name for the rest of the list. Matthew on the other hand makes one small stylistic change[162] and continues the use of δέ throughout the genealogy.[163]

Except for this one stylistic difference and the five small orthographical differences, most of which are solvable by textual variants, these verses

---

[160] This would exclude some of the views on the use of at least these two women. The four Old Testament women are dealt with extensively in part 4.

[161] On the subsequent anarthrous references to activated participants, see Levinsohn, *Discourse Features of New Testament Greek*, 159, where he suggests "the genealogy develops by switches from one salient ancestor to the next."

[162] However, note the caution by Levinsohn, *Discourse Features*, viii, concerning the over-use of "stylistic variation" when further investigation is usually warranted, as it probably is with 1:2–16.

[163] Louw and Nida, *Greek-English Lexicon of the New Testament Based on Semantic Domains*, 1.789 (89.87) define the use of δέ as "markers of a sequence of closely related events."

from Ruth 4 are taken directly into Matthew's genealogy. Such close verbal and structural agreement with Ruth 4:18–22 fully justifies classifying it as a quotation by Matthew. This use of Ruth is straightforward and easily accounted for when the two texts are compared.

The second way that Ruth has been utilized is far less obvious and has unfortunately been overlooked by scholarship. Recalling the previous work from an earlier section on Ruth and the classification of the genealogy of David as teleological, this insight leads directly into observing the same usage by Matthew for his genealogy of Jesus. Clearly, the most striking similarity between these two genealogies is this use of a teleological genealogy. Through the classification of Old Testament genealogies, the above analysis came to determine that within Ruth a teleological genealogy is employed with a numerical significance for Boaz and David.[164] In Ruth 4:22, David is placed at the climactic tenth position of this teleological genealogy that began with the less known Perez. As observed in sections 1 and 2 above, the entire story of Ruth had been leading to this climax of God providing a king for the otherwise hungry, needy nation that desperately required a king following the disastrous period of the judges.

This use of a numerical structure and significance, although not explicitly highlighted in Ruth as it is in Matthew, nevertheless indicates another key relation between these two genealogies. Hearers and readers of Ruth's story would no doubt realize the important count of ten individuals, and it appears that Matthew did as well. By adding the crucially important Abraham, Isaac, and Jacob, as well as including Judah (Ruth 4:12), Matthew had a genealogy totaling fourteen generations.[165] Matthew explicitly points to fourteen as significant at verse 17, structuring the three parts of the genealogy with fourteen generations in each.[166] Previously, it was observed

---

[164] The Greek manuscripts of Ruth, as well as the Targum and Peshitta, that contain the further addition of 'the king' after David's name also further help to see that this genealogy was possibly read by earlier translators and interpreters as teleologically driven. Possibly this addition of τὸν βασιλέα influenced Matthew's use of it in 1:6. Cf. Allen, *Matthew*, 3, suggests this as a possibility, or the use of ἐβασίλευσεν in 1 Chronicles 3:4.

[165] Rasco, "Matthew I–II: Structure, Meaning, Reality," 224, takes this to be the compositional procedure, 224. Cf. Davies, "The Jewish Sources of Matthew's Messianism," 500, considers that Matthew observed the fourteen generations from Abraham to David in the Old Testament and then constructed the genealogy on this pattern. However, as demonstrated above, Ruth 4 was determinative in this regard.

[166] Ostmeyer, "Der Stammbaum des Verheissenen: Theologische Implikationen der Namen und Zahlen in Mt 1.1–17," 175–192, argues that the persons placed in the seventh positions are significant, which is possible, but not exegetically obvious. Wright, *New Testament and the People of God*, 385, thinks the three periods of fourteen "hint at *six* periods of *seven* generations, so that Jesus starts the seventh seven." Cf. Hendrickx, *The Infancy Narratives*, 23–24; Witherington, *Matthew*, 40. Eloff, "Exile, Restoration and Matthew's Genealogy," 84, however, doubts this.

that Ruth 4:18–22 involved numerical symbolism utilizing Perez first so that the genealogy would arrive at the important name David at the key tenth position. This aided in classifying this as a teleological genealogy. Matthew has all ten of these names plus the earlier four, making the total fourteen,[167] which has been widely observed as a play on the numerical significance of David's name in Hebrew, a *gematria* (דוד = 4+6+4).[168] However, less observed is how this fourteen came about initially using Ruth 4. Thus, in Matthew's genealogy, David's name is in the fourteenth position, an element that is further pointed out by verse 17, which triples the significance of fourteen generations.[169] This kind of numerical symbolism, already noted structurally in Ruth, and the use of *gematria* in Matthew is certainly possible.[170] The prominence of David in 1:1–17 is evidence, given that his name appears five times, more than any other name. The kingship of Jesus, not only within the genealogy, but also throughout the Gospel, is a prominent theme (cf. 2:2; 21:5; 25:34, 40; 27:11, 29, 37, 42). A final aspect that would strengthen observing this use of *gematria* is the teleological form of the genealogy. It has been argued that the purpose for teleological genealogies is to point toward a key individual. Matthew, utilizing the teleological genealogy of Ruth, has adapted it to point beyond David to Jesus Christ as the mathematical fulfillment of David.

As observed in the above analysis in relation to genealogies in Ruth and Genesis, Matthew's genealogy is not a slavish repetition of preceding genealogies, but a creative rewriting in light of the paramount subject whom he seeks to portray. This rewriting primarily involves structuring the genealogy teleologically in similarity to Ruth, but transcending that genealogy in light of redemptive history. This use of Ruth's teleological genealogy involves a fundamental adaptation in pointing beyond David to one who is υἱοῦ Δαυίδ. Thus, Ἰησοῦς ὁ λεγόμενος Χριστός is the one toward whom Matthew points as the goal of Israel's history, and the one with whom he intends to climactically end, another manner of emphasizing the fulfillment so prominent in the entire Gospel. Matthew's genealogy of Jesus stands in

---

[167] 1 Esdras 8:1–2 contains a genealogy for Ezra with fourteen names, however in ascending format.

[168] Jeremias, *Jerusalem in the Time of Jesus*, 292, among many that have noted *gematria*. Cf. Rev. 13:18; *Barn.* 9:8. See Davies and Allison, *Matthew*, 1.163–165 on use of *gematria* among Jews and Christians. The most recent work from France, *Matthew* NICNT, 31, expresses doubt about a use of *gematria* here in Matthew.

[169] Meier, *Vision of Matthew*, 53, observes an apocalyptic pattern to 3X14, but this appears tenuous. McNeile, *Matthew*, 5, notes a possibility that the numerical structure is due to oral use for memory purposes.

[170] Knowledge of Hebrew would therefore be necessary, unless this would be pointed out to the wider congregation by the reader of the text. Cf. Note the pun on the Hebrew meaning of Jesus' name in 1:21; also the probable Hebrew significance of 2:23.

obvious continuity with those he has used, hence the significance of βίβλος γενέσεως as an evocative link. However, for Matthew this important genealogy transcends them in light of the Christ he climactically ends with, the final ending that serves as the completion of that story the Old Testament genealogies could never achieve until the Christ came.[171]

Many scholars have rightly recognized the climactic thrust of Matthew's genealogy. Various commentators have even noted the *telos*-oriented nature of Matthew's genealogy,[172] yet unnoticed is the important connection between Matthew and Ruth, and the use and adaptation of Ruth by Matthew in this regard. Beyond the adaptation of a teleological genealogy, it should also be observed that Matthew also resembles Ruth by making his genealogy integral to the whole book. Whereas Ruth's genealogy ends the story, Matthew's genealogy of Jesus opens the story, by both linking the story of Jesus to the previous story of Israel, but also moving it forward teleologically to focus upon the Messiah who has come to fulfill and complete Israel's tragic story.

Many scholars have indicated the noteworthy difference between Matthew's genealogy and those found in the Old Testament, where those genealogies characteristically begin with the progenitor or ascend to him. In contrast, Matthew begins in verse 1, not with Abraham, technically the first ancestor of the list, but with Jesus Christ himself, temporally the last person of the list. Johnson has observed how the genealogy begins with the last person named, who is the "end-point and goal of the list."[173] The combination of this important aspect with the summary statement in verse 17 that further highlights the teleological momentum of verses 2–16, only makes explicit what stands implicit within verses 2–16. Matthew's genealogy in verses 2–16, like Ruth's, descends in a unilinear form toward a key individual. Moreover, Matthew, like Ruth, ends climactically with a key individual. The genealogy in Ruth pointed toward and ended with David, the heroic king of Israel. In like manner, the genealogy in Matthew also points toward a great and final king, Ἰησοῦς ὁ λεγόμενος Χριστός. Matthew causes the teleological thrust of the genealogy to become more obvious by the use of an *inclusio* at verses 1 and 17, a structure which emphasizes Christ. This would further support the contention for interpreting the form and purpose of this genealogy as teleological.

Matthew's genealogy, employing and adapting the genealogy of Ruth, finishes that genealogy by continuing the list of descendants born after

---

[171] Ostmeyer, "Der Stammbaum," 189, "Christus wird zum Kulminationspunkt der Heilsgeschichte."

[172] Hagner, *Matthew 1–13*, 9; Davies and Allison, *Matthew*, 1.187; Schweizer, *The Good News according to Matthew*, 21: "Jesus, the goal of God's history."

[173] Johnson, *Purpose of Biblical Genealogies*, 147.

King David, and continues to follow the Old Testament story downward
into the devastating exile, which fully ended the kingship and independent
nationhood of Israel. Then, Matthew finishes the story of Israel untold in
her scriptures by descending toward Messiah, and ending with Jesus the
Christ as the climax of Israel's history. From Matthew's perspective, mirroring undoubtedly the broader early Christian church, Jesus is the one in
fact toward which all of that history had been pointing. For Matthew and
his readers, Ruth's genealogy of David had ended with a genealogy that
tentatively concluded a story of one family's need for a son, set in the period of the judges when the nation of Israel needed a king. Matthew begins
his Gospel with the *definitive* conclusion to the Old Testament story, the
story of a nation's long but tragic history, again needing a king, which
through a teleological genealogy, Matthew proclaims has come.

2.4.3 The Use of Chronicles

All of the names in verses 1–12, with the exception of Ruth, appear within
the genealogy of 1 Chronicles 1:27–3:19. It has been shown that Matthew
utilized Ruth's genealogy to get the names Perez through David, adding
Abraham, Isaac, and Jacob. This becomes further evident when it is noted
that the names that Matthew uses from Abraham to David appear in scattered places of 1 Chronicles: Abraham (1:27–28, 34); Isaac (1:28, 34);
Jacob (1:34; 2:1); Judah (2:1); Judah's brothers (2:1–2); Perez and Zerah[174]
(2:4); Tamar (2:4); Hezron (2:5); Aram/Ram (2:9, 25); Aminadab (2:10);
Nahshon (2:10); Salmon (2:11); Boaz (2:11); Rahab[175] (2:55); Obed (2:12);
Jesse (2:12); David (2:15). Bathsheba, referred to by Matthew as the wife
of Uriah, ἐκ τῆς τοῦ Οὐρίου, is mentioned in 3:5 (Bathshua). Uriah is
mentioned by Chronicles in a list of David's thirty mighty men in 11:41.

Tracing the line scattered throughout the multilinear genealogy of 1
Chronicles 1:27–2:15, the count of generations from Abraham and David
is fourteen generations, matching Matthew's count. But unlike Ruth's unilinear genealogy, which lists ten generations from Perez to David, the
Chronicler's list is multilinear, uses various genealogical formulas, and the
generations are scattered throughout the genealogy, but clearly discernible

---

[174] Zerah is not mentioned in Ruth 4.

[175] Most scholars argue that Rahab was drawn from elsewhere by Matthew, however
Bauckham, "Tamar's Ancestry and Rahab's Marriage: Two Problems in the Matthean
Genealogy," 320–329; now in *Gospel Women*, 35–41, argues persuasively based on exegesis as commonly practiced among Jewish interpreters in that time period, that Ρηχαβ
from 1 Chronicles 2:55 (MT רכב), connected with Σαλωμων (סלמא) in 2:54, may have
been the reference used to get Ραχαβ (Mt. 1:5). More on this point below.

for an observant reader to count and use (1:34; 2:4–5; 9–15).[176] It is best postulated that Matthew utilized Ruth for the names up to David, based on the detailed argument above, with some regard to their use in Chronicles, especially for Rahab. Chronicles was mostly used for the remainder of the names from Solomon to Zerubbabel directly from Chronicles.

To get the names from Solomon to Zerubbabel, Matthew went to 1 Chronicles 3:10–19. These texts are listed below, making evident Matthew's utilization of the Chronicles genealogy.

וּבֶן־שְׁלֹמֹה רְחַבְעָם אֲבִיָּה בְנוֹ אָסָא בְנוֹ יְהוֹשָׁפָט בְּנוֹ׃
יוֹרָם בְּנוֹ אֲחַזְיָהוּ בְנוֹ יוֹאָשׁ בְּנוֹ׃
אֲמַצְיָהוּ בְנוֹ עֲזַרְיָה בְנוֹ יוֹתָם בְּנוֹ׃
אָחָז בְּנוֹ חִזְקִיָּהוּ בְנוֹ מְנַשֶּׁה בְּנוֹ׃
אָמוֹן בְּנוֹ יֹאשִׁיָּהוּ בְנוֹ׃
וּבְנֵי יֹאשִׁיָּהוּ הַבְּכוֹר יוֹחָנָן הַשֵּׁנִי יְהוֹיָקִים הַשְּׁלִשִׁי צִדְקִיָּהוּ הָרְבִיעִי שַׁלּוּם׃
וּבְנֵי יְהוֹיָקִים יְכָנְיָה בְנוֹ צִדְקִיָּה בְנוֹ׃
וּבְנֵי יְכָנְיָה אַסִּר שְׁאַלְתִּיאֵל בְּנוֹ׃
וּמַלְכִּירָם וּפְדָיָה וְשֶׁנְאַצַּר יְקַמְיָה הוֹשָׁמָע וּנְדַבְיָה׃
וּבְנֵי פְדָיָה זְרֻבָּבֶל וְשִׁמְעִי וּבֶן־זְרֻבָּבֶל מְשֻׁלָּם וַחֲנַנְיָה וּשְׁלֹמִית אֲחוֹתָם׃

υἱοὶ **Σαλωμων** Ροβοαμ Αβια υἱὸς αὐτοῦ **Ασα** υἱὸς αὐτοῦ Ιωσαφατ υἱὸς αὐτοῦ Ιωραμ υἱὸς αὐτοῦ Οχοζια υἱὸς αὐτοῦ Ιωας υἱὸς αὐτοῦ Αμασιας υἱὸς αὐτοῦ **Αζαρια** υἱὸς αὐτοῦ Ιωαθαν υἱὸς αὐτοῦ Αχαζ υἱὸς αὐτοῦ Εζεκιας υἱὸς αὐτοῦ Μανασσης υἱὸς αὐτοῦ **Αμων** υἱὸς αὐτοῦ Ιωσια υἱὸς αὐτοῦ καὶ υἱοὶ Ιωσια πρωτότοκος Ιωαναν ὁ δεύτερος Ιωακιμ ὁ τρίτος Σεδεκια ὁ τέταρτος Σαλουμ καὶ υἱοὶ Ιωακιμ Ιεχονιας υἱὸς αὐτοῦ Σεδεκιας υἱὸς αὐτοῦ καὶ υἱοὶ Ιεχονια-ασιρ Σαλαθιηλ υἱὸς αὐτοῦ Μελχιραμ καὶ Φαδαιας καὶ Σανεσαρ καὶ Ιεκεμια καὶ Ωσαμω καὶ Δενεθι καὶ υἱοὶ Σαλαθιηλ Ζοροβαβελ

Matthew 1:6b–13
Δαυὶδ δὲ ἐγέννησεν τὸν **Σολομῶνα** ἐκ τῆς τοῦ Οὐρίου, **Σολομὼν** δὲ ἐγέννησεν τὸν Ῥοβοάμ, Ῥοβοὰμ δὲ ἐγέννησεν τὸν Ἀβιά, Ἀβιὰ δὲ ἐγέννησεν τὸν **Ἀσάφ**, **Ἀσὰφ** δὲ ἐγέννησεν τὸν Ἰωσαφάτ, Ἰωσαφὰτ δὲ ἐγέννησεν τὸν Ἰωράμ, Ἰωρὰμ δὲ ἐγέννησεν τὸν **Ὀζίαν**, **Ὀζίας** δὲ ἐγέννησεν τὸν Ἰωαθάμ, Ἰωαθὰμ δὲ ἐγέννησεν τὸν Ἀχάζ, Ἀχὰζ δὲ ἐγέννησεν τὸν Ἐζεκίαν, Ἐζεκίας δὲ ἐγέννησεν τὸν Μανασσῆ, Μανασσῆς δὲ ἐγέννησεν τὸν **Ἀμώς**, **Ἀμὼς** δὲ ἐγέννησεν τὸν Ἰωσίαν, Ἰωσίας δὲ ἐγέννησεν τὸν Ἰεχονίαν καὶ τοὺς ἀδελφοὺς αὐτοῦ ἐπὶ τῆς μετοικεσίας Βαβυλῶνος. Μετὰ δὲ τὴν μετοικεσίαν Βαβυλῶνος Ἰεχονίας ἐγέννησεν τὸν Σαλαθιήλ, Σαλαθιὴλ δὲ ἐγέννησεν τὸν Ζοροβαβέλ

Matthew's direct use of 1 Chronicles involves utilizing the names from Solomon to Zerubbabel listed in 3:10–19. While some are noticeably skipped, as dealt with below, Matthew's use of this genealogical source is identifiable. The genealogical format of these verses in Chronicles differs from Ruth's genealogical formula, when it uses υἱὸς αὐτου.[177] In keeping with the teleological orientation, Matthew retains the format of Ruth 4:18–22, X ἐγέννησεν τὸν Y, but utilizes the names of the kings listed in the

---

[176] Johnson, *Purpose of Biblical Genealogies*, 152, maintains that Matthew had 1 Chronicles 2:1 before him based on the use of καὶ τοὺς ἀδελφοὺς in verse 2, an emphasis upon the whole people of God.

[177] However, 1 Chronicles 2:10–12, from Aram to Jessie, does utilize the X ἐγέννησεν τὸν Y format.

verses from Chronicles. As was the case with the use of the names in Ruth 4, there are several orthographical differences between Matthew and Chronicles highlighted above: Σολομὼν, Ἀσάφ, Ὀζίας, Ἀμώς. The usual explanation of differing texts as well as the fluidity of spelling can account for two of these names. This is obvious in the spelling of Σολομὼν and Ὀζίας.

In the case of Ἀσάφ and Ἀμώς, reasons for the orthographic differences are considerably more complex. Definitive explanations for these differences are therefore much harder to argue. The more reliable manuscripts, א B C have these spellings, with later texts, L, W, and Majority text, revealing tendencies to correct the two back to a traditional spelling, Ασα and Αμων. Although in these particular cases, these later texts may actually have the original spellings and א B C producing the variants at this point. Ἀσάφ and Ἀμώς are the harder readings. Appealing to some scholars is the possible reference to Asaph the Levitical temple musician, with followers in the guild ("sons of Asaph"), and Amos the prophet.[178] Asaph, whether the individual or guild, has several Psalms ascribed to him: Psalms 50 and 73–83. There is one quotation from a psalm of Asaph (78:2) in Matthew 13:35. Possible allusions to Asaph: Psalm 73:1 in Matthew 5:8; Psalm 73:13 in Matthew 27:24; Psalm 77:20 in Matthew 14:25; 78:36 in Matthew 15:8. There are no quotations from Amos in Matthew, but there are at least three possible allusions: Amos 3:5 in Matthew 10:29; Amos 7:4 in Matthew 3:11; Amos 8:9 in Matthew 27:45.

If one considers the textual evidence based on the earliest forms of the text, which in this case indicates that these two readings for Asaph and Amos should be favored,[179] then the use of them by Matthew would appear intentional. Access to 1 Chronicles 3:10 for Ασα and 3:14 for Αμων has been shown, unless one argues the differences were already in the texts which Matthew utilized, which is difficult to argue without textual evidence currently possessed. Thus having the Chronicles' spelling at hand would indicate an intentional change at this point. An error in this regard by Matthew would be considerably difficult to maintain, particularly so when especially these two separate names have such potential for alteration. The change could in this case be supposed intentional,[180] unless any differing textual traditions in Chronicles are forthcoming. If the change is considered intentional, the purpose for it is curious given that neither Asaph nor Amos appear as particularly dominant individuals in Israel's history, nor are they otherwise prominent within Matthew's Gospel. If Mat-

---

[178] Nolland, *Matthew*, 79–81; Davies and Allison, *Matthew*, 1.175, 177–178; Gundry, *Matthew*, 15–16; Schniewind, *Matthäus*, 10.

[179] Metzger, *Textual Commentary*, 1–2.

[180] Gundry, *Matthew*, 15–16.

thew sought to find and use subtle allusions to other aspects of Israel's history beyond kingship, presenting a psalmist and a prophet would be among chief material for such allusions.

Matthew generally appears to have no indication of completely fabricating a false ancestor for the sake of providing such connections, at least in regard to the names between Abraham and Zerubbabel. For arguing this intentional subtlety, appeals to standard Jewish exegesis that considered such crafting usual fare for a writer could account for such a practice,[181] all the more if Bauckham's theory to account for Rahab's presence in the genealogy is allowed, as will be argued below. Definite controls for such maneuvers as appealing to typical Jewish exegetical practice are necessary. Confidence in the case of Matthew's intentional use of Asaph and Amos in the genealogy cannot be high, but in this regard among the list of options, this may in fact be the least of the worst among all the explanations for their presence. Of all the names in the list that Matthew had reasonable ability to change slightly enough such that the initial ancestor was not completely lost, but allude to someone that evoked an aspect of Israel's history, these two names Asa/Asaph and Amon/Amos appear to be the most likely candidates for such a procedure. Within the list of later ancestors, Abiud through Joseph, there are also a few possibly evocative names from Israel's history, especially Zadok, Jacob, and Joseph. At this point in the genealogy, the opportunity was considerably wider for inserting significant names, which apparently has not been the case here, as there are few prominent names listed from Israel's history. Placing substantial exegetical weight upon the use of Asaph and Amos is certainly precarious, but thus discounting the use altogether given the points above might prove too skeptical. In addition, with the use of Asaph and Amos, Matthew might also be giving further evidence for his prominent "fulfillment" theme in which Jesus fulfills the Psalms and prophets.[182] Appealing to Matthew 13:52 in this regard is common, as a signature of the author and as an indication of his practice.

Matthew's genealogy omits three kings between Joram/Jehoram and Azariah/Uzziah: Ahaziah, Joash, and Amaziah.[183] It is not directly understood why these were skipped, whether they were omitted as an error, whether this error appeared in the text used by Matthew or was committed by Matthew himself. A more probable reason is that the omission was intentional to keep the list to fourteen names between David and the exile. Furthermore, there is a possibility that the omission might also be inten-

---

[181] Keener, *Matthew*, 76–77, defines it as midrashic allusions that connect Jesus to priests and prophets.

[182] Schniewind, *Matthäus*, 10. Cf. Schweizer, *Matthew*, 24.

[183] Also skipped is the short reign of Athaliah (2 Kgs 11:1–3), not mentioned in Chronicles either.

tioned because the line associated with the house of Ahab was cursed (1
Kgs 21:21) and due to their idolatry.[184] These two reasons are not mutually
exclusive and both could certainly be maintained.[185] The most probable
reason is one based on the teleological nature of the genealogy that seeks
to adhere to fourteen generations within each section; hence, some names
must be left out.[186] The fact that these were part of a cursed line may have
made them the most probable candidates for exclusion, although there are
certainly other kings, evil to a greater or lesser degree, in the list that are
retained. No definite decision in regard to the omission can be made other
than that they are obviously skipped. The omission appears intentional, at
minimum for numerical reasons, keeping the list is kept at fourteen as a
result. Based on the defendable presumption that Matthew used Chronicles, and other texts as well, an error in this regard should be discounted
and intentional omission maintained. The fact that Matthew can quote texts
from the Old Testament that are not amply used in other writings of the
New Testament, as well as in non-canonical Jewish and Christian literature, further indicates an ability to navigate these texts most capably. Also
skipped is Ιωακιμ, father of Ιεχονιας (3:16).[187] Again, as with the omission
of the three kings, it appears that Matthew has omitted him to keep the
fourteen in the second section between Solomon and the exile.

Beyond the use of names, Matthew also resembles the Chronicler's
work by starting the Gospel with a genealogy, as an introduction to the following narrative.[188] Matthew's opening is not as abrupt as 1 Chronicles
1:1, but the fact of beginning a book with a genealogy is similar. Like
Chronicles, Matthew proceeds with a narrative that follows his genealogy.
Moreover, like Chronicles, Matthew's genealogy is closely integrated to
the narrative. The integration of genealogy with narrative in Chronicles[189]
was extensively dealt with above. Matthew resembles Chronicles in this
regard when the genealogy is structurally integrated to narrative, initially
in 1:18–25 by δε and the subsequent material of that pericope that explains
verse 16, and further beyond by telling the story of Jesus. A basic characteristic of this integration involves the interlocking of theological motifs
between both parts. Matthew's genealogy of Jesus serves to introduce the

---

[184] Gaechter, *Das Matthäus-Evangelium*, 38.

[185] Nolland, "Jechoniah and His Brothers (Matthew 1:11)," 172, says it was for both
reasons.

[186] Davies and Allison, *Matthew*, 1.166, defend intentional omission as the best explanation. They also note that omission was common practice in genealogies, especially for
brevity, 1.176.

[187] See Nolland, "Jechoniah," 172–177.

[188] Goulder, *Midrash*, 228, thinks the Chronicler has directly influenced Matthew in
this regard.

[189] Johnson, *Purpose of Biblical Genealogies*, 47–55, 210–228, 253.

story of Jesus, and ground the subsequent narrative with the prior story of Israel. The prior discussion of considering genealogy as a compressed narrative, retelling Israel's history, also appears to have influenced Matthew. In this regard, Matthew appears to juxtapose two key aspects within his genealogy of Jesus, the teleological orientation taken from Ruth and the compressed narrative theologically recapitulating Israel's history from Chronicles.

One of the most obvious motifs in Chronicles is the strong emphasis placed on the dominance of David. This emphasis also appears within Matthew's genealogy. The name David appears five times and serves as a key dividing point in the summary statement in verse 17. Nolan points out that broadly within their books, the Chronicler and Matthew share similar theological themes: kingdom, Jerusalem, temple, David, the embrace of all Israel, and Gentile participation. He also posits that "phrases applied to 1 Chronicles 1–9 are equally true of Matthew, whose genealogy may be called a 'sermon' on the privileges of the messianic people, and a 'panegyric' on David".[190]

Alongside the similar theological motifs are the structural similarities. These structural similarities involve the key dividing points of Israel's history. Two key dividing points in both Chronicles and Matthew are David and the Exile (1:17).[191] Both Matthew and Chronicles make particular note of the exile within their genealogies (1 Chr. 3:17; 5:22; 8:6; 9:1; Matt 1:11,12,17).[192] Matthew utilizes the LXX μετοικεσία, found at 1 Chronicles 5:22. The related cognate form μετοικίζω occurs in 8:6.[193]

The ending of Matthew has also been observed by some scholars as resembling 2 Chronicles when it is claimed that Matthew 28:18–20 depends on 2 Chronicles 36:23.[194] However, not everyone is convinced by this connection.[195] While the connection is not especially strong, at the very least, by beginning with a genealogy and ending with an edict or commission, Matthew resembles Chronicles.

---

[190] Nolan, *Royal Son of God*, 27–28.

[191] Moreton, "Genealogy of Jesus", 223.

[192] Matthew's use of the Exile will be dealt with below.

[193] 2 Kings 24:16 also uses μετοικεσία, and the perspective of exile presented there could also possibly be considered in the background of Matthew's usage, particularly in the use of καὶ τοὺς ἀδελφοὺς αὐτου, a broadly conceived reference to all those taken into exile with Jeconiah/Jehoiachin. Further discussion about καὶ τοὺς ἀδελφοὺς αὐτου and the importance of it are below.

[194] Malina and Rohrbaugh, *Social-Science Commentary on the Synoptic Gospels*, 24.

[195] Davies and Allison, *Matthew*, 3.679.

Another key aspect of Chronicles easily overlooked is the inclusion of women,[196] which reveals that their inclusion in a genealogy is certainly not unprecedented. Tamar is named in 1 Chronicles 2:4[197] and Bathsheba is listed in 3:5.[198] The Chronicler therefore reveals no tendency to hide these women when they are placed thus within this genealogy. There is also no mention of any of these three women being foreigners, which is something that is stated for other women in the Chronicler's genealogy (2:3, 17; 3:1, 2; 4:17). Neither is there any indication of any wrongdoing on their part. As was also the case with Tamar and Ruth in Ruth 4, they are in fact presented positively. These women appear within the genealogies of Chronicles as individuals in Israel's history and their appearance is useful as a reminder that they are an important part of the story of Israel. Matthew follows Chronicles by naming these women as important parts of Israel's history.

Finally, the overall approach of both genealogies can be compared. Although Chronicles involves a multilinear genealogy and Matthew a unilinear genealogy, both are overviews, theologically construed, of Israel's history. Chronicles presents a comprehensive overview of Israel, involving all the tribes. It spans history from Adam until the postexilic period. This comprehensive historical overview is theologically interpreted by use of structure and by what is emphasized within the genealogy. Matthew likewise presents an overview of Israel's history through the genealogy itself as a compressed narrative, as well as through the summary of that history in verse 17, which structures Israel's history into a tripartite scheme. As with Chronicles, Israel's history in Matthew is theologically interpreted, and done so from a particular perspective. That perspective is teleological and narratival. It has been earlier observed how Chronicles integrates the genealogy with the narrative that follows it. Matthew also achieves integration between his genealogy and narrative, further supporting the understanding of genealogy as a compressed narrative. Johnson, after careful analysis of both Matthew's genealogy and narrative, concludes, "linguistically, structurally, and theologically, the genealogy and the Gospel are at one."[199] The integration observed between the genealogy and the rest of the Gospel narrative involves the use of Abraham, David, Israel's history, kingship, christology, as well as the teleological thrust toward Christ as the

---

[196] Mussies, "Parallels," 38, counts 14 women in 1 Chronicles 2 within the tribe of Judah. David's wives are mentioned in 3:1–10. Foreigners are also mentioned in the genealogy.

[197] Matthew reads Rahab at 2:55, as argued by Bauckham, "Tamar's Ancestry and Rahab's Marriage," 320–329; and Bauckham, *Gospel Women*, 35–41.

[198] Βηροαβεε in LXX and בת־שוע in MT.

[199] Johnson, *Purpose of Biblical Genealogies,* 255. Cf. Brown, *Birth of the Messiah*, 70 n. 19.

consummation of Israel's history. For Matthew's presentation of Jesus, the story of Israel is fundamental to not only the genealogy, but to the entire Gospel.

2.5 Matthew's Genealogy as Teleological

Matthew's genealogy of Jesus Christ is teleologically constructed. In an earlier section, various genealogies in the Old Testament were observed and classified. The structure, use, and purpose of these genealogies were analyzed, and attention was given to the integration of genealogy and narrative. It was also observed that the Old Testament contains one distinctive use at the end of the book of Ruth of a teleological genealogy. It has been shown that Ruth has influenced Matthew in this regard. Matthew incorporates and surpasses Ruth in light of the all-surpassing and climactic nature of his subject.

There has been little attention to the teleological function and structure of Matthew's genealogy, and this attention has only been very brief and cursory with no clear explanation as to how and why Matthew's genealogy is constructed as it is. Many have noted the thrust and climactic nature of the genealogy, but do not further discuss the nature of this phenomenon. Some have explicitly mentioned the *telos* aspect of the genealogy, but do not expand it, nor do they identify the genealogical structure as teleological.[200] Hagner does generally render it teleological, although he does not specifically classify the form of the genealogy as such. He states, "the teleological orientation is unmistakable."[201] One aspect that inclines Hagner toward this understanding is through a comparison with Old Testament genealogies that characteristically begin with progenitor. In contrast, the genealogy of Jesus in Matthew begins not with Abraham, technically the first ancestor, but with Jesus himself, technically last person of the list.[202] Hagner later observes the unique summary in verse 17 that further brings out the "teleological momentum" of verses 1–16.[203] As with many others, Hagner cites the climactic fulfillment of Israel's history and Old Testament expectation that Jesus Christ brings, but beyond the two instances cited

---

[200] Davies and Allison, *Matthew*, 1.182, 187; Kynes, *Christology of Solidarity*, 15.

[201] Hagner, *Matthew 1–13*, 9, 12.

[202] *Ibid.*, 9. Cf. Patte, *Matthew*, 18, notes how Matthew reverses the practice of Genesis in this regard.

[203] *Ibid.*, 12.

above, Hagner also falls short of fully expounding the teleological thrust of 1:1–17.[204]

An area of imprecision in regard to classifying this important genealogy is apparent. This study takes the discussion further by implementing many of the helpful insights others have brought to this material. However, it goes beyond these in further understanding the genealogy as teleological and by expounding this peculiar use.

2.5.1 Form

The genealogy in Ruth 4:18–22 was identified as a unilinear teleological genealogy. This genealogy in form and content influenced Matthew's genealogy. The genealogy in Matthew, like Ruth's, is unilinear, following the genealogical line that starts with Abraham through David and on to Jesus.[205] It must be observed that Matthew's genealogy is not strictly unilinear, as Ruth's is. At several points, it briefly branches off for particular reasons.[206] Matthew's genealogy at these key points digresses with pertinent annotations that are not only part of the teleological thrust of the genealogy but stand as part of the theological retelling of Israel's history that Matthew narratively summarizes and recapitulates.[207] Matthew's genealogy, like Ruth, descends toward a key individual; and Matthew, like Ruth, ends climactically at this key individual.[208] Unlike Ruth, Matthew starts with a very well known and key ancestor, Abraham. Nevertheless, the forward movement of the genealogy is observable.[209] In order that it not be missed, the teleological aspect of Matthew's genealogy is already made explicit in verse 1 where Jesus Christ heads his own genealogy, in contrast to those of the Old Testament. In verse 17 the teleological structure and thrust of this genealogy is further explicated where the Christ climactically arrives at the end of the third period of Israel's history. These aspects, along with all those that will be further explored in this section, help toward identifying Matthew's genealogy as a unilinear teleological genealogy.

---

[204] Neither does he observe the teleological genealogy in Ruth 4 and its relation to Matthew. None of the literature surveyed has made this connection.

[205] The genealogy in Luke 3:23–38 is also unilinear, but it ascends, starting with Jesus and moving backward to Adam and God.

[206] This will be discussed below.

[207] The narrative quality and theological aspect of the genealogy are discussed below.

[208] Ostmeyer, "Der Stammbaum," 190, "Mit ihm der Stammbaum des Heils an sein Ende gekommen."

[209] Waetjen, "Genealogy as Key to Gospel of Matthew," 205.

2.5.2 Content

The clear teleological focus of Matthew's genealogy of Jesus is made evident in all three parts of 1:1–17. It is made explicit in the opening verse which presents the theme and keynote for the genealogy as well as for the entire book: Βίβλος γενέσεως Ἰησοῦ Χριστοῦ υἱοῦ Δαυὶδ υἱοῦ Ἀβραάμ (1:1). Both the genealogy and the entire Gospel start with Jesus Christ, as he is the main character of the story that Matthew narrates.[210] As already noted, to start a genealogy with the last descendant is unique and unprecedented. Herein reveals the teleological thrust of this genealogy. In verse 1 Jesus Christ receives priority over even David and Abraham.

The actual genealogy is found in verses 2–16. The teleological format and thrust of the genealogy are implicitly evident. Within these verses the forward movement and teleological thrust is made apparent as one reads progressively through the list. This movement is carried forward through the mention of familiar names that evoke well-known stories from the Old Testament[211] that most of the first hearers and readers would have heard many times. Just as the Old Testament story itself proceeds forward through time, so also these verses take the hearer and reader forward through time. Nevertheless, to move forward is to imply some sort of finish, an ending appropriate to the movement recounted. Verse 16 reveals that finish. The thrust of movement within the genealogy in verse 2–16 builds toward the climactic ending with Ἰησοῦς ὁ λεγόμενος Χριστός (v.16). Without verse 16, the genealogy is incomplete. An ending is necessary. Verse 16 climaxes the set of verses from 2–16. This ending marks not only the definitive finish of the preceding verses; it implies the fulfillment and goal as well. For Matthew, the history of Israel is completed with the coming of Jesus the Christ.[212] Thus, the teleological focus is made prominent.

The final verse within this pericope (v. 17) again explicitly reveals the teleological nature of the genealogy that precedes it. It serves as a brief summarizing commentary on verses 2–16. Through this brief commentary, the Evangelist points out the threefold structure to the genealogy from Abraham to David, from David to the exile, and from the exile to the Christ. The numerical structuring of fourteen is emphasized,[213] which is probably a *gematria* on the name David (דוד). Verse 17 emphasizes there has been a structural order to the genealogy as well as an order to the his-

---

[210] Kingsbury, *Matthew As Story*, 10–13; Kynes, *Christology*, 9.

[211] Keener, *Matthew*, 77.

[212] Hummel, *Die Auseinandersetzung*, 134: "Auch der Stammbaum (1.1–17) will Jesus als Vollendung und Abschluss der Geschichte Israels erweisen."

[213] Beare, *Matthew*, 63, posits the numerical symbolism adds emphasis to the fulfillment theme.

tory of Israel that it recapitulates.[214] Keener has insightfully pointed out, "As the genealogies of Genesis 5 and 11 unify history between major figures (Adam, Noah, and Abraham) ... Matthew's genealogy unifies the defining periods of Israel's history and points them to Jesus."[215] Verse 17 makes explicit the thrust implicit in verses 2–16. Christ stands dramatically and climactically at the end of Matthew's teleological genealogy. For Matthew, the order of history through the providence of God has led to this point. Consequently, verse 17 intends that as one adds up the meaning of Israel's history, the only appropriate sum will be Jesus the Christ.[216]

2.5.3 Purpose

Having seen the distinctive use and purpose of a teleological genealogy in Ruth, the observations of Matthew's genealogy as teleological are better understood. The genealogy in Ruth pointed toward and ended with David, the great king of Israel. In like manner, the genealogy in Matthew also points toward a king. Matthew's genealogy makes the teleological thrust even more obvious by the use of an *inclusio* at verses 1 and 17 that further reveal the purpose of this genealogy as teleological. The title Christ is used three times (vv. 1, 16, 17). Emphasis upon Jesus as son of David, is evident. David's name is mentioned five times in vv. 1–17. All of these elements are used to emphasize and teleologically highlight Jesus Christ as the foremost character of the genealogy and thus for Israel's history as well.

The purpose of using a teleological genealogy is to emphasize the last named individual as unique and the one toward whom all prior ancestors prepared. Like Ruth's genealogy, Matthew's genealogy points toward and focuses upon one key individual. Both genealogies are similar in teleological structure because both end with a key individual. The fact that Ruth ends with the great king of Israel also lends support for seeing Matthew's use of Ruth. Matthew's genealogy especially emphasizes the kingship of Jesus Christ as one born to the house of David.

The point of the genealogy, through the use of a teleological genealogy, is that Jesus Christ is the goal and climax of Israel's history, "Kulminationspunkt der Heilsgeschichte,"[217] the one toward whom all of history has been pointing. Zahn summarizes Matthew's objective:

---

[214] Further narrative nuances of this will be observed in the next section.

[215] Keener, *Matthew,* 78.

[216] Davies, "Jewish Sources of Matthew's Messianism," 499: "For Matthew history had a messianic pattern. Each stage of Jewish history suggested the Messiah to him. The pattern leading to Jesus, the Messiah, is threefold."

[217] Ostmeyer, "Der Stammbaum," 189; cf. Luz, *Matthew 1–7* (2007), 85–88.

To bring before his readers in the shortest possible form- in the form of a genealogical table – the whole history of Israel from the founder of the race to the Messiah, in order to express the thought, already hinted at in the title of the book, that the Jesus who received the name Messiah (1:16) was the goal of the entire history of his people.[218]

As will be seen below, it is also evident that Jesus Christ is the one who will restore the kingship of David, lost at the exile, but regained through the coming of the Christ. It is through Matthew's use of a teleological genealogy that points toward the supreme person in whom all the answers to the failures of the past and the one who was looked toward in hope.

2.6 Matthew's Genealogy as Narrative

Beyond the teleological format of the genealogy, it also reveals definite narrative qualities. As was seen above in regard to Old Testament genealogies and the relationships they had with Old Testament narratives, Matthew's genealogy can also be observed to have narrative qualities as well as being closely integrated to the narrative that follows. Through the use of names, annotations, an office, an event, structure, plot, and commentary upon the genealogy (v. 17), Matthew succeeds in retelling and recapitulating the entire history of Israel in seventeen verses.

2.6.1 Identifying Narratival Aspects in the Genealogy

Several scholars have noticed some of the narrative aspects to the genealogy. Few have given detailed attention to this distinctive use of a genealogy as a narrative. Most scholars have rightly noted the extremely stylized nature of this pericope.[219] Nolland has recently observed the narrative qualities in regard to the annotations within the genealogy. He has rightly proposed seeing the genealogy as a compressed narrative that serves as an interpretation of Israel's history with Jesus as the climax.[220] Surprisingly, the one scholar who has most strongly argued for a literary understanding to Matthew, namely Kingsbury, never mentions the narrative characteristics of the genealogy in his key book on Matthew's Story.[221] Kingsbury's

---

[218] Zahn, *Introduction to the New Testament*, 534. Cf. Goppelt, *Theology of the New Testament*, 1.168; Schniewind, *Matthäus*, 10.

[219] Scott, "Birth of the Reader," 85.

[220] Nolland, "Jechoniah," 169. Cf. Nolland, *Matthew*, 73; Hendrickx, *The Infancy Narratives*, 23, "a condensed history of Israel."

[221] Kingsbury, *Matthew as Story*, rightly sees Jesus as the main character of the story but never integrates the genealogy with the narrative nor does he understand the narrative qualities of the genealogy. However, Kingsbury's more recent article in Aune's, *Gospel*

student, David R. Bauer, has closely analyzed the genealogy in an article
that provides both an excellent overview of study on the genealogy as well
as advancing his own perspective. However, he does not stress the genealogy as a narrative in its own right, albeit compressed and unlike what one
normally thinks of as a narrative. Bauer primarily observes the genealogy
as an introduction to the narrative, introducing the main character to the
audience.[222] D. B. Howell, who wrote one of the first narrative critical
monographs on the entire Gospel of Matthew, also overlooks the observation that the genealogy serves as a brief narrative. He posits that the genealogy functions as an exposition that serves to introduce the story by placing the main character Jesus within the prior history of Israel, as well as
establishing one of the temporal coordinates for the narrative world that is
projected by the Gospel story.[223]

A few scholars have noticed the narrative qualities of the genealogy.[224]
Both Waetjen and Rasco have rightly observed the genealogy as a narrative, telling a story with a clear plot and progression.[225] Dan Via has identified the genealogy as "a very sketchy narrative" that contains what every
narrative must contain: a beginning, a middle, and an end. He states that
this brief narrative does introduce the story of Jesus, functioning as *discourse* by which "the narrator is informing the reader that the story to be
narrated is related to an earlier history, and he is positing the gospel story
as the completion of the earlier history and thereby as the fulfillment of
God's purpose."[226]

2.6.2 The Genealogy as Compressed Narrative

As seen above in part 1, Matthew's genealogy was influenced by Genesis,
Ruth, and Chronicles. All three books were analyzed in section 3 and the
conclusions of that study revealed narrative qualities to their genealogies.
Genesis displays various narrative aspects within the genealogies and in

---

of Matthew in Current Study, 163 does very briefly acknowledge narrative aspects to the
genealogy.

[222] Bauer, "The Literary and Theological Function of the Genealogy in Matthew's
Gospel," 129–159. Cf. Davies *Matthew*, 30. Many scholars, such as Nolan, *Royal Son,*
advocate reading chapters 1 and 2 as the introduction to the Gospel. Many through the
influence of Kingsbury take 1:1–4:16 as an integrated unit that introduces the audience to
the person of Jesus.

[223] Howell, *Matthew's Inclusive Story*, 98–99.

[224] Weaver, "Rewriting the Messianic Script: Matthew's Account of the Birth of Jesus," 376–385, offers a perceptive narratival reading of the numerous ironies in chapters
1–2.

[225] Waetjen, "Genealogy as Key," 216–217; Rasco, "Matthew I–II," 225–226, 230.

[226] Via, "Narrative World and Ethical Response: The Marvelous and Righteousness in
Matthew 1–2," 131. Cf. Carter, *Matthew and the Margins*, 55.

the use of the genealogies to link and unite narratives. It is apparent that Matthew has used his genealogy as an opportunity to unite Jesus to the entire history of Israel and to the Old Testament story much as Genesis unites key individuals.[227] The primary influence of Ruth was in the teleological thrust of the genealogy, although a further influence can be observed from the tight integration of the genealogy with the entire narrative. The primary influence of Chronicles was in the narrative aspects that this large multilinear genealogy displays. As detailed above, there are various places within the genealogy where the Chronicler adds brief annotations and narratives within the genealogy that help toward viewing the entire genealogy as a narrative and this has influenced Matthew's presentation.

Matthew's genealogy serves as a highly compressed narrative[228] that recapitulates the history of Israel in a teleological manner. All of this will need to be unpacked for deeper analysis and ultimately a better understanding of the genealogy and its role as introduction to the Gospel. Matthew's genealogy should be read as a compressed narrative for a variety of reasons. The primary evidence to begin with is verse 17, which serves as a brief commentary on the genealogy.[229] Many scholars have only regarded it as a summary or conclusion.[230] While the verse is quite brief, it nevertheless serves as a narrator's privilege in directly interpreting the preceding genealogy. Through this brief commentary, the author makes explicit what was only implicit within the genealogy itself. Some, like Bauer, have wrongly read verses 2–16 as a straightforward list without the divisions indicated by verse 17.[231] This is mistaken because the descending unilinear structure of the genealogy unfolds a story by retelling Israel's history. This is also evident by noting the use of two key annotations: τὸν βασιλέα (v.6) and μετοικεσίας Βαβυλῶνος (v.11,12), which imply breaks within the genealogy. Thus, verse 17 comments on this structural division, making explicit this understanding of the genealogy.

Verse 17 indicates the structure of the genealogy, and in that sense also points to the narrative qualities inherent in the genealogy. The structure is broken into historical periods that are significant for the author. These historical periods serve as key moments in the history of Israel.[232] It starts

---

[227] Keener, *Matthew,* 78.

[228] Smith, *Matthew,* 34, calls the genealogy a "highly compressed history of God's people." Cf. Luz, *Matthew 1–7* (2007), 81–82.

[229] See Eloff, " Ἀπό ... ἕως and Salvation History in Matthew's Gospel," 85–107 for the importance of this verse toward understanding Matthew's theology.

[230] Bauer, "Literary," 139; Kotze, "The Structure of Matthew One," 4.

[231] *Ibid.,* 139.

[232] On David and exile, Zahn, *Introduction to the New Testament,* 535, states, "the first indicates the highest, the second the lowest point in the historical development from

with Abraham, the father of the nation and the beginning of God's covenant relationship with his people. With David, Israel's history reaches a
climax by receiving "the king" who had been promised in the Torah (Gen
17:6, 16; Deut 17:14–20; cf. Acts 13:20–22).[233] Following this high point,
Israel's history then takes a turn toward disaster that ends with the Babylonian exile.[234] Both kingship and full independent nationhood are ended.
But for Matthew the story has not ended because as both the genealogy and
verse 17 point out, another rise toward a new and final climax takes place,
ending with the Christ. Thus, one can observe the fundamental importance
of verse 17 for understanding Matthew's genealogy as a compressed narrative. The verse clearly reveals the narrative structure to the genealogical
story.

As mentioned above, verses 2–16 implicitly encourage the reader to
closely follow these names and the history that echoes in the use of these
names. The utilization of δέ as continuative throughout verses 2–16 supports this narratival reading.[235] Implicitly a story unfolds through the historical echoes that are evident when David the king and the deportment to
Babylon are mentioned. Further echoes resonate when the numerous annotations break the normal pattern of the genealogy.[236] These annotations further serve to bolster understanding the genealogy as a compressed narrative. Particularly, the mention of τὸν βασιλέα and μετοικεσίας Βαβυλῶνος
serve as structural narratival markers, evocative for hearers and readers,
one an obvious high point and the other the lowest point, within this story.
The climactic ending in verse 16, ὁ λεγόμενος Χριστός serves to climactically culminate the movement of the story. These aspects also coincide
with the teleological thrust of the genealogy, because a story needs an ending. The Old Testament, as a scriptural story read and valued by early
Christians, never really concludes with a clear and definitive ending, at
least from their christological perspective. Matthew's genealogy serves as

---

Abraham to Christ." Cf. Pesch, "'He Will Be Called A Nazorean': Messianic Exegesis in
Matthew 1–2," 146.

[233] This is obviously based on a reading of the Torah as practiced in the first century,
therefore modern critical understanding of the Pentateuch, while eminently important
scholarship, should not obscure what was the common viewpoint of early Christian writers.

[234] Wright, *New Testament and the People of God*, 385–386, states this third exilic era
is the context in which Matthew proclaims Jesus as the deliverer, "a new David, who will
rescue his people from their exile." Cf. Eloff, "Exile, Restoration and Matthew's Genealogy," 75–87, takes up this viewpoint in further detail. His article states that it is a sum-
marization of his larger unpublished DTh thesis at the University of Stellenbosch, South
Africa, *From the Exile to the Christ: Exile, Restoration and the Interpretation of Matthew's Gospel*, which has been unavailable for the present work.

[235] Cf. Robertson, *A Grammar of the Greek New Testament*, 1183–1184.

[236] The meaning of these annotations is dealt with below.

the supreme ending to all that the Old Testament and Israel's history had pointed toward and anticipated, at least from Matthew's perspective.[237] The forward movement of verses 2–16 reveals a narrative fabric within this genealogy. Therefore, these names are not a bare list of ancestors, but a teleologically-driven story that unfolds, with a beginning, a high point, a low point, and ending with a climactic high point. The genealogy follows Israel's historical ascent, descent, and re-ascent again to Jesus Christ. Furthermore, Craig Evans in considering use of exile in Matthew states, "The Matthean genealogy may have been intended to suggest that the exile did not really come to an end until the appearance of Jesus."[238]

Another aspect that supports this narrative understanding of the pericope is the chiastic structure that gives emphasis to the three key individuals of Israel's history.[239]

> Verse 1: Christ … David … Abraham
> Verse 2–16: Abraham … David … Christ
> Verse 17: Abraham … David … Christ

The inclusio, with Christ at the beginning and the end for emphasis, would therefore indicate a focus upon Christ as the foremost priority for the pericope's structure.[240] The teleological nature of the genealogy matches this priority. However, at first glance it might appear there is some incongruity between the chiasm and the structures of verses 2–16 and 17. In other words, the implicit structure revealed through verses 2–16 and the explicit structure revealed in verse 17 seems at odds with the chiasm begun at verse 1. The structures of verses 2–16 and 17 cohere with one another. Nevertheless, what becomes evident is that the chiasm emphasizes by inclusio the main character of the genealogical narrative and of the entire Gospel narrative.

A final characteristic that provides evidence for viewing the genealogy as narrative is the inherent plot that is manifested. The genealogy unfolds a story by recapitulating the history of Israel by means of a highly com-

---

[237] Matthew's emphasis upon fulfillment in his Gospel especially highlights this viewpoint.

[238] Evans, "Aspects of Exile and Restoration," 292. This intersects with a heavily disputed topic as the whether people thought Israel was still in exile or not. Matthew's genealogy certainly appears to indicate the exilic situation lasted *until* the coming of Jesus the Christ (1:17).

[239] Nolan, *Royal Son,* 99; Bauer, "Literary," 141; Hagner, *Matthew 1–13,* 5; Kotze, "Structure," 2, 5. However, Brown, *Birth of the Messiah,* 587 fn34, does not regard it as a chiasm because it is so uneven, but rather views it as an "artistic topical sequence."

[240] Nolan, *Royal Son,* 99, points out the link with the genealogy created by v. 18, where verses 18–25 serve as a narrative unfolding the implications of verse 16. He notes the emphasis on the name Jesus in verse 1, 16, 18, 21, and the climactic final position in verse 25, which serves to include the whole chapter.

pressed narrative. The plot, which both verses 2–16 and verse 17 make evident in their own way, involves a rise, a fall, and restoration. In a well-known line, Plummer follows this plot's progression by observing, "In David (ver. 6) the family became royal; at the Captivity the royalty was lost (ver. 11); in 'Jesus, who is called Christ' (ver. 16), the royalty is recovered."[241] Echoes of the smaller components of Israel's story are also important and are dealt with below. The larger fulfillment of God's promises to Abraham and David are additional elements that are narratively evidenced through the structure of the genealogy, which is further dealt with below. These observations of a plot manifest in these verses further helps toward perceiving the genealogy as a narrative.

2.7 Theological Interpretation of Matthew's Genealogy

2.7.1 A Teleological-Narratological Genealogy

At this point, the preceding work must be synthesized and used toward further elaborating what Matthew communicates through the teleological genealogy that serves as a compressed narrative of Israel's history. The foremost concern within this study is to delineate Matthew's view of Israel's history, how it is portrayed in the Gospel, and particularly how this interpretation of Israel's history is used in the presentation of Jesus Christ. Therefore, this section seeks to bring together the preceding work on the genealogy as teleological and narratological, and to use these insights toward understanding Matthew's view of Israel's history. The use of a teleological and narratological genealogy in Matthew is principally theological. Through the genealogy, Matthew retells and interprets Israel's history[242] and specifically portrays it in such a way as to point to the fulfillment Jesus Christ brings to that history and the climactic and definitive nature of this fulfillment. Through the genealogy's compressed narrative, Matthew's plot is connected with the larger plot of Israel's history.[243] Matthew's distinctive teleological genealogy interprets Israel's history as leading toward a goal, Christ, and the genealogy as a compressed narrative reveals that this was the point of Israel's story all along.[244] An adequate manner of conveniently phrasing this theological presentation is *recapitulation*; Matthew 1:1–17 is a recapitulation of Israel's history through a teleological

---

[241] Plummer, *Matthew*, 2. Cf. Allen, *Matthew*, 2; Van Elderen, "The Significance of Structure of Matthew 1," 8.

[242] Carter, *Matthew and Margins*, 53.

[243] Keener, *Matthew*, 73.

[244] Cf. Hill, *Matthew*, 74.

and narratological genealogy. This recapitulation involves the repetition, in summary manner as a highly compressed narrative, of Israel's history in the form of a genealogy. The results of this chapter have led toward better understanding this presentation and highlighting how this recapitulation is accomplished in the genealogy. As noted above, Matthew shares with Chronicles an overview of Israel's history that is interpreted theologically. Matthew provides the final ending to Israel's history in the scriptures. That story, according to Matthew, has pointed towards and now climactically ends with the coming of Jesus Christ. This section will further expound upon how all of this is achieved.

The genealogy in Matthew has attracted much attention, most often in relation to the genealogy that appears in Luke. An effort to harmonize these two genealogies was undertaken very early on in the church when Julius Africanus was one of the first to propose solutions to this problem.[245] Johnson has helpfully surveyed all the proposals for harmonizing these two genealogies throughout the history of interpretation.[246] Most scholars have now abandoned the effort to harmonize these genealogies, realizing that they serve independent purposes within the writer's intention, and they have turned toward understanding each of them in their own context.[247] For the purposes of this thesis, no attempt is made to harmonize the two genealogies, but rather the focus is directed toward understanding the achievement of Matthew's genealogy within the Gospel of Matthew.

From the earlier discussion about genealogy as narrative in section one, it was particularly observed that certain genealogies could serve a far greater role within a narrative than merely to list ancestors or descendants, but that the genealogy itself serves as a compressed narrative that presents historical and theological intentions of an author. The integration of genealogy and narrative helped to highlight this key aspect of a genealogy's role within a narrative. It served to unify the narrative, particularly in Genesis, providing continuity and flow. The use of βίβλος γενέσεως, as utilized from Genesis, serves to link the genealogy of Jesus with the story of Israel as told in the Old Testament. The debate about its use as a title for the Gospel, evoking the title Genesis, pointing to a new creation motif, and other aspects of this discussion have obscured this essential point. The genealogy recapitulates Israel's history as leading teleologically to Christ. Matthew reveals the fundamental continuity between Jesus and Israel by using a common linking phrase from Genesis.

---

[245] See *Ecclesiastical History* 1.7; 6.31 from Eusebius, *The History of the Church*, 20–23, 204–205.

[246] Johnson, *Purpose of Biblical Genealogies*, 140–145.

[247] Cf. *Ibid.*, 144–145; Bauer, "Literary," 129.

Matthew's genealogy of Jesus serves as a compressed retelling and re-capitulation of Israel's history. The broad contours of the genealogy indi-cate a divine ordering, particularly noted in the summary of verse 17.[248] The teleological genre of the genealogy also serves a 'reverse-legitimating' function, as Israel's history is retold because it is precisely that story which bears repeating and it is that story which is properly concluded in the com-ing of the Messiah, the goal of Israel's history. From Matthew's perspec-tive, the coming of Messiah cannot be understood without the prior history of Israel, and yet that history is, in light of the coming of Messiah, only properly concluded with Messiah. Each will now need to be read in light of one another; the two are forever intertwined, enmeshed into one single story of God's people. Matthew's genealogy and the subsequent narrative serve as a proclamation of this theological presentation. Therefore, the ge-nealogy should be read as a key component of Matthew's christology. Carter grasps the importance of the genealogy to Matthew's christology when he writes, "the genealogy co-opts and reframes Jewish traditions and history to serve its christological perspective."[249] The teleological format of the genealogy has brought focus to this perspective and set Jesus Christ as the goal of Israel's history.

2.7.2 Israel's History Retold through Names

Each name in the genealogy is significant, not merely because each person is listed as being a part of the line of the Messiah, but each name serves as a reminder of stories from the Old Testament. Most of the names are famil-iar,[250] being a part of the scriptural story of God and his people, the meta-narrative of Israel's history. These individuals had served as subjects of narrative in that scriptural history, which the genealogical list in com-pressed fashion alludes to, and these names furthermore serve to remind the hearer/reader of particular events within Israel's history.[251] Therefore, each section of the genealogy will be discussed as these Old Testament *subjects of narrative* are highlighted.

The first section includes names, taken from Ruth 4, with Abraham, Isaac, and Jacob added. Most of the individuals are subjects of narrative in

---

[248] On οὖν as summary, see Levinsohn, *Discourse Features*, 126.

[249] Carter, *Matthew and Margins*, 55.

[250] The exception being those in the third section, who also serve a reminding func-tion, albeit quite different in terms of the exilic and post-exilic period that it brings to memory. This will be discussed below.

[251] Neyrey, *Honor and Shame in the Gospel of Matthew*, 94–104, has analyzed the ge-nealogy from a cultural and rhetorical perspective and concludes that through the geneal-ogy Jesus is rooted to a list of noble ancestors, which makes him 'a person of exalted status and honor'.

the early history of Israel. Many of these names evoke larger stories in Israel's history.[252] All of the named individuals served a role by being a part of the broader story of Israel's history. In addition, Keener proposes that through the use of these names which evoke stories and heroes of the past, this would especially appeal to Matthew's audience.[253]

The historical period spanned in the first section covers the era from the Patriarchs, as recorded in Genesis, to the establishment of the monarchy as depicted in 2 Samuel and 1 Chronicles. These individuals of Israel's early history came to be used as examples for later Israelites to emulate or as rebukes for their unfaithfulness. The historical periods covered in this section start with the Patriarchs, the Egyptian bondage, the exodus, wilderness wanderings, conquest, time of the judges, and the establishment of the monarchy in the kingship of David.

From Abraham to David

The story of Israel's history begins with Abraham in Genesis 11:29, earlier placed tenth in the genealogy of 11:10–26, and it continues in Genesis until the record of his death in 25:8. The pivotal role of Abraham as both forefather and a chief example of faith and commitment for the nation of Israel cannot be underestimated (Deut 9:27; Josh 24:2–3; 1 Chr 20:7; Neh 9:7; Isa 41:8; 51:2). The promises made to Abraham are often repeated throughout the Old Testament to inspire faith, challenge perseverance, and rebuke unfaithfulness. In the following narrative of Matthew, the importance of Abraham appears in three separate passages 3:9; 8:11;[254] and 22:32. One manner of reading the genealogy is to note the fulfillment of God's promise to Abraham to make of him a great nation with many descendants (Gen 12:2; 15:5). Davies summarizes the impact of Jesus as son of Abraham when he writes, "thus as son of Abraham, Jesus is in Mt 1:1 an Israelite indeed, a true member of the people of Israel. Matthew makes him bring to its culmination the history which began with Abraham: the genealogy underlines his Jewishness."[255] In addition to the rooting of Jesus in Abraham's family as a true Israelite, there are also ramifications for the mission to Gentiles through the naming of Abraham.[256]

---

[252] Carter, *Matthew and Margins*, 53.

[253] Keener, *Matthew*, 77.

[254] The inclusion of Gentiles, as a fulfillment of the promise to Abraham (Gen 12:3), is prominent here, and it climaxes with Jesus' command in Matt. 28:18–20.

[255] Davies, "Jewish Sources of Matthew's Messianism," 502.

[256] See Wilk, *Jesus und die Völker*, 83–153, 240–242, for recent work on the importance of the Gentile mission in Matthew; and Sang-In Lee, *Mission to the Jews and the Gentiles in the Gospel of Matthew*.

Often repeated throughout the Old Testament are the three patriarchs, Abraham, Isaac, and Jacob (cf. Matt 8:11; 22:32). These three men served as the forefathers of the nation that had received covenant promises from Yahweh (Gen 50:24; Exod 2:24; 6:3; Num 32:11; Deut 1:8; 6:10). By these three names, God designated himself as the God of Abraham, Isaac, and Jacob (Exod 3:6, 15, 16; Matt 22:32). The nation of Israel began in fulfillment to the promise made to Abraham, with the birth of the child of promise, Isaac. Isaac was the "miracle" son given to Abraham and Sarah in their old age as God had promised the patriarch years earlier (Gen 18:9–15; 21:1–7). Isaac's story is narrated from his birth in Genesis 21 through 35:29 when his death is recorded. Jacob was the second son of Isaac, and his story is narrated from Genesis 25:22 until his death is recorded in 49:33.

Judah was the fourth son of Jacob (Gen 29:35). Although not the first-born son, he came to have prominence through failures of his older three brothers, and was the one through whom kingship came (Gen 49:8–12; cf. 1 Chr 5:1–2). After the name Judah is added καὶ τοὺς ἀδελφοὺς αὐτοῦ. This phrase is repeated with Jeconiah in verse 11.[257] The brothers referred to in verse 2 are the other eleven sons of Jacob, hence a general reference to the twelve tribes of Israel.[258] During the famine, these brothers at the invitation of Joseph, along with their father Jacob, move to Egypt, where in later generations Joseph is forgotten. Exodus begins the story of Israel's travail as slaves in Egypt. The genealogy appears to connect these two references to brothers, as a corporate concept for Israel, and the people of God as a brotherhood and unity.[259] These two annotations are related by their exact phraseology and the corporate unity implied in both usages.[260]

A further parallel between these two uses can be noted. In verse 2, it refers to the Egyptian bondage, when the twelve brothers had gone to Egypt and a few generations later were enslaved. In verse 11, it refers to the Babylonian bondage, when the people were taken as captives to Babylon. Both events are times of oppression and bondage, "analogous phenomena."[261] Exodus and exilic themes will reappear in chapter two when Jesus is taken to Egypt and the young Bethlehem boys are slaughtered by a tyrannical Herod resembling another tyrant, Pharaoh of Egypt.

---

[257] Eloff, "Exile, Restoration and Matthew's Genealogy," 82, considers this phrase an *inclusio*.

[258] 1 Chronicles 2:1 names all twelve brothers. Cf. Matthew 19:28 refers to the twelve tribes of Israel.

[259] Gundry, *Matthew*, 14. Cf. Eloff, "Exile, Restoration and Matthew's Genealogy," 83.

[260] Nolan, *Royal Son*, 118.

[261] Japhet, *I and II Chronicles*, 47.

For the first time in the genealogy, a multilinear break occurs when Perez's brother, Zerah, is named along with his mother, Tamar. We have already noted that this indicates the genealogy is more than a mere list of names, but is in fact a compressed narrative. Perez and Zerah are brief subjects of narrative in Genesis 38:27–30. In addition, birth of twins evidences a special blessing for Tamar.

The four much debated women,[262] five when Mary is properly included, must be dealt with in this section chronologically as used by Matthew, primarily because each of them also serves as a subject of narrative within the Old Testament story. As seen above, each of the women were drawn from the two genealogical lists utilized by Matthew.[263] Other probable reasons for their inclusion, noted below, are subsidiary to this larger explanation: they are drawn from the two genealogical sources and they all serve as subjects of narrative. Their inclusion in Matthew is fundamentally the initial result of having been included previously in the two genealogical contexts that Matthew utilized, which was ultimately the result of their having been a productive part of Israel's history. The women are included in the Old Testament precisely because they played a role in Israel's history. As demonstrated above, it is not altogether accurate to say that presence of named women in a genealogy is completely unique (e.g. Gen 22:20–24; 25:1–6; 36:1–14; 1 Chr 2:3–4, 16–19, 46; 3:1–9).[264] By specifically naming the women, their narrative is called to memory.[265] Richard Horsley has rightly claimed that these women were "remembered for their crucial roles in the deliverance of the people," and they enabled the line to continue.[266] There is further significance to these women in that they all bore children in the line of David.[267] Therefore, their role in serving as subjects of narrative within Israel's history is the primary reason for their being named in the genealogy.[268] From Matthew's perspective, all of them

---

[262] For summaries of the various views see Johnson, *Purpose of Biblical Genealogies*, 152–179; Brown, *Birth of the Messiah*, 71–74, 591–596; Davies and Allison, *Matthew*, 1.170–172; Carter, *Matthew and Margins*, 59–61.

[263] Rahab is drawn from 1 Chronicles 2:55, as noted and argued below. Cf. Bauckham, "Tamar's Ancestry and Rahab's Marriage," 320–329; and *Gospel Women*, 35–41.

[264] Jewish tradition continued to add women's names to genealogies, as evidenced in Jubilees (e.g. 4:7–33) and Ps.-Philo (e.g. 1:1–19).

[265] Loubser, "Invoking the Ancestors: Some Socio-Rhetorical Aspects of the Genealogies in the Gospels of Matthew and Luke," 133.

[266] Horsley, *The Liberation of Christmas*, 85.

[267] Cf. Menninger, *Israel and the Church in the Gospel of Matthew*, 76.

[268] Wainwright, *Towards a Feminist Critical Reading of the Gospel According to Matthew*, 67.

were used as part of a divine plan.[269] The women are thus named simply because they were a part of the story.[270]

Other subsidiary components in their usage include the Gentile status[271] of especially Rahab and Ruth, and with less confidence Tamar and Bathsheba. The "irregularity" of the stories, which is mirrored by the "irregularity" of Mary and Joseph's situation (Matt 1:16, 18–25), could possibly be a subsidiary component. Primarily, Matthew named them as an important part of the story of Israel,[272] just as he names Mary who played an important role in the birth of the Messiah. What then ultimately unifies all five of these women in the presentation of Matthew's genealogy is their role in the story of Israel.[273] Joachim Jeremias summarizes they were "all women to whom God's power was revealed, therefore types of Mary."[274] The Evangelist continues to include various women, some named and others not named, throughout the Gospel narrative as important parts of the story of Jesus (8:14–15; 9:18–26; 12:46–47; 13:55–56; 14:3–11; 14:21; 15:21–28; 15:38; 20:20–23; 21:32; 26:6–13; 26:69–72; 27:55–56, 61; 28:1–10).[275]

All four of the women were named in Matthew's two sources, Ruth and Chronicles. Tamar and Ruth are named in Ruth 4. Tamar and Bathsheba are named in 1 Chronicles 2–3, and Matthew also reads Rahab in Chronicles.[276] It appears therefore that these women were not simply drawn from a widely available pool of women's names that Matthew would have had access to throughout the Old Testament material. Instead, each of these appeared within the two genealogies that Matthew used and adapted. Thus, indications as to their use by Matthew should start within the material from

---

[269] Witherington, *Matthew*, 50; cf. Lohmeyer, *Das Evangelium des Matthäus*, 5–6; Bruce, *Synoptic Gospels*, 63.

[270] Levine, *Social and Ethnic Dimensions*, 277, argues against their use as Gentiles or because of irregular sexual situations and in favor of all four women as the powerless overcoming cultural obstacles to fulfill their role in Israel's history.

[271] Obviously, it should be noted that Mary is not a Gentile. Gentile emphasis is prominent in Matthew 4:13–16; 8:5–13; 12:18–21; 15:21–38; 21:33–46; 27:54; 28:18–20. See Wilk, *Jesus und die Völker*, 83–153; however Wilk only very briefly discusses these women as Gentiles on page 84. Cf. Schnabel, *Early Christian Mission: Paul and the Early Church*, 1494–1495.

[272] Further women from the Old Testament that are cited in Matthew: Rachel (2:18); Queen of the South (12:42).

[273] However, Heckl, "Der biblische Begründungsrahmen für die Jungfrauengeburt bei Matthäus," 161–180, argues the four women are contrasted with Mary through an intertextual relationship with Gen. 5.

[274] Joachim, *Jerusalem in the Time of Jesus*, 293.

[275] See Bauckham, *Gospel Women*; and Witherington, *Women in the Ministry of Jesus*.

[276] Bauckham, "Tamar's Ancestry and Rahab's Marriage," 320–329; and Bauckham, *Gospel Women*, 35–41.

which Matthew received them. Had their names not appeared in these two sources, then other immediate reasons would need to be posited as to their inclusion, but given the fact that all four are named in the sources that Matthew utilized, the most evident reason for their inclusion by Matthew is they were already named in his source.

Furthermore, in conjunction with the previous point, all of these women are subjects of narrative. Each played a role in the story of Israel and the unfolding of the Messianic line, and they are forever encapsulated within the meta-narrative of Israel's history as recorded in the Old Testament.[277] This narratival use of them should also be noted in coming to a better understanding of their use in Matthew. Too easily, a presumption of their use is initially assumed, based on certain interpretations of their use in a number of Old Testament texts, with no attention to their use in Matthew's sources. In this case, it has yielded some notably unhelpful elements, particularly the over-moralizing interpretation of them as "sinners,"[278] whether by earlier interpreters or the more recent discussion of irregularity and scandal. This option has proven to not coherently match all four women, five when Mary is rightly included. The help needed for understanding their role is found elsewhere, and thus it is imperative to consider the context of these women in the two genealogies from which they were drawn. An author can highlight any number of aspects about a person, whether positive, negative, or both. In the case of these four Old Testament women, the context of Ruth unambiguously indicates a strongly positive use of both Tamar and Ruth, as argued in detail above. The context of Chronicles implies nothing negative about Tamar, Rahab, or Bathsheba,[279] and at minimum, their use is neutral. However, it could certainly be argued that here too they are positive figures by the very fact that they are specifically named in Chronicles, intentionally placed there as persons worthy to be named.[280] The "irregularity" of their situations is therefore subsidiary to this primary point, just as it is with Mary.

Tamar is drawn from the narrative that precedes the genealogy in Ruth 4:11. She is named in a prayer of blessing uttered aloud by the witnesses of Boaz's public commitment to marry Ruth. The use of Tamar in this prayer

---

[277] Nolland, *Matthew*, 77, concludes that "each is included primarily because of her unique individual potential for evoking important aspects of the story of Israel." Cf. Hutchison, "Women, Gentiles, and the Messianic Mission in Matthew's Gospel," 152–153, argues they are used as references to four key periods in Israel's history.

[278] Brown, *Birth of the Messiah*, 595, offers an important corrective that there should also be proper attention to the plentiful failures of males in the genealogy.

[279] The use of ἐκ τῆς τοῦ Οὐρίου, indicates even more narratively and will be discussed below.

[280] Wainwright, "The Gospel of Matthew," 635–644, has many further perceptive insights on the women that go beyond what this study could reasonably include.

is overwhelmingly positive, in her exemplary role as the mother of the house of Perez, through whom ultimately came David, as the reader is soon made aware. There is no indication on the part of those who uttered the prayer in the story, nor on the part of the narrator, of what frequently is recalled, specifically the "immoral" incident of Judah and Tamar as recorded in Genesis 38. Knowledge of Genesis 38 by the first century audience that heard and read Matthew was probably commonplace, but information about their perceptions must not be too readily assumed, and modern overmoralizing avoided.[281] Moreover, it would certainly behoove the modern interpreter of the Genesis narrative to be more cautious in too-readily implicating Tamar of wrongdoing based on a straightforward reading of that text. She is explicitly called "righteous"[282] by Judah himself when he states, 'She is more righteous than I', ויאמר צדקה ממני (Gen 38:26). She also receives a special blessing of God in her bearing of twin sons. Therefore, for better understanding Matthew's inclusion of Tamar in this genealogy, the immediate context of Ruth and Chronicles should be determinative. From Ruth 4, the reader is only given a positive portrayal of a woman whom God used to bring forth the house of Perez, ultimately blessing the entire nation who would benefit from the king to be born in this family line (Ruth 4:17, 22).

Tamar is named within the Chronicler's genealogy at 1 Chronicles 2:4, where the reader is reminded that Tamar bore twins to Judah, Perez and Zerah. Matthew also names both brothers, Perez and Zerah, in contrast to the remainder of the genealogy that does not specifically name a brother. The birth of twins to Tamar is a particular aspect Matthew keeps, further highlighting the blessing of God and her role in Israel's story.

Although Tamar is frequently assumed to be Canaanite, strictly maintaining the Gentile status of Tamar is problematic.[283] In Genesis 38, there is no explicit mention of where Tamar is from, although she is obviously not from the immediate "people of Israel" because at this point it includes only a family of three generations. Tamar may have been from among the Canaanite group from which Judah had also chosen his own wife Shua (Gen 38:2), but this is not made explicit in the text. She could have hailed

---

[281] Cf. France, *Matthew* NICNT, 37. No wrongdoing is mentioned of her in Jubilees, where like Genesis 38:26 she is called righteous (41:19); in contrast it is Judah who repents (41:23–24; cf. *T. Jud.* 12). In Ps.-Philo 9:3–5 she is used as a positive example, "our mother Tamar," by Amram within the Moses birth narrative. She is a virtuous proselyte in Philo *Virt.* 220–222; *Deus Imm.* 136–137. LeD'eaut, *The Message of the New Testament and the Aramaic Bible*, 34–35, notes the use of Tamar in the targums as positive.

[282] Cf. Joseph is explicitly called "righteous" in 1:19, and Mary is implicitly "righteous" in 1:18 and 20.

[283] Levine, *Social and Ethnic Dimension*, 73.

from the same area Rebekah was raised.[284] According to Jubilees 41:1 she
hails from the daughters of Aram, and she is especially hated by Er because she is not a Canaanite like his mother was (cf. *T. Jud.* 10:2–3). In
addition, from the important contexts of Ruth and Chronicles, a Gentile
nationality of Tamar is not mentioned. In the case of Judah's wife Shua
(Bath-Shua in 1 Chr 2:3) the Chronicler explicitly mentions that she was a
Canaanite. In other places, the Chronicler also records the Gentile status of
a person (2:3, 17; 3:1, 2; 4:17). With Tamar there is no such indication,
neither from Ruth or 1 Chronicles, and only a possible general inference
from Genesis 38. While she is not directly Israelite, as that family remains
quite small at this point, she is probably no more of a Gentile than Rebekah or Rachel according to the important contexts in Genesis and
Chronicles.[285]

Matthew's use of Tamar in his genealogy should therefore be seen as
positive and views that primarily consider her otherwise are faulty when
portraying her negatively in this text based on weak exegesis. She was an
important part of Israel's history, a "subject of narrative," and on that
count was considered by Matthew, as drawn from both Ruth and 1 Chronicles, to merit inclusion in his list of Jesus' ancestors. Her role in Israel's
history is sufficient reason for mentioning her here. The "irregularity" of
her situation is therefore subsidiary to the considerations above. She was
an important part in the continuation of the family line of God's people,
albeit in a way that appears "odd" to subsequent readers, thus resembling
in some ways the 'oddity' of Mary's situation.

Continuing to sequentially follow the names, many of those from Perez
to Boaz are considerably less known, some of whom are only referred to in
genealogies. They are less subjects of narrative individually, other than as
evocations of the period of history they cover: from the journey of Jacob's
family to Egypt, the exodus, the wilderness wandering, the conquest, to the
era of the Judges. The broader story evoked is Israel's wait for a king, a
story localized within the book of Ruth, set during the time of the judges
(1:1). This period of Israel's early history can be regarded in large part as a
time of need and anticipation of a king to lead God's people, based on accepting a straightforward reading of the scriptures as would have been
practiced by first century believers. It is also apparent that generations
were skipped in this account, just as they had been in Ruth 4. Telescoping
a genealogy to keep a certain number of names, in Ruth kept at ten, and in
Matthew fourteen, for each section was in keeping with the teleological
purpose. Thus reconciling individuals with a certain period is problematic

---

[284] Rebekah was from Abraham's country and relatives (Gen 24:4), the city of Nahor
(Gen 24:10).

[285] Nolland, *Matthew*, 74. Other sources *might* have influenced Matthew in this regard, for or against Tamar as a Gentile, but this would need careful arguing.

but unnecessary. Hezron was the son of Perez (Gen 46:12; Num 26:21; 1 Chr 4:1), among those in Jacob's large family that went to Egypt during the famine in Canaan (Gen 46:1–27). Aram/Ram is only mentioned in Ruth 4:19 and 1 Chronicles 2:9, 10.

Rahab is named in Matthew's genealogy, having been drawn from the genealogy in 1 Chronicles 2:55, where she is read as such by the Evangelist in relation to Salma. Bauckham has argued convincingly that Matthew drew the name Rahab from Chronicles, based on common Jewish exegetical practice of that period.[286] There is no other account in the Old Testament of the marriage of Rahab to Salmon;[287] unless it is supposed that Matthew wished to include Rahab as a part of the genealogy and by scanning the Old Testament for suitably appropriate examples for his theme, Matthew picked Rahab and inserted her at an appropriate point. This is perhaps more difficult to argue given the close attention Matthew had to the two genealogical sources. Arguing that Matthew fabricates ancestors when he has been shown to closely utilize sources otherwise is problematic and difficult to maintain exegetically. A better explanation is that especially given Matthew's certain use of 1 Chronicles 2 and 3, she was drawn from there as well.[288] The proximity of רכב in 2:55, the last verse of chapter 2, to the very next verses in 3:1–9, which list David's sons is also helpful evidence for this conclusion. Her inclusion in the genealogy could then be seen as the result of being found by Matthew in a source.[289] Matthew writes ʽΡαχάβ, whereas Chronicles has Ρηχαβ. The standard spelling of Rahab in the LXX is ʽΡαάβ (cf. Heb 11:31; Jas 2:25; 1 Clem. 12:1). In the MT Rahab is spelled רחב (Josh. 2:1, etc.) and 1 Chronicles 2:55 has רכב, commonly taken as the house of Rechab. Matthew's ʽΡαχάβ transliterates both Hebrew spellings, and differs by only one letter, a vowel, from the LXX Chronicles' Ρηχαβ.

Bauckham argues that through standard Jewish exegesis, Matthew found Rahab, and used her primarily in regard to a Gentile emphasis in the use of the four women in the genealogy. His former point of Matthew finding Rahab in Chronicles is upheld, especially after the previous observations of Matthew's usage of Chronicles. In addition, her having served a significant role in Israel's story is important to emphasize as well. Her Gentile status is a subsidiary bonus to this larger point, where it should be

---

[286] Bauckham, "Tamar's Ancestry and Rahab's Marriage," 320–329; and Bauckham, *Gospel Women*, 35–41.

[287] Rabbinic material states that Rahab was Joshua's wife (*b. Meg.* 14b–15a.). However, the later date for Rabbinic material is problematic, not to mention a lack of support from other sources that would have been available to Matthew.

[288] This is certainly not to argue that the Chronicler intended Rahab in 2:55. This issue cannot be discussed within the confines of this work.

[289] Or it was possibly inherited by Matthew, orally or written.

observed that a Gentile nationality for Ρηχαβ is not mentioned in Chronicles,[290] although certainly from her mention in Joshua, Rahab is a Canaanite living in Jericho (Josh. 2:1–2). The larger point that unifies all five of the women in Matthew's genealogy is their role in Israel's story, in conjunction with being taken from the genealogical sources Matthew utilized. Rahab was a noteworthy person in the story of Israel, a subject of narrative at the time period which the genealogy is unfolding, and her inclusion is fully comprehended on that basis. Her Gentile status is a subsidiary bonus for Matthew's overall purpose in the rest of his Gospel narrative.

Rahab was the Canaanite resident of Jericho who hid the Israelite spies and thus was a key individual in Israel's victory over that city (Josh 2, 6). Her occupation as a prostitute, spoken of within the story as told in Joshua, is explicitly referred to in Hebrews 11:31, James 2:25, and 1 Clement 12:1, Ραὰβ ἡ πόρνη. However, in all of these contexts, she is explicitly commended for her faith.[291] In regard to her occupation, Matthew makes no mention, although her story must have been known. The "oddity" of her occupation might possibly serve a subsidiary role in Matthew's purpose of the genealogy when compared with the "oddity" of Mary's situation. Nevertheless, her Gentile status appears to be the stronger subsidiary element, as evidenced by the emphasis on Gentiles in the rest of Matthew.

Through Salmon and Rahab comes Boaz. Again, as practiced in Ruth and Chronicles, and so Matthew, generations are skipped. Boaz and Ruth are the memorable heroes of the book of Ruth. Boaz commits himself to fulfill the duty to raise up a seed for a deceased relative, and the result is Obed. The book of Ruth narrates this story and the significant role that Ruth and Boaz ultimately play in Israel's history, specifically in the birth of King David.

Ruth is named here primarily as a result of being included in the genealogical source used by Matthew, and then also because she played a role in the story of Israel as a subject of narrative. Her Gentile status as a Moabite is a subsidiary point to this, a bonus for Matthew's Gentile emphasis later in the Gospel. Any "irregularity"[292] about her situation is less obvious compared to the other women in the genealogy, especially when she is portrayed as overwhelmingly courageous and virtuous throughout the story. As with the other women in the genealogy, her use is fundamentally be-

---

[290] Again, it must be admitted that the Chronicler was not directly referring to Rahab. Nevertheless, the use of רכב/Ρηχαβ in 2:55 is still not connected to a foreigner.

[291] Josephus portrays her as an innkeeper (*Ant.* 5.1.8) and she wins Joshua's admiration in *Ant.* 5.1.30.

[292] Usually this is based on Ruth 3:6–14, undoubtedly ambiguous and seemingly provocative. However, within the overwhelming context of the story, Ruth is virtuous, as noted explicitly in that pericope (3:11). In Josephus' account, he conveys that nothing wrong was done by Ruth and Boaz (*Ant.* 5.9.3).

cause she played an important role in the story of Israel. Matthew names her, having used the genealogy in Ruth 4, because she, along with the other named women, was an actor in Israel's story. Through her actions came a son who became the grandfather of King David, the one toward whom the teleologically driven genealogy of Ruth 4 points. Matthew has utilized this within his genealogy and reoriented it toward the son of David, the Christ.

Obed is only mentioned in Ruth 4:17, 21–22 and 1 Chronicles 2:12, serving as a small subject of narrative in Ruth 4 as the son of Boaz and Ruth, the one whom Naomi rejoices to hold (4:16). Obed's son Jesse is a brief subject of narrative in 1 Samuel 16. Through Jesse comes David the king. Within this section of the genealogy, the goal of kingship is realized with the coming of David.[293] The importance of David is self-evident, certainly highlighted by the pericope where his name appears five times (1:1, 6a, 6b, 17a, 17b). This focus was adapted from Ruth, where that genealogy teleologically focused on David, ending climactically with him as the tenth named person. The story of David dominates 1 Samuel 16–1 Kings 2.[294] To David was given the promises of 2 Samuel 7 establishing his throne. Attributed also to David are many psalms, accepted as such by the early church (cf. Matt 22:43). The importance of David for the Chronicler is also apparent considering the significant amount of space given to his story (1 Chr 9:35–29:30). The genealogy has reached a zenith with David, particularly noted by the annotation, τὸν Δαυὶδ τὸν βασιλέα (v.6).

From David to Exile

Nevertheless, this ideal King David, at fourteenth position in the first section, becomes the David of reality in the second section.[295] Discussion as to how the generations should be counted has long occupied scholars. It is not at all certain whether Matthew intended such mathematical precision be demanded of his genealogy. Therefore, it might then be possible that having thirteen names in the last section may not have mattered, and that Matthew was not willing to simply fabricate a name for the sake of numerical precision,[296] unless a name has dropped out.[297] However, there

---

[293] David is referred to by Matthew beyond this pericope in 1:20; 9:27; 12:3, 23; 15:22; 20:30, 31; 21:9, 15; 22:42–46.

[294] Neither the genealogy nor the rest of Matthew makes any comment upon the reign of Saul, who was nevertheless deemed a failure within the Old Testament story as portrayed by 1 Samuel and 1 Chronicles.

[295] Chronicles largely portrays an ideal David, whereas in 2 Samuel a more realistic presentation is offered. 1 and 2 Kings also differs similarly from 1 and 2 Chronicles. The tensions inherent in the different Old Testament accounts cannot adequately be dealt with given the confines of this study.

[296] Cf. Davies and Allison, *Matthew*, 1.186; Keener, *Matthew*, 74.

[297] As claimed by McNeile, *Matthew*, 3.

have been other explanations for counting the names and keeping the four-teens. Aside from some exegetically unconvincing explanations, such as counting Mary[298] or counting Jesus thirteenth and Christ fourteenth,[299] there seem to be two reasonable options. One could recount Jeconiah as fourteenth in the second section and first in the third section,[300] being sepa-rated by the narrative annotation about the deportation to Babylon. Nolland considers the Jeconiah of the third section to equal Jehoiakim.[301] Thus, counting Jeconiah twice is a possibility;[302] however, indications in the text point toward another option that will be argued here. David can be counted as fourteenth in the first section and then recounted as first in the second section.[303] His name also is separated by an annotation, 'the king'. Further conclusive evidence for counting David twice comes from the important summary in verse 17 where David closes the first section, from Abraham to David, and then begins the second section, from David to the exile. Je-coniah is never mentioned in verse 17, which verifies he should not be counted twice. Counting David twice would fit with the genealogical story ascending from Abraham to David, the ideal, but descending from David the reality, to exile. The turning point would then be David himself. A look to the next important annotation as well as the broader Old Testament story should provide further confirmation for reading the genealogy this way.

David is the father of Solomon by Bathsheba, the wife of Uriah. Here the genealogy introduces an ominous reference unlike any of the proceed-ing annotations. All the other women are referred to by name. Matthew's source, 1 Chronicles, lists Bathsheba's name in 3:5,[304] with no reference to Uriah as her husband.[305] Matthew does nevertheless clearly refer to Bath-sheba, ἐκ τῆς τοῦ Οὐρίου. Moreover, as with the three previous women, her inclusion by Matthew was fundamentally because she was named in his genealogical source and she played a role in Israel's history, being a subject of narrative as the other women were. In addition, her role in the story of Israel was significant in that through her, and not the other wives of David (1 Chr 3:1–9), came the birth of the next king, Solomon. 2 Sam-uel 12:24 records his birth, noting that 'the Lord loved him'. 1 Kings 1 re-

---

[298] Filson, *Matthew*, 53; Gundry, *Matthew*, 19.

[299] Stendahl, "Matthew," 770–771; Meier, *Matthew*, 5.

[300] Hagner, *Matthew 1–13*, 6; Eloff, "Exile, Restoration and Matthew's Genealogy," 80; Hendrickx, *The Infancy Narratives*, 23.

[301] Nolland, *Matthew*, 86.

[302] Cf. Mussies, "Parallels," 45. A few variants reveal corrections of what was per-ceived as either a genealogical error, a numerical error, or both, by adding Ιωακιμ.

[303] Cf. Schweizer, *Matthew*, 23; Schöllig, "Die Zählung der Generationen im matthäischen Stammbaum," 263–264; Wilk, *Jesus und die Völker*, 83.

[304] LXX Βηρσαβεε; MT בַּת־שׁוּעַ.

[305] Uriah appears in the list of David's mighty men in 1 Chronicles 11:41.

cords the choice by David himself that Solomon was to succeed him, when there were other older sons that had vied for that coveted position. Bathsheba played an important role in this change of leadership. As Adonijah jockeyed for taking David's place, she stepped forward to ask about this momentous decision (1 Kgs 1:15–31). Bathsheba played a significant role in Israel's history and thus mention of her by Matthew is warranted based on this fact.

As with Tamar, the Gentile status of Bathsheba is problematic.[306] Nowhere is her racial identity directly identified, and within the Chronicles genealogy she is not referred to as Gentile, whereas other wives of David are identified in this way (3:1–2). Her marriage to a Gentile does not overtly make her a Gentile. In addition, lack of "the Hittite" with Uriah's name might further weaken a reference to Bathsheba's Gentile status. The "irregularity" of the situation, primarily due to the fact that she suffered as a victim of David's twisted use of power, might play a subsidiary role. Nevertheless, her inclusion, as with the other women, is sufficiently explained by the mention of her in Matthew's genealogical sources and her role in Israel's story. 1 Chronicles 3:5 mentions her because she played an important part in the Davidic dynasty as the mother of Solomon. She is a subject of narrative in 2 Samuel 11–12 and 1 Kings 1–2. Matthew keeps her in the genealogical list precisely because she played an important role in the story of Israel.

However, there is certainly more that is meant by this short evocative phrase, ἐκ τῆς τοῦ Οὐρίου. The annotative twist made by this reference to Uriah is significant. Some scholars have taken the reference here to Uriah as an indication of his Gentile status, which was Hittite, thus portraying Bathsheba as such.[307] This viewpoint most often coincides with the assumption that all four women are Gentiles, which noted above is somewhat problematic in the case of Tamar and Bathsheba. The naming of Uriah appears to point in a different direction by evoking a larger story that primarily implicates David. Often noted by many scholars with the unusual annotation ἐκ τῆς τοῦ Οὐρίου is the evoking of David's failure in regard to the adultery with Bathsheba and the murder of Uriah.[308] This appears defendable because a story is provocatively being evoked. The peculiar way of referring to Bathsheba (ἐκ τῆς τοῦ Οὐρίου) indicates far more is meant, and this especially in regard to what it says of David than of Bathsheba. The genealogy, when narratively read, states that David was the father of Solomon, through Bathsheba, who was the wife of Uriah. Both Bathsheba and Uriah are mentioned because both were a part of Israel's history. Fur-

---

[306] Levine, *Social and Ethnic Dimension*, 73.

[307] Davies and Allison, *Matthew*, 1.174; Gundry, *Matthew*, 13.

[308] Johnson, *Purpose of Biblical Genealogies*, 153; Nolland, *Matthew*, 75.

thermore, upon this reading, the subtle way it alludes to what was David's downfall cannot be missed. The narrative of 2 Samuel 11 and 12 is evoked, and a key verse within this narrative identifies this event as a downfall never to be recovered from by David or his house (2 Sam 12:9–11).[309] This annotation when read in light of the summary of Israel's history given in verse 17 corroborates this interpretation. From Abraham to David there was an ascent, but from David to Exile, there is descent, in which the initial descent *toward* exile began with David himself. The subsequent narrative of David's life in 2 Samuel reveals the downward spiral and tragedy that befell his house following his failure.

The first section of the genealogy, from Abraham to David proceeded positively toward the goal of reaching David. Then as recounted within the Old Testament itself, a shocking turn takes place through egregious failures on the part of David himself. The summary statement again proves determinative in that the general sweep of the second fourteen names is downward from David to exile. Something turns this story toward this horrible end with exile. A clear indication within the genealogy reveals that it had started with David, proceeding through the line of his sons, among whom stand a number of outstanding leaders, as well several horrible leaders, but none formidable enough individually to avert the disaster of exile.

The list of kings from David to Jeconiah follows the list of 1 Chronicles 3:10–17. Each name recalls a narrative, having been a significant part in Israel's history: David (1 Sam 16–1 Kgs 2; 1 Chr 9:35–29:25); Solomon (1 Kgs 2–11; 2 Chr 1–9:31); Rehoboam (1 Kgs 12–14; 2 Chr 10–12); Abijah (1 Kgs 15:1–8; 2 Chr 13); Asa (1 Kgs 15:8–24; 2 Chr 14–16); Jehoshaphat (1 Kgs 15:24; 22:1–50; 2 Chr 17:1–21:3); Jehoram (1 Kgs 22:50; 2 Kgs 8:16; 2 Chr 21:4–22:1); Uzziah/Azariah (2 Kgs 14:21; 15:1–7; 2 Chr 26:1–23); Jotham (2 Kgs 15:5–38; 2 Chr 27:1–9); Ahaz (2 Kgs 15:38–16:20; 2 Chr 28:1–27); Hezekiah (2 Kgs 16:20; 18:1–20:21; 2 Chr 29:1–32:33); Manasseh (2 Kgs 20:21–21:18; 2 Chr 33:1–20); Amon (2 Kgs 21:18–26; 2 Chr 33:21–25); Josiah (2 Kgs 21:26–23:30; 2 Chr 34:1–35:27); and Jeconiah[310]/Jehoiachin (2 Kgs 24:6–17; 25:27–30; 2 Chr 36:8–10).

From Rehobam onwards the list follows the kings of the southern kingdom, Judah. Some of these kings were exemplary in many ways, such as Asa (1 Kgs 15:11; 2 Chr 14:2), Jehoshaphat (1 Kgs 22:43; 2 Chr 17:3), Hezekiah (2 Kgs 18:3–7; 2 Chr 29:2; 31:20–21), and Josiah (2 Kgs 22:2; 2 Chr 34:2, 33). Many however were horrendous leaders and serve as examples of evil for later generations: Rehoboam (1 Kgs 14:21–24; 2 Chr 12:14), Ahaz (2 Kgs 16:2–4; 2 Chr 28:1–5, 22–23), Manasseh (2 Kgs

---

[309] 1 Kings 15:5 provides a summary of David's life, explicitly identifying the case of Uriah as the one downfall. In the MT, the Uriah incident is recounted, but curiously not in the LXX.

[310] 1 Esdras 1:34 also calls Jeconiah son of Josiah.

21:2—9, 16–17; 2 Chr 33:2–9), Amon (2 Kgs 21:20–22; 2 Chr 33:22–23), and Jeconiah (2 Kgs 24:9; 2 Chr 36:9). The trajectory from David to exile is depicted tragically as a story of failure and rejection of God's word, most notably highlighted throughout the narrative of 1 and 2 Kings, and climactically in 2 Chronicles 36:15–16. The narrative flow of the second section (vv. 6b–11) is downward toward that stunning event of Judah's deportment to Babylon. The summary verse 17 explicitly points out this narrative flow of the genealogy, from David, the dramatic height of the first section, to the exile, the lowest point in Israel's story. At this point in their history, the people of God were taken into captivity and the kingship that David's house had held for generations is extinguished. This annotation records the only event that is explicitly listed in the genealogy.

From Exile to Christ

Jeconiah (Jehoiachin in 1 Chr 36:8–10) was carried into Exile as a captive,[311] taken to Babylon in the second deportation of 597 B.C.E. The annotation καὶ τοὺς ἀδελφοὺς αὐτοῦ has already been discussed above. In sum, it reveals the unity of all Israel, as well as thematically connecting the exodus and exile events, which becomes an important interpretive key for understanding Matthew 2. The genealogy in 1 Chronicles 3:17–19 LXX continues to follow the royal line of Jeconiah to his son Shealtiel, and from Shealtiel[312] to his son Zerubbabel. Having reached the nadir of the exile, the third section begins a new ascent that climactically ends with the last fourteen, mathematically totaled as דוד, the Christ.[313]

Shealtiel is only discussed within genealogical accounts, primarily as father of Zerubbabel (cf. Ezra 3:2). Zerubbabel is a well-known figure of the post-exilic community, a subject of narrative in Ezra-Nehemiah, and particularly attributed with promises for the future (cf. Hag; Zech 4). Beyond Zerubbabel, the source utilized by Matthew for the names of the third section, from Abiud to Jacob is completely unknown.[314] Speculations for the source(s) of this list of ancestors are uncertain without some textual clues. Although unknown names, Matthew follows this royal line, while no longer retaining kingship, it nevertheless remains alive. Where the Chronicler stops, bringing the genealogy down to his time, Matthew continues. Consequently, Matthew affirms that Israel's story has not stopped at the

---

[311] Note MT refers to Jeconiah as such, יכניה אסר, which is wrongly read by the LXX as a name, Ιεχονια-ασιρ (1 Chr 3:17).

[312] LXX Σαλαθιηλ; MT פדיה.

[313] Matthew's explicit use of the exile here demonstrates an inaccuracy in Wright, *God Who Acts*, 69, who thinks the exile is not used in the New Testament.

[314] Matthew's list of names also differs considerably from Luke's genealogy here.

exile but continues, albeit in a humble, subjected state until the Christ arrives.

The summary verse 17 further highlights this subjected condition, ἀπὸ τῆς μετοικεσίας Βαβυλῶνος ἕως τοῦ Χριστοῦ. The names in the third section, other than being common names found in various parts of the LXX, do not remind the hearer and reader of particular stories, as did the familiar names in the first and section sections, because at this point the scriptural narrative goes silent. These names used by Matthew only indicate the "silence" of this period in terms of God's intervention.[315] The story may be uncompleted, but in no way is it ended, as Matthew affirms through this list that continues the royal line, teleologically oriented toward the coming one. Matthew's genealogy links the story of Jesus Christ to Israel's history in tight continuity, proclaiming that the story is not uncompleted because Messiah has come. With Jesus the Christ, the fourteenth generation has come, the υἱοῦ Δαυὶδ has arrived.[316] The positive affirmation that this indicates in regard to Matthew's perspective of Israel's history should be underscored. Despite the failures within the line, particularly in terms of kingship, for Matthew the line nevertheless continues (cf. 2 Sam 7), and Israel's history and the promises to her are affirmed and completed in the Messiah. From Matthew's perspective, Israel's history and story are a crucial component in fully understanding Jesus' story. The genealogy serves to recapitulate this history of Israel in a highly compressed theological interpretation.

With verse 16, following the mention of Joseph, a final annotation is added, Ἰακὼβ δὲ ἐγέννησεν τὸν Ἰωσὴφ τὸν ἄνδρα Μαρίας, ἐξ ἧς ἐ γεννήθη Ἰησοῦς ὁ λεγόμενος Χριστός. Mary is the fifth woman named in the genealogy, and as previously discussed, her inclusion here is precisely because she played a significant role in the birth of the Messiah. She is obviously not immoral,[317] something much emphasized in the next pericope (verses 18–25). She is definitely not a Gentile, which sets her completely apart from the other four women within a strictly Gentile interpretation.

---

[315] Nevertheless, there certainly were many dramatic and important stories of the Jews during this period, particularly the Maccabean books. However, Matthew does not highlight these well-known stories in the genealogy.

[316] υἱοῦ Δαυὶδ is used beyond this pericope in Matthew 1:20; 9:27; 12:23; 15:22; 20:30, 31; 21:9, 15. Matthew 22:42–46 is an important discussion about the son of David.

[317] Freed, *The Stories of Jesus' Birth*, 32, implausibly states that Matthew included the women "to counter a Jewish accusation that Jesus was the illegitimate son of Mary." Cf. Schaberg, *The Illegitimacy of Jesus*. While both Freed and Schaberg present many perceptive insights, the illegitimacy viewpoint simply cannot be sustained from the text of Matthew itself, but assumes a certain historical context that really only appears later. See Ben Witherington, "Birth of Jesus," 66; and Van Voorst, *Jesus Outside the New Testament*, 127–129.

However, as argued above, the Gentile view is somewhat problematic in regard to Tamar and Bathsheba, and probably a bonus in the case of the Gentiles Rahab and Ruth. The "irregularity" of her situation might be matched with some of the "irregularities" of the other four women. However, like the other four women, Mary's inclusion within the genealogy primarily highlights her key role in the coming of Messiah, and Matthew regards her inclusion important, just as he will continue to narrate the involvement of women in the ministry of Jesus throughout the remainder of the Gospel. The subsequent pericope will explain the rather odd way that Jesus has arrived, ἐγεννήθη, the "divine passive,"[318] where God is observed as the active agent in Jesus' birth. The genealogy in this regard could be regarded at a horizontal and human level, in that the coming of Messiah is produced through Israel.[319] Nevertheless, Matthew emphasizes through this brief hint in verse 16, and then subsequently unpacked narratively in 1:18–25, Israel's history alone cannot produce the Messiah. That involves a vertical and divine intervention by God who brings about the deliverance needed, within the context of Israel and through her. The zenith of the genealogy is the phrase, Ιησοῦς ὁ λεγόμενος Χριστός (v. 16). This annotation climaxes the teleological genealogy, closing the inclusio of 1:1, with reference to Jesus as the Messiah, an evocative kingly title clearly linked with David's kingship.

Verse 17 interprets the genealogy, serving as a hermeneutical and theological key and summary, by noting the structure already inherent within the genealogy itself. Four primary events, three of which are from the Old Testament story, are highlighted. Abraham, David, exile, and Christ are highlighted for emphasis. This is how Matthew recapitulates Israel's history. The previous story of Israel, as told in the scriptural narrative, is encapsulated in this one verse. Matthew indicates his reading of Old Testament history through this fundamental verse, having just recounted the story of Israel genealogically in the compressed narrative of verses 2–16. Unpacking verse 17 has been important for understanding the genealogy, and it is imperative for understanding Matthew's view of Israel's history and the subsequent story he tells. The story of Jesus that Matthew narrates cannot be understood without verse 17, and certainly not without the genealogy. These are fundamental to the story Matthew tells, a fact easily overlooked by scholars that too easily fail to integrate the genealogy with exegesis of the entire Gospel. The story of Israel is vitally important for Matthew, and having provided the matrix from which Messiah has arisen, Mat-

---

[318] Hagner, *Matthew 1–13*, 4, 12.

[319] The genealogy is technically Joseph's, son of David (1:20), who adopts Jesus into the royal line (1:25); cf. Davies and Allison, *Matthew*, 1.185.

thew goes on to tell the story of Jesus in continuity with Israel's story and as the proper conclusion to it.

2.8 Chapter Conclusions

The narratological genre of Matthew's genealogy of Jesus, along with the teleological orientation, lends the best insight into explaining the purposes of the genealogy. The genealogy should consequently be read as a theological retelling of the history of Israel, a recapitulation of Israel's story through a teleological and narratological genealogy.

Three key elements are to be concluded from Matthew's genealogy:

1. Teleology: For Matthew, Israel's history and story has been oriented toward a goal. The goal, as noted in the genealogy by where it starts, was promised to Abraham. The goal was to give a king, a ruler for God's people, to provide the leadership to fulfill Israel's call and mandate. Matthew announces that goal has finally arrived in Jesus the Christ. This is an important component of Matthew's christology where the teleological format of the genealogy is matched to the fulfillment that Matthew emphasizes throughout the Gospel. The summary of verse 17 further reveals the teleological orientation of the genealogy, which was adapted from Ruth, and symbolically equated by the fourteen generations as a *gematria* on the name David (דוד). For Matthew, Israel's history can be structured according to the name David, with whom definitive kingship in Jesus Christ has been finally realized.

2. Narrative: The structure of verse 17 reveals the plot of Israel's story that Matthew wants to emphasize. From Abraham to David was the anticipation and *ascent* toward kingship, an objective toward which Israel's history was moving, a promise and a call to be fulfilled, realized in David the king. However, once this climax in the story was reached, the goal and call were not adequately fulfilled. For beginning with David himself, and then through his sons that followed him as kings, there is a tragic *descent*, a failure to fulfill God's call for Israel. This tragic failure ends with the catastrophic event of Israel's history, the exile, when kingship ceases and the people are subjected to foreign rulers. The Old Testament story effectively ends here according to Matthew's scheme. Although the Old Testament records that a return takes place, a modest temple is rebuilt, and some basic aspects of national identity are maintained, there nevertheless continues "exilic" conditions without a king and independent nationhood. Matthew indicates that the story is suspended here, but that it is by no means over, in that a new *ascent* has taken place, unknown to Israel until Messiah's coming. The scriptural story of Israel ended with exilic condi-

tions, a story essentially incomplete and without conclusion. Matthew adds the crucial ending with the goal and climax of Israel's history in the coming of Messiah, son of David, son of Abraham. As Witherington observes on 1:21, "Jesus' mission is to an Israel that is lost or has gone astray."[320]

3. Christological: Israel's story is essential to Matthew's story and his christology. The story of Jesus cannot be understood or narrated without it. To effectively narrate the story of Jesus, Matthew must first begin with Israel; hence, that story is retold, recapitulated, through a compressed narrative, and set at the beginning of the Gospel as an introduction for the proceeding narrative. Continuity between the story of Jesus as narrated by Matthew and Israel's story is firmly established by the genealogy. This is a significant aspect of Matthew's christology that can too easily be overlooked. Jesus is firmly planted within the matrix of Israel,[321] a formative point for the subsequent story that unfolds in Matthew. This positive affirmation of Israel's story, recapitulated as it is through a genealogy of Jesus Christ, is significant. Although the plot of the story is tragic, the overall affirmation of that story reveals an overwhelmingly positive stress upon the fact that the ultimate goal has been reached in the coming of Christ. Matthew's genealogy recapitulates and theologically interprets Israel's history, with an added summary as further interpretive help for properly reading the genealogy. This introduction to the Gospel retells and recapitulates the story of Israel precisely because the story of Jesus cannot be understood without it,[322] nor for Matthew can Israel's story be understood without Jesus. According to the theology and narrative of Matthew's genealogy, the eschatological restoration of the kingdom is fulfilled in the Son of David, Jesus the Christ.[323] He is the climax and completion of Israel's history.[324]

The importance of this pericope for understanding Matthew's Gospel will continue to occupy the remainder of this thesis. This chapter has argued at length that the history of Israel is fundamental to the story that Matthew goes on to tell. Placing it at the beginning as an introduction is

---

[320] Witherington, *Matthew*, 46.

[321] Luz, *Matthew 1–7* (2007), 82: the "genealogy puts Jesus at the center of Israel's history".

[322] Cf. Swartley, *Israel's Scripture Traditions and the Synoptic Gospels*, 282: "Jesus' story is told within the structure and language of Israel's faith story. Israel's story shapes Jesus' story, as presented in the Synoptics. Indeed, the OT is a precondition for the Synoptics' story of Jesus."

[323] On the close connection in Matthew between Christ and Son of David, see Head, *Christology and the Synoptic Problem*, 181–186.

[324] Wright, *God Who Acts*, 56–57.

hermeneutically important for the subsequent interpretation of Matthew.[325]
Appearing at the beginning of the book, the theme of the Gospel is encapsulated, Jesus as the fulfillment of Israel's history.[326] As Boris Repschinski
has recently mentioned, "The christology of Matthew's Gospel, viewed
from beginning to end rather than from end to beginning, implies a reader
who is firmly rooted in the traditions of Israel."[327] The argument of this
entire chapter is precisely that the genealogy introduces the Gospel with an
interpretive key, Israel's history recapitulated.

The conclusion of this chapter has identified that the genealogy is a
theological recapitulation of Israel's history. Israel's story is the presupposition and foundation to the entire Gospel story, as well as being the story
that it seeks to definitively conclude. Thus, the hermeneutical importance
of Israel's history as the introduction to Matthew's Gospel, and to the story
of Jesus it tells, can be rightly emphasized and used for the subsequent interpretive work to be done in the rest of the Gospel of Matthew that this
study seeks to explain.[328]

---

[325] Carter, *Matthew and Margins*, 55, in considering the discourse states that "for the
narrative, the genealogy provides an interpretive framework which shapes the understanding of the rest of the story." Cf. Barnet, *Not the Righteous but Sinners*, 22.

[326] Johnson, *Purpose of Biblical Genealogies*, 210–228, provides a detailed examination of the relation between the genealogy and the rest of the Gospel, noting similarities
in form, language, and theology.

[327] Repschinski, "'For He Will Save His People From Their Sins' (1:21) Christology
for Christian Jews," 265.

[328] As noted in a previous footnote, although filled with Old Testament influence and
christological implications, Matthew 1:18–25 does not directly contain a clear recapitulation element and thus it is not analyzed for the purpose of this study.

Chapter 3

Passive Recapitulation of Israel's History

3.1 Introduction

Having observed the recapitulation of Israel's story in the first chapter, this chapter will proceed with attention to Matthew 2. The argument this chapter will advance is that Jesus is depicted as passively recapitulating Israel's history. The recapitulation that is indicated here involves the repeating and reliving of Israel's history by the child Jesus, who is moved according to the actions of both God and Joseph. Therefore, Jesus passively relives Israel's history. Primary to the narrative of the Matthew 2 is the exodus background variously portrayed, which will be closely detailed in this chapter. Essential to maintain is the continuity this chapter has with the proceeding. Jesus' genealogy is constructed in a manner that recapitulates Israel's history. For Matthew, Jesus' life emerges from within the matrix of Israel, and in Matthew 2 Jesus is manifested as passively recapitulating Israel's history in his early movements as a child. This chapter will unpack evidence for observing this recapitulation as well as the manner in which it is narrated. As with the previous chapter, primary consideration will be given to the use of the Old Testament and the christological features of Matthew 2.

3.2 Use of the Exodus Motif in Matthew 2:1–23

Delineating the many Old Testament allusions, resonances, and background of Matthew two is no small feat.[1] The chapter as a whole presents a host of unique exegetical challenges. Carefully weighing all the evidence for one's understanding of the material involves a complexity of issues. There is the ever-present subjectivist tendency toward reading into the text

---

[1] Nellessen, *Das Kind und seine Mutter*, is a wide-ranging work on Matthew 1:18–2:23 that delves into a variety of areas such as structure, form criticism, comparative analysis, and theology. Also important is the work by Prabhu, *Formula Quotations in the Infancy Narrative of Matthew.*

motifs that are only marginally present, if at all, or those motifs altogether fanciful. It proves to be a formidable exercise. As Hengel and Merkel aptly point out, chapter two is one of the most peculiar (*eigenartigste*) passages in the New Testament.[2] France quips concerning this chapter, "It is a mine-field littered with exegetical corpses."[3] Entering this exegetical minefield with care toward navigating and cautiously attending to the text itself, the present section seeks to extricate a profitable understanding of what is tex-tually communicated, particularly highlighting the important ways it re-lates to the history of Israel. Significant to restate and keep foremost in mind is that the predominant focus of the Gospel is on Jesus and his story. In particular, these beginning chapters of Matthew's Gospel introduce Je-sus[4] utilizing the Old Testament scriptures and the scriptural history of Is-rael for the proclamation of Jesus' story.

When the individual details and broader whole of Matthew chapter two are examined, weighed, and related, it can be shown that the exodus, as an event, formative and paradigmatic within Israel's history, and as an overall theme, appears as a dominant overarching motif.[5] This will be demon-strated broadly through the overriding plot of the chapter, as it closely re-sembles the Exodus period. Individual aspects within the text also utilize the Exodus in various ways and this will be examined and demonstrated. Israel's experience in Egypt, the distinctive role of Moses as the divinely ordained deliverer, and the deliverance of the people from that land of op-pression; all of these encompass the exodus event as recounted in the scriptural account, which stands as the major formative event in the history

---

[2] Hengel and Merkel, "Die Magier aus dem Osten und die Flucht nach Ägypten (Mt 2) im Rahmen der anitiken Religionsgeschichte und der Theologie des Matthäus," 139: "Die eigenartigste Erzählung bei Matthäus, ja vielleicht im ganzen Neuen Testament überhaupt, ist die Geschichte von den μάγοι ἀπὸ ἀνατολῶν."

[3] France, "The Formula-Quotations of Matthew 2 and the Problem of Communica-tion," 233.

[4] Brown, *Birth of the Messiah*, 585, comments on the importance of chapters 1–2, stressing that "the theological motifs of these chapters anticipate the theology of the rest of the Gospel."

[5] This in no way discounts other legitimate motifs, especially the use of Davidic chris-tology and Kingship, as argued by Nolan, *Royal Son of God*, 38. Cf. Deines, *Die Gerechtigkeit der Tora im Reich des Messias*, 469–478. On the Mosaic/Exodus back-ground of Matthew 2, Davies, *Setting*, 82–84; Brown, *Birth of the Messiah*, 586, judi-ciously defends the Mosaic background, although he acknowledges Davidic motifs as well; Keener, *Matthew*, 107; Harrington, *Matthew*, 46. Allison very strongly defended the Mosaic aspects of the entirety of Matthew in *The New Moses*. Cf. Teeple, *The Mosaic Eschatological Prophet*. Daube, *The New Testament and Rabbinic Judaism*, 189–192, argued that Jacob and Laban are the analogous material for Matthew 2, which could pos-sibly be a subsidiary motif for some readers. Witherington, *Matthew*, 55–56, denies the use of the Moses story and exodus in Matthew 2 in keeping with his sapiential reading, with Jesus as son of David like Solomon.

of Israel. Indeed, Israel's history in the exodus period could be observed as the virtual birth and infancy period of the nation. According to the scriptural account, when they went down to Egypt, they were a family of people, but by the time of the exodus, their numbers had grown to the size of a nation. The deliverance from Egypt became over time the prototype for the future redemption of Israel.[6] The background that the exodus contributes to chapter two, particularly in terms of plot, characterization, verbal allusions, and themes, as adapted and utilized by Matthew for retelling Jesus' story, will become apparent throughout the following sections. The argument will thus focus upon how Jesus recapitulates Israel's exodus history in this chapter.

3.2.1 Past Scholarship on Matthew 2:1–23

The prevailing scholarly understanding of chapter two regards the geographic aspects of the portrayal to be the primary meaning and focus for Matthew's presentation of Jesus' early years. The impetus for this geographic perspective was initiated through an important article by Krister Stendahl where he noted the prominence that geography plays within the chapter as a whole, particularly through the four fulfillment quotations,[7] all of which have place names: Bethlehem, Egypt, Ramah, and Nazareth.[8] Beyond these geographic locations cited within the fulfillment quotations, there are further aspects of this geographic focus outside these quotations in the manner that Jesus' early years are followed through the various movements from location to location. He is born in Bethlehem, taken by Joseph out of Judea to seek refuge in Egypt, brought back to the land of Israel, and finally taken on to Nazareth in Galilee.[9] It will be demonstrated

---

[6] Davies, *Setting*, 26.

[7] Schnelle, *The History and Theology of the New Testament Writings*, 229, calls them "reflection citations" (*Reflexionszitate*). Cf. Strecker, *Theology of the New Testament*, 36. Stanton, *Gospel for a New People*, 347–348, argues for "formula quotation" as the standard translation of *Reflexionszitate* to be retained. Fulfillment quotation (*Erfüllungszitate*) also adequately describes the distinctive group of citations that Matthew emphasizes, especially since it utilizes a translation of the important Matthean verb πληρόω that is used in each case. All of the terms are useful descriptions, but "fulfillment quotation" appears to be the best general term. Cf. Rothfuchs, *Die Erfüllungszitate des Matthäus-Evangeliums*, 27–56; Kümmel, *Introduction to the New Testament*, 110; Luz, *Matthew 1–7* (2007), 125–131.

[8] Stendahl, "Quis et Unde?," 70. Cf. France, "Formula-Quotations," 240, maintains, "the geographical theme is the warp, the main organizing principle of the chapter, into which the woof of the Mosaic and Exodus typologies (together with other possible scriptural elements) is woven."

[9] Garland, *Reading Matthew*, 27, calls this "messianic topography," being directed at dealing with an apparent problem in that Jesus is associated with Galilee and Nazareth when it was known that the Christ was to originate in Bethlehem.

how this is an important aspect within the overall exodus motif of the passage in that Israel as a nation experienced various geographical movements within her scriptural history. Also important for understanding the geographic background of chapter two, is the observation that Israel's leader Moses also experienced in his early years various geographic movements, all of which are relevant for understanding Matthew's distinctive portrayal of Jesus' early movements as a passive recapitulation of Israel's history. Stanton summarizes the theological impression of Matthew 2 as "christological geography."[10]

In the subsequent sections of this chapter, Matthew will be shown to parallel and relate both Israel's history and Moses to Jesus, particularly through the use of recapitulation. By the comparing and paralleling of Israel's movements as a nation and Moses' movements as their leader with Jesus' movements, one can begin to ascertain the theological impression made through this narrative that presents Jesus as recapitulating, as a repetition and corporate representative experience, both the history of Israel and Moses. The distinctive use of the fulfillment quotations further emphasizes this theological intention, and as Garland helpfully indicates, these quotations should be seen to serve as "interpretive statements." Consequently, the fulfillment quotations in Matthew's narrative "freeze the action and explain its significance." Matthew utilizes these because "it is the Scripture that authoritatively clarifies who Jesus is," and these citations serve to "create a set of resonances for the reader," and they "demonstrate that the things that Jesus did and that happened to him were predetermined components of an agelong design of God."[11] The use of these quotations serves to highlight Matthew's programmatic emphasis on Jesus' life and ministry as the fulfillment of God's will.[12] These quotations are subsumed within the broader geographic portrayal, and as will be shown below, all of this is propelled through the employment of the exodus motif in this narrative.[13]

Raymond Brown has added to Stendahl's insights when he makes the helpful distinction between Matthew's *apologetic* use of geography, deal-

---

[10] Stanton, *Interpretation of Matthew*, 72.

[11] Garland, *Matthew*, 28–29, who also notes the interesting ways that Matthew utilizes Scripture "to taper it to fit the context of his account," 28–29. This will become exceedingly important below when the fulfillment quotation of Hosea 11:1 is discussed.

[12] Beaton, *Isaiah's Christ in Matthew's Gospel*, 23; cf. Jones, "Matthew," 60.

[13] Discussion concerning the possible midrashic nature of chapter two is not a particular concern for this chapter due to continued problems with its use. Meier, *A Marginal Jew*, 236, asks whether chapter two is properly midrash, and he considers it debatable because it "largely depends on how wide or narrow a definition of midrash one allows." Cf. Wright, "The Literary Genre Midrash," 454–456, asks whether the infancy narratives are midrash and based on detailed work determines they are not; Childs, *New Testament as Canon*, 69–70; Davies and Allison, *Matthew*, 1.195.

ing with the various objections in that regard, and the *didactic* purpose of the geographic, which both informs and strengthens faith.[14] Brown goes on to perceptively indicate the fundamental importance of these place names, in that all are of decisive significance in Israel's history and "offer a theological history of Israel in geographical miniature," exodus, kingship, and exile. He adds, "just as Jesus sums up the history of the people named in his genealogy, so his early career sums up the history of these prophetically significant places."[15] Brown's insights are brief and suggestive, and many other scholars speak similarly, albeit general and brief, in this regard. Unfortunately, none have followed this up with closer attention to the text in light of this important theological history of Israel's geographic movements. Added to this oversight is the lack of continuity that scholars regularly exhibit between the genealogical introduction to the Gospel and the pericopes that are fundamentally grounded and conceptually influenced by it, a significant oversight that has taken place in regard to the importance of Israel's history for Matthew.

Bethlehem, the birthplace and city of David,[16] is also where Jesus is born, a detail Matthew seeks to make evident when it was widely known during Jesus' adult years that he came from Nazareth (Matt 21:11). Egypt, the land of the exodus, also plays a significant role in Jesus' early years. Ramah, the place of quintessential mourning during the exilic period to Babylon, is evoked, utilizing a quotation from Jeremiah, to voice the extreme sorrow of those weeping in nearby Bethlehem. All three of these decisive moments in Israel's history were encompassed within the genealogical retelling of Israel's history dealt with above in chapter one.

The broader exodus period is implicitly referenced through the annotation, "and his brothers," attached to Judah (1:2), paralleled by the later reference to the exile in 1:11. It was Judah and his brothers, the 'twelve tribes' that went down to Egypt with their father Jacob/Israel, and while dwelling there within a few generations they became so numerous that a tyrannical Pharaoh instituted organized oppression of the hated Israelites. Kingship is explicitly indicated through the conspicuous addition of βασιλέα that appears in 1:6 following David's name. This annotation serves to note the beginning of the monarchy in Israel's history. Finally, the exile is explicitly referred to through the annotation, μετοικεσίας Βαβυλῶνος (1:11, 12, 17b, 17c). Like the earlier annotation to Judah's name, "and his brothers" is attached to Jeconiah's name (1:11), referring to those Israelites that were exiled in Babylon. This also serves as a unique way of paralleling these two events, the exodus and the exile, both of which involved se-

---

[14] Brown, *Birth of the Messiah*, 97, 179–180.

[15] *Ibid.*, 217.

[16] Bethlehem is also the setting for the story of Ruth (1:1, 2, 19, 22; 2:4; 4:11).

vere oppression of Israel, where in each event they are dislocated to a foreign land.[17] In each event, they are also brought out of that foreign land
and led back to the land of Israel. This paralleling of the exodus and exilic
events will become especially significant in the final sections of this chapter that deal with the latter part of Matthew chapter two.

3.2.2 Israel's History in Matthew 2:1–23

The exodus, kingship, and exile were fundamental events in Israel's history, and these events can rightly be observed as almost spanning the entire
scriptural history of Israel, albeit in a distinctive and concise theological
portrayal, already evidenced in the genealogy (1:17). Thus, from a broad
standpoint, it could be argued that Jesus passively recapitulates the whole
of Israel's history in chapter two. Brown incisively observes that the goal
of Matthew's infancy narrative is "to be inclusive of the whole story of Israel with overt references to the great salvific events of the exodus and the
exile."[18] Jesus passively experiences and repeats the movement, providence, and tragedy of Israel's history, but he is dramatically preserved as
the deliverer, with both Mosaic and Davidic overtones, that emerges to redeem an Israel (1:21) still in exile (1:17).

This perspective on the importance of Israel's history within chapter
two can best be understood, although not by any means minimizing the
above insights, when the fundamental backdrop for the chapter is recognized to primarily highlight the exodus. The subsections below will provide evidence for this interpretation. Within the broader exodus theme,
these other important geographical and historical events are submerged,
both broadly in terms of plot and individually within the various details
that will be expounded below. As noted above, exodus and exile are analogous, and hence the reference to both is necessary, while fundamentally
the overall orientation of the chapter is exodus. Exile is subsumed within
this exodus depiction. The unique symbolic portrayal of these geographic
locations must be examined closely for understanding their use within the
whole of the chapter as well as understanding the role each quotation has
in connection with the geographic location, all of which is portrayed
through an overarching exodus motif.

3.2.3 Understanding the Narrative of Matthew 2:1–23

To enter the narrative's portrayal and recapitulation of the Exodus, it will
prove essential to briefly recount how the chapter itself unfolds as a narra-

---

[17] Japhet, *I and II Chronicles*, 47, remarks how the Chronicler regards the exodus and
exile as "analogous phenomena."

[18] Brown, *Birth of the Messiah*, 586.

tive. Chapter 2 opens with a weighty introductory statement, τοῦ δὲ ᾿Ιησοῦ γεννηθέντος ἐν Βηθλέεμ τῆς ᾿Ιουδαίας ἐν ἡμέραις ῾Ηρῴδου τοῦ βασιλέως. The birth of Jesus, one whom the reader already knows as "Christ" (1:1, 16, 17), occurred in Bethlehem, which is a detail not indicated in the earlier two pericopes. However, this birth of the Christ has ominously occurred during the days of Herod the king.[19] This provides a significant narratival setting, the background and plot for a conflict between two kings.[20] Matthew's narrative account portrays King Herod discovering about the birth (τεχθείς)[21] of another king through the report of magi from the east, who have seen a star, "his star" (αὐτοῦ τὸν ἀστέρα), that in their perception signifies the arrival of a new king of the Jews. They arrive in Jerusalem and end up generating an unexpected reaction. At their report, Herod, and indeed all Jerusalem, is troubled (ἐταράχθη), and a meeting of the chief priests and scribes is duly organized so that Herod can determine where this rival king might be located. Ascertaining from these leaders that the scriptures say that the Christ would be born in Bethlehem,[22] Herod stealthily sends the magi to Bethlehem expecting them to report back to him when they have found this newborn king. Although seemingly fooling the magi with his pretended interest, the hearer and reader probably begins to suspect that Herod clearly has ulterior motives.[23]

Departing from the king, the magi once again see the star, which helps them locate Jesus in Bethlehem, and there they pay homage (πεσόντες προσεκύνησαν αὐτῷ) to this newborn king. However, the magi subsequently fail to report back to Herod, which the reader fully understands would mean disaster for the child. Having been warned in a dream not to return to Herod, the magi return home by another route. Joseph is then

---

[19] The historical circumstances that this narrative purports to represent, while interesting and important, are outside the concern of this work, being much discussed in all critical commentaries and other works. The focus is on the Matthean narratival account and attending to the unique appropriation of Israel's scriptural history in this highly compact theological portrayal of Jesus' early life.

[20] For more on this conflict see Schlatter, *Matthäus*, 25; cf. Frankemölle, *Matthäus Kommentar 1*, 161–165. Further insights on the contrast between Jesus and Herod are in Bauer, "The Kingship of Jesus in the Matthean Infancy Narratives: A Literary Analysis," 306–323.

[21] Turner, *Matthew*, 80, notes that the participle "functions as a attributive adjective that portrays Jesus as the 'born-king' of the Jews," which serves to contrast him with Herod who came to his appointed kingship by political shrewdness.

[22] This is the first quotation in chapter two, which although not explicitly a fulfillment quotation, nevertheless retains it implicitly. It is also submerged into the narrative as a response the chief priests and scribes give to Herod.

[23] The hearers and readers of Matthew's Gospel would no doubt have been fully aware of the Herodian era and Herod's notorious reputation. Cf. Josephus *J.W.* 1.8.9– 1.33.8; *Ant.* 14.7.3–17.8.1.

warned through a dream that Herod seeks the child's life, is told he must flee with the child and mother to Egypt, and must stay there until the death of Herod. The reader is then informed that this event fulfills scripture.

At some point after the magi have already set off toward their homeland and after Jesus has already been taken by Joseph to Egypt, Herod becomes outraged, realizing that he has been tricked (ἐνεπαίχθη) by the magi that never report back to him. Based on information he had received from them, he sends to have all boys (πάντας τοὺς παῖδας) in Bethlehem age two and under eliminated. Through this massacre, he hopes to get rid of this newborn king the magi have "warned" him about. These shocking murders by a tyrannical king, the reader is informed, are shown also to have fulfilled scripture, in that they provoke extreme lamentation among those mourning their dead. After the death of Herod, Joseph through a dream is instructed to take the child and mother and return to the land of Israel, which Joseph promptly obeys. However, fearing Archelaus' reign in Judea, Joseph is warned through a dream to relocate in Galilee, which he obeys by settling in Nazareth. The reader is again informed that this fulfills that which was written by the prophets.

3.2.4 Identifying the Exodus Motif in Matthew 2:1–23

Throughout the subsequent sections, the exodus motif, particularly how the exodus is recapitulated, will be dealt with broadly as a background motif. This can be shown in the characterization and plot of the narrative that encompasses the whole of chapter two. Alongside this analysis, there must also be close attention to the details of the text that make this exodus motif a valid interpretation of the chapter. This focus upon the whole of the narrative, as well as the parts, in conjunction with following the flow of the narrative as unfolded by Matthew is an important component in this presentation. Other studies have helpfully emphasized the whole, others the parts, yet others the narrative, but rarely have all three been taken into consideration, and particularly in continuity with the theological interest in Israel's history throughout these pericopes. This focus keeps attention to the fundamental trajectory set in motion by the genealogical introduction that recapitulated Israel's history through a compressed narrative (1:1–17). The ways that Matthew chapter two highlights the exodus and Jesus' passive recapitulation of Israel's history will be examined in five subsections. These five subsections are structured according to the flow of the narrative as presented by Matthew.

The first section will seek to illuminate the exodus background of the narrative, particularly how the plot is set in motion and advanced, as well as highlighting the unique characterization that is achieved. Herod receives an ominous signal from two sources that serve to drive the action of the chapter forward through a conflict between two kings. *Prophetic warning* will be demonstrated as a useful characterization of this material as portrayed in Matthew. Help from other Jewish sources during this period will also aid the search for better understanding this chapter as a recapitulation of the exodus.

The second section will continue to follow the narrative, as due warning is received by Joseph to flee the harm Herod intends, and thus their flight to safety is narrated. The portrayal of this event will be shown to parallel both Israel's early history and Moses' early life. This unique exodus portrayal can be understood as a recapitulation of Israel and Moses.

The third section will look closer at the puzzling way that Egypt is employed in this narrative, and the distinctive characterization and subtle reversal thereby achieved when Judea under Herod resembles Israel's experience in Egypt under Pharaoh. Again, a recapitulation can be observed, albeit in a rather surprising manner that must be closely examined. Following this examination, a further discussion as to particular use and meaning of the fulfillment quotation will be undertaken.

The fourth section will examine the role of the Rachel lament within the overall narrative. Its placement and role will be demonstrated to well serve the exodus recapitulation of the entire narrative. Again, the astounding reversal must be noted, in that within the land of Israel an oppression resembling the exodus period has occurred, a recapitulation of that period within the early life of Jesus.

Finally, in the fifth section the return to the land of Israel will be examined. This also recapitulates the exodus, both the nation of Israel's movement from Egypt to the land of Israel, as well as the life of Moses who returns to Egypt to take up his vocation as deliverer in leading God's people out of Egypt. The surprising geographic reversals will be noted and the recapitulation again highlighted in this final pericope of the infancy narrative.

3.3 Prophetic Warning

The focus of this section will be upon the utilization of what will be termed "prophetic warning,"[24] and this will prove useful for identifying the exodus motif in Matthew 2. Prophetic warning is the characterization of the role of the magi in their communication of what turns out to be ominous news for Herod. This communication by the magi, the role of the star they have seen, and the task of the chief priests and scribes, are signs of

---

[24] Cf. France, *Matthew: Evangelist and Teacher*, 188.

prophetic warning, at least from the perspective of Herod and the narrative. This prophetic warning serves to drive the action of the entire narrative and its employment makes the exodus motif of chapter two fully evident. The appearance of the magi who enter Jerusalem announcing the birth of a king, having seen his star, shocks Herod[25] and all Jerusalem. Herod gathers the chief priests and scribes for further information regarding the birthplace of the Christ, and it is confirmed by scripture from Micah 5 that the Christ is to be born in Bethlehem, which the majority of Matthew's audience would know is near Jerusalem. Combining the magi with the chief priests and scribes, one can best understand the role of these characters as that of a prophetic warning, particularly by the manner in which Herod himself receives it. This prophetic warning serves to initiate the unfolding action in a way similar to the exodus account, thereby portraying Jesus as the passive recapitulation of Israel in Matthew 2.

The action and plot of the narrative involve conflict. When the narrative opens with the notice of Jesus' birth, already called Christ three times in chapter one, during the days of king Herod, the underlying plot of conflict is introduced. Here the two key individuals are named and set up for contrast throughout the remainder of the narrative. Herod reacts with shock, threatened by the report of the magi that a king of the Jews has been born, and he institutes measures to eliminate this rival. The narrative unfolds an account of this event utilizing the exodus as a fundamental backdrop and motif throughout. The exodus event and the Moses story are the major influences upon the material of chapter two.[26]

To help identify the exodus motif, comparison of Matthew's narrative to the book of Exodus is necessary. The book of Exodus begins by recounting how the children of Israel came to grow in Egypt to the size of a nation and how they were subsequently enslaved, oppressed, and killed by the king of Egypt (βασιλεύς Exod 1:8). The portrayal of this event in Exodus particularly focuses upon Moses and the means undertaken to preserve his life from the dangers of Pharaoh's extermination efforts. This provides helpful background for a greater understanding Matthew's narrative of Jesus and Herod, and the text of Exodus will be especially utilized later in this chapter providing evidence that Israel's history is recapitulated passively by Jesus. However, for directly identifying the exodus motif of 2:1–12, the text of Exodus is less helpful, other than a few brief points that will be made in the paragraphs below, because the extermination plans under-

---

[25] ἀκούσας can be taken as causal, "because Herod heard this." See Hanna, *A Grammatical Aid to the Greek New Testament*, 12.

[26] Brown, *Birth of the Messiah*, 600. Cf. Davies and Allison, *Matthew*, 1.194, and 1.265 (fn 16): "When one takes away from Mt 2 all the items with parallels in the Moses materials, little more than a few lines about magi remain." As demonstrated below, even the magi serve an exodus role.

taken by Pharaoh are only general measures to control the population of Israelite males.[27]

3.3.1 Comparison with Jewish Sources

Understanding the wider Jewish traditions that expand upon the Exodus material will prove enlightening for further understanding the exodus motif of Matthew's narrative. Lou Silberman has examined the importance of oral traditions for understanding Matthew and writes, "there existed a large body of thematic materials within the thought of the Jewish communities; that these materials came into expression for particular occasions at various times, in various ways, with various emphases."[28] These Jewish writings build upon the narrative account in the book of Exodus, filling in further details about Pharaoh's actions, and especially focusing upon Moses, whose stature in post-exilic Judaism grew in importance. This development led to further pondering upon infancy traditions of Moses.[29] These expansions reveal a general proclivity toward expanding the Exodus material about Moses. Many of these traditions were widely known in the first century, and Matthew's indebtedness to them for his construction of this narrative will become apparent.[30]

One of the primary places to find information on the traditions about Exodus and Moses available in the first century is the Jewish writer Josephus.[31] Although his writings are well known to be the mixed result of personal and political motivations beyond merely recounting Jewish history,[32] his works nevertheless provide a wealth of material that can help

---

[27] Jubilees 46:11–47:4, Ps.-Philo 9:1, Ezekiel the Tragedian 1–31, and Philo's *De Vita Mosis* 1.8 resemble Exodus in this regard, and are unlike the expansions evidenced in Josephus and the *Targum Pseudo-Jonathan.*

[28] Silberman, "Habent Sua Fata Libelli: The Role of Wandering Themes," 195.

[29] Brown, *Birth of the Messiah*, 114.

[30] Cf. Crossan, "From Moses to Jesus: Parallel Themes," 18–27, helpfully lays out some of these parallels for a more popular reading audience; however the work below is undertaken differently and without following Crossan's anachronistic use of the 12th century *Sefer ha-Zikronot.*

[31] There are further expansions upon the Exodus material in the vast Rabbinic literature, but due to problems of dating this material, it is far more difficult to argue that a certain tradition was known in the first century. What clearly matches datable material, such as Josephus, might be useful as further evidence of knowledge of certain traditions. Therefore, there is some reference to Rabbinic material in footnotes as well as some pertinent references to other literary material.

[32] Hengel, *The Zealots*, ix, "Josephus was a thoroughly tendentious writer and we have to weigh what he says and what he omits in the light of his own interests."

scholars determine wider traditions about biblical history available among the Jewish people in the first century world.[33]

The infancy material on Moses can be found in Josephus' *Jewish Antiquities* (2.205–237), and it contains some relevant similarities to Matthew's depiction of Jesus' infancy stories.[34] Josephus expands upon Exodus 1:15–22 in several interesting ways. This expansion was probably based on material that had developed over time and was inherited and utilized by Josephus. It was material that was known to the wider Jewish world of the first-century, as evidenced by the similarities of Josephus, Matthew, and as dealt with below, the *Targum Pseudo-Jonathan* on Exodus 1:15. The parallels between Josephus' narrative and Matthew's narrative in regard to this basic shared knowledge are the primary focus of the following material. However, no textual relation between Matthew and Josephus is being made, i.e. Matthew utilizing Josephus' works directly or vice-versa. Hence, the differences between Matthew and Josephus will be less of a concern because no direct literary relationship is being made. What is to be observed is merely the utilization of extra-biblical traditions that existed among the Jews in the first century. Comparison of Matthew with these traditions will help make evident that the dominant plot and motif of chapter two is the exodus.

In his *Jewish Antiquities*, Josephus retells and expands upon the infancy material in Exodus concerning Moses, appropriating aspects that would reach the audience he was seeking to engage through his book. After relating the oppressive mistreatment and tremendous hardships faced by the Israelites in Egypt, Josephus begins to narrate the shift toward a greater extermination of their race as a result of an ominous prediction. He writes that one of the sacred scribes ('ιερογραμματέων), skilled in predicting the future, warned Pharaoh (βασιλεύς) that an Israelite would be born who will be a threat to Egypt and elevate Israel (2.205). Josephus writes,

A certain one of the sacred scribes for they are skilled in their ability to predict the future accurately, announced to the king that someone would be begotten at that time to the Israelites who would humble the rule of the Egyptians and would elevate the Israelites; and having been reared he would surpass all men in virtue and acquire a reputation held in everlasting memory (2.205).[35]

---

[33] Josephus' literary activity, occurring as it does between 70 and 100 CE, was therefore contemporary to the composition of Matthew. *Jewish Antiquities* is generally regarded as being composed shortly after 100 C.E.; cf. Evans, *Noncanonical Writings and New Testament Interpretation*, 87.

[34] Cf. Schlatter, *Matthäus*, 32–37; Davies and Allison, *Matthew*, 1.192–194. Bourke, "The Literary Genius of Matthew 1–2," 161–164, after rigorously pointing out every difference between Josephus and Matthew, still must conclude they are analogous.

[35] All translations are from Feldman, *Flavius Josephus: Translation and Commentary*, 188–189; where he adds, "There is a similar prediction by Pharaoh's astrologers in the

Josephus refers to the Egyptian prophet as a sacred scribe who predicts the rise of a threat to Pharaoh and the kingdom of Egypt. Feldman comments on this section,

It is particularly effective that at the very beginning of his long narrative of Moses, one of the Egyptian sacred scribes, a non-Jew, who, as Josephus remarks, "possessed considerable skill in accurately predicting the future, foretells the birth of a child who will surpass all men in virtue and who will win everlasting renown." [36] This prediction and threat alarms the Pharaoh, and he orders that every male born to Israelites be cast into the river with the obvious intent of eliminating this potential threat. Unlike the canonical account as related in Exodus, Josephus expands upon this scene by making Pharaoh's extermination project a direct response to this prophetic warning from a sacred scribe. Josephus narrates the terrible suffering and misery resulting from this massacre, an event resembling in many ways the terrible lament recorded in Matthew 2:18. Yet, Josephus triumphantly notes,

No one, however, can overcome the will of God, not even if he contrives countless devices for it. For the child, whom the sacred scribe foretold, was nurtured having escaped the surveillance of the king, and the one who had made the prediction was found true in the things that would happen through him, and it happened thus (2.209).[37]

At this point Josephus goes on to narrate the story of Moses' birth. Moses' father, Amram, is greatly troubled at the prospect of his wife's pregnancy during this harsh period of extermination.[38] He prays to God for deliverance, and God responds to Amram by appearing to him in his sleep.[39] Through this dream, God reassures Amram by first recalling past activities through Abraham and Jacob, and then directly assuring Amram that the child will be protected because he is destined to deliver the Hebrews from

---

rabbinic tradition." Cf. Davies and Allison, *Matthew*, 1.195, note that Pharaoh learns of the birth of Moses from astrologers in *b. Sanh.* 101a and *Exod. Rab.* on 1:22.

[36] Feldman, *Josephus*, 188 fn 576.

[37] *Ibid.*, 190.

[38] Josephus characterizes Amram as a major figure in his retelling of Moses birth, whereas Exodus in fact does not mention the name Amram or Jochebed until 6:20. Moses' parents are mentioned, but unnamed in Exodus 2, where it is his mother that hides him for three months and goes on to place him in a basket on the river. In Matthew 1 and 2, Joseph is the primary character that acts within the narrative, whereas in Luke's account Mary's role is more pronounced.

[39] This detail is a Josephan addition to the Exodus narrative. Matthew 1–2 records several dreams that Joseph has (1:20; 2:13, 19, 22). Similarities to Matthew 1:18–25 could also be noted. Joseph is troubled at the pregnancy of Mary, ponders this situation, and during his sleep an angel of the Lord appears to him with instructions regarding Mary and the child.

the Egyptian distress (cf. Matt 1:21) and will be forever remembered.[40] Amram awakes, conveys this news to Jochebed, and the birth happens as prophesied with a providential gentleness so as to escape notice. Moses is successfully hidden for three months until Amram begins to fear his discovery, and thus decides to leave the care of the infant to God's preservation. Believing God's care, they make a basket for Moses, place it upon the river, and leave his welfare to God. This providential care is demonstrated as God oversees the subsequent unfolding events. Pharaoh's daughter sees the basket, orders swimmers to retrieve it, and upon seeing the beautiful child becomes enchanted by him. Miriam, who had been carefully watching all of this, advises that a Hebrew mother nurse the child, because Moses had already refused the breasts of many Egyptians. The princess agrees and Miriam brings Moses' mother, who was unknown to Pharaoh's daughter, and the child clings to her breast. The name Moses is bestowed upon him because he was saved (*eses*) out of the water (*mou*).[41]

Josephus then goes on to relate the greatness of Moses, being seventh from Abraham,[42] extraordinary in understanding, and handsome in appearance. The princess seeks to adopt Moses, being childless herself, thus making him a part of Pharaoh's family. She brings Moses to her father the king, places Moses in his hands, whereupon the king, in order to please his daughter, sets his crown upon Moses head. Moses, while playing with this crown, shockingly throws it down and stamps upon it. Josephus then relates,

This seemed to indicate an omen for the kingdom. The sacred scribe who had predicted that his birth would lead to the humiliation of the kingdom of the Egyptians, after uttering a dreadful scream, rushed headlong to kill him. "This is that child, O King," he said, "Slaying whom, God revealed, we would be free from fear" (2.234–45).[43]

The princess acting quickly snatches Moses from the danger and thereafter carefully nurtures him, although he continues to be regarded with suspicion by the Egyptians. Thus, Moses is raised and matures to become the leader he was predicted by the scribe to be.

---

[40] Feldman, *Josephus*, 192, discussing the fame of Moses, states, "Indeed, he was the one figure in Jewish tradition who was well known to the pagan world," and in fact apparently so well known that some did not have to refer to him by name (Ps-Longinus and Quintilian). This may have significance for Matthew here as well, in that Moses is never directly named in this chapter. Accepting Feldman's point, one could suppose it would not have been necessary for Moses to be named here when there are plenty of other indicators pointing in his direction. Moses is named in Matthew 8:4; 17:3, 4; 19:7, 8; 22:24; and 23:2.

[41] Cf. Matthew 1:21 where Joseph is told to name the child Jesus, "Yahweh saves."

[42] Note the significance of positioning Moses at the seventh place, resembling Matthew's numerical focus in structuring the genealogy.

[43] Feldman, *Josephus*, 199.

Josephus' account parallels several aspects of Matthew's exodus motif and these parallels deserve further elucidation for best understanding Matthew's narrative and Jesus' recapitulation of Israel's history. It proves crucial to note that Josephus' colorful rendition of Moses' infancy significantly introduces a key aspect never apparent in the Exodus text itself. In the Exodus account, Pharaoh responds generally to the threat that numerous male Israelites pose to his kingdom and never to one particular person.[44] However, in Josephus' account, Pharaoh's extermination plan is directly attributed to the prophetic warning received through one his prophetic advisors. To eliminate this one potential threat to his kingdom, he must initiate a widespread plan executing all males born to Israelites to be sure that he rids himself of this rival. The prophetic warning sets up the action for Josephus' rendition of Moses infancy and the exodus.

Matthew's narrative also begins similarly through a prophetic warning, from ostensibly non-Jews[45] that come to Herod proclaiming a king to have been born. Although they are not direct advisors to Herod, and their own intent is in fact to pay homage to this newborn king, their message is nevertheless taken by Herod as an ominous and prophetic threat, one that he becomes greatly alarmed at and must seek to eliminate. Herod turns to other advisors in the chief priests and scribes, who turn out to further confirm what the magi have related, that a king will arise in Bethlehem. Davies points to the similarity between the sacred scribes and the magi when he writes, "The sacred scribes here fulfill the role of the Magi, and like them they make the ruling monarch aware of the impending danger."[46] Herod's response to the prophetic threat corresponds to Pharaoh's response in Josephus, with a plan to eliminate this rival, first by sending the magi to find the child, and when they fail to return, he sends others to kill all the boys of Bethlehem age two and under. As with Josephus' account, there is extreme misery at the loss of life, and like Josephus, the deliverer is preserved from this destruction to fulfill the role prophesied by the scribes. The similarity of motif between Josephus and Matthew involves the prophetic threat that a ruler is coming, the reaction of a king by decreeing death of all newborn males, a massacre that results in much misery, and the providential preservation from this imminent threat of the one who will emerge as a deliverer of God's people. These similarities have helped fur-

---

[44] Only later when Moses is an adult is there focus on eliminating him specifically, as dealt with below.

[45] This is never explicitly stated, but assumed by most scholars as they come from the East. Matthew does exhibit definite Gentile focus in 8:5–13 and 15:21–28. More on the magi below.

[46] Davies, *Setting*, 80. Davies then goes on to show similarity to the Targum material, which is dealt with below.

ther identify the exodus motif in Matthew's account, and it has added support for understanding the narrative as a recapitulation of Israel's history.

Another helpful Jewish tradition alongside Josephus' retelling of Exodus is the *Targum Pseudo-Jonathan* on Exodus 1:15.[47] This paraphrastic translation expands the biblical portrayal in several aspects. As with the Josephus material, no direct literary relationship between this Targum and Matthew is being made, other than merely the observable relation of oral traditions that could have had a wide circulation among first century Jews. The purpose for looking at this Targum is to present what probably was traditional material known during the time that the infancy traditions about Jesus began to develop and take form, as well as at the time of the Gospel's final composition. The expansion upon this episode from Exodus in both Josephus and the Targum, while similar and different in several ways, serves as helpful evidence for seeing this material as relevant toward understanding the Gospel of Matthew, a late first century document. In addition, it is important to state that there is definitely no argument being made as to the existence of this Targum as a written text during the first century, a highly disputed point in New Testament studies as well as the broader study of Aramaic in the first century. That important discussion extends far beyond the constraints of this study. The point that is being made is that the material that underlies the Targum can reasonably be supposed to have existed as an oral tradition, particularly a tradition of expanding the Exodus material about Moses. This expanding tradition is clearly evidenced by Josephus who wrote his work in the late first century. What underlies the Targum probably also existed in some form as a tradition in the first century.

Targum Pseudo-Jonathan on Exodus chapter one opens with a basic translation of the Hebrew account, with occasional extra words or phrases. As with the Exodus account in the Hebrew, Pharaoh instigates an oppression of the Israelites to reduce their power and potential uprising through an enforced slavery building fortifications. However, they continue to increase in number, adding that "the Egyptians lived in dread" of the Israelites. The Egyptians therefore increase their harsh labor, making life further difficult for the Israelites. At this point, the Targum expands upon the Hebrew narrative by describing a dream that comes to Pharaoh. This dream threatens doom for both the Pharaoh and the nation of Egypt.

Pharaoh has a dream where he sees weighing scales, with the land of Egypt on one side and a lamb on the other. Ominously the lamb weighs heavier upon the scales than Egypt. Pharaoh rises and summons the magicians of Egypt to hear this significant dream, seeking an interpretation of

---

[47] Maher, *Targum Neofiti Exodus*, *The Aramaic Bible*.

it. Jannes and Jambres,[48] who are chief magicians, declare to Pharaoh, "A son is to be born in the assembly of Israel, through whom all the land of Egypt is destined to be destroyed" (*Tg. Ps.-J.* Exod. 1:15).[49] The dream and interpretation serve as a prophetic warning, a threat that inspires the subsequent actions as recounted in canonical Exodus. Here, it is observed that Pharaoh's extermination plans are the direct result of this prophetic warning, unlike the Hebrew account of Exodus, and he thus takes counsel and instructs the Jewish midwives to kill all male children, which they proceed to disobey out of fear of the Lord.

The expansion upon the Exodus material in this Targum and in Josephus appears to be unrelated literarily, and while there are some general similarities, they clearly differ in several respects. However, both provide key evidence of expansion of the Exodus traditions among the Jewish people. The resemblances between them are nonetheless valuable to highlight. In both the Targum and Josephus, Pharaoh receives an ominous warning, a prediction of one who threatens his kingdom. Advisors instruct Pharaoh in regard to this prophetic warning and Pharaoh acts upon this threat with the intent to destroy this child. Prophetic warning serves to unfold the subsequent events of Israel's life in Egypt and the infancy of Moses. The importance this serves for understanding Matthew's recapitulation of exodus becomes evident when these traditions are dealt with in detail.

This broader plot, where Pharaoh receives a prophetic warning, his reaction and plan to exterminate the rival by killing all Israelite boys, with the subsequent preservation of Moses, as recounted in Josephus and the Targum, strikingly resembles Matthew's narrative in a variety of ways. Herod receives a threatening report from magi, which here in a way serves as a form of royal counsel appearing as a prophetic warning, that another king has been born within his realm. He is alarmed, as is all of Jerusalem. Herod calls on the counsel of chief priests and scribes (πάντας τοὺς ἀρχὶ ερεῖς καὶ γραμματεῖς τοῦ λαου) to determine what the scriptures indicate about the Christ's birthplace so as to swiftly eliminate this threat. They reply with a quotation conflating Micah 5:2 and 2 Samuel 5:2/1 Chronicles 11:2.[50] There can be shown here an interesting verbal similarity between these counselors to Herod and those that counsel Pharaoh in *Antiquities* 2.205 ('ιερογραμματέων). The report to Herod, the alarm it causes, and the measured plans to eliminate this threat all resemble the plot in *Antiquities*

---

[48] Jannes and Jambres were well known from Jewish, Christian, and pagan sources. They are also mentioned in *Tg. Ps.-J.* Exod 7:11; *Tg. Ps.-J.* Num 22:22. Cf. CD 5:17–19; "Jannes and Jambres," *OTP*, 2.427–36; 2 Tim 3:8.

[49] Maher, *Targum Neofiti Exodus*, 162.

[50] Davies and Allison, *Matthew*, 1.243, maintain "Moses was remembered as a shepherd (Isa 63:11; Ps.-Philo 19:3, 9; *Mek.* on Exod 14:31; *Exod. Rab.* on 2:2), so the quotation nicely fits Matthew's Moses-Messiah typology."

and in the Targum. Therefore the reader of Matthew's narrative, realizing
this background and plot, and also possibly aware of the expanding traditions such as discussed above, would perceive Herod characterized as a
"Pharaoh," reacting with oppressive power to squash all contenders to his
kingdom. In this specific instance, Herod reacts just as Pharaoh does in
Josephus' account and in the Targum. What these parallel resources provide is enough similarity with Matthew toward viewing King Herod as a
"Pharaoh," and perceiving Jesus as the "Moses" whom this king seeks to
destroy. In response to a threatening report, a prophetic warning from royal
counsel, both Pharaoh and Herod sought to eliminate rivals.

The pursuit by Herod of this rival king pervades the entire narrative. At
the end of the narrative, the newborn king Jesus has been delivered from
the threat and the oppressive king Herod is dead.[51] In Exodus 2:23 and
4:19, the Pharaoh is pronounced dead and Moses remains alive, having
been preserved from execution.[52] Matthew chapter two resembles this conflict between Pharaoh and Moses, in that both involve the pursuit of eliminating a threat. God is depicted as providentially preserving Jesus' life
from the threat of death throughout the narrative, and in contrast to the
preservation of Jesus, the reader is told of Herod's end in death, something
repetitively mentioned on three separate occasions in the narrative (2:15,
19, 20). Like Moses, Jesus emerges victorious to take up his vocation of
deliverance (1:21).

The prophetic warning is actually doubled in Matthew in that the initial
information about a new king is received from the magi and further information from scripture about where the Christ is to be born is received from
the chief priests and scribes. The Targum also had two forms of prophetic
warning: Pharaoh's dream and the interpretation of that dream by Jannes
and Jambres. Through information related through the magi that they had
seen a star,[53] and through the scriptural testimony related by the chief
priests and scribes, Herod is portrayed as receiving extremely unsettling,
threatening news. The threat Herod perceives is made clearer in light of the
means he undertakes to eliminate the Christ. The hearer and reader can
perceive the unfolding plot of the narrative and ascertain the theological
significance Matthew underlines through this double prophetic warning. A
sign of threat for Herod, a sign of hope for those hearing and reading this

---

[51] Keener, *Matthew*, 107, notes of Josephus' *Antiquities* that he exalts Moses, as Matthew exalts Jesus, and through this, "divine protection could function as divine vindica-
tion in ancient narratives."

[52] This account involves Moses as an adult, and it will be dealt with in closer detail
below.

[53] According to the narrative, it is not clear whether Herod and Jerusalem actually saw
the star. They are troubled not by the star but by the news they heard from the magi (2:2–
3).

narrative, much like the underlying purpose for the beginning of the Exodus story, which especially highlights the preservation of Moses for his future delivery of Israel.

3.3.2 The Magi and the Star

It can now be better understood how the magi[54] and star are relevant for the overall exodus background to this narrative. Brown's exhaustive analysis of chapter two identified various traditions that are utilized and fused in this chapter. Although this enterprise can become an overly speculative endeavor, he examines the data and proposes an estimate of the origin of this material. One of the traditions Brown identifies is the magi story, initially separate from the Herod story, but fused at some point to this Moses story. Consequently, through the prophetic warning instigated by the magi, this problem can thereby become the initiation for the action of the story present in Matthew chapter two.[55] On this theory, for the story to work, Herod has to discover the threatening information through some source, and utilizing the magi tradition, fusing it together with the overall exodus plot, was a way of bringing the two traditions together for a coherent narrative.[56] Proposals on the origin and composition of this narrative, while worthwhile endeavors, can only arrive at rough estimates at best. For the purpose of this study therefore, the narrative is interpreted as a whole, coherent text.[57]

---

[54] They are never specifically called "wise," and it appears best to retain the Greek by simply calling them magi. Cf. Powell, "The Magi as Wise Men: Re-Examining a Basic Supposition," 1–20, has rightly argued against the predominance of scholarship's regular characterization of the magi as wise men. Their use is also significant for those with a Greco-Roman background; see Davies and Allison, *Matthew*, 1.230.

[55] Brown, *Birth of the Messiah*, 190–194; Cf. Davies and Allison, *Matthew*, 1.229; Luz, *Matthew 1–7* (2007), 102: "Without 2:1–12, 2:13–23 would not be understandable." Via, 'Narrative World and Ethical Response', 134, says two plots are fused, structure determined their placement here. Bourke, "Literary Genius," 172, cites a conflation of two stories: "The magi's seeking out the King of the Jews and offering him his gifts has nothing to do with either the Moses or the Israel typology. But in the text as we now have it, their questionings (2:2) are the point of departure of the entire flight and massacre complex."

[56] Gundry, *Matthew*, 26–27; and Keener, *Matthew*, 99, propose that Matthew gets the magi from the book of Daniel (Dan 2:2, 10 LXX Theod. uses μαγος). Meier, *Matthew*, 11, considers that Matthew took the motif from the Balaam story in Numbers as "a literary and theological motif."

[57] Cf. Patte, *Matthew*, 30, observes that chapter two as it now stands "constitutes a complete literary section," 30; and Davies, *Setting*, 62, who states that the entirety of Matthew chapters one and two are "a unity wrought by the Evangelist."

Many scholars understand the magi and star tradition as an allusion to Numbers 22–24, where Balaam the prophet[58] sees a star come forth out of Jacob (Num 24:17). Two key words, ἀστέρα and ἀνατολῇ, are used in Matthew 2:2 that indicate this possible relationship. In addition to these words, the emphatic position of αὐτοῦ[59] may also further evidence an allusion to Numbers 24:17.

εἴδομεν γὰρ αὐτοῦ τὸν ἀστέρα ἐν τῇ ἀνατολῇ (Matt 2:2)
ἀνατελεῖ ἄστρον ἐξ Ιακωβ (Num 24:17)

This event takes place during the time of Israel's wilderness wanderings, having been delivered from Egypt, and can thus be viewed as broadly within the Exodus period of Israel's history. This utilization of the magi material then could yield far more than an initial set up for a coherent plot, it further succeeds in adding color, particularly in terms of the fulfillment that pervades the whole of Matthew's Gospel. Matthew can therefore allude to this prophecy and place Jesus as the fulfillment of it, although it is only an implicit fulfillment and never directly stated as the others.[60] Balaam had been employed by the king Balaak to curse the Israelites, but instead he blessed them, giving them a hopeful and significant prophecy for a future deliverer, which from Matthew's perspective, Jesus fulfills. In addition, it is important to note that the prophecy of Balaam was viewed as messianic by various Jewish interpreters.[61]

A further possible parallel that would provide additional evidence is discussed by Brown. He observes a relation between Balaak and Herod, and that may possibly linger in the background. Balaam's resistance to the king and his blessing of Israel may also be compared to the magi's behavior.[62] They had tricked Herod by not returning to him with information about the child and then went home by another route. The magi's actions may therefore allude to Balaam's, who also hailed from the east (Num 23:7).[63] Consequently, Davies and Allison allege, "Matthew probably thought of the magi as 'Balaam's successors'."[64] Balaam infuriated Balaak

---

[58] Philo calls him a μαγος in *Mos.* 1.276.

[59] Hanna, *Grammatical Aid*, 12.

[60] See Instone-Brewer, "Balaam-Laban as the Key to the Old Testament Quotations in Matthew 2," 207–227, for a recent argument that sees the story of Balaam in the Old Testament and early Jewish sources as the background to Matthew 2.

[61] Num 24:17 LXX ἄστρον; ἄνθρωπος (MT כוכב; שבט); in Tg Neofiti: for *star* and *scepter* it has *king* and *redeemer*; in Tg Ps-J *king* and *messiah*. Dunn, *Jesus Remembered*, 340, states that Numbers 24:17 "was a popular source of speculation and hope in Jewish thought of the time, not least at Qumran." Cf. 1QM 11:4–9; 4Q175 1:9–13; CD 7:18–20.

[62] Brown, *Birth of the Messiah*, 193–194.

[63] *Ibid.*, 610, indicates that the church fathers interpreted the magi in resemblance of Balaam.

[64] Davies and Allison, *Matthew*, 1.231.

by not following his orders to curse Israel by blessing Israel instead. Thus, Herod resembles both Pharaoh and Balaak.[65] Another additional significance that might be relevant is to point out that the midwives' also do not follow Pharaoh's orders in the Exodus account. They fail to kill the newborn Israelite boys, because they feared God (Exod 1:17), "deceiving" Pharaoh about it (1:18–19).[66] This results in Pharaoh instituting a second plan by commanding all the people to throw the newborn boys into the Nile (1:22), which is similar to Herod's subsequent move to kill all the boys in the surrounding region of Bethlehem.

The role of the star[67] in this narrative has long puzzled scholars, whether it was a natural astronomical phenomenon or miraculous,[68] and how it could guide the magi.[69] Other scholars would rather understand the star symbolically.[70] Gnilka has also indicated that the function of the star is analogous to Exodus 13:21 where Israel is guided in the wilderness with a cloud by day and fire by night.[71] Matthew keeps the star as a part of the tradition, even if it troubles subsequent interpreters, for it apparently serves the pervasive fulfillment purpose Matthew is so fond of explicitly citing, here allowing its presence as an implicit fulfillment of Numbers 24:17.[72] In short space, Matthew can retain the broader exodus motif and have an added bonus of a fulfillment of the prophecy of a star and kingship. Furthermore, the homage and gifts given to the child Jesus is utilized to keep this kingship motif prominent in the narrative. Moreover, in Josephus' *Antiquities*, Moses is visited by various people who are enamored with his beauty (2.230–231).

---

[65] Brown, *Birth of the Messiah*, 193.

[66] God is said to deceive or mock (ἐμπέπαιχα) Pharoah and the Egyptians in Exodus 10:2 LXX.

[67] Matthew apparently favors "natural" phenomenon that exhibit a literary and theological quality for the story of Jesus, as seen in darkness (27:45) and an earthquake at Jesus' death (27:51). Astrological signs also played a role in Greco-Roman literature (e.g. Suetonius *Aug.* 94). For astrological signs generally in the ancient world, see Davies and Allison, *Matthew*, 233–234.

[68] Luz, *Matthew 1–7* (2007), 105, thinks Matthew portrays it as miraculous.

[69] See Allison, *Studies in Matthew*, 17–41, for a cogent argument that the "star" is an angel.

[70] Schnackenburg, *Matthew*, 22–23, perceives the star as a literary symbol, where "graphic oracle becomes an actual star arising in the heavens." Cf. Frankemölle, *Matthäus*, 166–168.

[71] Gnilka, *Matthäusevangelium*, 40. Cf. Keener, *Matthew*, 104, notes that if the star did move, there may be an allusion to the pillar of cloud that guided Israel in the wilderness (Wis 10:17; 18:3); Meier, *Matthew,* 12.

[72] Ellis, *The Making of the New Testament Documents*, 346, thinks that the repetitive use of star (2:2, 7, 9, 10) further supports an allusion to Numbers 24:17.

As a final comment upon this section, it might prove useful to consider Matthew's possible restraint[73] in regard to this material.[74] Far more could have been done, explicitly and implicitly, in making this material evoke a host of themes and correspondences. However, this in fact has not occurred here, and this may result from some constraints and reserve among the Christian community, reticent to retell Jesus' story for the sake of utilizing every conceivable connection with past scriptures and themes. Jesus' story is fundamental and his story is the main purpose for the writing of this Gospel. As Witherington helpfully summarizes the "story of Jesus itself has led the author to the Old Testament text looking for an explanation, rather than the story being generated out of Old Testament quotations."[75] Jesus' life was known through the variety of traditions available in the Christian communities, and where his story can be presented in correspondence with past scriptures and traditions, this no doubt proves a bonus.[76] The discussion above has shown that the exodus theme is prominent enough within the narrative, as well as Jesus' recapitulation of Israel's history. Constrained by his own convictions and the traditions at hand, much of which was already known throughout the Christian communities, Matthew retains these with plenty of clues to evoke the exodus theme and recapitulation. However, the Evangelist apparently will not overly transcend the basics of Jesus' story for the sake of a parallel.

Thus far, prophetic warning has been discussed by highlighting the important ways this parallels the exodus tradition. The evidence presented above in regard to prophetic warning will continue to undergird the following material in various ways. It plays a significant role in the plot of the narrative throughout the chapter as well as involving the overall characterization in the narrative, especially Herod as a Pharaohic figure. Continuing to follow the narrative account, the next subsection will focus on the flight to safety in response to Herod's murderous intent, while continuing to demonstrate the important ways this links with the exodus tradition.

---

[73] Cf. Witherington, *Matthew*, 73.

[74] This restraint can also be said for the community that passed on these traditions prior to the final redaction, as well as whoever fused this material together. It is nevertheless a difficult and speculative endeavor to chart this process. Due to necessary restrictions, this study has nevertheless placed emphasis primarily upon interpretation of the final text.

[75] *Ibid.*, 52.

[76] Holmgren, *Old Testament and the Significance of Jesus*, 13: "Early Christians did not discover Jesus as the result of an initial study of the Old Testament. Rather the movement was in the opposite direction; that is, from their 'meeting' with Jesus Christians looked back to the Old Testament, their scripture, in order to gain understanding of what took place."

3.4 Flight to Safety

The magi finally achieve their goal by coming to the child led by the star. They then offer their homage and gifts fit for a king (cf. Ps 72:10, 15; Isa 60:6). They are warned not to return to Herod, and therefore return by another way. In response to the threat upon Jesus' life, having been warned of this through a dream,[77] Joseph must retreat[78] from the danger of Judea for refuge in Egypt.[79] This subsection will examine this pericope, and it will become evident that the exodus motif continues to be utilized throughout this material. Both Israel the nation and Moses the individual were involved in flights of escape from dangers that threatened their survival. The flight of Jesus to safety will be shown to resemble both Israel and Moses, and thereby demonstrate his passive recapitulation of Israel's history.

At this point in the narrative, the allusions are closer to the book of Exodus itself, both for Israel's flight to safety and Moses' as well. It should be observed that Matthew here conflates the two early accounts of Moses' life. Moses escapes Pharaoh's threat twice, once as a child in the basket incident and second as young man fleeing the wrath of Pharaoh after Moses had murdered an Egyptian. Parallels in language, which will be demonstrated below, make evident this exodus background. Beyond the Exodus account, there may also be further traditions linked to Josephus' *Antiquities* 2.210–216 where Amram receives instruction through a dream about Moses' future and warning about Pharaoh's plans to destroy him. As a result, Amram hides the child and Moses is preserved from death. This is woven by Josephus into the Exodus account of Moses' episode in the basket and being found by Pharaoh's daughter.

There are thus two significant and distinctive ways that Jesus' flight to Egypt and return back to Israel correspond to previous stories recounted in the book of Exodus, one corresponding to Israel's movements and the other corresponding to Moses' movements, involving literal geographic recapitulations of both.[80] Corresponding to Israel's movements, Jesus' journey down to Egypt (v. 14) and back to the land of Israel (v. 21) paral-

---

[77] See the helpful excursus in Keener, *Matthew*, 95–96, on the importance of dreams for both Jewish and Greco-Roman readers.

[78] BDAG, 75, "take refuge" (cf. 2:22; 4:12; 15:21). Metzner, "Der Rückzug Jesu im Matthäusevangelium: Ein literarisches Déjà-vu-Erlebnis," 258–268, identifies and discusses this as a literary motif in Matthew's story.

[79] Dibelius, *From Tradition to Gospel*, 130, notes that the motif of threat and saving of child hero was widespread, citing Suetonius, *Vita Caes.* 2, *Aug.*, 94; cf. Bultmann, *History of Synoptic Tradition*, 293, who adds *Nero*, 36.

[80] Davies, *Setting*, 78, briefly covers repetition of both Israel and Moses, and regards these two aspects as legitimate interpretations.

lels exactly Israel's movement in the exodus period, which is recounted in
Genesis and Exodus. Israel, as a family/nation go down to Egypt as the
sons of Jacob/Israel. After a period of several generations, they are brought
out of Egypt, and they return to dwell in the land of Israel as recounted in
Joshua. This exodus theme can thus be seen explicitly to encompass verses
14 and 21, noting the paralleling of language that serve as brackets for the
intermediate material of the narrative.

Verse 14
ὁ δὲ ἐγερθεὶς παρέλαβεν τὸ παιδίον καὶ τὴν μητέρα αὐτοῦ νυκτὸς
καὶ ἀνεχώρησεν εἰς Αἴγυπτον
Verse 21
ὁ δὲ ἐγερθεὶς παρέλαβεν τὸ παιδίον καὶ τὴν μητέρα αὐτοῦ
καὶ εἰσῆλθεν εἰς γῆν Ἰσραήλ

Threat resulted in Israel's movement to Egypt, specifically the famine in
the land at that time, and Egypt served as a place of refuge where food
could be found. Egypt was not the ultimate land promised for Israel, and
Exodus narrates the considerable difficulties they had in leaving Egypt,
having become enslaved during their time there. Their return to the land of
Israel takes place many years later, as recounted in Joshua. The parallel
wording of verses 14 and 21 as shown above make evident the exodus
theme that has already pervaded the earlier verses, and serve to keep the
exodus theme prominent throughout the narrative up to verse 21. These
parallel statements serve as the brackets into which the intermediate material is placed, as well as providing an important setting for understanding
the exodus background and purpose of these verses in the overall narrative.
The quotation of Hosea 11:1 in verse 15 explicitly connects Jesus with Israel, the "son" now called from Egypt, reliving and recapitulating their experience.

Brown comments about the background of these verses and regards not
only the geographic movement, but also the dreams, as significant for
identifying Matthew's Joseph resembling the Old Testament Joseph, who
not only went to Egypt, but also was involved with dreams.[81] The Old Testament Joseph brings his father Jacob/Israel and family to Egypt to save
them from the devastating famine.[82] This resemblance, while not pedantically exact, is sufficiently close enough to observe and understand the correspondences. Joseph in response to threat takes his family, the child Jesus
and mother Mary, to Egypt for refuge (v. 14). After the threat of Herod's
murderous intentions has passed, Joseph takes Jesus and Mary, and they
return to the land of Israel (v. 21). Therefore, the exodus is recapitulated

---

[81] Brown, *Birth of the Messiah*, 112, 598.
[82] Nolan, *Royal Son*, 35: "it is again a Joseph, son of Jacob and Rachel (Matt 1:16, and note 2:18–19), who brings the heir of the promise to safety in Egypt."

both geographically and experientially through the arrangement of the material. This is manifested explicitly through the quotation of Hosea 11:1, and Jesus is thereby portrayed as reliving the experience of the exodus and passively recapitulating Israel's history. It proves important to fully identify what is done here. Matthew can be observed as constructing the narrative to portray Jesus repeating the exodus, which apparently is an important theme that needs to be emphasized in completely telling Jesus' story.

Jesus is also depicted as reliving the experience of Moses, who fled from a threatening situation twice, once as a child and later as a young man, when he had to flee from the wrath of Pharaoh.[83] The second flight to safety involved fleeing Pharaoh's anger as a result of murdering an Egyptian. Matthew alludes to this account in several ways. First, in verse 13 by the use of ζητεῖν which appears in Exodus 2:15 (ἐζήτει). Just as the Pharaoh *sought* to kill Moses because he was now a threat to this kingdom, so also another Pharaoh-like figure *seeks* to kill one who is a threat to his kingdom. Second, Herod intends to eliminate this rival and accordingly sends to kill (ἀνεῖλεν) the boys in and around Bethlehem (2:16). Exodus 2:15 also uses ἀνελεῖν for Pharaoh's intent to kill Moses. Third, Moses flight from Pharaoh's anger is in Exodus 2:15 called ἀνεχώρησεν, also used in Matthew 2:14. The verb ἀναχορέω can be used in the sense of taking refuge (Matt 2:14, 22; 4:12; 12:15; 14:13; 15:21).[84] At a broader level, the thematic links correspond in that a king seeks to destroy a rival.

Herod seeks Jesus with the same intent on eliminating a deliverer, one whom he explicitly calls the Christ (2:4). The reader would have gained this narratival depiction explicitly through 1:1, 16, 17, 18, as well as the broader deliverance motif in 1:21. While Jesus himself has done nothing that resembles Moses' inept action, one might suppose that the magi provide this element by their failure to obey Herod's orders. The realization of their trickery, as perceived by Herod (2:16), results in the orders to kill all the boys around Bethlehem in the hopes of killing the one Herod seeks. Here Moses' flight is recapitulated by Jesus, as is Moses' return,[85] dealt with below. Through these two juxtaposed elements, Matthew presents Jesus as recapitulating both Israel's history and Moses experience.[86]

Thus far, two important elements in highlighting the exodus parallels have been covered: prophetic warning and flight to safety. Both of these have been shown to parallel the exodus traditions in various ways, particu-

---

[83] Stanton, *Gospel for A New People*, 77–84, has an interesting discussion regarding the use of the rhetorical strategy σύγκρισις, "comparison." He cites Matthew's comparison of Jesus to Moses as an illustration of this device.

[84] BDAG, 75.

[85] "The final redeemer is as the first," a Rabbinic saying, Davies and Allison, *Matthew*, 1.254; Hengel and Merkel, 'Die Magier', 158.

[86] Vogtle, "Die matthaische Kindheitsgeschichte," 176–177.

larly utilized so as to present Jesus as recapitulating Israel's history, as well as some of Moses' movements. These recapitulations were shown to be literal geographic repetitions of Jesus' movements in the narrative. At this point, the analysis must now focus upon the distinctive characterization of Jesus' movements in light of the exodus history. Explicit citation of the exodus is achieved through the fulfillment quotation recorded in verse 15. However, the role of this citation within the narrative must be carefully examined because there are several intriguing textual nuances. What will unfold is an argument for observing Matthew's characterization of Judea under Herod as parallel to Israel's experience in Egypt under Pharaoh. This involves several unexpected reversals of the exodus story, easily missed by many scholars that have focused upon other aspects that have unfortunately excluded what Matthew subtly has achieved.

3.5 Judea under Herod = Israel under Pharaoh

The characterization of Judea under Herod is colored by motifs drawn from the exodus story of Israel under Pharaoh. The achievement of this portrayal is accomplished in a distinctive manner. To fully understand this portrayal, there must be detailed attention to a number of areas. Therefore, this section must first illuminate how the quotation of Hosea 11:1 is misplaced within the narrative based on the geographical movements of Jesus. Second, there will be an overview of the commonly given explanations for this placement. Third, several reasons will be offered as to why these explanations are inadequate. Finally, a proposal will be advanced for understanding why the quotation appears where it does within the narrative, where it is argued that this is achieved by the use of a subtle geographical reversal.

3.5.1 A Misplaced Quotation?

A brief examination of where the quotation appears in relation to the narrative is necessary to fully understand the oddity about this quotation's position. In Matthew 2:15 a quotation from Hosea 11:1 is utilized, Ἐξ Αἰγύπτου ἐκάλεσα τὸν υἱόν μου. Matthew's text follows the Hebrew rendering, ממצרים קראתי לבני, and not the LXX, ἐξ Αἰγύπτου μετεκάλεσα τὰ τέκνα αὐτου.[87] It serves as one of the fulfillment quotations that Matthew

---

[87] Unless a more literal Greek text was used. See Gundry, *Use of the Old Testament*, 93; Lindars, *New Testament Apologetic*, 216–217.

characteristically uses.[88] However, the location of this quotation within the narrative is logically and geographically out of place because Jesus is taken *to* Egypt not out of Egypt. Within the preceding section of the narrative (vv.13–15), Joseph has been warned in a dream that Herod is seeking to kill Jesus, thus they are to flee to Egypt and stay there until told otherwise. Joseph rises and does as he has been ordered, and then it is stated that they *stay* in Egypt until Herod's death. Immediately following this section the reader is given this quotation, following the Evangelist's important formula, "in order that it might be fulfilled what was spoken by the Lord through the prophet" (ἵνα πληρωθῇ τὸ ῥηθὲν ὑπὸ κυρίου διὰ τοῦ προφήτου). The reader appears to be instructed that "Out of Egypt I have called my son" is fulfilled by what has just occurred. Yet, at this point in the narrative, the reader has only been told that Jesus went *to* Egypt and continues to reside there until later in the narrative. It is not until verse 21 that the reader is told about Jesus leaving Egypt and his return to the land. Logically, the calling out of Egypt quotation should follow verse 21, when Jesus actually leaves Egypt and returns to the land of Israel. Thus, the placement of Hosea 11:1 at the end of verse 15 is indeed peculiar and deserves a thorough investigation.

It would be unremarkable to make no comment about the odd position of the quotation because it is easy to overlook, and overfamiliarity with the text can often affect such an oversight. Nevertheless, several scholars have given brief notice of this puzzling placement. For example, Harrington notes the peculiarity but offers no further discussion about it.[89] Similarly, Luz states that the quotation simply does not fit the context, but also presents no further discussion.[90] A few scholars do go further and rightly regard it worthy of discussion. The encyclopedic commentary by Davies and Allison notes with surprise, "It is exceptional for a formula quotation to refer forward to an event yet to be narrated" and they go on to offer an explanation for this exceptional use.[91] Stendahl, Brown, France, Gnilka, Frankemölle, and Hagner make various comments on this oddity, offering similar explanations for this peculiarity that must now be delineated.[92]

---

[88] On fulfillment in Matthew see Stanton, *Gospel for a New People*, 346–363; France, *Matthew: Evangelist and Teacher*; McConnell, *Law and Prophecy in Matthew's Gospel*, Rothfuchs, *Die Erfüllungszitate des Matthäus-Evangeliums*; Segbroeck, "Les citations d'accomplissement," 107–130.

[89] Harrington, *Matthew*, 44.

[90] Luz, *Matthew 1–7* (2007), 118.

[91] Davies and Allison, *Matthew*, 1.262.

[92] It appears a distinct possibility that to some degree these explanations might be part of the general lore of information that is passed on from commentary to commentary without much serious thought about it.

3.5.2 Overview of Common Explanations

The primary explanation for the placement of this quotation concerns the geographical focus of the chapter. Geography plays an important role in the chapter, from Jesus' birth in Bethlehem, his flight to Egypt, return to the land of Israel, the relocation to Galilee, and finally the settlement in Nazareth. Many scholars answer the oddity of placement based on the geographic focus of this section comprising verses 13–15. Because Egypt is the focus of these verses, the quotation was needed here with the first mention of Egypt.[93] The explicit mention of "Egypt" in the quotation made it useful for rooting the childhood movements of Jesus in the prophetic scriptures as a fulfillment of them. Thus, according to these scholars, the reason the quotation could not be placed following verse 21 is due to the fact that the geographic focus of that section is on the land of Israel[94] or especially to focus on the final destination as Nazareth.[95] Therefore, for these scholars the explanation is quite simple, geographic locations are the determinative factor and not the movement itself.[96] In sum, Hosea 11:1 is utilized primarily for the mention of Egypt, and for geographic reasons the quotation must appear at verse 15 when Egypt is the focus of this section.[97] These scholars acknowledge the oddity of the quotation as *logically* out of place in terms of the movements of Jesus, but the geographic orientation of the chapter leads them to consider the quotation's necessary use here.

Beyond the geographic explanation, which for the most part predominates in most discussions about the placement of this quotation, there have been several other points made to further explain why the quotation is placed where it appears in the text. Hagner offers a theological reason in conjunction with the geographic focus. He proposes that the quotation *anticipates* the following narrative, in that 'the premature quotation serves as the signal of the theological import of the presence of the holy family in Egypt by its explicit reference to the exodus'.[98] Similarly, Davies and Allison regard the formula quotation as a reference forward, anticipating what will be narrated in verses 19–21.[99] Brown makes a further point when he

---

[93] Stanton, *Interpretation of Matthew* (Edinburgh: T&T Clark, 1995), 71. In reply to why the quotation does not actually follow the first mention of Egypt in verse 13, Davies and Allison, *Matthew*, 1.263, answer that this would destroy the parallelism between 13–14 and 19–21.

[94] Stendahl, "Quis," 71. France, "Formula-Quotations," 243; Schweizer, *Matthew*, 41; Carter, *Matthew*, 84; Gnilka, *Matthäusevangelium*, 51; Frankemölle, *Matthäus*, 169–170.

[95] Strecker, *Der Weg*, 58; Carson, *Matthew 1–12*, 91; France, *Matthew* (NICNT), 79–80.

[96] Davies and Allison, *Matthew*, 1.262–263.

[97] Turner, *Matthew*, 91.

[98] Hagner, *Matthew 1–13*, 36. Cf. Garland, *Matthew*, 29.

[99] Davies and Allison, *Matthew*, 261.

supposes that the exodus focus of these verses therefore requires the quotation about Egypt to appear here because of his assumptions about the latter verses' focus on the exile. He observes an exilic motif for verses 16–18, and therefore regards a reference to the exodus as necessary and understandable only among verses 13–15.[100] Hagner concurs by noting the appropriateness for the theological structure of the narrative, so that the exodus motif must precede the exilic.[101] Reference to Egypt after verse 21 would distort this particular theological structure. Important for this explanation is an assumption that an exodus motif dominates verses 13–15 and an exilic motif dominates verses 16–18, something that is argued against below.

There are two alternatives to the above explanations. One is offered by Nolland who observes a possible conflict between the quotation and the angel's words in verse 20. Therefore, the quotation is placed where it appears rather than after verse 20, "because close juxtaposition of the angel's words and the quotation would have tended to put the two items of quoted speech in competition."[102] While this is remotely possible, given the analysis and argumentation of this section, it will prove improbable. Gundry offers an altogether different interpretation of the quotation and its use in verse 15. He regards the emphasis of the quotation in this section, not as a reference to the geographical movements of Jesus, but as an emphasis on the divine preservation of Jesus while in Egypt.[103] To do so he translates the preposition temporally, rendering it "since Egypt (i.e., from the time he dwelt there)."[104] The Hosea quotation based on this explanation by Gundry is not actually out of place, since the geographic movements are not involved.

3.5.3 Why These Explanations are Unsatisfactory

While the above explanations may reasonably satisfy those scholars that employ them, they simply fall short of adequately explaining several significant details of the text. Six aspects must be highlighted that make the common explanations appear less likely. They are cumulative arguments, and therefore must overlap one another to some degree. Together these as-

---

[100] Brown, *Birth of the Messiah*, 220.

[101] Hagner, *Matthew 1–13*, 36.

[102] Nolland, *Matthew*, 123, where he also adds that the quotation is thus located so that the fulfillment quotations link each subdivision of 13–23, which coincides with some of the argumentation below.

[103] Gundry, *Matthew*, 34.

[104] Gundry, *Use of Old Testament*, 93–94. Yet, he still allows the geographic aspect to be legitimate as well for "a deliberate play on the double meaning."

pects will lead to a search for another way of explaining the quotation's odd presence in verse 15.

1. The quotation is oddly placed and it appears to be intentional.

The foremost aspect that is rightly to be highlighted and one point in which the above scholars agree with is the fact that the quotation is indeed in the wrong place. Based on the geographic movements of Jesus' family, it should logically appear after verse 21 when they actually come out of Egypt and return to the land of Israel. However, these scholars appear to misunderstand the relation of geography and movement in the story as it unfolds. Important to note, is that the narrative follows the *movements* of Jesus, and the geographical locations that are cited are a part of this movement. The movements and geographical locations are obviously interconnected. Therefore, simply to emphasize the locations themselves as determinative for the placement of the quotation fails to convince. The quotation would still make sense after verse 21 because they have to go out of and leave Egypt to get back to the land of Israel. Verse 19 explicitly mentions that Joseph is in Egypt. Verse 21 relates this movement back to the land of Israel, and the quotation of Hosea would make complete sense following this statement.

2. An Exodus motif prevails throughout the entire chapter.

Brown and others observe an exodus focus in verses 13–15 and an exilic focus for verses 16–18.[105] This also fails to adequately deal with the text overall. The exodus as a motif and background actually serves as the fundamental backdrop for the whole of Matthew 2, as argued throughout this present chapter. Primarily the exilic motif is thought to be highlighted by the quotation of Jeremiah 31 in verse 18 as well the literal exit of Jesus from the immediate area of his birth in Judea. But this concerns a misunderstanding of the use of the Jeremiah quotation, dealt with in detail below, that essentially serves as a quintessential lament of God's people in a time of extreme suffering and oppression. Note the context. Herod, like the Pharaoh of exodus, kills the Israelite boys and Rachel (*Stammütter*)[106] weeps. The whole of the chapter resembles aspects of both Israel's experience in the exodus period as well as Moses' experiences. Further, verses 19–21 closely parallel Exodus 4:19–20, dealt with in detail below.

3. The Greek text exhibits several parallels that help to identify the prevailing exodus motif of the chapter.

Further help can be gained for understanding the placement of the quotation, as well as the Exodus theme encompassing a larger section of the chapter, by attending to details within the Greek text. On the next page, there is an outline layout of the Greek text that helps toward identifying

---

[105] Brown, *Birth of the Messiah*, 219; Hagner, *Matthew 1–13*, 36.
[106] Schlatter, *Matthäus*, 43.

the exodus motif throughout the entire chapter. Through placing the Greek text into phrases in an outline format, attention to details in the text can be better observed toward noting important aspects of the exodus theme throughout verses 13–21.

Matthew 2:13–21
13 Ἀναχωρησάντων δὲ αὐτῶν
    ἰδοὺ ἄγγελος κυρίου φαίνεται κατ᾿ ὄναρ τῷ Ἰωσὴφ λέγων,
      Ἐγερθεὶς παράλαβε τὸ παιδίον καὶ τὴν μητέρα αὐτοῦ
    καὶ φεῦγε εἰς Αἴγυπτον
        καὶ ἴσθι ἐκεῖ ἕως ἂν εἴπω σοι·
        μέλλει γὰρ Ἡρῴδης ζητεῖν τὸ παιδίον τοῦ ἀπολέσαι αὐτό.
14 *ὁ δὲ ἐγερθεὶς παρέλαβεν τὸ παιδίον καὶ τὴν μητέρα αὐτοῦ νυκτὸς*
    καὶ ἀνεχώρησεν εἰς Αἴγυπτον,
15   καὶ ἦν ἐκεῖ ἕως τῆς τελευτῆς Ἡρῴδου·
    ἵνα πληρωθῇ τὸ ῥηθὲν ὑπὸ κυρίου διὰ τοῦ προφήτου λέγοντος,
      Ἐξ Αἰγύπτου ἐκάλεσα τὸν υἱόν μου.
16 Τότε Ἡρῴδης ἰδὼν ὅτι ἐνεπαίχθη ὑπὸ τῶν μάγων ἐθυμώθη λίαν,
    καὶ ἀποστείλας ἀνεῖλεν πάντας τοὺς παῖδας τοὺς ἐν Βηθλέεμ
        καὶ ἐν πᾶσι τοῖς ὁρίοις αὐτῆς ἀπὸ διετοῦς καὶ κατωτέρ
        κατὰ τὸν χρόνον ὃν ἠκρίβωσεν παρὰ τῶν μάγων.
17   τότε ἐπληρώθη τὸ ῥηθὲν διὰ Ἰερεμίου τοῦ προφήτου λέγοντος,
18   Φωνὴ ἐν Ῥαμὰ ἠκούσθη,
            κλαυθμὸς καὶ ὀδυρμὸς πολύς·
            Ῥαχὴλ κλαίουσα τὰ τέκνα αὐτῆς,
            καὶ οὐκ ἤθελεν παρακληθῆναι, ὅτι οὐκ εἰσίν.
19 Τελευτήσαντος δὲ τοῦ Ἡρῴδου
    ἰδοὺ ἄγγελος κυρίου φαίνεται κατ᾿ ὄναρ τῷ Ἰωσὴφ ἐν Αἰγύπτῳ
20 λέγων,
      Ἐγερθεὶς παράλαβε τὸ παιδίον καὶ τὴν μητέρα αὐτοῦ
    καὶ πορεύου εἰς γῆν Ἰσραήλ·
            τεθνήκασιν γὰρ οἱ ζητοῦντες τὴν ψυχὴν τοῦ παιδίου.
21 *ὁ δὲ ἐγερθεὶς παρέλαβεν τὸ παιδίον καὶ τὴν μητέρα αὐτοῦ*
    καὶ εἰσῆλθεν εἰς γῆν Ἰσραήλ.

It is crucial to note the parallel wording of verses 14 and 21 (in italics), serving as brackets for the intermediate narrative material. In verse 14, Joseph takes Jesus and Mary *to* Egypt. In verse 21, Joseph takes Jesus and Mary back *to* the land of Israel. This is the literal exodus movement in the narrative, and thus Jesus passively recapitulates that literal geographic movement. The return to Israel should be taken as an exodus, in that Jesus is *literally* brought out of Egypt and taken to Israel. The intermediate material comes within this broader exodus structure. The literal aspect to this exodus movement will be further discussed below, as well as the role verse 15 plays within the narrative.

    4. The fulfillment quotations in Matthew 2 *conclude* each section.

It has been noted above the surprise that some scholars have had in regard to the way this fulfillment quotation is utilized because it is exceptional for a fulfillment quotation to refer *forward*.[107] Given the postpositioned[108] use of the other fulfillment quotations in this chapter, all of which follow the event they refer to, the Hosea quotation certainly warrants a second look. Three scenes comprise verses 13–23: 13–15, 16–18, and 19–23.[109] At the end of each of these scenes, there is a fulfillment quotation.[110] A look at Matthew's other fulfillment quotations reveals a similar pattern, in that they serve to conclude a section (4:15–16; 8:17; 12:18–21; 13:35; 27:9).[111] Therefore, does verse 15 prove an exception to this pattern by referring *forward*? Based on the cumulative evidence gathered in this section this becomes less likely. The quotation should properly be regarded as a commentary on the preceding material, which is how the other quotations are used elsewhere in Matthew, and especially in Matthew 2.[112]

5. Ironically, Egypt is a place of refuge while Judea is a land of oppression.

It deserves observation that Egypt, the land of oppression for Israel in the past, here serves as a place of refuge and safety for Jesus and his family.[113] The threat and oppression, mirroring the account in Exodus of Pharaoh's extermination plan, is now in the land of Israel itself. Herod poses as a tyrannical threat, resembling Pharaoh, seeking to destroy the child.[114] A complete, ironic reversal has taken place, something the original hearers and readers of Matthew's Gospel could perceive, no matter when or where they were.[115] They would surely have noted this point given the notorious reputation of Herod and the narratival contrasts, noted above, that are evi-

---

[107] Davies and Allison, *Matthew*, 1.262.

[108] Luz, *Matthew 1–7* (1989), 143.

[109] Davies and Allison, *Matthew*, 1.257; Luz, *Matthew 1–7* (2007), 117, Hagner, *Matthew 1–13*, 33; Hengel and Merkel, 'Die Magier', 140–142.

[110] Frankemölle, *Matthäus*, 169. Cf. France, "Formula-Quotation," 237: "One selected proof-text for each episode of his narrative." Strecker, *Theology of the New Testament*, 367: "each stage of the birth story is concluded with a reflection citation." Cf. Neusner, *Judaism in the Matrix of Christianity*, 90.

[111] The apparent exceptions are 1:22–23 and 21:4–5.

[112] Commenting on the formula quotations as a whole Luz, *Matthew 1–7* (1989), 156, "In the majority of cases they have the character of a commentary, i.e. they are appended to the end of a narrative section and comment on it." The Hosea quotation appears to serve exactly this function as well.

[113] Cf. Luz, *Theology of Matthew*, 24; Carter, *Matthew*, 83; Garland, *Matthew*, 28. It should be noted that Egypt served as a place of refuge at various times (cf. 1 Kgs 11:40; 2 Kgs 25:26; Jer 41:16–18; 43:1–7).

[114] Gnilka, *Matthäusevangelium*, 51: "Gottes rettender Eingriff bewahrt dieses vor dem Zugriff des Tyrannen."

[115] Discussion of this Gospel's date and audience is outside the confines of this study; however, Herod's reputation would have been widespread, common knowledge throughout the areas that could be proposed as Matthew's audience; cf. Luz, *Matthew 1–7* (2007), 112.

denced in this chapter. This reversal will prove important in the proposal below.

6. Joseph takes his family and flees at night.

Another aspect worth highlighting is the mention that Joseph leaves at night (v. 14). Granted, he rises from his sleep, having been warned in a dream, and wastes no time by fleeing, which is further aided by the cover of night. Yet given other clear exodus motifs in the passage, and the chapter as a whole, the aspect of haste and flight from danger as an echo of the Passover tradition (Exod 12) might also be posited.[116] The intentional use of night in verse 14 would help prove further that Judea is now being made out as "Egypt," the land of oppression and murder from which the family must flee.

3.5.4 A Subtle Reversal

Having observed how other scholars have accounted for this odd placement, and then offered several significant areas that make these reasons suspect, another proposal altogether different must now be advanced. Given the above details, a better understanding of the use of Hosea 11:1 in Matthew 2:15 is to take it as *metaphorical*. The text demands a literal geographical movement to Egypt in verses 13–14 and a literal movement back to the land of Israel in verses 19–21. The Greek parallels noted above make this patently evident. However, the placement of the Hosea quotation at the end of the section comprising verses 13–15 should be seen as a metaphorical understanding of "Egypt." Judea under Herod is characterized as resembling Egypt under Pharaoh. Just as Pharaoh killed the Israelite boys, so too Herod repeats the same type of massacre.

Before this subtle reversal in Matthew 2 is further discussed, it might prove useful to highlight another text where a similar metaphorical understanding occurs. Although no textual relation between Matthew 2 and Revelation 11–12 is being made,[117] noting a similar use of Egypt would prove helpful and serve as possible evidence that this metaphorical understanding of Egypt existed as tradition late in the first century. Revelation 11:8 describes Jerusalem, the place where the Lord was crucified, as a "spiritual" Sodom and Egypt (ἥτις καλεῖται πνευματικῶς Σόδομα καὶ Αἴγυπτος, ὅπου καὶ ὁ κύριος αὐτῶν ἐσταυρώθη). Not only is Egypt metaphorical in this instance, it is explicitly used to indicate something about Jerusalem; much like what Matthew appears to be doing. Also relevant is to observe that later in Revelation 12:5–6, the text goes on to narrate some-

---

[116] Keener, *Matthew*, 109 says this departure at night might recall the Passover tradition (Exod 11–14); Cf. Davies, *Setting*, 82; Patte, *Matthew*, 37.

[117] Bultmann, *History of the Synoptic Tradition*, 293, cites Revelation 12 as relevant background for Matthew 2:1–23; cf. Nepper-Christensen, *Das Matthäusevangelium*, 168.

thing like an apocalyptic infancy narrative. This type of material may thus have existed as a part of the various ways that Christians recounted Jesus' birth and early childhood.[118] In Revelation 12, a dragon pursues the woman who is about to bear a child, seeking to devour this child. She gives birth to a son who is to rule all the nations. Both the son and woman escape the dragon. The son is snatched to God and the woman flees into the wilderness. Again, no direct relation between these texts is being posited, other than to note a similar threat motif and reversal in regard to Egypt and Jerusalem. The key observation to note from this comparison is the use of Egypt metaphorically in Revelation 11:8.

In Matthew 2, Egypt is to be regarded as a literal geographic location in verses 13–14, as well as in verse 19. But through the use of irony and geographic reversal, as understood through the pervading exodus themes saturating the narrative, Egypt in verse 15 is metaphorical. Jesus indeed comes out of a metaphorical Egypt when he is taken by Joseph away from the dangers that Herod, a Pharaoh-like character now poses.

To understand the unique portrayal of events in these verses one can compare the geographic movements. First, Israel's Exodus involved *leaving* Egypt, fleeing the dangers and oppressive bondage there, going into the wilderness, and *returning* to the land of Israel. Similarly, Moses' flight from Pharaoh also involved *leaving* Egypt and fleeing the danger there, going to Midian, and later *returning* to Egypt. Yet, in a completely opposite direction, Jesus' flight from Herod involves *leaving* the oppression of Judea and fleeing *to* the refuge of Egypt.[119]

B. B. Scott has detected this ironic aspect and he considers this metaphorical alteration an ideology of paradoxical reversal, symbolically presented. Egypt, the symbol of enslavement, now protects, while Judea is a place of murder.[120] This metaphorical use of Egypt, albeit seemingly odd, appears a far more reasonable interpretation, given the cumulative arguments that have been made, as opposed to merely perceiving it as the above scholars indicated. The following points will further advance this

---

[118] This is evidenced by the differences between the infancy narratives in Matthew and Luke, as well as the development of further infancy narratives that continued to occupy the attention of writers in the second century and beyond. See Schneemelcher, *New Testament Apocrypha*, 363–417; Elliott, *The Apocryphal New Testament*, 46–122.

[119] Crossan, "From Moses to Jesus," 27, also characterizes the odd placement of the quotation as subtle work, but thinks Jesus' flight from Israel to Egypt parallels Moses' flight from Egypt to Israel; therefore, the purpose is to highlight Jesus' significance for the Gentiles as Savior.

[120] Scott, "The Birth of the Reader," 95. Unfortunately, Scott includes no more discussion about this symbolism in his article. Cf. Garland, *Matthew*, briefly adds, "Jesus, the son of David, is rejected in the land of Judah and therefore must find refuge in Egypt, the symbol of bondage," 28; Patte, *Matthew*, 38.

argument and highlight the importance of it in light of the recapitulation of exodus in this chapter.

Help can be culled from a few other scholars, cited as evidence this metaphorical aspect has been previously observed, although only cursorily and not to the degree argued in this section. To date there has not been detailed attention to this irony, neither has there been a study that has brought all the above aspects together. From the brief attention this irony has generated, we can note the following as examples. Nolan speaks to this metaphorical understanding of Egypt in his discussion of 2:15, although only briefly, when he notes this viewpoint as a possibility in two separate places of his work on the infancy narrative. He comments, "that the bitter metaphorical understanding of Egypt as Jerusalem is not to be dismissed out of hand ... if Egypt in 2:15 implies Jerusalem, it explains why the quotation is inserted at the departure from Judea, and is in the past tense."[121] Earlier in a footnote, he states that possibly one could see this as an exodus of Jesus from Jerusalem: "Now Jerusalem is 'Egypt,' as the peculiar position of 2:15b could imply."[122] In his commentary on verses 19–21, Gundry also briefly notices the reversal when he writes, "Whether or not Israel has ironically become a new Egypt because of the Jewish leaders' cooperation with that new baby-killing Pharaoh, Herod, the parallel between Moses and Jesus comes out even more clearly than before."[123] These scholars have detected an important point, although it is not expanded upon in their works other than these brief remarks. It is easy to miss the subtle reversal, especially when one too easily accepts the common explanations of most scholars in regard to why it appears in verse 15. Closer attention to the exodus themes, as well as the details of the text, has shown these explanations inadequate, and they in fact miss a feature Matthew appears to have deftly presented though subtly communicated.

Beyond these thematic aspects, textual evidence, as previously noted, can also be re-gathered for further acknowledgement of this reversal. Placement of the quotation at verse 15 is fundamental. It appears meant to arouse the attention of any careful hearer and reader of the narrative. Without this placement, the reversal, if the Evangelist still intended it, would be far more difficult if not impossible to pick up. However, placed at verse 15, long prior to the narratival recounting of the literal exit from Egypt, makes this intent fully comprehensible. In verse 13, Joseph is

---

[121] Nolan, *Royal Son of God*, 209.

[122] *Ibid.*, 37. However, he says nothing more than this brief comment.

[123] Gundry, *Matthew*, 38. Note that the exodus motif prevails in these verses, a key point argued below. Keener, *Matthew*, 109, states in a footnote how the family does not *leave* Egypt here and adds, "yet this divergence is intentional, for by presenting Herod as a new Pharaoh Matthew has purposely and ironically inverted the ethnic perspective of the tradition."

warned in a dream to flee to Egypt (εἰς Αἴγυπτον) because Herod, continuing to be characterized as Pharaoh, seeks to kill the child. Joseph promptly gets up to do just this at night, a significant detail that alludes to and evokes the exodus of Israel from Egypt by night.[124] Thus, Joseph leaves to go to Egypt (εἰς Αἴγυπτον). Verse 15 begins by recording that they stay in Egypt until the death of Herod, and then appears the quotation of Hosea 11:1, "Out of Egypt ('Εξ Αἰγύπτου)" probably retaining the aorist tense as found in the quotation because it can refer to the preceding mention of the movement out of metaphorical Egypt. As with Matthew's other fulfillment quotations in this chapter, this quotation also should be seen to *follow* the event and geographic location, serving as a scriptural commentary for this section. Matthew's practice is consistent and Hagner is mistaken to posit this as a "premature quotation."[125] The quotation rightly follows the point made, albeit fundamentally *reversing* the Exodus event in terms of the literal geographical movement. Now the refuge occurs in Egypt and the threat happens in Judea.[126] Moses fled from Egypt to escape Pharaoh, and there are several allusions to this event in this chapter. Israel as a nation left Egypt, fleeing the oppressive bondage of Egypt and Pharaoh, and there are several allusions to this event in this chapter. The text as originally evoked in Hosea certainly refers back to this formative event, a literal meaning for Egypt as well as a literal reference to the whole people of Israel, God's son that left Egypt. However, the metaphorical usage in Matthew, though subtle, is evident. While Jesus does follow the literal geographic movements, Matthew utilizes this quotation to refer to the exodus, recapitulated by Jesus, the Son of God, where the repetition is geographically reversed. Unmistakable is the outright contrast between the literal going *to* Egypt and the subsequent quotation, to be thus taken metaphorically, a going *out* of "Egypt."

3.5.5 *Judea as a Metaphorical Egypt*

The common explanations, while possible, appear deficient because they do not adequately satisfy what appears in the text, nor do they take into account what appears an intentional subtlety by Matthew. There are clear indications that there is far more to this quotation, and this is initially evi-

---

[124] Davies and Allison, *Matthew*, 1.261, argue against observing an exodus allusion here when they write, "If this were pertinent, the note of time should come in 2.21, when the family *leaves* Egypt, not here, when they enter it." However, that is exactly the point for its provocative occurrence here at this position in the narrative.

[125] Hagner, *Matthew*, 36.

[126] Chrysostom, *Gospel of Matthew*, Homily 8.2, as quoted in Simonetti, *Matthew 1–13*, 32, long ago recognized the irony, "Isn't this remarkable: While Palestine plots, it is Egypt that receives and preserves the One for whom the plots are designed."

dent due to its odd placement within the narrative appearing after Joseph goes *to* Egypt and long before the leaving of Egypt in verse 21. The explanation for its placement here has deserved closer attention. Further, given the prominence of exodus themes in Matthew, the clear characterization of Herod as a Pharaoh-like king, and Jesus as both an Israel-type and Moses-type character, a better understanding of the formula quotation is to read it as a fundamental *reversal* of the geographical movements in Exodus.[127] The explicit parallel of verses 14 and 21, the wider Exodus themes, the textual allusions noted above, and the specific placement of the Hosea quotation must bear weight in regard to this point. It is important to emphatically state that Matthew is referring to Israel's *literal* geographic movements from Israel to Egypt (v. 14) and from Egypt back to the land of Israel (v. 21). But the specific placement of the Hosea quotation, appearing where it does within the narrative, seemingly out of place, alongside the narratival characterization that has already unfolded, it points toward a *metaphorical* understanding of Egypt as well.

In short space, Matthew has employed a variety of images.[128] Israel's history has been passively recapitulated, in that Jesus literally goes to Egypt (v. 14) and returns to the land of Israel (v. 21). In addition, Jesus' exodus from Judea, the metaphorical Egypt, also passively recapitulates Israel's history in that Jesus escapes by night the terrors of a new Pharaoh, an oppressive period resembling Israel's history in Egypt. Moses' experience has been passively recapitulated, in that Jesus relives the threatening Pharaoh that seeks his life, the one having been born king of the Jews, and as the reader already knows is destined to redeem his people (1:21).[129]

It has been made abundantly evident that the quotation is oddly placed. Should the common explanations regarding this placement be accepted? Given the details outlined above, a persuasive case can be made for accepting the quotation as a subtle reversal, a geographical juxtaposition, whereby Judea is a metaphorical "Egypt" and Herod a metaphorical "Pharaoh" in this story. Within the narrative movements, the Hosea quotation is

---

[127] It is not unknown for Matthew to practice interesting reversals, as seen in the conspicuous addition of οὐδαμῶς to the quotation of Micah 5:2 in verse 6, which France, "Formula-Quotations," 242 observes, "emphatically reversing the original description of Bethlehem's insignificance." Cf. Hagner, *Matthew 1–13*, 29. In addition, one should note that this reversal appears within the same narrative and also concerns a geographic location.

[128] Cf. France, "Formula-Quotations," 250: "We have seen reason at each point to believe that Matthew had more in mind than the 'surface meaning'; that he had bonus points to offer to those whose acquaintance with the Old Testament ... deliberately composing a chapter rich in potential exegetical bonuses." Cf. Davies, *Setting*, 92; L. Hartman, "Scriptural Exegesis in the Gospel of St. Matthew."

[129] France, *Matthew* NICNT, 77, observes both the Israel and Moses motifs, adding it "has for Matthew two scriptural resonances which do not fit neatly together."

"misplaced" *logically*, and it would appear that the Evangelist has intentionally done this with an ironic subtlety one ought not overlook.[130] This
peculiar and provocative use of subtlety might also help interpreters understand Matthew's Gospel overall, particularly in regard to the use of the Old
Testament in the Gospel with the possibility that there is a far greater
flexibility and creativity to the Evangelist's use of prophecy and fulfillment as exemplified in the use of Hosea 11:1 in Matthew 2:15. This is
given further attention in a section below.

3.5.6 Jesus as Son of God

Crucial to note in regard to the Hosea quotation is that this is the first explicit mention in Matthew's Gospel of Jesus as Son of God, τὸν υἱόν μου,
which in the context of the pericope in Matthew is clearly utilized as an
address of God to his Son. Many scholars, preeminently Kingsbury, have
regarded "Son of God" as the key title for Matthew's Gospel, predomi-
nantly denoting his filial relation to God.[131] The meaning of "Son" in Matthew's utilization of the Hosea quotation indicates more, while not negating what that title might mean elsewhere in Matthew as a title denoting filial relation to God (e.g. 11:27), or even here as a subsidiary aspect. When
the use of Son of God is properly understood in the context of its use here,
it indicates another type of relation. In this context, Jesus' sonship is directly related to Israel's sonship, and here it is posited as a relation that
corresponds by his recapitulation of Israel's exodus history, both "sons"
having been called out of Egypt by God. Brown considers this essential
when he states, "It is significant that Matthew's first reference to Jesus as
God's Son, which comes in the Hosea reference, sets him in the history of
God's people."[132] Israel's sonship was undoubtedly a filial type relationship to God, and that underlies the use here; but the fullest understanding
of the Hosea quotation brings the immediate focus of attention to Jesus'
connection with Israel, especially in terms of recapitulation, with the subsequent narrative of Matthew unfolding further the meaning of Jesus as
Son of God.

---

[130] Stanton, *Gospel for a New People*, 360, may thus be correct to regard the formula
quotations in chapter 2 a part of the Evangelist's own work. Cf. Davies, "Jewish Sources
of Matthew's Messianism," 507; Stendahl, *School of Matthew*, viii: "I find it difficult to
separate the author of Matthew 2 and the originator of the formula quotations in that
chapter." Schnackenburg, *Jesus in the Gospels*, 111, thinks the introductory expression
should be traced back to the evangelist, however the quotations are from a collection of
testimony. Schnelle, *History and Theology of the New Testament*, 229–230, disagrees and
thinks the entire citations are part of a pre-Matthean *testimonia* collection.

[131] Kingsbury, *Matthew as Story*, 54–58; and *Matthew: Structure, Christology, Kingdom*, 162.

[132] Brown, *Birth of the Messiah*, 616.

Davies and Allison have observed how Jesus repeats Israel's history and write, "For Matthew, 'Son of God' must have to do in part with Jesus as the personification or embodiment of true, obedient Israel."[133] This is exceptionally important for adequately charting Matthew's christology, something which this study has sought to especially highlight through close attention to Jesus as the recapitulation of Israel. As a result of the arguments demonstrated above, through the subtle use of a quotation from Hosea, while directly evoking the Exodus, and paradoxically reversing the geography, Matthew also introduces an important element to his christology. Through synthesizing the various elements observed above, Jesus is thus depicted as the embodiment of Israel, the one who both relives and recapitulates that history, and *is* Israel in some sense.[134] The genealogy has already prepared the hearer and reader to begin to perceive Jesus in this way, with the history of Israel recapitulated utilizing a compressed narrative. Through names of a genealogy, which serve as a retelling of Israel's history, and now through an infancy narrative in which the exodus predominates, Matthew interconnects the story of Jesus with the story of Israel, especially by recapitulation.[135] William Kynes aptly summarizes, based on the use of Hosea in 2:15, "It recalls the exodus, suggesting, perhaps, the attending notion that Jesus is a new Moses, but more importantly it puts Jesus in the place of Israel as he assumes the filial relationship with God once predicated of the nation (cf. Exod 4:22; Deut 8:5; Hos 11:1; Jer 31:9, 20)."[136]

In Exodus 4:22 Israel is called God's son (υἱὸς / בֵּן). While Matthew can quote freely from the Septuagint, as he does in quoting Isaiah 7:14 in 1:23, here when he quotes Hosea 11:1, he appears to directly translate from the Hebrew text,[137] which explicitly has בֵּן, while the Septuagint has τέκνα.

---

[133] Davies and Allison, *Matthew*, 1.263–264. They add in a footnote (10) that Kingsbury "has failed to develop this aspect of Matthew's Son of God Christology," 264. Garland, *Matthew*, 29, rightly observes the use of 'my son' from Hosea, saying, "Matthew takes it to refer to Jesus because he understands Jesus to embody true, obedient Israel as the son of God. Jesus will enact a new exodus."

[134] Pesch, "Der Gottessohn," 412. Cf. Meier, *Vision of Matthew*, 55 regards Jesus, and only Jesus, as a new and true Israel: "What Israel was has now been absorbed into the person of Jesus." He thinks that for Matthew, the church is the new people of God, and Israel a reference to the people of the Old Testament and Judaism; Meier, *Matthew*, 14; Bourke, "Literary Genius," regards Jesus-Israel predominant in chapter two, and Jesus is the new and true Israel, 166, 172–173; Gibbs, "Son of God as the Torah," 38–39. These aspects of sonship will further become important when Matthew 3:1–4:11 is examined.

[135] Harrington, *Matthew*, 49: "The Moses-typology roots Jesus in the history of Israel; indeed his divine sonship is specifically tied to Israel's experience as a people."

[136] Kynes, *Christology of Solidarity*, 20.

[137] It might also be possible that a more literal Greek translation was utilized. Cf. Stendahl, *School of Matthew*, 101; and Menken, *Matthew's Bible: The Old Testament*

כי נער ישראל ואהבהו וממצרים קראתי לבני:
διότι νήπιος Ισραηλ καὶ ἐγὼ ἠγάπησα αὐτὸν
καὶ ἐξ Αἰγύπτου μετεκάλεσα τὰ τέκνα αὐτοῦ

Use of "son" here is of utmost importance given the theological recapitulation that Matthew sets forth. Contrary to Kingsbury and others that almost exclusively observe Sonship in terms of Jesus' filial relation to God, while not negating that as a legitimate inference given the christology of Matthew overall (cf. 11:25–27), the primary intent of Matthew's utilization of υἱός here is to reveal solidarity with Israel, also called God's son.[138] Longenecker rightly observes that "the prophet was using 'my son' as a collective term for the nation Israel."[139] By utilizing this collective inherent in Hosea 11:1, Matthew reveals Jesus as a corporate solidarity. By recognizing this corporate solidarity, Matthew then can be rightly understood as characterizing Jesus as the recapitulation of Israel using the quotation in relation to Jesus' movements, literal and metaphorical, within the narrative. Through use of the fulfilment quotation, Jesus is fully paralleled with Israel.[140] Furthermore, as Anderson and Freedman note, Hosea 11:1 refers to "the most critical period in Israel's history, its childhood."[141] This expands an understanding of the applicability of the Hosea text to Jesus' early life.

Luz considers Matthew's attraction to Hosea the result of two catchwords, Egypt and son. The catchword Egypt will remind readers of the exodus which is being repeated anew.[142] Hence, in a short phrase, a host of images is allowed to color the reader's understanding of who Jesus is,[143] which is a substantial aspect to the purpose of the entire Gospel narrative focus upon presenting the story of Jesus Christ. The sonship of Jesus is explicitly tied to his bond with the people of Israel, and as their deliverer, like Moses formerly also experienced, here Jesus is preserved and escapes death so that he can achieve the purpose for which he has been called (1:21). However, at the end of the Gospel, it will involve him going to Jerusalem for his death.

Text of the Evangelist, 133–142. The complexities of these textual issues are not always grasped, as Stanton rightly points out, *Interpretation of Matthew*, 21.

[138] This is a key aspect to Kynes' work *Christology of Solidarity*.

[139] Longenecker, *Biblical Exegesis*, 128.

[140] Strecker, *Der Weg*, 58. However, Verseput, "The 'Son of God' Title in Matthew's Gospel," 553, only sees the parallel at sonship.

[141] Anderson and Freedman, *Hosea*, 577.

[142] Luz, *Matthew 1–7* (2007), 121. On the possibility that the wider context of Hosea is also included, see Garbe, *Der Hirte Israels*, 31–32.

[143] Sand, *Matthäus*, 53, regards verse 15b to serve as an important function within the pericope as the "Zeilpunkt der Perikope."

3.5.7 Jesus' Fulfillment of Hosea 11:1

Thus far in this discussion, there has been little mention of the *fulfillment* aspect Matthew explicitly declares by the use of the Hosea quotation, ἵνα πληρωθῇ τὸ ῥηθὲν ὑπὸ κυρίου διὰ τοῦ προφήτου λέγοντος, Ἐξ Αἰγύπτου ἐκάλεσα τὸν υἱόν μου.[144] This lack of attention has been intentional because Matthew's use of Hosea and the fulfillment he intends to point out in Jesus' experience cannot be understood apart from the subtle components of the narrative as recounted above. Having observing Matthew's subtle use of the quotation, attention and discussion of the fulfillment aspects can now be undertaken.[145] Hence, now the oft-asked question can be addressed: did the Evangelist understand Hosea's text as a prediction, now fulfilled in Jesus? In fact, the use of this quotation as a straightforward prediction could actually be the result of two different viewpoints.[146] On the one hand, he may have thought of Hosea as predicting this event that Jesus fulfills. Therefore, he directly utilized this quotation from Hosea as a prediction that Jesus then fulfilled.[147] On the other hand, it could have been understood by Matthew as originally non-predictive, but for the purposes of Matthew's apologetic, he presented it within the Gospel as a prediction that Jesus fulfilled. He could have clearly understood Hosea's original referent to Israel's literal exodus out of Egypt but reapplied it to Jesus in a unique way, which would certainly be appropriate within the framework of presenting Jesus recapitulating Israel's history.[148] There are no means for answering this question except from the text of Matthew itself and attending to every possible detail in the text.[149]

---

[144] Luz, *Theology of the Gospel of Matthew*, 30, 35, states that with the addition of "the Lord" to the fulfillment quotation (cf. 1:22, the only other use) "God himself is cited as the author of the quotation."

[145] This discussion must nevertheless be brief given the vast amount of literature on the subject and the magnitude of it for interpreting Matthew.

[146] It bears mention that these viewpoints might have been part of the tradition that Matthew then included in the Gospel and not necessarily of his own direct initiative, something outside the purview of this study.

[147] Luz, *Matthew 1–7* (2007), 121. Cf. Edgar, "Respect for Context in Quotations from the Old Testament," 57, sees it this way in his article where he states that "it is in the synoptic gospels that the most outstanding instances of contextual inaccuracy are found." See Mead, "A Dissenting Opinion About Respect for Context in Old Testament Quotations," 279–289 for criticism of Edgar's approach.

[148] Cf. France, *Matthew* NICNT, 80.

[149] Brown, *Birth of the Messiah*, 221, favors Matthew's originality in applying Hosea to Jesus here. Cf. Davies and Allison, *Matthew*, 1.262, likewise consider Matthew was the first to connect Hosea 11:1 with the story of Jesus via Numbers 24:8. Knowledge of the use of Hosea 11:1 within the early church is uncertain, especially given the paucity of textual help in this regard. Most scholars regard its use here a Matthean contribution. Based on the textual evidence currently available, this is all that can be said.

Moody Smith's important summary article on the use of the Old Testament in the New commends the customary view, in terms of Matthew's use of Hosea as well as his other fulfillment quotations, "that all of these events happen according to prophecy and not fortuitously means, of course, that they are ordained of God and, moreover, that they constitute an extension of the holy history into the period of Jesus' life and ministry."[150] James Barr also summarizes this common view when he states that Matthew takes Hosea as a prediction, which involves Matthew ignoring the verb tense in the process.[151] However, it has been shown above how this frequent understanding of Matthew's use of Hosea cannot be justified by the text itself. The above details of Matthew's subtle work should dispel such overly restrictive analysis. The text itself would demand a far greater flexibility in regard to Matthew's use of the Hosea quotation here.[152] It therefore appears that the rigidity of understanding in terms of prediction-fulfillment resides less in Matthew's work than in modern scholars assumptions about his work.[153]

If Hosea 11:1 had been placed after verse 21, then there would be firmer support for thinking Matthew simply took this as a literal prediction. However, given that he places it in verse 15b, one must question prediction as an adequate explanation of what Matthew intends here. In fact, it appears Matthew's grammatical skills are more perceptive that Barr realizes, because given the above argumentation about the provocative use of this quote, the verb tense admirably fits the narrative at this point.[154]

As a result, having attended to the subtle and creative work of the Evangelist, a better understanding of fulfillment, as well as all of his utilization of canonical and noncanonical scriptures, should be advanced which properly observes the open, complex, and flexible exegetical procedure.[155]

---

[150] Smith, "The Use of the Old Testament in the New," 47.

[151] Barr, *Old and New in Interpretation*, 125. Cf. Hengel and Merkel, "Die Magier," 156–157; Luz, *Matthew 1–7* (1989), 146.

[152] As Carson, *Matthew 1–12*, 92, accurately emphasizes, πληρόω "has broader significance than mere one-to-one prediction."

[153] More research needs to be undertaken in this regard to better account for the data in Matthew, which exhibits a variety and flexibility that deserves more attention. It is imperative to undertake careful research with a critical methodology that strictly excludes anachronistic modern assessments of Matthew.

[154] Cf. Nolan, *Royal Son of God*, 209.

[155] von Rad, *Old Testament Theology*, 2.322–330, notes how an open and flexible exegetical practice characterizes the prophets' writings which carries on into the New Testament writer's practice as well; "the New Testament writers show the utmost freedom in their appropriation of Old Testament material." Such freedom is clearly evidenced in 2:6 (οὐδαμῶς) and 2:23, and it is the argument of this section that 2:15 is part of this exegetical freedom as well. Beaton, *Isaiah's Christ in Matthew's Gospel*, 192, concludes "Matthew's employment of the Old Testament is fundamentally theological

Yet, this is what has not generally been explicated about Matthew's fulfillment quotations.[156] It is therefore becoming more apparent that the
Evangelist is clearly not so easy to pin down. Based on the analysis of the
text to this point, some further exploration into determining Matthew's understanding of fulfillment can be observed.[157] The recapitulation, of Israel
and Moses, which Matthew subtly achieves, advances the understanding of
fulfillment beyond mere prediction. If this quotation really is intended as a
literal fulfillment of a prediction, then Jesus literally does not in fact fulfill
this prediction at all, because as already belabored above, he is taken to
Egypt and leaves the land of Israel, which is an opposite direction altogether. *Literal* fulfillment of the prediction, particularly at this point in the
narrative, must entail leaving Egypt and going to the land of Israel.[158] Had
the quotation appeared after verse 21, one could certainly regard a literal
fulfillment within the purview of intent.

It therefore appears that fulfillment must be more broadly construed to
include correspondence, repetition, and recapitulation.[159] The majority of
scholars that comment on verse 15 usually make some customary mention
that Jesus "repeats" Israel, although many continue to maintain that the
Evangelist merely takes Hosea as predictive.[160] Most would regard Hosea's

---

and best described as complex." Cf. Sanders, "Gospels and the Canonical Process," 223;
Wright, *God Who Acts*, 63–64.

[156] Brown's, *Birth of the Messiah*, 220–221, nuanced discussion is an exception,
where he never directly characterizes it as predictive, primarily satisfied with citing Matthew's attraction a result of the correspondences between past and present. Cf. Davies
and Allison, *Matthew*, 1.262–264 also provide a nuanced discussion; expanded in Allison, *The New Moses*, 140–142; and Hagner, *Matthew 1–13*, 36–37. However, further
methodologically careful work needs to be done on this.

[157] See Beaton's, *Isaiah's Christ in Matthew's Gospel*, 30–34, helpful analysis on the
rhetorical function of the quotations in Matthew.

[158] Certainly, Jesus does literally go to Egypt and return to the land of Israel, recapitulating the literal movements of Israel's history. However, the fulfillment quotation placed
at 2:15 is utilized in a more flexible manner through the subtle contrasts evidenced
above.

[159] Watts, *Isaiah's New Exodus in Mark*, 195, in a footnote briefly comments about
the use of the Old Testament in Matthew, where he states, "the NT authors are operating
with a conception of fulfillment which assumes the paradigmatic or typological significance of the OT – as Yahweh had done he would do again ... rather than the more commonly assumed literal prediction."

[160] As with many aspects of the modern encyclopedic commentary genre, these types
of customary statements become a generalized position that continues to be passed on
from commentary to commentary while never really receiving the attention it deserves.
This has been a major focus of this work by examining in greater detail this repetition,
filling a gap in the scholarship on Matthew.

original intent as a recollection of the exodus event of the past.[161] Did Matthew either not know the original context in Hosea, ignore it, or interpret it
altogether differently as prediction? The above analysis of Matthew's use
of Hosea here compels a different reading of Matthew altogether, one more
flexible and open to the creative use of Old Testament texts.[162] E. E. Ellis
has provided a careful and nuanced discussion of fulfillment in Matthew in
terms of analogy, in opposition to viewing it as a double prophecy, merely
illustrative, or a generalizing application.[163] Furthermore, Childs also helps
toward understanding Matthew's work here beyond merely predictive,
when he notes that all of the Old Testament was regarded as *prophetic* and
pointing forward: "Old Testament citations provide a theological context
within the divine economy of God with Israel by which to understand and
interpret the significance of Jesus' life and ministry."[164] Matthew's distinctive use of Hosea 11:1 within the overall context of the literary and theological motifs utilized in chapter two allows the whole of Israel's history to
be recapitulated, through a "telescoping" of several events of that history.[165]

The use of the Hosea text in 2:15 is particularly important for the work
of this thesis in regard to the overall argument that Jesus is the recapitulation of Israel. In regard to chapter two, it has been argued that Jesus *passively* recapitulates Israel's history. At the broader level, it becomes more
apparent that Jesus' recapitulation of Israel involves him as the representative of his people,[166] which is more heavily emphasized in 3:1–4:11. Writing in regard to Matthew's reference to Hosea, G. W. H. Lampe states,
"the pattern of God's dealings with Israel is recapitulated and fulfilled in

---

[161] Sailhamer, "Hosea 11:1 and Matthew 2:15," 87–96, is a rare exception, regarding
Hosea's intent predictive, which therefore explains Matthew's use of Hosea as a fulfillment of what Hosea meant. McCartney and Enns, "Matthew and Hosea: A Response to
John Sailhamer," 97–105, rightly criticize Sailhamer's article. Another evangelical discussion can be found in Howard, "The Use of Hosea 11:1 in Matthew 2:15: An Alternative Solution," 314–328.

[162] Lindars, "The Place of the Old Testament in the Formation of New Testament
Theology," 64, on the creative use of the Old Testament. Borgen, "Response to Lindars,"
67–75, critiques Lindar's article, but also provides helpful insights.

[163] See Ellis, *Old Testament Canon in Early Christianity*, 56, where he regards typological understanding to describe Matthew's meaning here, explaining his view of typology in 62–67. Cf. France, *Jesus and the Old Testament*, 38–80; and Holmgren, *Old Testament and the Significance of Jesus*, 37, 43.

[164] Childs, *New Testament as Canon*, 70. Cf. von Rad, "Typological Interpretation of
the Old Testament," 34; France, *Matthew* (NICNT), 80–81.

[165] Knowles, *Jeremiah in Matthew's Gospel*, 48.

[166] Kynes, *Christology of Solidarity* is given entirely to this subject.

the story of the representative head of the new Israel, who sums up in himself the covenant people of God."[167]

This section has dealt with the characterization of Judea under Herod as resembling Israel's experience under Pharaoh in Egypt, as well as Moses' early experiences. This has involved recognizing the distinctive geographic reversal Matthew has portrayed while also focusing upon the theological portrayal of Jesus passively recapitulating Israel's history and Moses' as well. The next subsection will continue to follow the narrative, with Jesus having been rescued from the danger that Herod poses, and the strikingly evil and oppressive slaughter of the boys around Jerusalem. This characterization continues to follow the exodus motif of oppression, sorrow, and the need for deliverance, which for the hearer and reader of the Gospel has already been programmatically announced in as Jesus' role and mission (1:21).

3.6 Rachel's Lament

As the flow of the narrative continues to be followed, after Matthew records the Hosea quotation, he goes on to recount Herod's explosive response to the magi's failure to return. The young boys of Bethlehem and the surrounding area are murdered, a scene that strikingly resembles the murder of the Israelite boys under Pharaoh. Additionally important to recall is the prior discussion of Jewish literature undertaken in detail above that revealed various further exodus traditions that Matthew has utilized in his portrayal of Jesus in this narrative.

After narrating the tragic death of the Bethlehem boys, Matthew then notes another fulfillment that this event corresponds to, utilizing a quotation from Jeremiah 31:15 (LXX 38:15)[168] that highlights the oppression motif that has dominated the entirety of Matthew chapter 2.

τότε ἐπληρώθη τὸ ῥηθὲν διὰ Ἰερεμίου τοῦ προφήτου λέγοντος, Φωνὴ ἐν Ῥαμὰ ἠκούσθη, κλαυθμὸς καὶ ὀδυρμὸς πολύς· Ῥαχὴλ κλαίουσα τὰ τέκνα αὐτῆς, καὶ οὐκ ἤθελεν παρακληθῆναι, ὅτι οὐκ εἰσίν.

The quotation, as it appears within the context of Jeremiah 31, refers to the exile of the people when many had been killed and others were forced to leave the land. The oppression and sorrow of the exilic period is highlighted throughout the book of Jeremiah, as well as in the book of Lamen-

---

[167] Lampe, "Typological Exegesis," 203–204.

[168] The textual issues in regard to this quote are numerous. See Stendahl, *School of Matthew*, 102–103; Gundry, *Use of the Old Testament*, 94–97; and Menken, *Matthew's Bible*, 143–159.

tations, traditionally attributed to Jeremiah. Nevertheless, the utilization of the quotation in Matthew should be observed as remaining within the over- all exodus motif that the entire narrative continues to maintain. Structur- ally this can be argued by observing again the placement of the quotation, occurring as it does *between* the parallel of verses 14 and 21 that record the literal going to Egypt and subsequent return to the land.

Verse 14
ὁ δὲ ἐγερθεὶς παρέλαβεν τὸ παιδίον καὶ τὴν μητέρα αὐτοῦ νυκτὸς
    καὶ ἀνεχώρησεν εἰς Αἴγυπτον
Verse 21
ὁ δὲ ἐγερθεὶς παρέλαβεν τὸ παιδίον καὶ τὴν μητέρα αὐτοῦ
    καὶ εἰσῆλθεν εἰς γῆν Ἰσραήλ

Much is made of the placement of the Hosea quotation, which has already been observed, in that it should logically come after verse 21; that is if it is intended literally. Beyond this point, many scholars have wrongly ex- plained the placement of Hosea 11:1 at verse 15 as a result of the exilic focus of these latter verses. However, continuing the argument from the above sections, this Jeremiah quotation in fact occurs within the exodus focus, bracketed as it is by verses 14 and 21. The quotation as taken in the context of Jeremiah is certainly a reference about the exilic period, but its utilization here is somewhat different. The structural considerations should help toward observing this alongside the broader exodus motif that charac- terizes the whole of the chapter. Herod's action in killing the boys resem- bles Pharaoh's oppression in Exodus. The quotation, as utilized and adapted by Matthew, serves as a quintessential lament of oppression and sorrow[169] that the period of the exodus itself exemplifies.

Not only was the redemption from Egypt paradigmatic of God's salva- tion as discussed by subsequent generations, but the oppression of the exo- dus period also served as a model of oppression,[170] and the exile resembled the exodus experience in many ways, was characterized like it,[171] and was undoubtedly a foundational event for the Jewish people.[172] Exodus and ex- ile are clearly paralleled within the genealogy (1:2, 11), something the reader and hearer would probably have remembered. In addition, Jesus is depicted as being born into the exilic period in 1:17. Matthew continues to depict this "exilic" situation in which Jesus is born by characterizing the period within an overall exodus motif in chapter two. Knowles concludes

---

[169] Cf. Louw and Nida, *Greek-English Lexicon*, 530 (52.3), for κλαυθμός as "ritualized wailing and crying as an expression of grief and sorrow at funerals."

[170] Daube, *The New Testament and Rabbinic Judaism*, 6, states that "in the eyes of the Rabbis, of all causes for distress that the Israelites had in Egypt, the destruction of the male children was the most terrible, and Josephus, for example, thinks the same."

[171] Japhet, *I and II Chronicles*, 47.

[172] Nolland, *Matthew*, 125.

that Matthew's use of Jeremiah 31:15 "is a synthetic, conflational, or 'tele-scoping' view of sacred history." This involves the conflation of geography, Ramah and Bethlehem, and the temporal synthesis of exodus and exile. He goes on to note that this synthetic exegesis is typical of contemporary Jewish exegesis at that time.[173]

Both the exodus and exile involved a harsh life in a foreign land, among those that worshipped other gods and who directly oppressed the people of God. Matthew utilizes this quotation within the broader exodus motif that dominates the chapter. Herod's action resembles Pharaoh's, particularly as seen in the Jewish traditions noted above, in that to rid himself of a rival he seeks to eliminate this person. However, due to the failure of the magi to return with information about the child, Herod does not know exactly who that child is and therefore must have all the boys in that area killed. Further evidence for observing the reversal of verse 15 is evidenced in these verses, particularly in the oppression and sorrow among the people in Bethlehem and the surrounding regions (2:16). Joseph has fled Bethlehem, and the region of Judea, which is now a metaphorical Egypt, and which verses 16–18 graphically depict in the massacre of the Israelite boys by another oppressive Pharaoh-like figure seeking to eliminate the Christ. The quotation utilizes the name Rachel,[174] the favored wife of Jacob, the representative mother of all Israel (*Stammütter*),[175] and one whose children *literally* went to Egypt and subsequently became that oppressed people of the exodus period. As Schnackenburg has observed, Rachel who weeps "stands for Israel, which is seen in its continuity through all generations and in solidarity of its lot."[176]

The irony of the quotation as utilized here, continuing the paradoxical reversal Matthew highlights, is that the oppressive Pharaoh and the experience of Israel in Egypt are now found *within* the land of Israel itself.[177] Rachel now weeps in her own land, not because her children leave the land through death and exile, but because they are dying within the land itself, a land that now resembles Egypt.[178] Like the use of Hosea, Matthew utilizes the quotation ironically to reveal the extreme "exilic" situation within an

---

[173] Knowles, *Jeremiah in Matthew's Gospel*, 51.

[174] Rachel, according to Genesis 35:19, is said to have died in "Ephrath, that is Bethlehem" (cf. Jub. 32:34).

[175] Cf. Schlatter, *Matthäus*, 43; Bruce, *Synoptic Gospels*, 76. Note that Rachel's name also appears in Ruth 4:11 as one who with Leah built up the house of Israel.

[176] Schnackenburg, *Matthew*, 26.

[177] Cf. Gundry, *Matthew*, 38.

[178] Jesus leaving the land is a type of exile, but the way the overall narrative characterizes the oppression within the land, Jesus' return to the land and removal to Galilee actually resembles more closely the exilic period. However, this "exilic" situation remains within the broader exodus motif.

overall exodus-type narrative. The oppression of exile Jeremiah referred to involved another nation entering Israel to kill and take; Matthew twists or reverses the Jeremiah quotation so that the reader, who would already be reading the narrative as exodus-like, now understands Herod and his realm as the new Egypt, that kills God's people.[179] Thus, Jesus' preservation from this massacre is set forth as resembling Moses, one who is delivered from extermination, recapitulating that experience of the Exodus, in solidarity with his people, here preserved for the fulfillment of his calling of delivering his people (1:21). Although the boys of Bethlehem and the surrounding vicinity are murdered and Jesus' life is preserved, he too receives death at the hands of oppressors as an adult, done willingly for his people (20:28).

This subsection has dealt with the role that Rachel's lament serves within the narrative. The Jeremiah quotation was a particularly useful exilic lament in this regard to undergird the oppressive and painful sorrow that had also characterized the exodus period.[180] Matthew narrates Jesus' story in light of the exodus, and the oppressive conditions that characterized Israel's experience in Egypt are now reoccurring, recapitulated, within the land of Israel itself. As Nolland has observed, "The recapitulation of the life of the nation in the life of Jesus is in some way, for Matthew, foundational for Jesus' significance in the purposes of God."[181] This has been the primary argument of this work, describing this aspect of Matthew's christology.

The final subsection will deal with the return to the land of Israel, and the ways this recapitulates both Israel and Moses will be discussed. Also important to remain aware of as this chapter comes to a close is the significant juxtaposition of both a literal and metaphorical exodus that Jesus passively recapitulates.

3.7 Return to the Land of Israel

Following the death of Herod, Joseph is instructed to return to the land of Israel.[182] The angel of the Lord appears to Joseph while he is in Egypt, in-

---

[179] Stanton, *Gospel for a New People*, 361, observes, "There is little doubt that in 2:17–18 Matthew intends to link the story of Jesus with the exodus and the exile experiences of Israel: just as the machinations of the opponents of God's people were thwarted of old, so too will Herod fail to overturn God's purposes."

[180] The quotation may also include the wider context of hope in Jeremiah 31. Cf. Witherington, *Matthew*, 69; France, *Matthew* (NICNT), 87.

[181] Nolland, *Matthew*, 125.

[182] The γῆν Ἰσραήλ of verse 20 and 21 are the only uses of this phrase in the entire New Testament. Luz, *Matthew 1–7*, 147, comments that land of Israel is "chosen deliber-

structing him to return to Israel because "*those* who sought the child's life are dead" (τεθνήκασιν γὰρ οἱ ζητοῦντες τὴν ψυχὴν τοῦ παιδίου). Within the narrative, Herod alone has been the only one seeking Jesus' life, although one might argue he "sent" helpers (ἀποστείλας ἀνεῖλεν πάντας τοὺς παῖδας) that carried out his plan to eliminate the rival. But the verbal link that this has with Exodus 4:19 should be noted, when Moses, who had fled Pharaoh's murderous anger, is instructed after the death of Pharaoh to take his wife and children and go back to Egypt.[183]

The close verbal parallels between Exodus 4:19–20 (LXX) and Matthew 2:19–21 can best be illustrated side-by-side.[184]

Exodus 4:19–20a	Matthew 2:19–21
μετὰ δὲ τὰς ἡμέρας τὰς πολλὰς ἐκείνας	
ἐτελεύτησεν ὁ βασιλεὺς Αἰγύπτου	Τελευτήσαντος δὲ τοῦ Ἡρῴδου
εἶπεν δὲ κύριος πρὸς	ἰδοὺ ἄγγελος κυρίου φαίνεται
	κατ' ὄναρ
Μωυσῆν	τῷ Ἰωσὴφ
ἐν Μαδιαμ	ἐν Αἰγύπτῳ
βάδιζε ἄπελθε	λέγων, Ἐγερθεὶς παράλαβε
	τὸ παιδίον
	καὶ τὴν μητέρα αὐτοῦ
	καὶ πορεύου
εἰς Αἴγυπτον	εἰς γῆν Ἰσραήλ·
τεθνήκασιν γὰρ πάντες οἱ ζητοῦντές	τεθνήκασιν γὰρ οἱ ζητοῦντες
σου τὴν ψυχήν	τὴν ψυχὴν τοῦ παιδίου.
ἀναλαβὼν δὲ Μωυσῆς	ὁ δὲ ἐγερθεὶς παρέλαβεν
τὴν γυναῖκα καὶ τὰ παιδία	τὸ παιδίον
	καὶ τὴν μητέρα αὐτοῦ
ἀνεβίβασεν αὐτὰ ἐπὶ τὰ ὑποζύγια	
καὶ ἐπέστρεψεν	καὶ εἰσῆλθεν
εἰς Αἴγυπτον [MT: ארצה מצרים]	εἰς γῆν Ἰσραήλ

As these texts are viewed side-by-side, the various parallels between these texts can easily be observed. The verbal parallels are close enough to justify a continued understanding of Matthew's narrative with an exodus motif. H. A. W. Meyer allows that due to such resemblance it appears "intentionally selected in the consciousness of being a historical parallel."[185]

Again, the reversal aspects to the geographic juxtapositions should be examined because both Israel's movements and Moses' are recapitulated.

---

ately: Jesus the son of David and of Abraham returns into the land of the people for whom he is sent." It would then appear to serve an evocative role as the conclusion of this narrative. This means a return to land of Israel, strongly characterized like Egypt. Such threat continues into Matthew 3, a point taken up in detail below.

[183] Stendahl, *School of Matthew*, 136.

[184] Cf. Davies and Allison, *Matthew*, 1.271; although they for unknown reasons only illustrate the parallels by presenting the English translation, whereas the Greek in fact reveals the various parallels far better.

[185] Meyer, *Matthew*, 68.

At the literal geographic level, Jesus passively recapitulates Israel's exodus movements. Like Israel, Jesus literally goes down to Egypt (v. 14) and returns to the land of Israel (v. 21). Jesus' return to the land of Israel in verse 21 is a completion of the movements that recapitulate Israel's literal geographic movements in the exodus, having been taken to Egypt and now returning to the land of Israel.

Jesus also recapitulates Moses' movements, which continues within the narrative based on the earlier observations on 2:15 and the parallels observed above in regard to use of Exodus 4. Like Moses, Jesus flees "Pharaoh," seeking refuge in another land.[186] However, unlike Moses, his refuge is in literal Egypt, having fled the metaphorical Egypt in Judea. Moses was instructed after the death of Pharaoh to return to Egypt, but here Joseph is instructed after the death of Herod to return to the land of Israel. The ironic reversal undoubtedly continues, because Joseph is returning to what continues to be metaphorical Egypt. In fact, it still contains similar dangers and threat for Joseph's family, now through a son of Herod, which mitigates his removal to Galilee, and finally his settlement in Nazareth.[187]

With these parallels, Matthew can both evoke the larger movements of Israel, who had gone down to Egypt (v. 14) and returned to the land (v. 21), and evoke the Moses parallel in which Jesus flees danger and returns to "Egypt." The broader exodus motif has continued throughout the narrative, and the infancy narrative ends with Jesus in the land of Israel. However, as seen above, his return to Israel includes a return to a place of danger and threat, a metaphorical Egypt, which puts Jesus in place to fulfill the calling of 1:21, something that chapters three and four consequently proceed to unfold.

3.8 Chapter Conclusions

This central argument of this chapter has been that Jesus passively recapitulates Israel's history in Matthew 2:1–23. The predominant background for Matthew 2 is the exodus, and this chapter has sought to highlight every aspect in which this can be observed. Israel's exodus history and Moses' infancy and early adulthood were demonstrated as the history that Jesus repeats in his own life and movements. The book of Exodus as well as other Jewish traditions helped to make this evident.

---

[186] Jesus "flees" by being taken by Joseph. Also important is the reminder that Moses' movements are being telescoped: as a child "fleeing" danger in the basket, as an adult fleeing Pharaoh's anger.

[187] This event is followed by another fulfillment quotation (v. 23) that has been notorious and widely debated. However, this discussion is outside the confines of this study.

A subsidiary argument of the chapter centered on Jesus' fulfillment of Hosea 11:1 in Matthew 2:15. Literal prediction was found inadequate to describe the manner in which Matthew creatively utilizes the Old Testament in his fulfillment quotations. Recapitulation fits within this flexibility. This focus on Israel's history in Matthew 2, carried over from the genealogy that recapitulated Israel's history, will continue into Matthew 3:1–4:11 as again it will be demonstrated that Jesus recapitulates Israel's history.

Chapter 4

Active Recapitulation of Israel's History

4.1 Introduction

Having observed Israel's history recapitulated in the genealogy and then Jesus' passive recapitulation of Israel's exodus, the use of Israel's history continues into the next narrative section of 3:1–4:11. This section of Matthew begins by introducing John the Baptizer and his prophetic ministry to Israel. John serves a key preparatory role in Matthew as a forerunner at the beginning of Jesus' ministry. At this point in the Gospel narrative the reader and hearer directly experiences Jesus' baptism and testing, events which are integrally related in Matthew. This is also the first time in the Gospel narrative that Jesus speaks and acts of his own prerogative. Previously Jesus had been a passive character in the narrative, a young child that moves according to the actions of his parents, passively recapitulating Israel's history in the events of his early life. Following his move to Nazareth as a child, the narrative quickly leaps over many years to a time when Jesus is an adult.[1] Through this introduction to the adult Jesus (3:1–4:11), which amounts to a fundamental preparatory period beginning Jesus' early ministry, the reader learns an important key in understanding who Jesus is, what he has come to do, and how this is crucially interwoven with Israel's history as recounted in her scriptural history. Jesus is active in the narrative in that he initiates and reacts within the narrative, thereby actively recapitulating Israel's history, reliving and representatively embodying it through his actions. The use of Israel's history is continued from chapters one and two, and the narrative further sets forth Jesus as the embodiment of Israel in an active recapitulation of Israel's history, especially the exodus period.

The plan for part three is to follow the narratival flow of 3:1–4:11, without forgetting the important continuity this has with 1:1–2:23; Jesus recapitulating Israel's history. This is important for understanding how the focus of the Gospel comes to center upon Jesus as the representative embodiment of Israel, recapitulating Israel's scriptural history. Although there

---

[1] Cf. Exodus 2:10–11 also moves quickly from Moses' childhood to his adult life.

has been much energy expended on understanding the literary aspects of Matthew, there has not been appreciable in-depth focus on how Jesus recapitulates Israel's history as unfolded in this narrative. Many scholars regularly mention concerning 3:1–4:11: Jesus recapitulates Israel's history, embodies her history, is a corporate personality, identifies himself with Israel, and represents Israel. As an example, Gundry writes, "Jesus is the representative Israelite in whose individual history the history of the whole nation, apart from its sin and apostasy, is recapitulated and anticipated."[2] All of this is indeed true and exceedingly important, but regrettably, this has become too often a mere stock generalization that is passed on from commentary to commentary with far too little attention toward how this is actually set forth and communicated in Matthew's narrative. Jesus as the passive recapitulation of Israel's history has already been explicated and argued in the previous chapter, where it was confirmed that he passively recapitulates Israel's history, with particular focus upon the exodus. In the section of 3:1–4:11, Jesus actively recapitulates Israel's history, a viewpoint that can be substantiated through a detailed examination of the narrative.

Hagner probably best summarizes the bulk of what has been discussed among scholars regarding Matthew's depiction of Jesus as recapitulating Israel. He notes how Matthew follows a similar sequence. After Jesus returns from Egypt, there is his baptism, which resembles Israel's crossing of the sea. Following Jesus' baptism, he is divinely declared to be God's Son, and then he enters the wilderness for a time of testing, fasting forty days and nights. The parallel with Israel is heightened in that Jesus answers from Deuteronomy 6–8, which describes Israel's experience in the wilderness. Hagner goes on to conclude that Jesus embodies Israel and is the fulfiller of her hopes, repeating in his own experience the experience of Israel, with the major difference that where Israel failed in wilderness, Jesus succeeds, demonstrating the perfection of his own sonship.[3]

This summary, while helpful and at a general level reasonably correct, needs to be refined and greatly expanded through an in-depth analysis of Matthew 3:1–4:11. The connections between Israel's story and Jesus' story are more than mere coincidences, indeed as Allison has demonstrated, "When a catena of New Testament texts alludes to biblical passages that

---

[2] Gundry, *Use of Old Testament*, 210. Witherington, *The Many Faces of the Christ*, 144–45, writes, "Christ's messiahship is furthermore closely connected with his role as acting for and perhaps even in some sense as Israel, fulfilling the roles Israel had failed in … All of these titles, then, are ways of showing Jesus to be not only the fulfiller of Old Testament prophecy but also the fulfiller of Israel's mission on earth. In Jesus, Israel's history is recapitulated and climaxed." Cf. Donaldson, *Jesus on the Mountain*, 91–92, 200; France *Matthew: Evangelist and Teacher*, 299.

[3] Hagner, *Matthew 1–13*, 62.

are all part of the same story, then, we may surmise, that whole story should be called to mind: plot is recapitulating plot."[4] Therefore, this chapter will seek to focus as closely as possible on this theme of recapitulation, highlighting in detail the various aspects that indicate an Israel/Jesus connection, in particular through the way the narrative unfolds, chronological aspects, and especially the use of scriptural texts, key words, titles, and themes. The focus will primarily be upon Israel and the scriptural account of her history, how Jesus recapitulates Israel's history. The Mosaic aspects are an important subsidiary motif,[5] which many have rightly discussed as important to Matthew.[6] Moses was obviously the key leader and representative in Israel's formative history; therefore, Israel's early history is directly intertwined with him.[7] As seen above, Moses was a key background character in chapter 2 within the larger exodus motif, where it was observed that Israel's history most dominates that narrative as well. The focus of this chapter will remain upon delineating the use of Israel's history and how Jesus recapitulates that history. The Mosaic aspects of 3:1–4:11 fall within the wider use of Israel's history and should be taken as a subsidiary aspect within the overarching theme of Israel's history recapitulated.[8]

4.2 The Narratival and Theological Unity of 1:1–4:11

It proves crucial to observe the connection of pericopes within the entire narrative from 1:1–4:11, which is the focus of this study. An obvious but easily overlooked point within the study of Matthew, indeed the entire New Testament, is the fact that the authors did not write the verse and chapter divisions within their text as is placed in the critical Greek texts used today. Therefore, these verse and chapter divisions can prove to be a serious distraction and distortion by breaking up material that was originally meant to be read together. While eminently useful today as a precise identification for easier discussion of where and what particular text one is

---

[4] Allison, *New Moses*, 310.

[5] Longenecker, *Christology of Early Jewish Christianity*, 36, observes the primacy of the Israel parallels and where the Mosaic serves within this larger framework.

[6] Meier, *Matthew*, 30, observes both Mosaic and an Israel typology in Matthew. Moses in Matthew is exhaustively dealt with in Allison, *New Moses*.

[7] Fox, *Genesis and Exodus*, 235, cited in Allison, *New* Moses, 199–200 n. 141, says almost every event of Moses' life foreshadows Israel's experience in the book of Exodus.

[8] Cf. Kynes, *Christology of Solidarity*, 31, interprets Matthew here as less Mosaic and more as Israel; however, his work necessarily contains too little detailed attention to 1:1–4:11 because it considers the whole of Matthew within the word-limitations of a thesis. Donaldson, *Jesus on the Mountain*, 98, focuses on Israel more than Moses as well.

using, this study will remain focused on the text itself, seeking to avoid the distorting effect of the verse and chapter divisions. This study focuses upon 1:1–4:11 as a coherent whole, within the larger story of Matthew's Gospel, which utilizes various connectors that unfold the narrative.[9] As one finishes 2:23, whether reading or hearing, the text continues with 3:1, "in those days." The narrative at a literary and theological level is seamless, unfolding an important perspective upon Jesus as the recapitulation of Israel in these chapters. The way the narrative achieves this viewpoint will be the focus of this chapter.

Beyond the obvious fact that 3:1 directly follows upon 2:23 within a narratival hearing and reading of this Gospel, there are other noticeable connections and parallels between chapters 1–2 and chapters 3–4 that deserve comment. This will aid the overall approach to this chapter as an argument that the christological perspective maintained in 1:1–4:11 is a cohesive whole that is to be interpreted as such.[10]

1. The use of the particle δέ in 3:1 links that section to the proceeding narrative of chapters 1–2.[11] A. T. Robertson considers this use of δέ a resumptive use "to go on with the main story."[12]

2. Abraham appears within the genealogical material at 1:1, 2, 17, and then he is mentioned again at 3:9 within John's rebuke of the Pharisees and Sadducees concerning their descent from Abraham.

3. The Holy Spirit is mentioned five times, mostly as a personally acting agent within the narrative. The first appearance of the Holy Spirit is in 1:18 when the Evangelist discloses Jesus' unusual origin. The narrative then further relates the Holy Spirit's role in Jesus' origin when this is communicated to Joseph (1:20). The Holy Spirit later appears in 3:11 when John declares that the stronger one after him will baptize by the Holy Spirit. The Holy Spirit descends upon Jesus in 3:16, and then he leads him out into the wilderness in 4:1.

4. Six times angels are mentioned in the narrative (1:20, 24; 2:13, 19; 4:6, 11).

---

[9] It would also bear stressing that reading among the ancients was a public, oral practice, even more so with a liturgically important document such as the Gospel of Matthew; cf. Cartlidge and Dungan, *Documents for the Study of the Gospels*, 1–4; cf. Acts 8:27–30. Therefore, oral, public reading is presupposed throughout this study in regard to exegesis and the impact and interpretation of the overall narrative.

[10] Matera, "The Plot of Matthew's Gospel,' 238, observes 1:1–4:11 as the first narrative block of Matthew. Cf. France, *Matthew* (NICNT), 25. See Kingsbury, *Matthew as Story*, 43–45 and Carter, *Matthew and Margins*, 555, on 1:1–4:16 as a narrative block. See Luz, *Theology of the Gospel of Matthew*, 22–23, on unity of 1:1–4:22.

[11] Sabourin, *Matthew*, 53; cf. Kingsbury, *Matthew: Structure, Christology, Kingdom*, 13–14.

[12] Robertson, *Grammar of the Greek New Testament*, 1185.

5. At 1:21 the angel proclaims to Joseph that the son to be born to Mary should be named Jesus "for he will save his people from their sins" (αὐτὸς γὰρ σώσει τὸν λαὸν αὐτοῦ ἀπὸ τῶν ἁμαρτιῶν αὐτῶν). In 3:6 the people are baptized in the Jordan river by John "confessing their sins" (ἐξομολο γούμενοι τὰς ἁμαρτίας αὐτῶν).

6. A very large proportion, in comparison with the entire Gospel, of the section 1:1–4:11 contains Old Testament quotations (1:3b–6[13], 23; 2:6, 15, 18, 23[14]; 3:3, 4:4, 7, 10). There are also many allusions to texts and motifs that have already been dealt with above, and the use of allusions and motifs continue into 3:1–4:11.

7. Of the ten fulfillment (πληροῦν) quotations in Matthew's Gospel,[15] four of them appear in the section 1:1–2:23 (1:22–23; 2:15, 17–18, 23). At Matthew 3:3, there is an implicit fulfillment quotation,[16] not explicit possibly due to the citation's role as referring to the ministry of John the Baptizer. In addition, Jesus' first spoken words in the Gospel programmatically pronounce his intent to fulfill (πληρῶσαι) all righteousness (3:15).

8. There are several similarities and continuities between 2:1–2 and 3:1–2. Ἐν δὲ ταῖς ἡμέραις ἐκείναις (3:1) continues and links with the use of ἐν ἡμέραις Ἡρῴδου τοῦ βασιλέως (2:1).[17] Kingship is an important theme within these chapters. In 2:1 Herod is described as king (βασιλέως), however, magi then arrive asking where the king (βασιλεὺς) of the Jews has been born, which sets up the key conflict within the narrative. Later as Joseph returns to Israel, he hears that Archelaus is ruling (βασιλεύει) Judea in place of his father Herod (2:22), whereupon he must flee this potential threat and withdraw to Nazareth. Immediately following this, the narrative proceeds to introduce John who appears in Judea proclaiming the nearness of the kingdom of heaven (ἤγγικεν γὰρ ἡ βασιλεία τῶν οὐρανῶν), where

---

[13] The quotation of Ruth 4:18–22 in Matthew 1:3b–6 is argued in detail in chapter one above.

[14] The phrase in 2:23, ὅπως πληρωθῇ τὸ ῥηθὲν διὰ τῶν προφητῶν ὅτι Ναζωραῖος κληθήσεται, should be understood as a quotation from the prophets, at least from Matthew's perspective, although the direct identification of which text(s) being quoted is not definitively clear.

[15] Simply counting the explicit use of the verb πληροῦν, there are ten fulfillment quotations. Other possible texts for inclusion: 13:14–15, which uses ἀναπληροῦν; 3:3 where the idea of fulfillment is implicit without the use of πληροῦν; 2:5, 11:10, and 26:31 which implicitly stresses fulfillment utilizing γέγραπται, and a general fulfillment without a quotation in 26:56 (cf. 26:54), τοῦτο δὲ ὅλον γέγονεν ἵνα πληρωθῶσιν αἱ γραφαὶ τῶν προφητῶν.

[16] Stanton, *Gospel for a New People*, 348.

[17] See Blass and Debrunner, *A Greek Grammar of the New Testament*, 240 (§459.3), for ἐν δὲ ταῖς ἡμέραις ἐκείναις (3:1) as a connective phrase. Cf. Levinsohn, *Discourse Features*, 206–207, suggests the phrase is part of an episode within a larger whole. More on this very important continuity of motif is discussed below.

again the kingship motif is mentioned. The text goes on to uphold John as the fulfillment of Isaiah 40:3, the forerunner to the coming of the Lord. Both the magi and John arrive (παραγίνομαι),[18] the magi arrive in Jerusalem and John arrives in the wilderness of Judea. Both the magi and John are concerned with kingship, the magi asking where the king has been born and John proclaiming the nearness of the kingdom, which undoubtedly entails kingship. In addition, the realm for most of the action in these four chapters is Judea (2:1, 5, 6, 22, 3:1, 5). Jerusalem is also mentioned in both sections (2:1, 3; 3:5).

9. The magi arrive from the East to pay homage (προσκυνῆσαι) to the newborn King of the Jews (2:2), which they actually perform in verse 11. The devil in 4:9 tells Jesus that he can have all the kingdoms of the world if he will fall down and worship him (ἐὰν πεσὼν προσκυνήσῃς μοι). The magi had already done that, πεσόντες προσεκύνησαν αὐτῷ, to the child Jesus (2:11).

10. Jesus as Son of God serves a crucial role within both sections as a thematic unity.[19] At 2:15, by utilizing a quotation from Hosea 11:1, Matthew includes this scriptural text within his narrative. Though the quotation within the context of Hosea dealt with God speaking of Israel, here Matthew utilizes what God had said of Israel in Hosea to focus solely upon Jesus, "Out of Egypt I have called *my son* (τὸν υἱόν μου)," which clearly identifies Jesus as the Son of God.[20] The divine voice reappears at 3:17 to explicitly proclaim, "This is *my son* (ὁ υἱός μου), the beloved, with whom I am well pleased." The tempter twice specifically tests Jesus as the Son of God, Εἰ υἱὸς εἶ τοῦ θεοῦ (4:3, 6).

11. A voice (φωνή) emerges in three places: the voice in Ramah of Rachel weeping for her children (2:18); the voice crying in the wilderness from the Isaiah 40:3 quotation referring to John's role as forerunner (3:3); and the divine voice that declares approval to Jesus as Son of God (3:17).

12. An interesting geographical parallel occurs in the two sections that serves to bind them together. At 2:22, upon his return to Israel, Joseph fears the threat in Judea that Archelaus poses. Through a dream, he is warned to withdraw to Galilee (ἀνεχώρησεν εἰς τὰ μέρη τῆς Γαλιλαίας), and then he obediently takes the child Jesus to Galilee (2:23). At 3:13, Jesus arrives at the Jordan from Galilee to be baptized by John and then in

---

[18] Davies and Allison, *Matthew*, 1.232, note how Matthew uses παραγίνομαι to introduce the magi (2:1), John the Baptizer (3:1), and Jesus (3:13); cf. Luz, *Matthew 1–7* (2007), 134.

[19] Sabourin, *Matthew*, 55; cf. Kingsbury, *Matthew: Structure, Christology, Kingdom*, 42–53.

[20] Kingsbury, *Matthew as Story*, 54, observes the important connection when he writes, "In the 'aside' of 2:15, Matthew quotes an Old Testament passage to the implied reader and applies it in such a fashion that God is made to refer to Jesus as 'my Son'."

4:12, hearing of the imprisonment of John, Jesus withdraws to Galilee (ἀ νεχώρησεν εἰς τὴν Γαλιλαίαν).[21] These movements reveal an underlying unity of geographic perspective within the narrative of these chapters.

While a few of these details might not appear as especially persuasive evidence, most of them are strong indicators of an underlying narratival and theological unity. The cumulative effect of these should provide ample evidence that at 3:1 one does not leave behind the perspective and background of chapters one and two, but instead a unified perspective continues throughout the section of 1:1–4:11.[22] Although it is obvious that there is a clear break at the *historical* level because many years have passed between 2:23, where Jesus was a child, and 3:1, where Jesus is an adult, the *literary* and *theological* seam is unbroken at this point in the narrative as one would experience it by reading and hearing it.[23] A unified approach to this section is therefore warranted, particularly in how Jesus recapitulates Israel's history throughout these chapters, which will be the primary argument and focus of this chapter.

In addition to this continuity literarily and theologically, a further argument at the literary level might prove persuasive toward observing the unity of the narrative as well as the continued focus on Jesus as the recapitulation of Israel's history. Above in chapter two it was argued that there is a metaphorical use of Judea as Egypt-like in 2:15, primarily because the quotation appeared at an odd and inappropriate point within the narrative from a strictly geographical standpoint. Joseph is warned to take Mary and Jesus and flee to Egypt, which he obeys. The fulfillment quotation referring to God's son being called out of Egypt from Hosea 11:1 is then placed at this point in the narrative after they had fled *to* Egypt. The geographic movement as strictly understood is not followed in that Jesus had not been called out of Egypt but taken there by Joseph. This was one of the crucial points that persuaded another reading to be considered where Judea is to be metaphorically understood as an Egypt-like place of threat and oppression. Through the larger characterization of Judea, and especially the child Jesus under King Herod as a recapitulation of Israel and Moses in Egypt under Pharaoh, it was concluded that the evidence of a metaphorical use of Judea as Egypt proved compelling.

Might this metaphorical use of Judea as "Egypt," a place of threat and danger continue into chapters 3 and 4? The pericope begins, "In those days," Ἐν δὲ ταῖς ἡμέραις ἐκείναις (3:1). The use of this particular phrase

---

[21] Nolland, *Matthew*, 10, points out that the two episodes are bracketed together at 3:13 and 4:12, 151. Cf. Kynes, *Christology of Solidarity*, 10.

[22] Contra Davies and Allison, *Matthew*, 1.287, where they overemphasize discontinuities in these chapters; later they directly contradict their own viewpoint as shown below.

[23] Luz, *Matthew 1–7* (2007), 71, 134, states that ἐν δὲ ταῖς ἡμέραις ἐκείναις (3:1) connects the infancy narrative to the baptism narrative.

is more than a vague time reference for the ministry of John or "a loose connecting link."[24] At issue here is the meaning of this particular phrase within the context of the narrative, whether it merely connects the following baptism narrative to what precedes it, or whether the phrase goes further by continuing themes expressed in chapter 2, evoking a dangerous context in which the ministry of John is set, which Jesus then continues (cf. 4:12, 17). Luz interprets the phrase as a connecting link between the two sections.[25] However, Hill takes the phrase as more than a vague time reference or a mere connecting link, but draws attention, as often done in the Old Testament, "to a period of historic interest ... equivalent to 'in those crucial days' or 'in that critical time'."[26]

These viewpoints appear inadequate for best understanding the meaning of the phrase within Matthew's narrative. Davies and Allison assert that the Evangelist adds Judea to wilderness (ἐν τῇ ἐρήμῳ τῆς Ἰουδαίας) which stands alone in Mark and Luke. This addition "takes the reader back to chapter 2 where Judea is a place of danger (1, 5, 22); so John's ministry is set in a hostile place."[27] Unfortunately, they do not further connect this motif with the preceding material at the narratival level,[28] but this observation is valuable evidence for better understanding the purpose of the phrase. Carter agrees with detecting a threat motif here, and he furthers this understanding when he interprets John's baptism with echoes of the exodus as "an act of liberation from the oppressive political and religious leadership exemplified in chapter 2."[29] This important point, when wedded to the metaphorical interpretation of Judea as Egypt that was advanced in the previous chapter of this study, helps toward recognition of the overall narrative context in which Jesus' entrance is set. Jesus accepts John's baptism, which recapitulates Israel's exodus, argued in detail below. Jesus does so as the one who will redeem his people, already programmatically expressed at 1:21 (cf. 20:28), but also, and this is fundamental for understanding 3:13–4:11, as an obedient Israelite, fulfilling a role that demands all righteousness (3:15). As will be observed below, the narrative focuses attention upon Jesus by narrowing down to him alone, one who recapitu-

---

[24] So Allen, *Matthew*, 22.

[25] Luz, *Matthew 1–7* (2007), 134, warns that "the phrase should not be theologically overextended." However, he refers especially to Strecker, *Der Weg der Gerechtigkeit*, who regards it as a "time of revelation"; Kretzer, *Herrschaft*, "time of judgment," and Kingsbury, *Matthew*, period of the "last times". Admittedly, Luz's warning has more to do with the eschatological understanding of the phrase than what is argued here.

[26] Hill, *Matthew*, 89.

[27] Davies and Allison, *Matthew*, 1.291; Cf. Carter, *Matthew*, 92–93.

[28] *Ibid.*, 1.287, are inconsistent here when they flatly stated, "no close seam has been sewn, no continuity of theme emphasized."

[29] Carter, *Matthew and Margins*, 95–96.

lates and embodies in himself Israel's history. The metaphorical aspects of the text have helped toward recognizing this, but the narratival aspects will also lead toward better recognizing this characterization of Jesus recapitulating Israel.

4.3 The Importance of the Unity of 3:1– 4:11

Having observed the larger connections and continuity in Matthew's narrative from 1:1–4:11, it is now necessary to examine the tight unity and interconnections of 3:1–4:11, which is essential toward understanding the overall narrative of Matthew as well as for understanding how Jesus is presented as Israel recapitulated. The treatment of the baptism and testing narratives together is important because it will become more obvious that the testing narrative colors one's reading of the baptism narrative when these two sections are rightly viewed together within an overall narratival framework.[30] Matthew 3:1–17 and 4:1–11 are closely interconnected in various ways.[31] This unity is exhibited literarily, geographically, structurally, and theologically. A list of these connections is essential for understanding how these are connected and how the pericopes when literarily combined interpret one another. Some of these details are more persuasive than others listed; however, the unity is clearly made evident. Furthermore, it will also prove helpful for demonstrating why this is especially important for examining the way the narrative presents Jesus as the embodiment of Israel in his recapitulation and representation of her scriptural history.

1. The temptation narrative begins in a way similar to the baptism narrative, making a connection between them.[32] Both the baptism and the testing are paralleled using an infinitive of purpose: τοῦ βαπτισθῆναι (3:13) and πειρασθῆναι (4:1).[33] Jesus came to John for the explicitly stated purpose of being *baptized* by John at the Jordan River, and Jesus was led to the wilderness by the Spirit for the explicitly stated purpose of being *tested*

---

[30] Moberly, *The Bible, Theology, and Faith*, 199, with primary attention to the context of Matthew states, "The testing of Jesus takes place immediately after his baptism and is to be understood as an essential corollary to it."

[31] In Mark 1:9–13 the baptism and temptation events also belong together; and Q is commonly understood to include the baptism and temptation at the beginning as the "call" of Jesus. Cf. Davies and Allison, *Matthew*, 1.350–351. However, Bultmann, *History of the Synoptic Tradition*, 251, is skeptical Q recounted the story of the baptism, although it included John's sermon.

[32] Cf. Lohmeyer, *Matthäus*, 55.

[33] Wilkens, "Die Versuchung," 481. See Blass and Debrunner, *Greek Grammar of the New Testament*, 197 (§390) on the infinitive of purpose (cf. 5:17); cf. Robertson, *Grammar of the Greek New Testament*, 989–991.

by the devil.[34] Both infinitives occur within the leading verse of the pericope that sets the scene for the subsequent narration.

2. Τότε is used in both 3:13 and 4:1 in a way that connects and unifies
the entire narrative.[35] Bultmann long ago observed this as a characteristic
of Matthew to form stronger links between passages, especially with temporal connections.[36] The use of τότε in 4:1 connects that pericope to 3:13–
16.[37] The use of τότε in 3:13 connects that pericope to 3:1–12. As a result,
the overall structural unity and cohesion[38] of the narrative is evidenced,
bound as it is through the continued use of τότε.

3. The baptism narrative and testing narrative are connected by a key title: υἱός (3:17; 4:3, 6). The Son of God title is important to both the baptism event, where the divine voice declares Οὗτός ἐστιν ὁ υἱός μου ὁ ἀ
γαπητός, ἐν ᾧ εὐδόκησα. In the testing event, the Tempter twice calls Jesus
υἱὸς τοῦ θεοῦ (4:3, 6). Moreover, the use of υἱός in the testing narrative
cannot be understood without its prior use within the baptism narrative.

4. The wilderness (ἔρημος) serves as the geographic setting for both the
baptism and the testing (3:1; 4:1).

5. Nolland observes a possible parallelism between John's humble diet
in the wilderness and Jesus' temporary fast in the wilderness.[39] This parallel would only be a general resemblance in that both John and Jesus were
in the wilderness and both were sustained through meager nourishment,
which in Jesus' case is greatly heightened in that he goes completely without food.

6. In 3:13 Jesus comes to John from Galilee (Τότε παραγίνεται ὁ
Ἰησοῦς ἀπὸ τῆς Γαλιλαίας) and in 4:12 he returns to Galilee (ἀνεχώρησεν
εἰς τὴν Γαλιλαίαν.). The two episodes are bracketed together by this mention of coming from and returning to Galilee.[40] This would reveal a further
structural and literary unity of this section in regard to geographical movements.

7. Both involve a divine response of approval (3:16–17; 4:11). This divine approval follows and responds to the active obedience exhibited by

---

[34] The Spirit acts in both pericopes, descending upon Jesus immediately following his
baptism and serving as the agent that leads Jesus into the wilderness for testing.

[35] Cf. Wilkens, "Die Versuchung," 481; and Kingsbury, *Matthew: Structure, Christology, Kingdom*, 15.

[36] Bultmann, *History of the Synoptic Tradition*, 351. Cf. Blass and Debrunner, *Greek
Grammar of the New Testament*, 240 (§459) for τότε "as a connective particle to introduce a subsequent event" (cf. 2:7, 16, 17; 3:5, 13, 15; 4:1, 5, 10, 11; etc.).

[37] Cf. Bruce, *Synoptic Gospels*, 88.

[38] For τότε providing cohesion, see Levinsohn, *Discourse Features*, 96.

[39] Nolland, *Matthew*, 140. Furthermore, John and Jesus are alike in their messages
(3:2; 4:17), which Witherington, *Matthew*, 77, considers an *inclusio*.

[40] Nolland, *Matthew*, 151.

Jesus, both acts of obedience involve obstacles that Jesus must overcome. In the baptism narrative, Jesus comes to John for baptism, and he is opposed by John (3:14). Jesus then states his intent to fulfill all righteousness (3:15), is baptized, and then an unexpected divine response occurs (3:16–17). Following Jesus' baptism the heavens open, the Spirit of God descends upon Jesus, and a divine voice from heaven responds with words of explicit approval of Jesus (3:17). In the testing narrative, Jesus is led into the desert to be tested by the devil (4:1). In response to each temptation, Jesus replies with scripture, indicating his steadfast intent to obey. Jesus states his intent: to live by the words of God (4:4), to not test the Lord (4:7), and to worship the Lord and serve only him (4:10). Following these three tests, another unexpected divine response occurs. Angels come and serve Jesus, implicitly a response of divine approval to his successful obedience (4:11). In addition, it is important to note the emphatic use of ἰδοὺ in both 3:17 and 4:11, both serving to highlight this divine response of approval.

8. Another possible connection is the use of λίθος in the plural form at 3:9 (τῶν λίθων τούτων) and 4:3 (οἱ λίθοι οὗτοι). Both verses deal with a transformation of stones into something else.

9. Both John and Satan have conversations with Jesus,[41] appearing to recognize to some degree who he is as they meet; but both John and Satan have inadequate conceptions about Jesus, which presents an obstacle that must be overcome by Jesus.[42] Within both events the same exact phrase is used, τότε ἀφίησιν αὐτόν (3:15; 4:11),[43] as a result of Jesus resisting these obstacles by his obedient fulfillment of God's will. Satan clearly tempts Jesus to disobey God, but John also "tempts" Jesus by his trying to prevent (διεκώλυεν)[44] Jesus from coming to his baptism because he assumes the need is for Jesus to baptize him.[45] Both John and Satan are thoroughly rejected by Jesus and both respond as demanded by Jesus; John allows his

---

[41] Wilkens, "Die Versuchung," 481, states, "Man könnte den kurzen Dialog zwischen dem Täufer und Jesus ein Präludium zu dem Dialog zwischen Jesus und dem Versucher nennen." The various connections between these two pericopes are used as justification for Wilkens' proposal that the Evangelist composed this material himself.

[42] Bailey and Vanderbroek, *Literary Forms in the New Testament*, 115, classify 3:13–15 as an objection story, "where an objection calls forth the response from the main character."

[43] Wilkens, "Die Versuchung," 481; cf. Powery, *Jesus Reads Scripture*, 120 (fn 165).

[44] See Blass and Debrunner, *Greek Grammar of the New Testament*, 169 (§326) on the conative imperfect: "wanted to prevent, tried to prevent." Cf. Brooks and Winbery, *Syntax of New Testament Greek*, 93.

[45] Davies and Allison, *Matthew*, 1:355; cf. Przybylski, "Role of Matthew 3:13–4:11 in the Structure and Theology of the Gospel of Matthew," 224; Boring, *Matthew*, 162; and Keener, *Matthew*, 132 (fn 172): "suggesting that John unwittingly had taken the devil's side in seeking to deter Jesus' mission." (Cf. 4:10 and 16:23).

baptism and Satan leaves Jesus. These two obstacles serve to further high-light the obedience of Jesus even when faced with different types of formi-dable opposition.

10. Jesus' Sonship is declared following his baptism, and then that Son-ship is immediately tested as a divinely orchestrated event, through the Spirit's leading of Jesus into the wilderness.[46] This aspect aligns sequen-tially with Israel's scriptural history where Israel's sonship is declared in her exodus from Egypt (Exod 4:22), they pass through waters in their exo-dus (Exod 14:21–22), and then they are led into the wilderness, which serves as a divinely orchestrated test for Israel to demonstrate her sonship through faithfulness to God's commands (Deut 8:2). The use of Deuteron-omy in Jesus' quotations further makes this explicit as will be seen below, especially in regard to the use of Deuteronomy 8. In addition, the further parallels that will be shown between Jesus and Israel in 3:1–4:11 will serve as additional proof that this section must be observed as a whole.

These ten reasons should prove more than adequate to demonstrate the suitability of viewing the baptism and testing as connected events, with 3:1–4:11 seen as a narrative section to be read as a whole. In addition, as the unity of 3:1–4:11 is recognized, a fuller understanding of Jesus as the recapitulation of Israel can be established. What this chapter seeks to ex-plicate is that it would appear that one should therefore read the wilderness testing of Jesus as the Son, which comes prior to his ministry that begins at 4:12ff, as closely related to Israel's history in the exodus and wilderness events. The connections that Jesus' testing has with Israel's testing in the wilderness are obvious and widely recognized, but because within Israel's scriptural history the exodus and wilderness events are chronologically and sequentially related, one should also observe Jesus baptism and testing as mirroring this aspect of Israel's history. Israel crosses through the sea and then is tested, prior to their task of taking the land. Jesus is baptized[47] and then he is tested prior to his ministry in the land of Israel.

Having examined the unity of 3:1–4:11 and the assistance that supplies toward observing Jesus recapitulating Israel's history at a broader level, it is important to consider much more closely the baptism narrative and how Jesus is presented as the recapitulation of Israel.

---

[46] Goulder, *Midrash*, 245, notes, "the close link between Baptism and Temptation may be gauged from the fact that both Paul in 1 Cor 10 and the author of Hebrews in chapter 5 draw baptism/sonship into their sermons on temptation."

[47] Cf. how Paul in 1 Corinthians 10:1–11 relates Israel's crossing the sea and baptism, probably traditional material the early church utilized.

4.4 The Baptism Narrative

The wilderness of Judea and the Jordan River serve as the setting for John's baptism of Jesus. This geographic setting has been observed by some scholars as an echo of the exodus.[48] Davies writes concerning the wilderness setting, it was "no mere geographic accident, this was intended to recall the exodus from Egypt in accordance with those Jewish expectations of a Messianic Age, which would reproduce the conditions of the Mosaic period."[49] Many have observed a new exodus motif, particularly as a result of the Isaiah quotation in verse 3.[50] Davies and Allison have especially noticed this motif with Jesus as the inaugurator of the new exodus, and they find that because 3:13–17 is followed immediately by the Temptation narrative, Jesus thus repeats the experience of Israel. "In other words, 3:13–17 is coloured by what comes after, and this suggests, as we shall see, new exodus. Like Israel of old, the Son comes out of the waters to enter the desert and suffer temptation."[51] The river Jordan also reminds alert readers of scripturally significant history in that this river was part of the eastern boundary of Israel and the crossing of Jordan was the beginning of Israel's conquest (Num 34:10–12; Josh 3; Jub. 50:4). Beyond the general points, much more can be observed through how the narrative unfolds to focus exclusively upon Jesus and this will be the primary argument of this section. Attention will be centered on how the Evangelist centers upon Jesus through narrowing the focus on Jesus as Israel embodied and recapitulated.

A primary purpose of 3:1–12 is to set the stage for Jesus' baptism in 3:13–17: John prepares for Jesus,[52] something that the construction of the narrative unfolds. John's role, as explicated in the quotation of Isaiah 40:3 in 3:3, is preparatory, a role which he clearly fulfills (cf. 11:7–15). The reader is introduced to John the Baptizer, his prophetic message and special lifestyle that sets him apart as a prophet. Crowds appear from Jerusalem, all Judea, and all the surrounding area, coming to John for baptism.

---

[48] Meier, *Matthew*, 17; Garland, *Matthew*, 34; and Keener, *Matthew*, 116, 118.

[49] Davies, *Setting*, 27. He goes on to state his view that John's baptism adapted proselyte baptism, which was suffused with exodus imagery, whereby a Gentile was made a member of Israel, "by recapitulating in baptism, and in other aspects of the ceremony, those historic acts whereby Israel was constituted as a people," 34–35.

[50] Saldarini, "Matthew," 1009. Koester, *History and Literature of Early Christianity*, 2.77, states, "If the theme of the renewal of the people in the wilderness also played a role in John's prophecy, the baptism that John offered should be understood in the context of the exodus typology (passage through the Red Sea)."

[51] Davies and Allison, *Matthew*, 1.344–345.

[52] *Ibid.*, 1.343.

Then many Pharisees and Sadducees come to the area of John's baptism.[53] Finally, Jesus comes for the purpose of being baptized by John. The manner in which this narrative unfolds and the successive groups that come to John indicate a narrowing, from "all" the people of Jerusalem, Judea and the surrounding area, to the religious leaders, down to Jesus alone. The primary goal of the narrative narrows through these successive groups to focus upon Jesus, Israel recapitulated, the Son of God.[54] The means by which Matthew narrates this event serves a purpose that has gone largely unnoticed. The narrative slowly narrows its focus, from the crowds, to the Jewish leaders, down to Jesus alone, and this is important for both the baptism narrative as well as the testing narrative, where Jesus is alone tested. Indeed Jesus is the last person baptized by John. It is important to see this narrowing unfold because it will directly impact how Jesus is presented as the recapitulation of Israel, the embodiment and vicarious representative of Israel.[55]

4.4.1 Narrowing Down to Jesus Alone

1. All the People Come Out for John's Baptism

Matthew narrates that the people come to John's baptism, from Jerusalem, all Judea, and all the surrounding area of the Jordan.[56] The "all" appears to be emphasized, being repeated twice in verse 5. Davies and Allison consider the possibility that "all" the region is employed to increase the geographic impact of John's ministry with some exaggeration.[57] Through Matthew's depiction, all the people come for John's baptism, confessing their sins as they are baptized.[58] This takes place over a period of time as indicated by the use of the ingressive imperfect (ἐξεπορεύετο) that stresses the beginning of an action that continued for some time.[59] It is also evident through the use of a distributive iterative imperfect

---

[53] The specific way that this is phrased is highly significant, as demonstrated below.

[54] Note that the genealogy also served a similar goal in focusing upon Jesus teleologically.

[55] Cf. Kynes, *Christology*, 20–21, states "Jesus is presented as the representative of Israel in his response to John's ministry."

[56] Hill, *Matthew*, 91, "the regions are personified (cf. 2:3)." Cf. Carson, *Matthew 1–12*, 102.

[57] Davies and Allison, *Matthew*, 1.297–298; Cf. Filson, *Matthew*, 65: hyperbole.

[58] Malina and Rohrbaugh, *Social Science Commentary on Synoptic Gospels*, 38, state that, "According to Matthew, John the Baptizer seeks out group repentance, that is, the repentance of Israel."

[59] Also called Inchoative and Inceptive, see Wallace, *Greek Grammar*, 544–545; cf. Hagner, *Matthew 1–13*, 49: "describing a repeated process over some time"; and Levinsohn, *Discourse Features*, 172–175.

(ἐβαπτίζοντο), used for repeated action in past time.[60] The narrative therefore gives the distinct impression of a tremendous response to John's preaching.[61]

In contrast to what will be observed in 3:17, the people do not receive a direct divine response, although John, as the divinely legitimated prophet of God, does receive them as they have come for his baptism. They are merely mentioned as coming for baptism, confessing their sins. Unlike the leaders who receive fierce criticism from John, the people receive no direct verbal response at all. However, in a roundabout way, a response could be considered implicit in John's response to the Jewish leaders, i.e. the people came to repent but the leaders did not. It could also be argued that the people, at least those that happen to be there when the leaders come, are understood to be an audience to John's sermon, although this is clearly not fully directed at them.[62] Of course, the leaders too could have come to John over a period of time. Nevertheless, Matthew here depicts their coming to John together as a unified group and John's response is a one time sermon directed at these leaders. Therefore, while the people receive no direct divine response, they are received by John and baptized by him. The lack of focused response to the people is differentiated from the radically different responses the leaders and Jesus receive.

2. Many Pharisees and Sadducees Come to the Place of John's Baptism

Following the narration of the crowds coming for John's baptism, the Evangelist narrates that many of the Pharisees and Sadducees come to John.[63] Some scholars have assumed that like the crowds, they came to John for baptism.[64] This assumption is by no means explicitly substantiated by the text, because it is never directly stated that they ever are actually baptized by John. Compare what is written of the people who come to John and are baptized by him (vv. 5–6) with what is written of the Jewish leaders (v. 7). Unlike the leaders, the text explicitly states that the people were

---

[60] Wallace, *Greek Grammar*, 547; cf. Blass and Debrunner, *Greek Grammar of the New Testament*, 169 (§325,327).

[61] Hagner, *Matthew 1–13*, 49.

[62] Contrast Luke, who has John responding harshly to the crowds, calling them brood of vipers. What John says in Matt. 3:7b–10 to the Pharisees and Sadducees, is said to the crowds in Luke 3:7b–9.

[63] The article unites these two groups, although they were obviously distinct parties that opposed one another concerning a variety of issues. Many have noted the unlikely alliance here between these two groups, but that clearly appears to be the point for Matthew, who wants to group them together as a united front of the religious leadership against Jesus. They are again united in opposition to Jesus in 16:1, 6, 11, 12. Cf. Hill, *Matthew*, 92, who observes, "the combination is a literary device used to denote representatives of Israel."

[64] Nolland, *Matthew*, 142; Ridderbos, *Matthew*, 51; also many translations clearly give this connotation (RSV, NEB, NRSV, NJB).

baptized, καὶ ἐβαπτίζοντο ἐν τῷ 'Ιορδάνῃ ποταμῷ ὑπ' αὐτοῦ (3:6). Compare what is written of Jesus (v. 13, 16) with what is written of the leaders (v. 7). The text states Jesus comes for John's baptism and then explicitly states that Jesus was baptized, βαπτισθεὶς δὲ ὁ 'Ιησοῦς εὐθὺς ἀνέβη ἀπὸ τοῦ ὕδατος (3:16). In regard to the Pharisees and Sadducees, the text only states they simply *come to* John's baptism, πολλοὺς τῶν Φαρισαίων καὶ Σαδδουκαίων ἐρχομένους ἐπὶ τὸ βάπτισμα αὐτοῦ (3:7).[65] Thus, the text indicates they simply come to the area of John's baptism, possibly to observe or investigate John and his baptism rather than to be baptized by him.[66]

The people were coming out to John and were being baptized by him while confessing their sins. Jesus specifically came to John for baptism, although there is no mention of him confessing his sins. The leaders on the other hand were merely coming to his baptism, ἐρχομένους ἐπὶ τὸ βάπτισμα αὐτοῦ, with no mention of confession. McNeile rightly observes that the phrase does not necessarily mean that they came for the purpose of baptism,[67] as is stated directly in regard to Jesus (3:13). Certainly, John's outright condemnation of them (3:7–12) indicates that if they did come for baptism they are rejected and disallowed. However, they are never said to actually be baptized, nor do they confess their sins. The preposition ἐπι with accusative most frequently refers to place, answering where.[68] The range of options for its meaning here includes to the place of John's baptism, for the purpose of John's baptism, or against John's baptism.[69] Several scholars have observed its ambiguity here and they interpret the coming of the Pharisees and Sadducees variously ranging from excitement,[70] curiosity,[71] and mixed motives[72] to outright opposition.[73] For example, Davies and Allison consider the possibility that their coming was a discovery mission for critical observation.[74]

---

[65] Cf. Gaechter, *Das Matthäus-Evangelium*, 91; Witherington, *Matthew*, 112; France, *Matthew* NICNT, 110.

[66] Boring, *Matthew*, 157.

[67] McNeile, *Matthew*, 27; but he does note that the Syriac says, "to be baptized."

[68] Blass and Debrunner, *Greek Grammar of New Testament Greek*, 122 (§233).

[69] BDAG, 363–366.

[70] McNeile, *Matthew*, 27.

[71] Hill, *Matthew*, 92; Hagner, *Matthew 1–13*, 49.

[72] Bruce, *Synoptic Gospels*, 82.

[73] Carter, *Matthew*, 96–97, who takes ἐπι as against, "coming against the baptism," but France, *Matthew* NICNT, 110, doubts this.

[74] Davies and Allison, *Matthew*, 1.304. Cf. McNeile, *Matthew*, 26; Gundry, *Matthew*, 46; Boring, *Matthew*, 157. However, Davies and Allison's claim of imperfect editing here is unconvincing. It is never adequately proven in their analysis of the pericope, and, if the argument regarding the characterization in this narrative is correct, also mistaken.

In addition to the possible use of ἐπι as a discovery mission, the manner in which their coming is narrated could be distinctly important:

Ἰδὼν δὲ[75] πολλοὺς τῶν Φαρισαίων καὶ Σαδδουκαίων ἐρχομένους ἐπὶ τὸ βάπτισμα αὐτοῦ εἶπεν αὐτοῖς, Γεννήματα ἐχιδνῶν, τίς ὑπέδειξεν ὑμῖν φυγεῖν ἀπὸ τῆς μελλούσης ὀργῆς; (3:7).

Seeing the leaders come to his baptism, with emphasis on the initial use of Ἰδών, John then calls them "brood of vipers." The manner that this is narrated gives a distinctly negative impression; certainly if they come in opposition to John's baptism, but even if they come merely to discover what is going on in the wilderness where "all" the people have gone for John's baptism.

As one reads the narrative as it unfolds, the immediate impression is that they merely come to the place of John's baptism, and the reader might perhaps have a neutral impression. However, when John responds to their coming with condemnation and judgment, then the text indicates an outright negativity in their coming. Their real motivation in coming to John still appears unclear, whether curiosity or opposition, but obviously John's negative response indicates where they stand generally. Later in the Gospel, the leaders grow in their opposition to Jesus (9:3, 34; 11:19; 12:2, 10, 14, 24, 38; 15:1–2; 16:1, etc.), often coming to him for the purpose of testing and condemning him, and that further tilts this coming to John toward the negative. A key text in this regard is Jesus' response to the chief priests and elders of the people, who had come to question Jesus' authority. Jesus in his conclusion to the parable of the two sons says, ἦλθεν γὰρ Ἰωάννης πρὸς ὑμᾶς ἐν ὁδῷ δικαιοσύνης, καὶ οὐκ ἐπιστεύσατε αὐτῷ (21:32).[76] This further reveals their refusal to repent in light of John's special ministry. The primary point here in 3:7 is that they are not baptized, they do not confess their sins, and they receive a condemning rebuke from John.

In contrast to the positive divine response Jesus will receive, the singular response that the Pharisees and Sadducees receive is a stinging rebuke from John. The reader and hearer would understand this negative response as coming from God through his appointed prophet John. It has already been established that John has a distinctive role as a voice crying in the wilderness (3:3). The quotation from Isaiah 40:3 serves as a divine legitimization and authorization for his prophetic ministry, and thus his words of response, here a rebuke and judgment, are therefore, words from God.

The leaders have no reply or defense whatsoever to John's rebuke, leaving the reader with the distinctly negative impression that they are rightly condemned. Patte, through his use of a structuralist perspective, notes an

---

[75] Turner, *Matthew*, 110, considers the particle as contrastive between the people (3:5–6) and the Pharisees and Sadducees (3:7).

[76] Cf. Luke 7:30.

opposition in the text between the people of verse 5 and the leaders of verse 7.[77] Nevertheless, this opposition is clearly superseded by the tremendous contrast between Jesus and the leaders in terms of the response both receive. Moreover, Beare may be correct when he states that calling them poisonous snakes might indicate, "the religious leaders are accused of poisoning the people committed to their charge."[78]

Up to this point, the narrative has dealt with the people in general, and now the narrative has focused specifically upon the Jewish leadership. The text can thus be read as narrowing its focus from all the people down to the leadership, and then further narrowing the focus down to Jesus alone. This sequential narrowing clearly ends with Jesus, and the response he receives clearly marks him as unique. The leadership has been roundly condemned and the reader is now left with Jesus. Garland notes the distinct impression left upon the reader when he writes, "if the Pharisees and Sadducees are unworthy to be baptized by one who is unworthy even to serve the one who comes after him, they are clearly chaff that has been winnowed out and will be burned with an unquenchable fire."[79]

3. Jesus Alone Comes to be Baptized by John

"All" the people have come for John's baptism, with no divine response, and many Pharisees and Sadducees have come to John, receiving a distinctly negative divine response. Now the reader is left with Jesus alone coming to John for baptism. In contrast to the Pharisees and Sadducees, Jesus comes specifically to be baptized.[80] As observed above, 3:11 resembles 3:1, in that Jesus arrives (παραγίνεται) at the Jordan. He has come from Galilee[81] to the Jordan to be baptized by John. Jesus' clear purpose for coming is to be baptized by John, and even in the midst of John's resistance (3:14),[82] Jesus demands baptism because it fulfills all righteousness (3:15). Consequently, the reader is left with a distinct impression that Jesus pursues obedience even to the point of countering John himself.

Immediately following Jesus' baptism, a divine response of tremendous magnitude takes place. The heavens open, the Spirit of God descends like a dove and comes upon Jesus, and a voice from heaven says, Οὗτός ἐστιν ὁ

---

[77] Patte, *Matthew*, 46.

[78] Beare, *Matthew*, 93.

[79] Garland, *Matthew*, 36.

[80] Cf. Bruce, *Synoptic Gospels*, 85.

[81] While Jesus is the only person from Galilee mentioned, as all the others had come from Jerusalem and the broader region of Judea, the significance, if any, of this point is uncertain. Cf. Nolland, *Matthew*, 152.

[82] This is a Matthean addition, which the hearer and reader would understand in terms of John's humility before the greater figure of Jesus; nevertheless, Jesus emphasizes his determined pursuit of all righteousness, which includes being baptized by John.

υἱός μου ὁ ἀγαπητός, ἐν ᾧ εὐδόκησα.[83] This dramatic response is completely opposite to what the leaders had received. The leaders were condemned as snakes and chaff; Jesus is affirmed by God himself as the Son of God, the Beloved, in whom God is pleased. Here Jesus directly receives a response of divine approval to his voluntary humility in baptism[84] and an open acknowledgement of who he is, the Son of the one that speaks from heaven, hence the Son of God. As Luz states, "God gives *his* answer to this perfect obedience."[85] The narrative has narrowed its focus exclusively upon Jesus. Through this arrangement, Matthew signals Jesus' unique role, and it is fundamentally a representational role, embodying Israel in his recapitulation of her history. Jesus alone accomplishes this, and the indications that he alone is Israel will be further dealt with below. In addition, there must be detailed analysis of this divine approval.

4.4.2 The Baptism of Jesus

Before the divine approval is further discussed, reasons for Jesus' baptism itself should briefly be discussed. Why is Jesus baptized and why did Jesus submit to John's baptism? The text succinctly answers that question when Jesus replies to John's opposition, Ἄφες ἄρτι, οὕτως γὰρ πρέπον ἐστὶν ἡμῖν πληρῶσαι πᾶσαν δικαιοσύνην (3:15). Although a very short and tantalizingly succinct answer, it has nevertheless provoked tremendous discussion and a multitude of explanations have been given as to what Jesus' baptism means.[86] In addition, there has been much debate and discussion regarding the meaning of "to fulfill all righteousness."[87]

Within the narrative of Matthew, Jesus responds to John's call and presents himself for baptism. Kynes helpfully encapsulates the effect of this presentation when he writes, "John gives the prophetic call to Israel, and Jesus, the true representative of Israel, gives the righteous response."[88] In

---

[83] Both Mark and Luke have 2nd person singular as a direct statement to Jesus whereas Matthew uses 3rd person singular as a direct statement about Jesus. Hagner, *Matthew 1–13*, 58, considers this intentional, "objectifying it and making it more suitable as catechetical material for the church." Garland, *Matthew*, 38, considers the voice from heaven "a narrative aside directed to the reader." Luz, *Theology of the Gospel of Matthew*, 36, says the voice is directed "at the assembled people and the listening community." Cf. Keener, *Matthew*, 134; and Schniewind, *Matthäus*, 26.

[84] Ridderbos, *Matthew*, 62.

[85] Luz, *Matthew 1–7* (2007), 144.

[86] Davies and Allison, *Matthew*, 1.321–323, present a thorough discussion of eight viewpoints.

[87] *Ibid.*, 1.325–327, offer seven viewpoints on this phrase. Cf. Eissfeldt, "Πληρῶσαι πᾶσαν δικαιοσύνην in Matthäus 3,15," 209–215; Luz, *Matthew 1–7* (2007), 141–143.

[88] Kynes, *Christology of Solidarity*, 26.

short, Jesus presents himself in solidarity with his people Israel,[89] a Messiah who is the representative embodiment of Israel, God's Son and Servant.[90] He obeys God's will by fulfilling all righteous because Jesus' calling was, as Ridderbos points out, "to comply with the demands that God imposed on every Israelite."[91] John was God's spokesman (3:3) calling people to repent in light of the nearness of the kingdom of God (3:1), and his baptism was an integral component of his call. Thus, Jesus' coming for baptism is a response of obedience to God's call for Israel. An important reminder to be noted is that Jesus has been depicted as recapitulating Israel's history throughout 2:1–4:11, which also leads toward observing Jesus as Israel in his baptism. The way the narrative uniquely narrows upon Jesus in 3:1–17 is part of this overall recapitulation of Israel. He alone is able to accomplish this representative task as Son and Servant, having received the anointing of the Spirit.[92]

Jesus submits to baptism because this action fulfills all righteousness, although baptism alone is not itself the full completion of that call to righteousness. Luz rightly observes, "'All righteousness' does not *consist* in the baptism by John, but the latter only belongs to it. The sentence receives a programmatic character: Jesus, obedient to the will of God, becomes the prototype and example of the Christians."[93] These are the very first words spoken by Jesus in the Gospel and serve as a programmatic statement (cf. 5:17–18),[94] utilizing two key terms πληρόω and δικαιοσύνη. Jesus fulfills the demands of God as an individual Israelite, and yet as the divine voice declares he is God's Son and Servant, the representative one through whom salvation is being enacted (cf. 1:21).[95] All righteousness is the accomplishment of the obedient life, which Jesus must exhibit throughout his ministry.[96] Garland aptly notes,

"in his baptism, Jesus is shown to be one who binds himself to the destiny of Israel and who is intent on doing what God requires. The contrast be-

---

[89] McNeile, *Matthew*, 31, "by ἡμῖν the Lord associates himself with the Jewish people."

[90] Cf. Hagner, *Matthew 1–13*, 57; France, *Matthew* NICNT, 120.

[91] Ridderbos, *Matthew*, 58. Cf. Filson, *Matthew*, 68; Hagner, *Matthew 1–13*, 60.

[92] Witherington, *Matthew*, 85–86, summarizes: "Jesus submits to doing God's loving will for humanity, and particularly for Israel, to be their deliverer in the way God intends, following God's salvific plan; thereby all righteousness is fulfilled."

[93] Luz, *Matthew 1–7* (1989), 178. Davies and Allison, *Matthew*, 1.325, concur, "rather is the baptism an example or instance of Jesus' fulfilling righteousness." Cf. Nolland, *Matthew*, 153.

[94] Davies and Allison, *Matthew*, 1.324.

[95] Schniewind, *Matthäus*, 27, thinks Isaiah 53:12 relevant here.

[96] Kynes, *Christology of Solidarity*, 26, concludes, "Jesus 'fulfills all righteousness' by fulfilling the role of a righteous Israel through his entire life and ministry." Cf. Nolland, *Matthew*, 154.

tween Jesus and the Pharisees and Sadducees who will not repent and do what God requires could not be clearer."[97] Jesus uniquely stands out, as the text has narrowed down to him alone and centers on him as the representative one who totally identifies with Israel, fulfilling God's demands of his Son.[98]

4.4.3 Divine Approval

The immediate response to Jesus' baptism, a baptism that was purposely undertaken to fulfill all righteousness in solidarity with his people and as the representative embodiment of Israel, is divine approval.[99] The baptism itself is only quickly mentioned by a participle because the dramatic symbolic events that follow are what the Evangelist clearly emphasizes. As Kupp recognizes, the voice from heaven is a "significant intrusion into the story," offering a heavenly seal of approval as depicted through the narratival portrait.[100] The redactional insertion of ἰδού, twice used, draws special attention to this dramatic climax and culmination of 3:1–17.[101] Through two revelatory events, a vision and a voice, God declares his approval to Jesus' action in a distinct way that, as noted before, those previously mentioned in the narrative had not received.[102] From God himself the hearer and reader learn that Jesus is the Son of God, in a way similar to the way God declares Jesus' Sonship in 2:15.[103]

Kingsbury notes how the first revelatory event is one of sight, where the heavens open "to permit the Spirit to descend and to signal that divine revelation is about to take place (Ezek 1:1). The descent of the Spirit upon Jesus denotes the divine act whereby God empowers him to accomplish the messianic ministry he is shortly to begin (Matt 4:17)."[104] The second revelatory event is one of sound where the voice that speaks from heaven is God himself, [105] utilizing words that are found in several passages from the Old Testament.[106] The dramatic combination of two revelatory events serves to emphasize and approve the status and role of Jesus within the

---

[97] Garland, *Matthew*, 37.

[98] Albright and Mann, *Matthew*, LXIV.

[99] Luz, *Theology of the Gospel of Matthew*, 36, "It is precisely in reference to this deed of righteousness that the voice of God now responds ... this, the man who consistently obeys God's will, is the Son of God."

[100] Kupp, *Matthew's Emmanuel*, 64; cf. Witherington, *Matthew*, 85: "Jesus as the chosen instrument of God."

[101] Davies and Allison, *Matthew*, 1.328, 335.

[102] Cf. Matthew 17:5.

[103] Wilk, *Jesus und die Völker*, 134.

[104] Kingsbury, *Matthew as Story*, 52.

[105] *Ibid.*, 52.

[106] These texts are dealt with below.

Gospel, although the fullest understanding of his status and role cannot be grasped until the cumulative impact of Jesus is gained from the whole of the Gospel text.[107] The subsequent testing narrative (4:1–11) following this divine approval will unfold further the meaning of these words (3:17), providing both an example of what Jesus' status and role clearly is not, and what it must purposely be (cf. 20:28). As attention is focused upon how this perspective is disclosed, it becomes more evident that Jesus is the recapitulation of Israel.

4.4.4 Jesus as Israel in the Baptism Narrative

It is commonly asserted that this baptism scene corresponds to Israel's exodus. The correspondence often observed is that when Jesus passes through the waters of baptism this relates to Israel passing through the waters in their Exodus from Egypt.[108] Frequently this point can merely be mentioned summarily, almost as information unquestionably true. It deserves greater attention and explication to support such a claim, which is an important component of the overall depiction of Jesus recapitulating Israel's history in Matthew 1–4. Crucial evidence toward observing Jesus as Israel is the overall structure of the narrative from 1:1–4:11 and the important relations between Jesus and Israel. The genealogy recapitulates Israel's history to focus teleologically on Jesus. Jesus passively recapitulates Israel's history in 2:1–23. The interrelationships of the narrative from 1:1–4:11 have been demonstrated in detail above. Also shown above, is the narratival unity of 3:1–4:11. The unity of 3:1–4:11 provides supportive evidence for observing Jesus as Israel recapitulated because 4:1–11 should therefore color one's reading of 3:1–17.[109] The unity of the overall narrative demonstrates the importance of this reading. The pericope 4:1–11 comes immediately after 3:13–17, is connected narratively with the τότε at 4:1, and therefore both pericopes should be used as mutually influential components for observing Jesus as Israel within the overall narrative. Thus, the wilderness testing that immediately follows Jesus' baptism should help one read the episode in 3:13–17 with an exodus motif. In addition, further insights observing Jesus recapitulating Israel in the baptism narrative will be detailed below.

---

[107] The scene in 17:5 resembles 3:16–17 in various ways, ἔτι αὐτοῦ λαλοῦντος ἰδοὺ νεφέλη φωτεινὴ ἐπεσκίασεν αὐτούς, καὶ ἰδοὺ φωνὴ ἐκ τῆς νεφέλης λέγουσα, Οὗτός ἐστιν ὁ υἱός μου ὁ ἀγαπητός, ἐν ᾧ εὐδόκησα· ἀκούετε αὐτοῦ, with a repetition of the key words of verse 17. Cf. 2 Peter 1:17.

[108] Davies and Allison, *Matthew*, 1.282, 402. Cf. Carter, *Matthew and Margins*, 107; and Boring, "Matthew," 146.

[109] Davies and Allison, *Matthew*, 1.344.

Unfortunately, very little evidence for Jesus as Israel can be garnered from the dove that appears in verse 16: καὶ εἶδεν [τὸ] πνεῦμα [τοῦ] θεοῦ καταβαῖνον ὡσεὶ περιστερὰν [καὶ] ἐρχόμενον ἐπ' αὐτόν. It obviously warrants mention that the dove is connected not to Jesus, but to the Spirit of God, who is described as descending upon Jesus like a dove. The dove has been the subject of much discussion, with a plentiful abundance of possibilities offered as to its possible meaning and frankly little agreement. Davies and Allison have provided an exhaustive list of these in their commentary, presenting sixteen options that have been offered in the history of interpretation.[110] There is indeed some indication that it can be taken in reference to Israel[111] (Ps.-Philo 23:7; 39:5; 4 Ezra 5:26). In Jewish literature, the dove is sometimes a symbol of Israel (Philo *Qu. Rer. Div.* 25, 48; also symbol of wisdom). In *Melkita* the Spirit rests upon Israel as she crosses the Red Sea and the people are compared to a dove (cf. Ps.-Philo 21:6) and are granted a vision.[112] Keener has observed that in Jewish literature there is frequent use of the dove to represent Israel (Ps.-Philo 39:5; *b. Ber.* 53b; *Shab.* 49a; 130a; *Ex. Rab.* 20:6; *Song Rab.* 1:15; *Mek Beshallah* 3:86ff; 7:27ff.).[113] However, such use of Rabbinic literature is especially problematic due to issues of dating.[114] Based on Psalm 74:19 and 2 Esdras 5:21–6:34, David Capes considers the dove a symbol of God's suffering people, signally Jesus' role as sufferer.[115] William Lane, in his commentary on Mark, thinks Jesus is portrayed as the one true Israelite, where "the descent of the Spirit 'as a dove' indicates that he is the unique representative of the new Israel created through the Spirit."[116] However, Capes and Lane do not offer enough persuasive arguments to conclusively interpret the dove as Israel. The dove is a symbol for Israel in Hosea 7:11, here called Ephraim, καὶ ἦν Εφραιμ ὡς περιστερὰ. However, the connection of the dove in Matthew 3:16 with Hosea 7:11 is tenuous and uncertain. The conclusion of Davies and Allison is that the dove in 3:16 is connected with the Spirit's

---

[110] Davies and Allison, *Matthew*, 1.331–334. Cf. L. E. Keck, "The Spirit and the Dove," 41–67.

[111] Gaechter, *Das Matthäus-Evangelium*, 102–103.

[112] Allison, "Matthew," 851, has pointed this out, although he prefers the new creation motif. However, Jeremias, *New Testament Theology*, 52, comments that "comparison of the spirit with a dove is quite unknown to early Judaism," and then he goes on to suppose that the Spirit "descended with a gentle sound 'like a dove'." Bultmann, *History of the Synoptic Tradition*, 250, does observe a connection of the Spirit and dove in Judaism, "in particular the *Tg. Song of Songs* 2:12 interprets the 'voice of the turtle dove' as the 'voice of the Holy Spirit'."

[113] Keener, *Matthew*, 133. Cf. Hill, *Matthew*, 96, notes that the dove in later Jewish literature is a symbol of the Holy Spirit and of the community of Israel.

[114] See Neusner, *Rabbinic Literature and the New Testament*.

[115] Capes, "Intertextual Echoes in the Matthean Baptism Narrative," 47–48.

[116] Lane, *Mark*, 57.

hovering in Genesis 1:2, thus serving as a new creation motif,[117] and they do not directly find in the use of dove evidence of a new exodus motif. Yet, they nevertheless cannot exclude the idea from Matthew's story because verses 13–17 are immediately followed by the temptation narrative where Jesus repeats Israel's experience in the wilderness.[118]

Although 4:1–11 is rightly observed as coloring the reading of 3:13–17, the use of the dove in verse 16 remains ambiguous and uncertain,[119] even granting the more conclusive evidence listed below. Therefore, it cannot be used as clear evidence for Jesus as Israel in this pericope. The clearer evidence garnered from the narratival unity, coloring from 4:1–11, and the evidence below might possibly incline closer toward interpreting the dove in connection with Israel. However, very little if any weight can be placed upon the dove interpretation because it is so unclear and uncertain.[120]

It is now possible to engage with the clearer evidence that Jesus is Israel in the baptism narrative, recapitulating the exodus. The overall dominance of recapitulation in Matthew 1–4 should rightly influence the understanding of the baptism pericope, which is closely united to 4:1–11. Within the baptism narrative itself there are numerous clues that can be listed which help toward identifying Jesus as the recapitulation of Israel's exodus. The geographic setting of John's baptism is in the wilderness (3:1), which is related to Israel's experience when they passed through the waters of the Red Sea while they were already in the wilderness (Exod 13:18). The quotation in verse 3 of Isaiah 40:3 further underscores that the exodus is being recapitulated. In Israel's exodus experience, God leads his people out of Egypt through water and into the wilderness[121] for testing (Deut 8:2–5), which is also the pattern recapitulated by Jesus in 3:13–4:11. The word water (ὕδατος) here is also a sufficient echo or motif evoking the exodus event of passing through the sea,[122] in conjunction with the other many details discussed here. All the people had come out to John for the baptism in the waters of the Jordan (3:5–6). Jesus the Son comes to John for baptism, where he experiences what the people had experienced as their representative, which is fully made explicit through the divine declaration of 3:17.

---

[117] Davies and Allison, *Matthew*, 1.344–345. Cf. Barrett, *The Holy Spirit and the Gospel Tradition*, 39.

[118] *Ibid.*, 1.344–345. Further on the new exodus motif in the baptism and temptation narrative see Davies, *Setting*, 34–45.

[119] Luz, *Matthew 1–7* (2007), 143: "the text leaves the question open."

[120] Indeed, it might possibly be intentionally unclear or multifaceted. Cf. Matthew 2:23.

[121] Cf. Davies and Allison, *Matthew*, 1.354.

[122] Again important to note is the comparison with 1 Cor 10:1–4 where Israel's crossing of the sea is related to baptism.

An additional observation is also possible. The element of threat, through the continued metaphorical understanding of Judea dealt with above (2:13–3:17), also might underlie the overall depiction of the people coming to John for baptism, seeking forgiveness and deliverance. Jesus comes to enact that deliverance, which is highlighted in 3:17, experiencing what the people experience, embodying in himself the recapitulation of Israel.

Further evidence can be garnered with the help of Rikki Watt's work on Isaiah's new exodus in the Gospel of Mark. Although Watts is primarily dealing with the Markan account of the baptism, his insights are nonetheless helpful toward identifying Jesus as Israel in the baptism narrative of Matthew. Watts' work especially highlights Mark's use of Isaiah and particularly the New Exodus theme in Isaiah. Beyond the exodus imagery that Watts observes in Mark's account, also evident in Matthew's, is the conception of Isaiah's account of Israel's exodus. He observes Isaiah 63 as relevant background with corresponding features, where Israel's exodus is remembered and the Spirit's involvement is especially highlighted (63:10–11, 14).[123] Within this remembrance of Israel's exodus, Isaiah 63:14 says κατέβη πνεῦμα, two words also used similarly in Matthew 3:16 within its exodus context.[124] A few verses later in 63:19, still within the exodus context, there is a plea that God would rend the heavens and come down, ἐφ' ἡμᾶς ἐὰν ἀνοίξῃς τὸν οὐρανόν.[125] This corresponds as well with the opening of the heavens in Matthew 3:16. Watts summarizes the overall viewpoint in the depiction of Jesus baptism with exodus motifs that are influenced by Isaiah, "if the memory of Yahweh's great redemptive act, from Isaiah 63's point of view, is characterised by his 'placing' of his רוּח- presence in the midst of his people then it is hardly surprising if the long-awaited repetition of the saving event should also be so characterised."[126]

The connection in the baptism narrative between Jesus and Israel, specifically as Jesus recapitulating Israel's exodus history, is both evidenced through what has been dealt with above as well as what is explicitly stated in the 3:17. The voice of God makes a dramatic declaration of who Jesus is, which is in response to his obedience in baptism, Οὗτός ἐστιν ὁ υἱός μου ὁ ἀγαπητός, ἐν ᾧ εὐδόκησα. The divine response, affirming Jesus' purpose to fulfill all righteousness, is fundamental for observing Jesus' recapitulation of Israel precisely because of the specific, evocative titles he is called.

---

[123] Watts, *Isaiah's New Exodus in Mark*, 103–108.
[124] *Ibid.*, 103–104.
[125] *Ibid.*, 106.
[126] *Ibid.*, 106.

Kynes, building upon Hooker's work,[127] makes an important observation that helps toward accepting this perspective when he notes how with the use of three special words in 3:17, υἱός, ἀγαπητός, εὐδόκησα, each has particular relevance to the relationship of God with Israel. Jesus is described in terms once used for the nation of Israel, or its representative. He also has pointed out that in aligning himself with the ministry of John, Jesus appears to embody the Israel John sought to restore.[128] In addition to this insight from Kynes, it bears repeating what was observed above in regard to how the structure and technique of the narrative in narrowing down upon Jesus makes it obvious that he alone does this as representative, recapitulating in himself Israel's scriptural history. These titles therefore affirm that Jesus is the embodiment of "Israel."[129]

Much of the work on 3:17 focuses almost exclusively upon the quotation of Psalm 2:7 and Isaiah 42:1.[130] These texts are certainly relevant and important for any discussion of verse 17, and this area of research has been amply delved into by many scholars. In addition, an article by Jeffrey Gibbs argues strongly that LXX Jeremiah 38:20 is directly utilized, and he consequently argues against observing the use of Psalm 2:7.[131] Nevertheless, while these verses are important scriptural background and provide some textual content for 3:17, they should not be the exclusive means of interpreting Matthew's narrative. As Stendahl rightly observes, 3:17 is "not a quotation in the true sense."[132] France agrees, questioning the pursuit of specific textual sources because the emphasis is on the declaration by God, that this man is his own Son in whom he delights.[133] The three key words are utilized and placed together within a text that has communicated Jesus' status narratively, and they continue to serve a fundamental role in the subsequent pericope in 4:1–11. The narrative's structure and content therefore provide an essential exegetical framework for understanding the meaning of these three key words, and equally the three key words also provide meaning for how one reads the narrative. The mutual, interactive

---

[127] Hooker, *Jesus and the Servant*, 73.

[128] Kynes, *Christology of Solidarity*, 27–28.

[129] Cf. Moberly, *Bible, Theology, and Faith*, 199: "the language resonates so richly with things said by God of people within Israel's scripture ... that it locates Jesus fully within the context of Israel's encounter with God as attested in scripture."

[130] Other possible texts included as relevant are Genesis 22:2, 12, 16; LXX Jeremiah 38:20.

[131] Gibbs, "Israel Standing with Israel: The Baptism of Jesus in Matthew's Gospel," 511–526.

[132] Stendahl, *School of Matthew*, 144.

[133] France, *Matthew* (NICNT), 123–124; cf. Watts, *Isaiah's New Exodus in Mark*, 108–109. Therefore, Turner, *Matthew*, 123, is all the more unconvincing when he unnecessarily argues for the primacy of Isaiah 42 in 3:17.

effect of these two hermeneutical components supports interpreting Jesus as the recapitulation of Israel in these chapters.

It is now important to discuss each of these three titles, the relation they have to Israel, and how it reveals Jesus as the recapitulation of Israel in this narrative.

1. Son of God (Οὗτός ἐστιν ὁ υἱός μου).

Son of God is certainly a key title in Matthew's Gospel, although as noted in the introduction, it is simply not necessary to go so far as to demand as Kingsbury proposes that it is the primary title in Matthew.[134] There are other titles, roles, and motifs that are utilized and important for understanding Matthew's Gospel and his christology, and there is never any indication that the reader should interpret Son of God as the one key title to the Gospel. Davies and Allison have rightly observed that the Son of God title receives meaning from the Jesus and Israel typology in chapters 1–5.[135] Jesus' relation to Israel, especially through the recapitulation of Israel's history, is an important element of Matthew's focus, especially at 2:15, 3:17, and 4:1–11. A key component in the use of Son of God here is the relation to Israel, who had been declared a son during the exodus period (Exod 4:22), and Jesus recapitulates that exodus event as the Son.

As one progresses through Matthew's narrative it is necessary to discern the cumulative effect of the uses of Son of God [τὸν υἱόν μου (2:15); ὁ υἱός μου (3:17); υἱὸς τοῦ θεοῦ (4:3, 6)], and how this develops and expands a proper understanding of the meaning and role of Jesus as Son of God. To exclusively interpret Son of God in Matthew as only a declaration of his deity through his relationship to God his Father is to misinterpret the larger context of these early chapters of Matthew.[136] At 2:15, it was observed how Jesus recapitulates Israel's exodus, literally and in a metaphorical manner, as the embodiment of Israel. What was said by God of Israel in Hosea, as God's son, is said by God of Jesus in Matthew; therefore, Jesus is Israel, God's Son. Both 2:15 and 3:17 communicate God's perspective upon Jesus, and both are related to Israel's exodus event, which Jesus recapitulates. In 2:15, τὸ ῥηθὲν ὑπὸ κυρίου διὰ τοῦ

---

[134] Kingsbury, *Matthew as Story*, 51–58.

[135] Davies and Allison, *Matthew*, 1.340; Allison greatly expands upon this in *New Moses*.

[136] It is nevertheless not altogether wrong to interpret Son of God in Matthew as referring to his divine status (cf. 28:19), but it is exegetically incorrect to interpret it exclusively so. However, Son of God as a divine title is outside the purview of this study. Cf. Wright, *Jesus and the Victory of God*, 485–486, provides an apt reminder when he writes, "We must stress that in the first century the regular Jewish meaning of this title had nothing to do with an incipient trinitarianism; it referred to the king as *Israel's representative*. Israel was the son of YHWH: the king who would come to take her destiny on himself would share this title."

προφήτου, what had been spoken by the Lord through the prophet, is implicitly the voice of God. In 3:17, φωνὴ ἐκ τῶν οὐρανῶν λέγουσα, Οὗτός ἐστιν ὁ υἱός μου ὁ ἀγαπητός, ἐν ᾧ εὐδόκησα, a voice from heaven said, 'This is my Son, the Beloved, with whom I am well pleased', is explicitly the voice of God.[137] Building upon 2:15, the meaning of 3:17 expands the understanding of Jesus as Son, Israel, in that he has come to fulfill all righteousness (3:15), obeying God's call through his prophet John, accepting the demands of God put upon his people. The dramatic divine response of approval to Jesus' obedience makes clear that he has fulfilled that righteousness and call demanded through the ministry of John. The narrative structurally narrows upon Jesus alone, marking him as the representative Israelite, the embodiment of Israel, who achieves and is divinely declared, Son of God. The pericope 4:1–11 goes on to present the testing of Jesus' Sonship, what it does not mean and what it must mean, through his words, actions, and then the divine approval he receives in response to his obedient success. The testing of Jesus' Sonship corresponds closely with Israel's testing in the wilderness, both through the direct use of texts from Deuteronomy and by the resemblance of Jesus' situation with Israel's experience in the wilderness.

Israel as a nation was called God's son in various texts (Exod 4:22–23; Hos 11:1; Isa 1:2; 30:1; 63:16; Jer 3:19–22; 31:20 [LXX 38:20]; Sir 4:10; *Pss. Sol.* 13:9; 17:27–30; 18:4; *Jub.* 1:24f; and Wis 2:13, 16, 18).[138] Watts notes that the relatively rare use of son in the singular often appears in exodus contexts (e.g. Exod 4:22–23; Deut 1:31; Hos 11:1 [MT]; Wis 18:13).[139] Furthermore, God is depicted as Father in his relations with Israel his son (Exod 4:22; Deut 8:5; Isa 63:16; Hos 11:1),[140] where in each of these verses there is also an exodus background. This is clear scriptural background for the use of υἱός in 3:17, which evidences the use of a title, role, and relation to Israel from these texts. The wider narrative of Matthew has presented Jesus as the recapitulation of Israel, and therefore his being called "my Son" links him with Israel, who was God's son. This scriptural background where Israel had been called God's son is the key to understanding the use in 3:17 rather than a specific text as often maintained by scholars. In addition, Israel's king was also called God's son, "God's anointed representative"[141] (2 Sam 7:14; Pss 2:7; 89:26f; 110:3 LXX).[142] This also provides relevant background for understanding use of

---

[137] See Kingsbury, *Matthew as Story*, 44, 51–55, for "Son of God" in 3:17 as the climax of chapters 1–4.

[138] *TDNT*, 8.354.

[139] Watts, *Isaiah's New Exodus in Mark*, 112.

[140] *TDNT*, 8.351–353.

[141] Longenecker, *Christology of Early Jewish Christianity*, 97.

[142] *TDNT*, 8.349–351.

Son here, as Jesus has already been identified as son of David and Messiah (1:1).

Many scholars have noted the use of Psalm 2:7, κύριος εἶπεν πρός με υἱός μου εἶ σύ ἐγὼ σήμερον γεγέννηκά σε. However, as noted above, demanding one specific text over another is unnecessary, especially given the fact that only two words are in common with Psalm 2:7.[143] How many words must there be to legitimately call it a quotation?[144] Another fact that warrants mention is that Psalm 2:7 involves the Lord speaking to his son, κύριος εἶπεν πρός με, which reveals a general commonality between 3:17 and Psalm 2:7. This would still not mean that this is the only text utilized when it is actually the word and title that is the focus and reason for use, which admittedly appears in various places of the Old Testament and other Jewish literature, more so than one single text. Two aspects of sonship are combined, Israel as God's son and Israel's king as God's son.[145] Longenecker has observed how a corporate idea of sonship was utilized and especially united in reference to Jesus.[146] This is especially important for understanding Jesus as the recapitulation of Israel and the embodiment of Israel as representative and king. The latter part of what the divine voice declares in 3:17 will also further evidence this representative understanding of Jesus' role.

2. The Beloved (ὁ ἀγαπητός)

While many scholars and translations regard "beloved" as an adjective,[147] which might be the correct interpretation, understanding it as an independent title is also a position that is worthwhile briefly to pursue.[148] McNeile defends beloved as an independent title, arguing that the titles "my Son" and "the Beloved" are distinct.[149] Hill comments that Beloved could be taken in two different ways. It may signify only or only-begotten, as done in Genesis 22:2 and 12, which would point to Jesus' uniqueness of relationship to God. On the other hand, it could be taken as an echo of Isaiah 42:1, a chosen one who is the special object of love. Hill considers the latter more likely, especially in light of the longer quotation of Isaiah

---

[143] Mark and Luke have four words in common with a slightly different order.

[144] Davies and Allison, *Matthew*, 1.336, rightly ask whether it might be "more properly an allusion."

[145] Cf. Watts, *Isaiah's New Exodus in Mark*, 112.

[146] Longenecker, *Christology of Early Jewish Christianity*, 99.

[147] Davies and Allison, *Matthew*, 1.340, state "this is probably an adjective, not a second title." Cf. *TDNT*, 8.367.

[148] This is not essential for the argument of this chapter, because neither position negates what has been argued above in regard to Jesus as the recapitulation of Israel.

[149] McNeile, *Matthew*, 32, also notes that syˢ and syᶜ separate these titles: "my Son and my beloved." Cf. Allen, *Matthew*, 29; Morris, *Matthew*, 67; Saldarini, "Matthew," 1010; and NRSV, in contrast to RSV, treats it as a distinct title as well.

42:1–4 in Matthew 12:18–20,[150] which utilizes ὁ ἀγαπητός μου as a title.[151] Therefore, the Beloved would be further allusion to Isaiah 42:1, which the remaining words of 3:17 utilize to some degree. In addition, as noted above, Israel was designated as ἀγαπητός (Pss 59:7; 107:7; Isa 5:1; Jer 38:20). Jesus being designated as ὁ ἀγαπητός μου would therefore further relate him to Israel as the recapitulation of Israel. In sum, whether one opts for one position over the other, it nevertheless continues to signal Jesus as the one who has been narrowed down to as Israel recapitulated and embodied.

3. With Whom I am Well Pleased (ἐν ᾧ εὐδόκησα)

The final phrase in the divine approval of Jesus' baptism is important in that it highlights another aspect of Jesus' role as Israel recapitulated: the Servant of Yahweh. The wording is close enough to recognize it as an allusion to Isaiah 42:1,[152] repeated in Matthew 12:18 in a slightly different form.[153] In response to his baptism, which is part of his fulfillment of all righteousness, Jesus is the one in whom God is well-pleased. Filson notes that the aorist εὐδόκησα is not a timeless approval but "probably expresses approval of the submission to baptism which has just occurred."[154] Brooks and Winbery further suggest this as a dramatic aorist "for emphasis or dramatic effect."[155] Jesus relation with Israel in this phrase can be observed in several texts where εὐδοκέω is used for Israel (Pss 43:4; 149:4). Divine approval of Jesus' baptism thus signifies the servant role of Jesus, who has submitted to baptism, and now goes forth with the approval of God to his mission. The representative role of Jesus is especially emphasized in the servant allusion. The Son of God takes upon himself the task of the servant,[156] being anointed by the Spirit to do so.[157] The coming of the Spirit upon Jesus also links with Isaiah 42:1 and the further context of that passage describing the role of the Spirit-anointed servant (cf. Isa 11:2;

---

[150] Hill, *Matthew*, 98; Cf. Beaton, *Isaiah's Christ in Matthew's Gospel*, 130–132.

[151] Davies and Allison, *Matthew*, 1.337, note "beloved" appears in the targum on Isaiah 42:1.

[152] Not all LXX manuscripts have it, although Davies and Allison, *Matthew*, 1.337, note that Theodotion and Symmachus translate it thus.

[153] See Beaton, *Isaiah's Christ in Matthew's Gospel*, for details on the complex textual issues.

[154] Filson, *Matthew*, 69.

[155] Brooks and Winbery, *Syntax*, 102–103.

[156] Hill, "Son and Servant: An Essay on Matthean Christology," 14.

[157] Turner, *Jesus, Master and Lord*, 97: "The coronation of the Messiah and the ordination of the Servant of God are here combined." Cf. Manson, *Jesus the Messiah*, 110; Gerhardsson, "Sacrificial Service and Atonement in the Gospel of Matthew," 29.

61:1).[158] Jesus is the one through whom deliverance is to take place (cf. Matt 1:21) which is dramatically announced in 3:17 by divine declaration.

The results of this portrayal of Jesus at the conclusion of his baptism is that he is divinely declared to be the Son of God, Israel recapitulated, who also represents Israel, his people, as the Servant of the Lord. He is the Son of God as an individual, as well as "Israel," Son of God "as an inclusive and 'summary' figure."[159] Through the narrowing down to Jesus alone, this representative role is further emphasized. C. H. Dodd accurately summarizes the impact of verse 17 when he writes,

> Here then is a summary of the essential purport of the life and work of Jesus in a kind of symbolic shorthand: he undertook his mission, our informants are saying, as Messiah, as Son of God, as the Servant of the Lord, in the power of the divine Spirit and this is "God's truth," affirmed by the divine voice whose echo can be caught by the inward ear.[160]

In Matthew's portrayal, Jesus recapitulates Israel's exodus history, re-enacting and embodying that history in his own experience and doing so as their representative.[161]

4.4.5 Summary

The baptism narrative was shown to narrow down the focus to Jesus alone. The crowds came to John and were baptized. The leaders came to the place of John's baptism and were rejected. Then Jesus alone came to John for baptism. Jesus' acceptance of John's baptism was done to fulfill all righteousness, where he fully identifies himself with his people as an Israelite obedient to God's call through his prophet John. John's baptism was shown to have resemblance to the exodus and the divine response to Jesus identifies him as the Son, which is what Israel had been called in the Exodus. Jesus actively recapitulates Israel's exodus and like Israel is led out into the wilderness to be tested.

4.5 The Testing Narrative

Immediately following Jesus' baptism and the dramatic events of divine vision and voice, as unfolded in the narrative of Matthew's Gospel, Jesus

---

[158] See Watts, *Isaiah's New Exodus in Mark*, 115–118 on the use of servant in Isaiah.

[159] Moule, *The Birth of the New Testament*, 87.

[160] Dodd, *Founder of Christianity*, 105–106.

[161] Cf. Watts, *Isaiah's New Exodus in Mark*, 102–120.

is led by the Spirit into the wilderness to be tested by the devil.[162] As noted above, the testing[163] event must be seen in light of the proceeding (3:1–17), allowing these pericopes to mutually affect the total understanding of this introduction to Jesus and his ministry, and as a whole unified narrative depicting Jesus as the recapitulation of Israel. As Dodd states, "now the Israel-to-be, in the person of the Messiah (the Servant of the Lord) is put to the test."[164] The text has narrowed upon Jesus alone as the Son, Israel embodied, and he now goes forth alone recapitulating Israel's wilderness testing. It is important to emphasize this aloneness. Jesus alone received the divine approval as the Son and now he is led into the wilderness to be tested alone as the Son. Thus, it is specifically the Sonship of Jesus that is tested.[165] The test that Jesus faces in the wilderness parallels Israel's test in the wilderness,[166] whereby Israel's sonship had been tested, as recounted in the books of Exodus, Numbers, and Deuteronomy. Here Jesus relives and recapitulates the testing Israel received, specifically recapitulating three testing events in her early history. The testing narrative presents Jesus as Israel, recapitulating her history, embodying Israel in himself, fulfilling that call in the obedient way she had failed to do as recorded in her scriptural history.[167] Here Jesus continues to fulfill all righteousness (3:15) in a way that will be further explicated through his programmatic statement in 5:17–18.[168]

4.5.1 The Genre of the Testing Narrative

The testing narrative has been the subject of much discussion in terms of its genre, often labeled as haggadic midrash or tale, because it appears to

---

[162] The many historical questions regarding this event are beyond the scope of this study, because all attention is on the narrative as presented in Matthew. It appears to be a visionary experience, recognized as such long ago by Calvin, *A Harmony of Matthew, Mark, and Luke*, 1.139–140.

[163] Testing is overall the better term. See Gibson, "Testing and Trial in Secular Greek Thought", 1207–1210. Cf. Jeremias, *New Testament Theology*, 74; Witherington, *Matthew*, 86–89; France, *Matthew* (NICNT), 126–127. However, both testing and temptation will be utilized throughout the chapter where one term is more appropriate that the other within the context of the point being made, i.e. God tests Jesus, the devil tempts Jesus.

[164] Dodd, *Founder of Christianity*, 107–108.

[165] Meier, *Matthew*, 29. Cf. Marshall, "Son of God or Servant of Yahweh?," 336, summarizes, "It is as the Son that Jesus is tempted, and the purpose of Satan is to destroy the relationship of trust and obedience between Jesus and his Father."

[166] Schniewind, *Matthäus*, 29.

[167] Cf. Tertullian, *On Baptism* 20; France, *Jesus and the Old Testament*, 51: "He was learning the lessons which God had intended Israel to learn in the desert."

[168] Deines, *Die Gerechtigkeit der Tora*, 257.

bear close resemblance that type of literature.[169] Davies and Allison conclude this to be a "haggadic tale spun largely out of Deuteronomy 6–8 and akin to rabbinic disputations, presumably its author was a sophisticated Christian scribe."[170] Gerhardsson calls it "an example of an early Christian midrash."[171] Form-critically, some of the closest parallels to the narrative are found in rabbinic sources where two rabbis cast Scripture back and forth.[172] One rabbinic text even has Abraham and Satan battling one another (*b. Sanh.* 89b).[173] Although important as finding an appropriate genre for this section is, this section must primarily focus upon what the Evangelist textually communicates through the narrative without prejudice being given to a specific label, and thus this study must give less attention to defining or labeling the genre of the testing narrative.

4.5.2 Interpretations of the Testing Narrative

Theissen has helpfully categorized the primary ways this pericope has been interpreted.[174] The first interpretation is salvation-historical where the central focus is how Jesus' testing recalls Israel's test in the wilderness. The second is the christological interpretation. Here a correct understanding of Jesus' messiahship is explicated, against contemporary political and military understandings of messiahship. The third is a parenetic interpretation. Jesus serves as a model to the Christian community for how a believer faces testing. While it would be terribly unwise and unnecessary to focus solely upon one interpretation to the complete exclusion of others, this study highlights the salvation-historical interpretation as primary, while accepting to a lesser degree nuances of the other two interpretations as possibly playing a part in Matthew's purpose.[175]

4.5.3 Importance of the Quotations from Deuteronomy

Crucial for correctly interpreting the passage is proper attention to the three quotations from Deuteronomy.[176] Luz concludes, "the three tempta-

---

[169] Gerhardsson, *The Testing of God's Son*, 7, 11; cf. Davies and Allison, *Matthew*, 1.352; Hagner, *Matthew 1–13*, 63; Boring, "Matthew," 163.

[170] Davies and Allison, *Matthew*, 1.353; they also doubt Gerhardsson's theory of rabbinic interpretation of the Shema as speculative.

[171] Gerhardsson, *Testing of God's Son*, 11.

[172] Bultmann, *History of Synoptic Tradition*, 254.

[173] Davies and Allison, *Matthew*, 1.352.

[174] Theissen, *The Gospels in Context*, 218–219; cf. Stegemann, "Die Versuchung im Matthäusevangelium," 30–35; Bonnard, *Matthieu*, 41–42.

[175] Cf. Allison, "Matthew," 851, accounts validity to all three interpretations, with primacy given to salvation history.

[176] Allison, "Son of God," 76.

tions make do with a minimum of narrative requisites; thus the weight falls on the central quotations of Scripture."[177] Indeed this is the primary key that overwhelmingly reveals Jesus recapitulating Israel's history in this pericope. Each quotation directly alludes to an experience of Israel during a formative period of her scriptural history. This point in particular would therefore suggest the Mosaic motifs within this pericope are subsumed to a lesser status in best understanding the narrative, with primacy placed on Israel as the key background.[178] The use of the scriptural quotations focuses attention upon Israel's history, and this key aspect of the narrative will be seen to especially confirm Jesus' recapitulation of Israel's history. There are other aspects that help to see recapitulation in this narrative, but the Deuteronomy quotations are undoubtedly the most explicit reason for doing so; and as has and will continued to be argued, this explicit recapitulation of Israel's history should also color our reading of the wider narrative (3:1–4:11) as a whole.

This section will primarily follow the narrative as it unfolds, giving attention to each of the temptations successively, while remaining mindful of the entire narrative and context. The three temptations follow the chronology as unfolded in Exodus (chaps. 16, 17, and 32);[179] and the quotations from Deuteronomy 6–8 therefore proceed backwards through that text.[180] Thus, it appears Matthew follows the chronological order of Exodus: the hunger theme of chapter 16, testing God incident of chapter 17, and the idolatry with the golden calf event of chapter 32. In addition, there are some who argue that Matthew worked backwards from the fasting text in Deuteronomy 9, to not living by bread in chapter 8, not tempting God in 6:16; and not worshiping any other in 6:13. By then working backwards one moves toward the Shema.[181] However, Goulder appears correct in thinking this too strained and hence unlikely, and he admits that Matthew

---

[177] Luz, *Matthew 1–7* (1989), 183. Cf. Kynes, *Christology of Solidarity*, 29.

[178] Cf. Keener, *Matthew*, 138; Kynes, *Christology of Solidarity*, 31, on the importance and correctness of the Israel connection states, "It was Israel who was tested; it was Israel who was caused to hunger, and it was Israel who was called 'son of God'."

[179] In Luke, the latter two temptations are reversed, either for his own purpose or by merely retaining the order from Q. Of those that accept the source Q, most argue that Matthew retains the order of Q; Davies and Allison, *Matthew*, 1.364; However Hengel, *Four Gospels and the One Gospel*, 182, proposes that Matthew used and alters Luke here, and thus he doubts the existence of "Q," 206–207. Wilkens, "Die Versuchung," proposes, 479, "Matt. 4:1–11 stammt nicht aus der Redenquelle Q, sondern ist eine eigene Schöpfung des Evangelisten."

[180] However, note that Deuteronomy 6:13 and 10:20 are essentially the same, a point fully discussed below.

[181] Gerhardsson, *Testing of God's Son*; Cf. Gundry, *Matthew*, 56; Saldarini, "Matthew," 1011; Malina and Rohrbaugh, *Social Science Commentary on the Synoptic Gospels*, 42.

simply follows the order of Exodus,[182] which makes sense as the chronological order experienced by Israel as depicted in Exodus. Primarily, each
test is linked to a text from Deuteronomy, and that text is linked to a failure by Israel as recounted in Exodus. This failure is also assumed in the
contexts from Deuteronomy Jesus quotes in that the setting of Deuteronomy depicts Moses speaking to Israel at the end of the wilderness period,
reminding them of their past failures and therefore challenging them to
loyalty and obedience. All of this will prove highly significant for understanding Jesus' recapitulation of Israel, and the obedience he exhibits in
light of Israel's failures.

Jesus quotes three specific texts from Deuteronomy, preceding his quotation of each with γέγραπται, which was a common method to introduce
scripture.[183] However, one aspect of this use of γέγραπται in regard to the
three quotations should be noted. Each text quoted from Deuteronomy is a
command, and by prefacing each command with γέγραπται, Jesus makes
evident their binding character upon his own life as ἄνθρωπος (4:4), his
own dependence as a human upon words from God.[184] In addition,
Donaldson has rightly stressed that one must not view the temptations as
three separate units, but must see all three together in relation to one another, "Jesus' responses, for example, are to be understood, not individually in the context of their respective temptation scenes, but together, as a
unified expression of a view of Sonship that incorporates a recapitulation
of the Israel wilderness ideal."[185] Thus, Jesus, the Son of God, is not outside the demand to follow the commands of Israel's scriptures, but hears
and obeys them as an Israelite; an important point that Matthew portrays
here narratively before they are programmatically stated by Jesus himself
in 5:17.

A further point in regard to the use of scripture in this pericope is the
importance of the context of the quotations.[186] This is most evident when
the parallels between Jesus' situation and Israel's situation are compared.
All three of the Deuteronomy texts refer to temptations Israel experienced
in the wilderness. Attention to the surrounding context will therefore be of
major concern as each temptation is examined and how they shed more
light upon how Jesus is the recapitulation of Israel in this pericope.

The section from Deuteronomy 6–8 depicts God speaking through
Moses to his son Israel while they are in the wilderness (Deut 1:1), as they

---

[182] Goulder, *Midrash*, 247.

[183] Fitzmyer, *Essays on the Semitic Background of the New Testament*, 8–10.

[184] Powery, *Jesus Reads Scripture*, 119–120.

[185] Donaldson, *Jesus on the Mountain*, 95.

[186] Cf. Keener, *Matthew*, 141; Albright and Mann, *Matthew*, LXI–LXII.

are poised to enter the land that had been promised to them;[187] and through the manner that Matthew has Jesus quoting from Deuteronomy, the Son is therefore portrayed as hearing and obeying God's voice in Deuteronomy.[188] Indeed Jesus is faithful at every point where Israel failed.[189] That failure had been a major point of Deuteronomy, warning Israel not to follow the failures of their past; it is also crucial for understanding Jesus' test in Matthew 4.

4.5.4 The Role of Deuteronomy 8

In addition to following the chronological order of Exodus, it also appears that Deuteronomy 8 bears a greater weight in regard to context and placement, occurring within the first temptation, and overall resembling the entirety of Jesus' testing in the wilderness. Indeed, as the narrative unfolds with Jesus' hunger leading into the first temptation and his quotation from Deuteronomy 8, one might suppose the period of fasting, which provoked extreme hunger, seemingly directed Jesus toward understanding this an experience 'designed by God to teach him the lesson of Deuteronomy 8:3'.[190] Thus, Deuteronomy 8 should be taken as relating more broadly to the entire testing narrative, and this can be clearly shown by a closer textual analysis of Deuteronomy 8.[191]

The overall background to the testing narrative closely corresponds to Deuteronomy 8. It is important to note this correspondence in language, content, and motifs because it influences the overall understanding of Matthew 4:1–11, which therefore colors the entire unit from 3:1–4:11. This correspondence between Deuteronomy 8:1–6, 14–16, 19 and Matthew 4:1–

---

[187] While the modern scholarly discussion of Deuteronomy, as well as all other ancient texts cited, is fully recognized by the present work, the conventional reading as understood in the first century must primarily guide much of the subsequent discussion. The Evangelist's use of Deuteronomy, as indeed in all of his use of other scriptural texts, was produced within the common understanding of that time period and careful distinction between their viewpoint and what is understood today must be maintained for careful exegesis of the Matthew's text. Evans, "The Old Testament in the New," 136, reminds twenty-first century interpreters, "We should assume that Matthew followed the exegetical conventions of his day, and therefore Matthean exegesis should be assessed accordingly." Cf. von Rad, *Old Testament Theology*, 330–332.

[188] Goldingay, "Old Testament and Christian Faith," 20: "Here in the wilderness the 'one true Israelite' takes seriously that set of principles given in the wilderness to Israel as a whole but never properly observed by her."

[189] Thompson, "Called-Proved-Obedient," 1, states "there is an implied contrast between the obedience of Jesus and the disobedience of the Israelites."

[190] France, *Matthew*, 98.

[191] Interestingly, Nelson, *Deuteronomy*, 107, has pointed out how Deuteronomy 8 repeats various aspects of 6:10–15, 107; cf. Weinfeld, *Deuteronomy 1–11*, 389, 396; Bultmann, "Deuteronomy," 143.

11 then lends further support for the necessity of recognizing Jesus as the recapitulation of Israel. An examination of the Greek text is therefore warranted.[192] Words in italics are key areas of correspondence that bear close attention, beyond the contextual relations discussed below.

1 πάσας τὰς ἐντολάς ἃς ἐγὼ ἐντέλλομαι ὑμῖν σήμερον φυλάξεσθε ποιεῖν ἵνα ζῆτε καὶ πολυπλασιασθῆτε καὶ εἰσέλθητε καὶ κληρονομήσητε τὴν γῆν ἣν κύριος ὁ θεὸς ὑμῶν[193] ὤμοσεν τοῖς πατράσιν ὑμῶν

2 καὶ μνησθήσῃ πᾶσαν τὴν ὁδόν ἣν *ἤγαγέν σε κύριος ὁ θεός σου*[194] *ἐν τῇ ἐρήμῳ* ὅπως ἂν κακώσῃ σε καὶ *ἐκπειράσῃ* σε καὶ διαγνωσθῇ τὰ ἐν τῇ καρδίᾳ σου εἰ φυλάξῃ τὰς ἐντολὰς αὐτοῦ ἢ οὔ

3 καὶ ἐκάκωσέν σε καὶ ἐλιμαγχόνησέν σε καὶ ἐψώμισέν σε τὸ μαννα ὃ οὐκ εἴδησαν οἱ πατέρες σου ἵνα ἀναγγείλῃ σοι ὅτι *οὐκ ἐπ' ἄρτῳ μόνῳ ζήσεται ὁ ἄνθρωπος ἀλλ' ἐπὶ παντὶ ῥήματι τῷ ἐκπορευομένῳ διὰ στόματος θεοῦ ζήσεται ὁ ἄνθρωπος*

4 τὰ ἱμάτιά σου οὐ κατετρίβη ἀπὸ σοῦ οἱ *πόδες* σου οὐκ ἐτυλώθησαν ἰδοὺ *τεσσαράκοντα* ἔτη

5 καὶ γνώσῃ τῇ καρδίᾳ σου ὅτι ὡς εἴ τις παιδεύσαι ἄνθρωπος *τὸν υἱὸν_αὐτοῦ* οὕτως *κύριος ὁ θεός σου* παιδεύσει σε

6 καὶ φυλάξῃ τὰς ἐντολὰς *κυρίου τοῦ θεοῦ σου* πορεύεσθαι ἐν ταῖς ὁδοῖς αὐτοῦ καὶ φοβεῖσθαι αὐτόν

14 ὑψωθῇς τῇ καρδίᾳ καὶ ἐπιλάθῃ *κυρίου τοῦ θεοῦ σου* τοῦ ἐξαγαγόντος σε ἐκ γῆς Αἰγύπτου ἐξ οἴκου δουλείας

15 τοῦ *ἀγαγόντος* σε διὰ τῆς *ἐρήμου* τῆς μεγάλης καὶ τῆς φοβερᾶς ἐκείνης οὗ ὄφις δάκνων καὶ σκορπίος καὶ δίψα οὗ οὐκ ἦν ὕδωρ τοῦ ἐξαγαγόντος σοι ἐκ πέτρας ἀκροτόμου πηγὴν ὕδατος

16 τοῦ ψωμίσαντός σε τὸ μαννα ἐν τῇ *ἐρήμῳ* ὃ οὐκ εἴδησαν οἱ πατέρες σου ἵνα κακώσῃ σε καὶ *ἐκπειράσῃ* σε καὶ εὖ σε ποιήσῃ ἐπ' ἐσχάτων τῶν ἡμερῶν σου

19 καὶ ἔσται ἐὰν λήθῃ ἐπιλάθῃ *κυρίου τοῦ θεοῦ σου* καὶ πορευθῇς ὀπίσω θεῶν ἑτέρων καὶ *λατρεύσῃς* αὐτοῖς καὶ *προσκυνήσῃς* αὐτοῖς διαμαρτύρομαι ὑμῖν σήμερον τόν τε οὐρανὸν καὶ τὴν γῆν ὅτι ἀπωλείᾳ ἀπολεῖσθε

The words in italics are just a part of the many varied relations between Matthew 4:1–11 and Deuteronomy 8 at the word and phrase level.

In addition, at a broader level, there are other important relations between these two texts:

1. The geographic setting of both is the wilderness (ἔρημος). Deuteronomy is set as a sermon to Israel in the wilderness (1:1) and chapter 8 refers specifically to Israel's previous experience of testing in the wilderness (8:2, 15, 16).

2. Deuteronomy 8 is presented as God speaking to Israel his son. Note the use of 2nd person singular throughout much of the chapter.[195] In Mat-

---

[192] There are a few differences between the MT and LXX that will be pointed out below.

[193] Note the 2nd plural here, whereas other verses use 2nd singular, which MT does throughout.

[194] LXX does not have 40 years where MT does, but LXX does have it in verse 4.

[195] MT is consistent in its use of 2nd singular whereas LXX fluctuates between singular and plural.

thew's narrative, God had spoken in 3:17, and the portrayal of Jesus' quoting from Deuteronomy reveals a person that hears God's words and seeks to obey them (4:4).

3. God led (ἤγαγέν) Israel in the wilderness to test (ἐκπειράσῃ) them as to whether they would keep his commands (Deut 8:2–5).[196] Jesus is led (ἀνήχθη) into the wilderness to be tested as to whether he will keep God's commands.

4. According to Deuteronomy 8:5, this was discipline as a father practices with a son (ὅτι ὡς εἴ τις παιδεύσαι ἄνθρωπος τὸν υἱὸν αὐτοῦ οὕτως κύριος ὁ θεός σου παιδεύσει σε). Jesus' fasting experience in the wilderness is a purposeful test of his obedience to God as the Son.

5. Israel was tested in the wilderness forty years (Deut 8:2) and Jesus was tested forty days and nights in the wilderness (Matt 4:2). Unlike Mark and Luke, only Matthew directly states that testing was the purpose of this wilderness excursion with his use of a infinitive of purpose,[197] which corresponds with Deuteronomy 8:2–5, especially 8:2 (ἐκπειράσῃ).[198]

6. God allowed Israel to be hungry as part of the wilderness test (Deut 8:3), just as Jesus also went hungry in his wilderness testing (Matt 4:2). Davies and Allison note that one can point ענה so as to mean God caused Israel to fast (cf. Lev 23:27, 29, 32; Ps 35:13).[199] In addition, Weinfeld states that the verb when joined with soul "indicates fast and hunger."[200]

7. A goal of the testing was to teach Israel that a person does not live by bread alone but by every word that comes from God (Deut 8:2–3),[201] which is what Jesus quotes back to the tempter when he is tested (Matt 4:4), revealing he too must learn and follow this principle.

8. At the end of Deuteronomy 8, Israel is warned of the danger of following other gods, serving and worshipping them (8:19). This is precisely the test that Jesus faced in the third temptation.

The closeness between these two texts demonstrates the use by Matthew of Deuteronomy 8 and the importance of attention to the wider context of Deuteronomy for understanding Matthew 4. Therefore, these relations should prove adequate for understanding Deuteronomy 8 as a key back-

---

[196] Bultmann, "Deuteronomy," 143, further observes how beyond the test of 8:2 there are actually several different interpretations of this wilderness period of Israel's history (Deut 1:31; 32:10–11; Jer 2:2; Hos 2:14–15).

[197] Gundry, *Matthew*, 54: "The testing of Jesus' obedience as God's Son becomes, then, the very purpose of the Spirit's leading him up into the wilderness ...; i.e., the Spirit descended on Jesus at his baptism in order to lead him in the way of righteousness, a way of obedience to the law, which he will quote in parrying the devil."

[198] Both Mark and Luke merely use the participle πειραζόμενος.

[199] Davies and Allison, *Matthew*, 1.359.

[200] Weinfeld, *Deuteronomy 1–11*, 388–389.

[201] Cf. Wisdom 16:26.

ground for the entire pericope, with Jesus himself as Israel, the Son, recapitulating the wilderness testing. Albright and Mann summarize the focus
of the narrative when they state, "Here the narrative *encapsulates* Israel in
the person of Jesus, and subjects him to the testing of covenant-loyalty in
Deuteronomic terms."[202]

4.5.5 Testing the Son of God

The test as presented in Matthew is primarily focused upon Jesus as the
Son of God and the relation he has with God in his recapitulation of Israel's history.[203] Son of God had been a significant title that Israel also was
called (Exod 4:22–23; Deut 1:31; 8:5; 32:5, 6, 18–20; Hos 11:1) and this
has already been important background in understanding Jesus as Son in
2:15 and 3:17. Summing up the cumulative effect of Jesus as the Son of
God, Meier concludes, "Matthew develops the title in terms of the obedient
servant who recapitulates the history of Israel, the son of God in the Old
Testament, and who proves he is the true Son and Israel by withstanding
temptation and doing the will of the Father."[204] The continued use of Son
of God therefore further helps toward perceiving Jesus as the recapitulation of Israel in this pericope. It also helps steer away from thinking that it
is only or even primarily the nature of Jesus' messianic status that is
tested.[205] Jesus is *alone* in the wilderness to face his test, and there are
never any spectators mentioned in any of the temptations, particularly in
regard to the second temptation. Furthermore, the manner that Matthew
exhibits the tempter's challenge of Jesus as Son is also important
(4:3,6),[206] and this is where many English translations unfortunately give a
false impression. The tempter is not denying the Sonship of Jesus, but
challenging him to prove it,[207] Εἰ υἰὸς εἶ τοῦ θεοῦ, εἰπὲ ἵνα οἱ λίθοι οὖ

---

[202] Albright and Mann, *Matthew*, LV.

[203] Since this is the broader focus of the test, Kynes, *Christology of Solidarity*, 33,
does not regard the test based solely on the unique messianic status of Jesus; a discussion
further dealt with below.

[204] Meier, "Matthew," 638; cf. Menken, "Deuteronomy in Matthew's Gospel," 49.

[205] Cf. France, *Matthew* (NICNT), 127. Exclusion completely of a messianic interpretation is unnecessary because Jesus, who is the Messiah (1:1, 16), is indeed tested, but he
is tested here as Israel recapitulated. Therefore, it appears improper to regard the messianic interpretation as the sole or even primary interpretation of the testing narrative due
to other indications in the text dealt with in this chapter.

[206] Cf. Matthew 27:40, where bystanders at the cross taunt Jesus to come down if he is
the Son of God. See France, *Matthew* NICNT, 127, for further links with the Passion narrative. Matthew 27:40 would be an important verse, among others (e.g. 16:1), that could
be utilized for further study of Jesus' tests throughout Matthew.

[207] Moberly, *Bible, Theology, and Faith*, "the if not of uncertain possibility, but of
definition and analysis," 199. Cf. Malina and Rohrbaugh, *Social-Science Commentary on
the Synoptic Gospels*, 41; Luz, *Matthew 1–7* (2007), 151.

τοι ἄρτοι γένωνται.[208] Use of a first class condition, in conjunction with the contextual clue from 3:17, indicates that the narrative portrays the tempter drawing upon those prior words for a temptation based on sonship. In addition, Meyer observes that there is special emphasis on υἱός given its position.[209] A better translation would then be: "*Since* you are the Son of God, command that these stones become bread."[210] This focus on Jesus as Son relates back to the divine voice in 3:17, which had earlier proclaimed Jesus' Sonship. As Kingsbury notes, "In testing Jesus, Satan cunningly adopts God's evaluative point of view according to which Jesus is his Son (4:3, 6)."[211]

Here the test is in regard to Jesus' Sonship, whether he will obey God's will, fulfilling the righteousness he had just announced to John in 3:15,[212] as well as a temptation for Jesus to abandon his mission as servant.[213] This testing, coming as it does prior to Jesus' ministry as narrated by Matthew (4:12ff.), was therefore preparatory for his ministry.[214] Donaldson has closely analyzed this passage, where he rightly weighs the use of Deuteronomy in each of the quotations, and concludes the temptation does not center on messianism[215] but on living as Israel was called to, "a pattern of Sonship that is given definition in terms of ideal Israel."[216] The focus of the testing narrative centers on Jesus' recapitulation of Israel's history, re-enacting their experience after the exodus.[217] Luz elucidates this interpretive approach regarding the testing narrative that

understands the Son of God, Jesus, typologically as the representative of the true people of God, who in the wilderness is victorious over precisely those temptations on which the

---

[208] See BDAG, 277, for εἰ with indicative, "to express a condition thought of as real or to denote assumptions relating to what has already happened." Cf. Brooks and Winbery, *Syntax*, 182.

[209] Meyer, *Matthew*, 94.

[210] Cf. Blass and Debrunner, *Greek Grammar of the New Testament*, 189 (§372). Davies and Allison, *Matthew*, rightly note, "Jesus' status as 'Son of God' is not questioned; rather it is the presupposition for the devil's temptation," 1.360. Cf. Hill, *Matthew*, 100; Kynes, *Christology of Solidarity*, 31.

[211] Kingsbury, *Matthew as Story*, 55.

[212] Gerhardsson, *Testing of God's Son*, 19.

[213] Davies and Allison, *Matthew*, 1.360.

[214] Allen, *Matthew*, 30. Cf. Carson, *Matthew 1–12*, 112, "the temptations legitimized Jesus as God's true Son."

[215] More evidence for excluding primacy of the messianic interpretation will be explicated under each temptation.

[216] Donaldson, *Jesus on Mountain*, 91–92.

[217] Allison, "Son of God," 76.

"son," Israel, foundered before the conquest. The typology may have christological or parenetical meaning.[218]

4.5.6 The Setting of the Testing Narrative

The setting for the testing of Jesus is the wilderness, τὴν ἔρημον, where he has been led by the Spirit (4:1). Although within each of the temptations there is a specific setting, the overall setting of the wilderness governs the narrative.[219] With the wilderness setting, one encounters a clear echo and parallel with the exodus story as recounted in Exodus, Numbers and Deuteronomy. Having just been baptized and divinely declared to be God's son, Jesus is led by the Spirit, ἀνήχθη εἰς τὴν ἔρημον ὑπὸ τοῦ πνεύματος. Davies and Allison suggest, "Perhaps Matthew's ἀνήχθη should recall the exodus from Egypt, to wit: just as God led Israel out of Egypt and through the waters and into the desert (Num 20:5; 1 Sam 12:6 LXX; Ps 80:1 LXX; etc., all using ἀνάγειν), so does the Spirit of God lead Jesus into the desert after he is baptized."[220] It was also thought that the Spirit of God was especially active during the exodus and wilderness period (Num 11:17, 25, 29; Neh 9:20; Ps 106:33; Isa 63:10–14; *Tg. Yer.* to Exod 15:2; *Mek.* on Exod 14:12 and 15; *b. Sota* 30b; *Num Rab.* on 11:17; *Exod Rab.* on 15:1).[221] It has already been observed above that Jesus' "passing through the waters" paralleling Israel's passing through the waters is a problematic viewpoint to take based on Matthew's text. Jesus' connections with Israel and his recapitulation of her history have therefore necessarily taken cues from other indications in the text. The varied parallels observed above were helpful observations toward understanding Jesus recapitulating Israel in this pericope and much further evidence in the text for this viewpoint will be outlined below. In addition, it should be added that whereas the scriptural portrayal of Israel's exodus was a dramatic divinely orchestrated event followed by a divinely orchestrated test (Deut 8), Jesus' baptism and the divine response he receives is also portrayed as a divinely orchestrated event (3:17–4:1). Thus with both Israel and Jesus, following dramatic events there is a time of testing, a testing of God's son.

Jesus is described as fasting[222] during his time in the wilderness, fasting forty days and nights. The number forty is significant in the Bible: the

---

[218] Luz, *Matthew 1–7* (2007), 149–150; however, it should be noted that he does not regard this interpretation as correct.

[219] Cf. France, *Matthew* NICNT, 128. Donaldson, *Jesus on Mountain*, 96, comments that although the settings of the three temptations are not brought together, usually wilderness dominates.

[220] Davies and Allison, *Matthew*, 1.354.

[221] *Ibid.*, 1.355.

[222] Allison, *The New Moses*, 168–169: "There may be a parallel of sorts in Deut, for according to Deut 9:18 and 25, Moses' fasting was occasioned by Israel's lapse into sin;

rains of the Flood in Genesis occurred for forty days and forty nights (Gen 7:4, 12); Moses met twice with the Lord on the mountain for forty days and forty nights (Exod 24:18; 34:28; Deut 9:9, 11, 18, 25, 10:10); the spies of Israel spent forty days spying out the land of Canaan (Num 13:25); Israel spent forty years in the wilderness until they came to the land of Canaan (Exod 16:35; Deut 2:7; 8:2, 4; 29:5; Neh 9:21; Ps 95:10; Amos 2:10); the forty years in the wilderness served as punishment for their lack of faith in response to the spies (Num 14:33–34; Josh 5:6; Ps 95:10); Israel spent forty years under the rule of the Philistines (Judg 13:1); Elijah was provided for in his flight from Jezebel forty days and forty nights (1 Kgs 19:8); Jonah prophesied that in forty days Nineveh would be overthrown (Jonah 3:4)[223]; and Ezekiel enacted a prophetic sign of Jerusalem's downfall by laying on his side forty days, a day for each year (Ezek 4:6). All of these reveal an importance of the number forty in Israel's history.[224] Nevertheless, beyond this general relation with Jesus' own testing, it is not immediately apparent thus far that any one of these serves as significant background for Jesus' testing in the wilderness. As will be explicated in detail below, the key to understanding the background is the quotation of Deuteronomy 8 in Jesus' reply to the tempter. While aspects of the other episodes in Israel's history noted above might have some possible connection, probably Moses forty day fast, and possibly Elijah's as well, it is the quotation of Deuteronomy 8 that makes abundantly clear the relation with Israel's forty year wandering in the wilderness.

According to their scriptural history, Israel's wandering was a punishment for their failure to follow the plan of conquering Canaan. Thus, they were punished one year for every day the spies spent in Canaan, forty years for forty days (Num 14:33–34). However, Jesus' period of fasting in the wilderness is by no means a response of punishment for any failure on his part. How does his forty-day testing relate to Israel's forty years? A clear answer is in Deuteronomy 8, which comes under fuller analysis within the discussion of the first test, where the close relation that Matthew 4:1–11 has with Deuteronomy 8 will become more evident at that point. In brief, it will be shown that Jesus' test resembles Israel's test, because in Deuteronomy 8 the aspect of punishment is lacking, and instead a disciplinary, educative purpose underlies the wilderness ordeal. This will be shown to be the important background to Jesus' testing, and the recapitulation he undertakes.

---

the refusal to eat and drink was a penitential act of the one for the many. The parallel is, obviously, inexact; but the Pentateuch does link the fast on Sinai to an episode of temptation."

[223] Three days in the LXX.

[224] Jeremias, *New Testament Theology*, 69, observes that "forty is a common symbolic number, which denotes times of oppression and of curse."

4.5.7 The First Test

The setting for the first test is the wilderness (ἔρημος), where Jesus has been led by the Spirit for the purpose of being tested. The text then narrates how Jesus had been spending his time since entering the wilderness, fasting forty days and nights. After such a prolonged period without nourishment, while Jesus is extremely hungry, the tempter approaches (προσελθὼν). The first test in regard to Jesus' Sonship concerns the hunger he experiences as a result of his forty day fast and what he should do to overcome this life-threatening hunger. At the point of such extreme weakness and hunger, the tempter approaches to suggest that Jesus provide himself bread. As noted above, the tempter does not doubt Jesus' Sonship, he presumes it in his suggestion, "since you are the Son of God, tell these stones to become loaves." In the midst of life-threatening hunger in the wilderness, the temper's suggestion links a need with a provision that is ostensibly acceptable, especially given the extreme hunger of Jesus and the impossibility of securing food in the desert otherwise. Indeed, it would appear that Jesus is near death and thus the securing of food for his obvious extreme need would be wise in this situation.

Jesus' Scriptural Response to the Temptation

Jesus responds to the tempter, Γέγραπται, Οὐκ ἐπ' ἄρτῳ μόνῳ ζήσεται ὁ ἄνθρωπος, ἀλλ' ἐπὶ παντὶ ῥήματι ἐκπορευομένῳ διὰ στόματος θεοῦ (4:4). This response utilizes words from Deuteronomy 8:3, emphasized as a written text that Jesus uses to answer the temptation. While it is not immediately apparent that the suggestion of the tempter is altogether wrong to act upon,[225] Jesus' reply makes evident a more fundamental concern for total dependence upon God alone by responding with a Scriptural quotation from Deuteronomy 8:3. Jesus quotes a scripture that had been addressed to Israel, utilizing γέγραπται, which he repeats in all three of his replies, the formal introduction to scriptural quotations. The quotation from Deuteronomy 8:3b, corresponds closely with the LXX in wording, especially seen in the use of ῥήματι, which is lacking in the MT.[226]

---

[225] This is in obvious contrast to the third temptation, which was fundamentally wrong for any Israelite ever to do.

[226] See Gundry, *Use of the Old Testament*, 67, on the Targums.

לא על־הלחם לבדו יחיה האדם
כי על־כל־מוצא פי־יהוה יחיה האדם:

οὐκ ἐπ' ἄρτῳ μόνῳ ζήσεται ὁ ἄνθρωπος
ἀλλ' ἐπὶ παντὶ ῥήματι τῷ ἐκπορευομένῳ
διὰ στόματος θεοῦ ζήσεται ὁ ἄνθρωπος

Matthew also extends the quotation beyond what appears in Luke when he keeps, ἀλλ' ἐπὶ παντὶ ῥήματι ἐκπορευομένῳ διὰ στόματος θεοῦ.[227] This extension of the quotation especially highlights Jesus' commitment to following God's law (cf. 5:17).[228] Reference to every word that proceeds from the mouth of God would most certainly include what the divine voice had just previously declared in 3:17.

Deuteronomy 8:3 and the Context

One must note the entire context of Deuteronomy 8 to demonstrate the presentation of Jesus as Israel recapitulated in Matthew. While much of the context of Deuteronomy 8 was discussed above as important broadly for understanding the entire testing narrative, much of it also applies to the first test. In addition to the discussion above, a few further comments here within the context of the first temptation are crucial for observing how Jesus recapitulates Israel's history in this test. Deuteronomy 8 calls Israel, God's son (8:5), to remember the past and the lessons that still needed to be learned. Israel's time in the wilderness served as a disciplinary test as to whether they would obey the commands of God (8:2). Tigay adds, "The reason for the test is not stated; perhaps it was intended to determine whether Israel was ready to enter the promised land."[229] If correct, this would have some correspondence with Jesus' experience as a test for whether he was ready for entering his ministry. To bolster this possibility, Weinfeld comments how a goal of punishment in the educative process is future improvement, "so God chastised Israel in the desert for its future benefit (cf. v 16)."[230] Consequently, a correspondence to Jesus' present test and future ministry is more evident.

This test directly involved the wilderness hardships, as Tigay indicates by literally translating verse 2, "that he might subject you to hardship so that he might test you."[231] This would closely correspond to Jesus' situation in the wilderness, having gone forty days without food. Jesus quota-

---

[227] Which is more original, what possibly appeared in Q, and/or other oral or written sources, is certainly an important question. However, it stands outside the scope of this study.

[228] Cf. Menken, "Deuteronomy in Matthew's Gospel," 46.

[229] Tigay, *Deuteronomy*, 92.

[230] Weinfeld, *Deuteronomy 1–11*, 390.

[231] Tigay, *Deuteronomy*, 92

tion from 8:3 reveals he realizes the kind of test he is undergoing, and he indicates the wrongness of seeking to secure by his own means the food he needs because his fundamental commitment and reliance is upon God. Jesus' response indicates he accepts his hunger as God's will.[232] Testing in the context of Deuteronomy 8 and this first test of Jesus is best summarized by Weinfeld when he writes, "by causing deprivation and lack of food, God tests man to see whether he really puts his trust in him."[233]

In contradistinction to the title Son of God used by the Tempter, Jesus' insists upon his humanity as ὁ ἄνθρωπος.[234] Jesus presents his standpoint as a human, required to obey the words of God as an Israelite. This emphasis upon Jesus' humanity also has broader implications for understanding all of the temptations. Each of the verses Jesus cites concerns God's call to his "son" Israel, as depicted in Deuteronomy. Jesus answers as one among them, as he had already exemplified when he submitted himself to John's baptism. This further complicates a strictly messianic interpretation in that Jesus' replies give no indication that his temptations are any different from those common to an Israelite.[235]

Exodus 16

A distinctive background to Deuteronomy 8:1–6 is the experience of Israel depicted in Exodus 16:1–36.[236] As the people continue their journey in the wilderness, as depicted in Exodus, they grumble against Moses and Aaron because they are hungry and have no prospect for food in the wilderness. The Lord responds to Moses that he will rain bread from heaven for them, which serves as a test as to whether they will follow his law or not. Especially evident for observing the connection between these texts is how Deuteronomy 8:2b–3 depends upon the account of Israel's manna experience in Exodus 16:4, with focus on the bread and the test involved. The reference back to the event is unmistakable. Bread (בֿחם/ἄρτος) is referenced in both texts (Exod 16:4, 32; Deut 8:3).[237] There is also a similar use of prove/test in Exodus 16:4 (πειράσω) and Deuteronomy 8:2 (ἐκπειράσῃ). Use of a testing theme in both verses indicates an important link that Deuteronomy uses to reference back to the manna episode. The fundamental concern in Exodus was Israel's dependence upon God alone for the provi-

---

[232] France, *Matthew* (NICNT), 131.

[233] Weinfeld, *Deuteronomy 1–11*, 389.

[234] Boring, "Matthew," 164, notes how Jesus insists on his humanity by juxtaposing human being to the devil's Son of God.

[235] Kynes, *Christology of Solidarity*, 32–33.

[236] Nelson, *Deuteronomy*, 111.

[237] Weinfeld, *Deuteronomy 1–11*, 388–389, notes "the manna, though coming from heaven, is called 'bread' (see Exod 16:2, 4, 32; Ps 105: 40; Neh 9:15)."

sion of their needs, something that Deuteronomy makes explicit. Sarna helpfully summarizes the episode, which also has clear correspondence with Jesus' test, when he writes, "God intentionally subjects Israel to hunger in order to demonstrate and inculcate the lesson of their absolute dependence upon him for sustenance."[238] Jesus recapitulates Israel's test in regard to absolute dependence upon God.[239]

Does Jesus' Test Differ From Israel's?

It is important to inquire whether this test is different from Israel's, in that Israel did not have the power to turn stones to bread. Hagner concludes it is indeed different because they had no power to turn stones to bread,[240] although he does accept some parallels with Israel. However, given the multitude of other parallels, especially giving due weight to the Deuteronomy quotations, one would be justified considering the test as basically similar in the setting of hunger and hardship. The fundamental issue, as indicated by Jesus' quotation, is whether he will depend upon God for nourishment. Both Israel and Jesus are put in a situation of hunger and the test is whether they will obey in privation or disobey with selfishness and self-sufficiency. Israel faces a lack of food and demands food from God, and thereby they express their essential lack of trust in God. Jesus faces a lack of food and the suggestion is presented that he demand bread.[241] Jesus' miraculous power is displayed later in the Gospel, but this power is understood to be only possible as he is empowered to do so (12:28). Jesus is faced with the same type of situation of hunger that Israel experienced, the possibility of death as a result of not receiving nourishment, and the same test of his relationship with and dependence upon God. Kynes rightly nuances the situation when he claims, "The devil is tempting Jesus to misuse, not his divine *powers*, but his *relationship* with his Father by failing to respond to his Father's love with trust."[242] Therefore, the first test should be understood as a recapitulation of Israel's wilderness test obeying a command that all Israel was expected to obey as the son of God.

---

[238] Sarna, *Exodus*, 86.

[239] Another possible text in the background is Psalm 78:18 where Israel is depicted as testing God "in their heart by demanding the food they craved." Although it is Israel testing God, their demand for food clearly references the manna episode as seen in verses 19–31. The temptation that the temper proposes resembles this situation in that Jesus is tempted to crave and demand bread.

[240] Hagner, *Matthew 1–13*, 65.

[241] Is Jesus to merely command that the stones become bread or is he to demand that they become bread, something God must do for him? Nolland, *Matthew*, 163, has also noticed this and likewise leaves it an open question.

[242] Kynes, *Christology of Solidarity*, 33, where he also notes a parallel with Wisdom 16:26.

A Messianic Temptation?

A brief discussion regarding messianic temptation is relevant because the central argument of this section is that Jesus recapitulates Israel's history, which precludes the temptation from being primarily focused on his messianic status. Many scholars have considered this a messianic temptation. However, this temptation to do a miracle cannot really prove his messiahship, because there is no one around to observe.[243] Jesus is alone, and he is thus the only one hungry.[244] This lack of a crowd present to observe Jesus proves true for all three temptations. Bultmann strongly emphasized that the temptations are not messianic, especially because nothing regarding Jesus' messianic role appears in the text.[245] Indeed, as Schniewind has noted, Jesus' answer to the temptation is not messianic.[246]

Donaldson best summarizes an understanding of the temptations that coincides and agrees with some of the conclusions of this study, as

> an attempt to induce Jesus to be unfaithful to a pattern of Sonship conceived in terms of the relationship between ideal Israel and the divine Father. It is a temptation away from Sonship, rather than towards any specific pattern of messianism. Jesus was called to live out in his own experience the Sonship that was to have characterized Israel – a relationship with God which involves dependence on him for the provision of needs, trust in his presence without the need for demonstration, and acceptance of sovereignty only on his terms.[247]

Jesus is tempted to wrongly utilize his abilities by acting on his own beyond the will of God.[248] The challenge concerns the Son doing for himself what God had done for Israel in the desert when they were hungry,[249] or at least demanding that it be done for him. The temptations therefore are not primarily focused upon his messianic status but involve the testing of his obedient relationship to God as the Son.[250]

---

[243] Beare, *Matthew*, 110.

[244] Moberly, *Bible, Theology, and Faith*, 201: "it is Jesus' own needs that area at stake; it is not a matter of providing food for others."

[245] Bultmann, *History of the Synoptic Tradition*, 254–257; cf. Luz, *Matthew 1–7* (1989), 185–186: "This means that the rejection of false hopes or conceptions, Jewish or Christian, is in my opinion not the main concern of the pericope. It is not possible to construct a unitary background against which our story polemicizes." It should be noted that later Bultmann allowed some messianic elements in *Theology of the New Testament*, 26–27.

[246] Schniewind, *Matthäus*, 30; cf. Bonnard, *Matthieu*, 42.

[247] Nevertheless, Donaldson, *Jesus on the Mountain*, 91, still wants to allow room for some messianic overtones. Based on the results of the present study, the messianic overtones are difficult to quantify and clearly define. Further careful work is needed that takes into account all the complexities.

[248] Davies and Allison, *Matthew*, 1.361–362.

[249] Garland, *Matthew*, 39.

[250] Cf. Kynes, *Christology of Solidarity*, 33.

4.5.8 The Second Test

The setting for the second test is the temple, although the broader wilderness setting, as an overall echo of Israel's experience indicated by the importance of Deuteronomy 8, remains in view throughout the entire narrative. Jesus is in the desert at verse 1, implicitly remains in the desert through and until verse 11 when he is cared for by angels, and then he leaves the desert to return to Galilee in verse 12. Thus, at a broader level, the wilderness setting continues and within that setting the remaining two temptations take place. Following the scriptural reply of Jesus to the first temptation, the devil proceeds to take (παραλαμβάνει)[251] Jesus to the Holy City and places him at the pinnacle of the temple (τὸ πτερύγιον τοῦ ἱεροῦ).[252] The second test describes the devil as enticing Jesus, since he is the Son of God, to cast himself down from the pinnacle of the temple because the angels will come to his aid and miraculously rescue him from harm. Jesus had rebutted the tempter's first temptation with a forceful quotation from scripture, and thus the devil undertakes his second temptation also quoting from scripture as a justification for the temple demonstration. Implied in the devil's response to Jesus' scriptural answer to the tempter's first temptation is a test of Jesus' loyalty to the scriptures: If you truly live by every word that proceeds from God's mouth then you will heed his promise in Psalm 91.[253]

The temptation directly deals with Jesus' trust and obedience, made obvious through the context of Psalm 91, of which the devil quotes two parts. The temptation parallels the experience of Israel in the wilderness, which is seen in the context of Jesus' reply when he quotes again from Deuteronomy. The broader point made in regard to the devil's implicit response to Jesus' previous answer from scripture is also very important. Jesus has stated that he lives by every word that comes from the mouth of God and the devil's second temptation connects with and builds upon Jesus' scriptural response. To fully understand the temptation it is important to examine both of the scriptural texts that are explicitly used: Psalm 91:11 and Deuteronomy 6:16, as well as the contexts of these verses. After the use of these texts has been demonstrated, as well as an examination of Exodus 17,

---

[251] Nolland, *Matthew*, 164–165, points out a parallelism between Joseph's protecting transport in 2:14 and 21 (παρέλαβεν) of Jesus and the devil's enticing transports in 4:5 and 8 (παραλαμβάνει).

[252] Moberly, *The Bible, Theology, and Faith*, 202, claims that "the symbolism of placement in 'the holy city' and the temple is that this is the place where God is specially present, the place above all others where one can be confident that God will be encountered and will not let his promises fail."

[253] Davies and Allison, *Matthew*, 1.365. Cf. Moberly, *The Bible, Theology, and Faith*, 202, asserts concerning the devil's use of scripture, "it is the plain meaning of scripture with which Jesus has to wrestle."

a clearer answer as to how this temptation recapitulates Israel's experience can be shown.

Psalm 91

Responding to Jesus' scriptural response, the devil says, 'since you are the Son of God, throw yourself down' and then he proceeds to also quote from scripture. To strengthen this suggestion that Jesus follow his advice, the devil even prefaces his quotation by repeating the same γέγραπται that Jesus had earlier used in verse 4, and then the devil quotes from Psalm 91:11–12. The broader context of this psalm speaks about the security of the person who trusts in Yahweh throughout the circumstances of life with some connections to the wilderness traditions.[254] This security promises protection from outward dangers (91:3, 5–8, 10, 12–13) as well as security in the person's endeavors (91:11–12).[255] The promise of the psalm is personalized in that throughout the psalm the second person singular is used.[256] This makes the devil's quotation even more apropos in regard to Jesus' situation individually.

Textually the quotation matches exactly the LXX wording of Psalm 91 (90): 11–12.

ὅτι τοῖς ἀγγέλοις αὐτοῦ ἐντελεῖται περὶ σοῦ [τοῦ διαφυλάξαι σε ἐν πάσαις ταῖς ὁδοῖς σου] ἐπὶ χειρῶν ἀροῦσίν σε μήποτε προσκόψῃς πρὸς λίθον τὸν πόδα σου.[257]

The quotation as narrated through the devil's temptation omits what has been bracketed above: to guard you in all your ways (τοῦ διαφυλάξαι σε ἐν πάσαις ταῖς ὁδοῖς σου), and consequently connects the first and second phrases of the scriptural quotations with καί.[258] Is this omission significant? The promise of guarding all your ways does not directly relate to the devil's suggestion that Jesus throw himself off the pinnacle of the temple, hence it might appear that the omission is insignificant because the devil only includes what is important for his temptation. However, this completely overlooks the glaring difference between the promise of guarding all the ways of the one who trusts the Lord and the suggestion to jump of the pinnacle. Taylor has noted this significance and states that "the omis-

---

[254] Stuhlmueller, "Psalms," 429–430.

[255] Gerhardsson, *Testing of God's Son*, 59, has suggested that the use of πτερύγιον in verse 5 was deliberately chosen as an allusion to the use of πτέρυγας in Psalm 91:4.

[256] This is true in both the MT and LXX.

[257] The Nestle-Aland text begins the italicized quotation with Τοῖς ἀγγέλοις, but the quotation should probably include the ὅτι which is part of the quotation from Psalm 91:11; cf. Meyer, *Matthew*, 97; McNeile, *Matthew*, 40.

[258] Nestle-Aland correctly observes this connective καί as the devil's speech and does not italicize it as part of the Psalm quotation.

sion is a part of the temptation, thus making the promise to apply to extraordinary circumstances only, rather than to the usual events of everyday living."[259] Indeed, the promise as utilized by the devil completely contradicts what the text actually states, i.e., the psalm promises the broader security of the person that trusts the Lord in the midst of life's experiences and it never advises a specific risky action such as putting oneself in the midst of a life-threatening danger. VanGemeren has noted an important structural arrangement when he states, "the promises of these verses (11–13) are conditioned on an appropriate response to v. 9."[260] Thus, true obedience to the advice of the psalm would radically preclude such a fundamentally unfaithful, risky move.

Although many scholars do regard the omission as insignificant,[261] in light of the context of the psalm as it relates to Jesus' situation on the pinnacle of the temple, and what the devil directly tempts Jesus to do, it does appear to be highly significant.[262] The temptation concerns Jesus faithfulness as Son, and in light of Psalm 91 which encourages trust in the Lord, the devil's temptation to test the Lord's protection is seen to be a clear violation of what the Psalm speaks about. This is further evidenced in Jesus' reply from Deuteronomy 6. Therefore, given the highlighted focus upon scripture, γέγραπται, within the overall narrative, as well as the devil's response to Jesus' scriptural response that he follows *every word* from the mouth of God, the omission is very significant, amounting to an outright distortion in that God's *every word* had not been rightly quoted by the devil. Jesus reply to the devil's temptation capitalizes on this omission and distortion when he replies again from Scripture, revealing his obedience to *every* word from God's mouth. Jesus' reply by quoting from Deuteronomy 6:16, "Again it is written, 'Do not put the Lord your God to the test'," identifies his faithful orientation and obedience of Psalm 91, that in all his ways as a faithful Israelite, he will not test the Lord's protection but trust his protection in the midst of his ways.

The Context of Deuteronomy 6

Jesus' response to the devil, Πάλιν γέγραπται, Οὐκ ἐκπειράσεις κύριον τὸν θεόν σου, once again utilizes words from Deuteronomy in such a way

---

[259] Taylor, "Decision in the Desert," 306–307.

[260] VanGemeren, "Psalms," 601.

[261] Hagner, *Matthew 1–13*, 6; Carson, *Matthew 1–12*, 113; Moberly, *Bible, Theology, and Faith*, 202, says the omitted words "make no difference to the sense."

[262] Gundry, *Matthew*, 57, rightly notes the significance when he states, "The deliberate throwing of oneself from a high perch does not correspond to accidental stumbling over a stone on one's path (as in the psalm)." Cf. Tasker, *Matthew*, 53–54; Carter, *Matthew and Margins*, 109.

as to make evident the action that the devil proposes to be illegitimate for an obedient Israelite. This obedience is best understood through an examination of Deuteronomy 6:16 and the broader scriptural and historical context. The immediate context within Deuteronomy is God communicating through Moses to his son Israel that they be careful to only worship and serve him. The quotation of Deuteronomy 6:16 as it appears in Matthew's Gospel matches exactly the second person singular wording of the LXX: οὐκ ἐκπειράσεις κύριον τὸν θεόν σου. The Hebrew text has second person plural: לא תנסו את־יהוה אלהיכם. The use of the second person singular closer matches the individual focus upon Jesus alone.[263] Matthew's use of the singular quotation from Jesus' lips makes Jesus obedient to the words of God addressed directly to the individual Israelite, again highlighting the faithfulness of Jesus, ὁ ἄνθρωπος, to every word from the mouth of God in contrast to the distortion of God's words by the devil.

It is important to note all of Deuteronomy 6:16,

לא תנסו את־יהוה אלהיכם כאשר נסיתם במסה

In the Hebrew text, God commands Israel, "Do not test (pl) the Lord your (pl) God, as you (pl) tested at Massah." As noted above, the plural is consistently used throughout. The verse is directed to the entire Israelite community, commanding them not to test the Lord as they had done at Massah, which is an event narrated in Exodus 17:1–7. Massah, a name that means test, was the name given to the place where Israel had tested the Lord when they quarreled and demanded water, testing the Lord.[264] The LXX is: οὐκ ἐκπειράσεις κύριον τὸν θεόν σου ὃν τρόπον ἐξεπειράσασθε ἐν τῷ Πει ρασμῷ. In the Greek text, God commands Israel, "Do not test (sg) the Lord your (sg) God as you tested (pl) in the Testing." The singular use has been noted above, but the second half of the verse is in plural form as it recounts Israel's demand for water in Exodus 17. Instead of retaining the name Massah, the LXX translates the meaning.

Attention to the detail of wording is important, because for Matthew's Jesus, *every* word from God's mouth is to be followed, as Jesus has explicitly stated.[265] Given the context of the quotation from Deuteronomy 6:16

---

[263] Rightly noted by Gundry, *Matthew*, 57. However, Hagner, *Matthew 1–13*, 67, thinks the difference between the MT plural and LXX singular is insignificant.

[264] Nelson, *Deuteronomy*, 93, observes, "Verse 16 is the reverse of the way the testing motif is used in 8:2, 16, where it is Yahweh who initiates the test." Similarly, for Matthew the first temptation involves Jesus being tested by God, whereas the second temptation Jesus is tempted to test God. Cf. Weinfeld, *Deuteronomy 1–11*, 396; Carter, *Matthew and Margins*, 107.

[265] A reminder of Luke 4:4 is appropriate, where it is observed that ἀλλ' ἐπὶ παντὶ ῥήματι ἐκπορευομένῳ διὰ στόματος θεοῦ only appears in Matthew. For Matthew's narra-

and the direct use of the incident of Israel at Massah as an example of how not to test the Lord, an examination of Exodus 17 is important for understanding the temptation of Jesus and how he recapitulates Israel's history. Exodus 17:1–7 is important because Jesus' quotation from Deuteronomy 6:16 directly refers to this particular incident from Israel's time in the wilderness. Deuteronomy 6:16 and Exodus 17:1–7 are also important in that they relate directly to the type of faithfulness exhibited by one who obeys Psalm 91, avoiding the distortion and test suggested by the devil's illegitimate use of Psalm 91.

Exodus 17

Exodus 17:1–7 relates an incident[266] that occurs some time after the event narrated in chapter 16 involving God's provision of manna which has been dealt with above in the first temptation of Jesus. Israel continued their journey through the wilderness and they come to Rephidim, which had no water for them to drink. Their response is to quarrel with Moses, demanding he give them water to drink. Moses answers, "Why do you quarrel with me? Why do you test (מה־תנסון את־יהוה /τί πειράζετε κύριον) the Lord?" (v. 2). The people continue to complain after Moses' warning that they were testing the Lord, and they ask why he has brought them out of Egypt to die of thirst. Moses cries out to the Lord and the Lord tells Moses to strike the rock and water will come out for the people to drink. Moses obeys and the narrative concludes with a theological summary of the event (17:7):[267]

ויקרא שם המקום מסה
ומריבה
על־ריב בני ישראל
ועל נסתם את־יהוה
לאמר היש יהוה בקרבנו אם־אין:

καὶ ἐπωνόμασεν τὸ ὄνομα τοῦ τόπου ἐκείνου
πειρασμὸς
καὶ λοιδόρησις
διὰ τὴν λοιδορίαν τῶν υἱῶν Ισραηλ
καὶ διὰ τὸ πειράζειν κύριον
λέγοντας εἰ ἔστιν κύριος ἐν ἡμῖν ἢ οὔ

"He (Moses) called the name of the place Massah and Meribah, because of the quarrel of the sons of Israel and because they tested the Lord, saying, 'Is the Lord among us, or not?'." Israel faced the difficult situation of

---

tive, every word from God's mouth is an important part of understanding his narrative and the obedience of Jesus exhibited throughout (cf. 5:17–19).

[266] The similar event recounted in Numbers 20:2–13 is less useful for helping understand the second temptation.

[267] There is a chiastic arrangement of this verse that can easily be seen by the arrangement above.

needing water, and instead of trusting the Lord to provide and protect them, they doubted and demanded from God in the form of a test the water they needed. "Is the Lord among us or not?," encapsulates this test that essentially proceeds from a heart of doubt and not a heart of trust (cf. Ps 95:7b–11). The Lord had promised his provision at various times prior to this incident, indeed miraculously demonstrated it through their deliverance from Egypt following the plagues, crossing the Sea, and the provision of manna. However, Israel doubted in the midst of a hard and dangerous situation, and they demanded a proof of God's presence and protection with the test that he perform a miracle of providing water. Jesus' situation mirrors this episode, as he recapitulates Israel's history as they had journeyed in the wilderness. Where Israel faced the temptation to doubt and test God, the devil comes to tempt Jesus with the same type temptation. The voice from heaven following Jesus' baptism had assured Jesus of who he was and of God's approval, but the devil tempts Jesus to doubt and test the Lord to perform a miracle for him since he is the Son of God. Consequently, the relation between Israel and Jesus can be observed in the similarity of the son testing God, with Jesus recapitulating this temptation experience.

Jesus' steadfast refusal to test the Lord reveals he had heeded the warning of Deuteronomy 6:16, which was a reflection upon the experience of Israel in Exodus 17, as well as truly heeding the intent of Psalm 91 that God protects the faithful.[268] Recapitulating Israel's history in the wilderness where they faced a temptation to doubt and test the Lord, Jesus faces the same type temptation but remains faithful where they had failed, which is explicitly the focus of the quotation of Deuteronomy 6:16 where they are warned not to test the Lord as they earlier had done. Therefore, Jesus recapitulated Israel's history in regard to the experience and test they had faced in Exodus 17, but his recapitulation exhibits obedience to Israel's scriptural history as delineated from Deuteronomy 6.

A Messianic Temptation?

As with the previous temptation, it is not at all obvious that this is a messianic temptation. However, a few scholars have argued that this is indeed a messianic temptation, because Jesus is tempted to show that he is the Son of God by making a spectacular demonstration at the temple complex.[269]

---

[268] See Luz, *Matthew 1–7* (2007), 152–153 for perceptive comments on how the 2nd temptation looks ahead to later scenes in Matthew.

[269] Pokorny, "The Temptation Stories and Their Intention," 125: *Schauwunder*. Cf. Gundry, *Matthew*, 56; Boring, "Matthew," 164, recognizes that spectators are not mentioned, nevertheless he still opts for Jesus demonstrating he is the Son of God by a spectacular demonstration, 164. Hill, *Matthew*, 101, thinks the evangelist understood Psalm

However, there are several major problems with this viewpoint. No spectators are ever mentioned.[270] With no public mentioned as present, a miraculous demonstration would be useless for one seeking to establish messianic
recognition among the masses. Indeed the devil makes no appeal whatsoever in this regard, as it would certainly add validity and persuasion to his
suggestion. Based on these points, the viewpoint that this concerns a messianic temptation is problematic. In addition, there appears to be no text,
tradition, or expectation that advances the idea that messiah would or
should undertake a demonstration such as casting himself off the temple to
be rescued by angels.[271] In fact, the context of Psalm 91 speaks generally
of any faithful Israelite and not specifically of a messianic demonstration.[272] The only possible messianic temptation might be in regard to Jesus' orientation for his future ministry: succumbing to this type of demonstration would thereby set a pattern for how he might achieve success.
Nevertheless, this still does not satisfy a straightforward reading of this
text when there is no specific appeal made to his future ministry as one of
miraculous demonstrations for the public's approval of his messianic
status. Nowhere does the devil state how Jesus might undertake his ministry through miraculous demonstrations. One should therefore conclude that
primarily this is not a messianic temptation because the text itself says
nothing in this regard that would indicate the temptation directly deals with
this.[273]

4.5.9 The Third Test

The setting for the narration of the third test is an unidentified very high
mountain,[274] where Jesus is taken by the devil for the third temptation. The
overall wilderness setting should not be forgotten as emphasized above.
From this very high mountain, Jesus is shown all the kingdoms of the
world and their splendor. Then the devil challenges Jesus that all those
kingdoms and splendor will be given to him "if you will fall down and
worship me."[275] This third temptation reveals a far more brazen attempt

---

91 as prophecy of the Messiah, thus the miraculous would vindicate Jesus' messianic
status.

[270] Luz, *Matthew 1–7* (2007), 152, briefly states that "in a temptation scene the public
is not appropriate, for stylistic reasons," with no further explanation as to why.

[271] Davies and Allison, *Matthew*, 1.366–367.

[272] Beare, *Matthew*, 110.

[273] Ridderbos, *Matthew*, 69.

[274] Davies and Allison, *Matthew*, 1.369, consider this a redactional addition, along
with the other mountain scenes (5:1; 8:1; 15:29; 28:16). Cf. Donaldson, *Jesus on the
Mountain*, especially focuses upon this aspect of Matthean theology.

[275] In the Old Testament, high places frequently involve idolatry (Lev 26:30; 2 Kgs
12:3; 2 Chr 34:3; Ezek 6:3–6, 13).

than the previous two temptations on Satan's part to entice Jesus to sin with an outright suggestion to commit idolatry. Presumably in light of that brazenness, Jesus therefore responds with a rebuke, Ὕπαγε, Σατανᾶ,[276] commanding Satan to leave, and then again he quotes from Deuteronomy, "Worship the Lord your God and serve only him" (Deut 6:13; 10:20).

Scriptural Background to the Third Test

Some scholars have observed a Mosaic motif particularly with this temptation given some of the possible similarities.[277] In Deuteronomy, Moses recalls going to the top of Pisgah where he looks in all directions and sees the promised land (3:27). Deuteronomy 34:1–4 contains the narrative of Moses seeing the promised land just before his death. He goes up to Mount Nebo, to the top of Pisgah, and the Lord shows him the whole land (ἔδειξεν αὐτῷ κύριος πᾶσαν τὴν γῆν); somewhat similar to the depiction narrated in Matthew 4:8, δείκνυσιν αὐτῷ πάσας τὰς βασιλείας τοῦ κόσμου. The Lord reminds Moses of his past promise of this land to Abraham, Isaac, and Jacob, that he would give it to their descendants (τῷ σπέρματι ὑμῶν δώσω αὐτήν); vaguely similar to the promise of Satan to Jesus, Ταῦτά σοι πάντα δώσω. However, Moses is not allowed to enter and he dies there in the land of Moab.

Beyond a few common aspects, such as a mountain, viewing the land, a promise of possession, these similarities are insufficient parallels for understanding the third test of Jesus in Matthew 4. Moses is merely shown the land, which was a promised possession to Israel and not just Moses. In addition, Moses faces no test whatsoever at the mountain. Indeed, it would have to be admitted that he had already failed his test as evidenced in the Lord's remarks to him regarding his inability to enter the land due to his previous failure in the wilderness (Num 27:12–14; Deut 32:48–52). The third test then should not be interpreted with a Mosaic background, much less as Mosaic typology.[278]

In addition to Moses, there have been a few other suggestions regarding the background for this test.[279] Abraham viewed the land from a mountain and the Lord promises to give it to him and his offspring (Gen 13:3–4, 14–18).[280] In Genesis 22, Abraham goes to a mountain and is tested by God,

---

[276] A similar rebuke is given to Peter in Matthew 16:23, Ὕπαγε ὀπίσω μου, Σατανᾶ.

[277] Allison, *New Moses*, 169–172; Cf. Hill, *Matthew*, 101.

[278] Cf. Donaldson, *Jesus on the Mountain*, 93; Nolland, *Matthew*, 166, doubts the links with Moses.

[279] Donaldson's study surveys and discusses many of these in greater detail than can be undertaken here.

[280] Cf. Jubilees 13:20–21. In 1QapGen 21:8–22 there is an expansion upon this, depicted as a vision Abraham receives where he goes up to the heights of Hazor.

where he obeys and is promised many descendants. Nevertheless, the parallels with Abraham are even weaker than with Moses.

Donaldson is convinced that the background to this mountain scene, as with the other mountain scenes in Matthew, is Mount Zion. By comparing Matthew's testing narrative with Psalm 2:6–8, an eschatological Zion theology is detected. His conclusion regarding this pericope, "the dominant feature in the background to the mountain setting of the third temptation is Mount Zion."[281] However, Donaldson has satisfied few scholars of this thesis.[282] The parallels he offers are not strong enough to bear the weight of his thesis for this pericope. While Donaldson's generalizations regarding the theology of Matthew are illuminating and constructive, the demand for Zion as the dominant feature of Matthean mountain theology is an over-reading of the evidence. The focus of Jesus as Israel remains throughout the entire pericope and should be understood as the principal motif in the third test as well.

Moberly has suggested a scriptural background where "there are specific resonances to a picture of universal dominion" in various texts such as Psalm 2:7–8; Genesis 22:17; 27:29; Numbers 23–24; Isaiah 45:14–25; 49:22–26; and Daniel 7. This appears to provide a better background for understanding the third temptation in terms of what Jesus is offered. Moberly concludes, "since God exercises his power and authority through those who are called by him to serve him, that is, Israel as a whole and Israel's human representative (king, son of man) in particular, then this expectation naturally devolves on Jesus as Son."[283] This provides a beneficial outlook for understanding Jesus' third test and how it relates to Israel's history. The following material will seek to make manifest this viewpoint by close attention to Jesus' scriptural reply to the devil's suggestion.

Jesus' Scriptural Response

As observed with the previous two tests, the primary indicator for understanding this test is the scriptural quotation Jesus utilizes against Satan, a text once again from Deuteronomy, which had also been spoken to Israel. As with the other two quotations, Jesus precedes the quotation from Deuteronomy 6:13 with γέγραπται. Most scholars focus sole attention upon the quotation from Deuteronomy 6:13, but as will be seen below, Deuteronomy 10:20 matches the wording and is particularly significant for further understanding this temptation and how Jesus recapitulates Israel's history at this point in the narrative. It is critically important to examine the context of Deuteronomy 6 and 10 for understanding this third test.

---

[281] *Ibid.*, 95.

[282] Davies, "The Jewish Sources of Matthew's Messianism," 504.

[283] Moberly, *Bible, Theology, and Faith*, 204.

Deuteronomy 6:13 (10:20) and the Context

Jesus quotes this text in response to Satan's suggestion that he fall down and worship him to gain all the kingdoms of the world, which obviously amounts to outright idolatry. Essential to understanding the third test is an analysis of the context of this quotation from Deuteronomy 6:13, as well as its repetition in 10:20. Deuteronomy 6:4 contains the *Shema*, commanding Israel to hear that the Lord is one and thus they are to love him completely by keeping his words. The pericope specifically focuses upon Israel's time in the land and their responsibilities before the Lord there. Verses 10–12 remind Israel that when they are in the land God promised, filled with the blessings, they must not forget the Lord who redeemed them from Egypt. Then verse 13 commands "Fear (only) the Lord your God and serve/worship him (alone)."

את־יהוה אלהיך תירא ואתו תעבד ובשמו תשבע

κύριον τὸν θεόν σου φοβηθήσῃ καὶ αὐτῷ λατρεύσεις [καὶ πρὸς αὐτὸν κολληθήσῃ]²⁸⁴
καὶ τῷ ὀνόματι αὐτοῦ ὀμῆ

Verse 14 goes in to warn Israel not to follow other gods. This verse is especially important for understanding the prior verse, in that idolatry would be a particularly egregious instance of failing to fear and only serve the Lord.²⁸⁵ Emphasis upon obedience and sole devotion to the Lord is the primary focus of this section in Deuteronomy.

In addition to this focus upon Deuteronomy 6:13, an analysis of the context of Deuteronomy 10:20 is also important, as will become apparent below. In Chapter 9 Moses is depicted as reminding Israel of the consequences of rebelling against God. To urge obedience and allegiance to God alone, Moses recalls the golden calf incident (Exod 32), which is used as a noteworthy illustration of Israel's rebelliousness (Deut 9:7–21, 25–10:5). That appalling episode of idolatry served as a poignant reminder of how easy it was for Israel to fail in the most fundamental command of God. Deuteronomy 10:12–22 concludes that section with a call that Israel only fear and serve the Lord. Verse 20 then repeats the command of 6:13.

Jesus' quotation of Deuteronomy in Matthew 4:10 is Κύριον τὸν θεόν σου προσκυνήσεις καὶ αὐτῷ μόνῳ λατρεύσεις.²⁸⁶ The quotation agrees with the LXX and MT except for two differences.²⁸⁷ Often scholars take the addition of μόνῳ as already implied in Deuteronomy 6:13 (10:20). Weinfeld

---

²⁸⁴ The LXX adds this here, whereas at 10:20 the MT and LXX agree in the use of the phrase.

²⁸⁵ Dupont, "L'Arriere-Fond Biblique Du Recit Des Tentations De Jesus," 291.

²⁸⁶ Gundry, *Matthew*, 58, proposes that "Matthew adds γάρ to γέγραπται to make Scripture the reason for refusing the temptation."

²⁸⁷ Luke 4:8 matches Matthew's wording.

states "although the adverb alone is missing, it is implied here, as it stands in opposition to the next statement in verse 14, 'do not follow other gods'."[288] It might be argued that here Jesus adds that emphatic adverb in light of the astounding attempt of Satan to dissuade his complete allegiance to God alone.[289] Moberly suggests that the word "alone" provides a key to the overall temptation, in that Jesus is not tempted to reject God and worship the devil, but instead is tempted to compromise that loyalty to obtain the glory God had promised by an easier means.[290] Jesus' scriptural reply with the addition of 'alone' would then emphasize the exclusive loyalty God deserves and his devotion to maintain the way ahead according to God's plan.

Another significant change is the appearance of προσκυνήσεις instead of the LXX φοβηθήση (MT תירא). Hagner notes how Jesus' use of προσκυνήσεις echoes the devil's words in verse 9.[291] Gundry goes further and considers it an assimilation of the verb "fearing" in Deuteronomy 6:13 to Satan's asking him to worship, although he also states that the meaning is close to fear, reverence, respect.[292] In addition, another possible reason for the use of προσκυνήσεις is the use of the same verb in Exodus 32:8, the golden calf incident. There the Lord tells Moses that the people of Israel, while Moses has been meeting with the Lord on the mountain, have made a calf and worshiped (προσεκυνήκασιν) it. Given this possibility in light of the context of the quotation from Deuteronomy 6:13 and 10:20, a few observations concerning Exodus 32 are necessary. Indeed, Exodus 32 is the quintessential precedent that exemplifies what Deuteronomy 6:13 had warned against. Deuteronomy 6:14 goes on to specifically warn Israel not to follow other gods. Later in Deuteronomy, the Exodus 32 event is explicitly referenced in 9:7–21, 25–10:5, concluding with a repetition of 6:13 in 10:20. The resemblances between the Israel event of Exodus 32 and the Jesus event in the third test are not pedantically exact, but given the context of the quotation that Jesus speaks to Satan, the parallel is sufficiently close enough to warrant attention. The wider focus of Jesus as Israel in the narrative helps confirm this viewpoint. Further evidence for viewing Exodus 32 as relevant background will be discussed below.

Exodus 32

The setting for the golden calf incident is at the bottom of Mount Sinai. The people remained at the base of the mountain while Moses had gone up

---

[288] Weinfeld, *Deuteronomy 1–11*, 336. Cf. Hagner, *Matthew 1–13*, 69.

[289] McNeile, *Matthew*, 42.

[290] Moberly, *Bible, Theology, and Faith*, 204.

[291] Hagner, *Matthew 1–13*, 69. Cf. McNeile, *Matthew*, 42; Gundry, *Matthew*, 58.

[292] Gundry, *Matthew*, 58, where he also notes 1 Samuel 7:3.

to receive the Law from the Lord. Due to the long absence of Moses, which lasted forty days and nights, the people grew restless. They ask Aaron to make gods who will go before them, presumably to provide for their needs and lead them in their journey through the desert. A golden calf is formed and they pronounce these as their gods, ascribing their deliverance from Egypt to them.[293] The Lord informs Moses of this terrible scene, revealing that not only had they made an image of a calf but they had worshiped (προσκεκυνήκασιν) it as their god (32:8). The swiftness of their rebellion in turning from the Lord, having so recently pledged their obedience (24:7), and then breaking the fundamental command of sole allegiance to God, strikes an ominous tone in the scriptural story about Israel.[294] As shown above, it is the classic illustration used by Deuteronomy 9 for warning against rebellion and idolatry.

This connection with Exodus 32 through the quotation from Deuteronomy 6:13; 10:20 helps toward understanding Jesus' recapitulation of Israel in this test. The resemblance is not exact, but analysis of the context of Deuteronomy 6:13 and 10:20, and how it reminds Israel of the Exodus 32 experience, helps tilt toward observing Jesus' test likewise resembling this event, particularly the outright idolatry. Jesus is tempted at a mountain to worship another god, just as Israel had been tempted at the mountain. However, whereas Israel failed, worshiping another god when they sacrificed to the golden calf to gain the promise, Jesus resisted the temptation and pronounced through his scriptural quotation his allegiance to God alone to gain what had been promised. This test recapitulates Israel history at the mountain, their temptation to worship another god to gain what was promised by God. The test, while recapitulating Israel's history reverses the outcome, in that Jesus fulfills the law of God by remaining obedient to God alone. The use by Jesus of Deuteronomy highlights his obedient hearing of that text, an obedience that had been demanded of Israel, and Jesus' quotations from Deuteronomy reveal that he had heard and learned from Israel's failures.

A Messianic Temptation?

The above observations made in regard to problems with a messianic interpretation to Jesus' testing continue to be relevant here. Again, there are no spectators mentioned. It is indicated that Jesus will gain all the kingdoms of the world and their glory if he worships the devil, a reality that

---

[293] Childs, *Exodus*, 576, notes that in several later Jewish works Satan tricked Israel to think Moses was dead and tricked them to shape a calf (*Ps-Jon, Exod Rabbah* 41:7, Rashi).

[294] Fretheim, *Exodus*, 279, comments regarding Exodus 32–34 that it is "likely these chapters function as a fall story for Israel."

seems unlikely that the devil can legitimately offer. This alone would be the closest indication of messianic interpretation in that Jesus is tempted to gain these kingdoms. The possibility of this interpretation is still subsumed under the prevailing narratival portrayal of Jesus as the recapitulation of Israel. Brief hints are nevertheless offered as to how Jesus proceeds upon his course and ministry, as an obedient Israelite focused upon fulfilling all righteousness (3:15). The central focus of the temptations is Jesus' active recapitulation of Israel's history.

4.5.10 Divine Approval

The immediate response to Jesus' rebuke and command that Satan leave is that he does indeed leave Jesus (Τότε ἀφίησιν αὐτὸν ὁ διάβολος).[295] Upon his departure, angels come to serve Jesus, presumably in the wilderness (4:1). The appearance of angels is introduced with the emphatic, ἰδού, last used in 3:17, where a divine response of approval had been proclaimed at Jesus' baptism. Here in response to Jesus' obedience in resisting Satan's temptations, another divine response of approval occurs. The angels' appearance reveals God's explicit approval to Jesus' test.[296] The Son is once again divinely approved. In fact, Jesus actually receives all that he had earlier resisted in the three temptations.[297] He had refused to take food in an illegitimate way, but here he receives the angels' service, which certainly included food.[298] Israel, God's son, had been tested and provided for in the wilderness (Exodus 16), and now Jesus, God's Son, recapitulates Israel's history, and is tested and provided for in the wilderness. Psalm 78:25 speaks of Israel eating the bread of angels through God's provision of bread for them in the wilderness.[299] Israel in the wilderness lacked water and was tempted to "test God" with a demand that he deliver them, and he provides the water they need with a demonstration of his deliverance. Jesus is tempted to test God with a demonstration of his deliverance, but he refuses to cast himself off the temple so that angels would come and deliver him. Then he receives the angels' help, God caring for his faithful Son through angels. Israel had been tempted to worship other gods at the mountain to gain the blessings they wanted. Jesus refused Satan's idolatrous offer of the kingdoms of the world, maintaining his sole allegiance to God and his will. His obedience to God enables him to exact an authority over

---

[295] As noted above, the wording resembles 3:15b.

[296] Garland, *Matthew*, 40, states, "their arrival is another token of God's approval of his son."

[297] See *ibid.*, 38, for a possible general chiastic structure of 1–11.

[298] Allison, *New Moses*, 169, where he notes that διηκόνουν is often used in connection with food, 8:15; 25:44; 27:55; Acts 6:2; cf. Elijah (1 Kgs 19:5–8).

[299] Cf. Wisdom 16:20; 2 Esdras 1:19.

Satan when at his command Satan leaves. Later Jesus at the end of the Gospel proclaims on a mountain that all authority in heaven and on earth has been given to him (28:18), a scene that has correlations with 4:8–10.[300]

However, as detailed above, whereas Israel had failed her wilderness tests in Exodus, as referenced in Deuteronomy, Jesus remained faithful throughout his tests, where he utilizes those key Deuteronomy passages in his resistance to his temptations.[301] According to Dodd, Matthew's theological purpose for the testing narrative is "that Jesus won his victory, not simply for himself as an individual, but as the representative of the people of God incorporate in him."[302] Jesus alone has proven himself faithful as Son to the call of God, living completely by the word God had addressed to his Son Israel, recapitulating her scriptural history, however reversing it in an obedient manner (cf. 1:21).

4.5.11 Summary

Moberly offers a helpful perspective on how to receive the resonances of Jesus and the story of Israel in scripture. He cautions a danger of interpreting this primarily as a "typology of the superiority of Jesus (faithful where Israel failed; on greater than Moses)," although he admits this has relevance. Within the context of Matthew's narrative at the outset of Jesus' ministry, "the point may be rather a typology of similarity; that kind of encounter with God which lies at the heart of Israel's story is what is taken up in the story of Jesus."[303] While Jesus certainly recapitulates Israel's history as the Son of God definitively and victoriously, his recapitulation penetrates further through the obedient use and application of scripture as an individual Israelite, ὁ ἄνθρωπος (4:4), affirming the scriptural history of Israel as a continuing authoritative source for the life of those who serve God. What Jesus in Matthew 5:17 makes explicit as a theological formulation, 3:13–4:11 narrates and exemplifies through the recapitulation actions of Jesus.

---

[300] Davies and Allison, *Matthew*, 1.404; Allison, *New Moses*, 171; Luz, *Matthew 1–7* (2007), 153; Moberly, *Bible, Theology, and Faith*, 190.

[301] Davies and Allison, *Matthew*, 1.354, add that "in Matthew's eyes, the victory of 4:1–11 will have been just as much a 'fulfilling of all righteousness' as the submission to John's baptism in chapter 3." In addition, Malina and Rohrbaugh, *Social Science Commentary on the Synoptic Gospels*, 42, add, "Whatever else Matthew tells about Jesus in the rest of his Gospel depends on Jesus' passing this challenge with his honor vindicated."

[302] Dodd, *Founder of Christianity*, 108. Garland, *Matthew*, 40, "Jesus' triumph over the devil settles the question about who can claim to be true Israel, the representative of God's people." Cf. Donaldson, *Jesus on the Mountain*, 92.

[303] Moberly, *Bible, Theology, and Faith*, 200.

4.6 Chapter Conclusions

The primary attention of this chapter has been focused upon explicating how Jesus actively recapitulates Israel's history in Matthew 3:1–4:11, which remains in continuity with the preceding material in Matthew that had begun with a clear orientation upon Israel's history. The first chapter of this study dealt with the genealogy and demonstrated the importance of Israel's history for the Gospel of Matthew, where two components are utilized: a teleological genealogy pointing toward Jesus as the fulfillment of Israel's history and a compressed narrative that recapitulates Israel's history. The second chapter dealt with Jesus' passive recapitulation of Israel's history, with the prominence of the exodus motif in that chapter highlighted and discussed. Matthew 3:1–4:11 builds upon the recapitulation of Israel, with Jesus as an adult. Retaining a continuity of focus from the previous chapters that reveals Jesus' continued connection with Israel's history, Jesus actively recapitulates Israel's history.

It has been shown how this section of Matthew (3:1–4:11) should be interpreted, with Jesus actively recapitulating Israel's exodus and wilderness period. The wilderness testing of Jesus as the Son, which comes prior to his ministry that begins at 4:12 is closely related to Israel's history in the exodus and wilderness events. The connections that this has with Israel's testing in the wilderness are more obvious, but because within Israel's scriptural history the exodus and wilderness events are chronologically related, one should also see Jesus baptism and testing as mirroring this aspect of Israel's history. Saldarini aptly summarizes the standpoint of Matthew when he writes, "The stories of the baptism and temptations recapitulate and reinterpret Israel's experience in reference to Jesus so that Jesus' rejection of the temptations affirms the Deuteronomic covenant and commandments."[304] Israel crosses through the sea and then is tested in the wilderness, prior to and in preparation for their task of taking the land; Jesus is baptized and then he is tested in the wilderness prior to and in preparation for his ministry in the land of Israel.

It was also shown how the narrative exclusively focuses upon Jesus through a narrowing, from all the people, to the leaders, down to Jesus alone. In response to Jesus' baptism, divine approval signals to the reader the role and status of Jesus as Son, Israel recapitulated and embodied. Jesus is then led into the wilderness to be tested as Son, which is also where Israel had been led following her exodus from Egypt. However, Jesus exhibits an obedient Sonship where Israel had failed in the duties of sonship, where again Jesus receives divine approval for his obedient actions.

---

[304] Saldarini, "Matthew," 1011.

Chapter 5

Conclusions

5.1 Summary

The purpose of this study has been to investigate and describe the use of Israel's history in Matthew 1:1–4:11, its viewpoint and theological interpretation of Israel's history, how it is variously portrayed in these chapters, and principally how this interpretation of Israel's history is utilized in the presentation of the story of Jesus Christ in Matthew. The term that was determined the most apt for describing this use of Israel's history is recapitulation. This recapitulation involves repeating and summarizing Israel's history, which is the primary focus of the genealogy, wherein Israel's history is summarized through a highly compressed teleological narrative. Recapitulation is also observed through how Jesus is portrayed as repeating, reliving, and representatively embodying Israel's history in Matthew chapters 2:1–4:11. In Matthew 2, Jesus passively recapitulates Israel's history, and in Matthew 3:1–4:11, Jesus actively recapitulates Israel's history. The recapitulation of Israel in Matthew 1:1–4:11 has therefore been the crucial argument of this work, ascertaining and describing how this recapitulation is communicated in these introductory chapters of the Gospel of Matthew.

Matthew opens with a genealogy of Jesus that introduces the Gospel and orients the hearer and reader to the primary focus of the entire Gospel story, the narration and proclamation of life and teaching of Jesus Christ. The first chapter of this study examined in detail the genealogy, which introduces the reader to Jesus' story by recapitulating Israel's history. Israel's history in Matthew's genealogy is theologically summarized and recapitulated through a highly compressed teleological narrative.

To best understand the genealogy in Matthew, its form and function, an extensive examination of Israel's scriptures, primarily the Old Testament, was conducted. Multilinear and unilinear genealogies are found in various places of the Old Testament. The genealogy in Matthew is primarily unilinear. A particular form of unilinear genealogy was found in Ruth 4:18–22 that led to identifying it as a teleological genealogy. This type of genealogy points toward and ends with a key person as the goal and climax of the genealogy. The teleological genealogy of Ruth 4 that focuses upon David is quoted in Matthew's genealogy, where the focus of the teleological genealogy is oriented upon Jesus Christ as the end and goal. From Matthew's perspective, Jesus Christ is the one toward whom the entire history of Israel points to as the ultimate goal and the climactic fulfillment of that history.

Further research into the genealogies of the Old Testament brought about a greater understanding of genealogies as compressed narratives, especially evidenced in both Genesis and 1 Chronicles. Genealogies were examined to yield narratival insights as well as summarative capabilities. The vast genealogy of 1 Chronicles 1:1–9:1 presents a theological interpretation of Israel's history through a compressed narrative. These insights led toward better identifying the genealogy in Matthew as a highly compressed narrative of Israel's history, where in brief, Israel's history is recapitulated through a teleological genealogy centered upon Jesus Christ that theologically interprets the history of Israel.

Matthew's utilization of names from the Old Testament, drawn primarily from the genealogies in Genesis, Ruth and 1 Chronicles, highlighted many of these individuals as subjects of narrative. Each of the names that Matthew includes was examined and the narratival aspects of the genealogy in regard to the use of these names, many of which were prominent individuals in Israel's scriptural history, were discussed in detail. In addition, the use of the four Old Testament women in the genealogy was discussed because they have figured prominently in many discussions of the genealogy. It was determined that frequently this discussion overlooks their primary purpose for being named in the genealogy. Their inclusion is fully understandable when it is recognized that each woman was named in the genealogical sources as utilized by Matthew. They are also important subjects of narrative elsewhere in the Old Testament, playing a significant role in Israel's history as recounted in the scriptural history. Subsidiary to this primary purpose is the bonus that the Gentile status of especially Rahab and Ruth can contribute to Matthew's Gospel. In addition, the varying 'irregularities' of the genealogy's five women might also contribute to Matthew's purpose as well. Nevertheless, the specific naming of the women in the genealogy of Jesus comes as the initial result of their appearance in the two genealogical sources, which makes their inclusion fully comprehensible. Their role in Israel's history was highlighted in Israel's scriptures because they were important individuals that contributed to that history, and Matthew keeps their names precisely because they were important persons in Israel's story. In addition, Mary's important role in Jesus' birth is also fully comprehensible in this manner as well and serves as corroborative evidence that all five women are named based on their role in Israel's story.

The recapitulation of Israel's history in the genealogy of Jesus affirms Israel's story. From Matthew's perspective, Jesus' story cannot be narrated or understood without retelling Israel's history; therefore, at the very beginning of the Gospel story, Israel's story is retold and recapitulated as an interpretive, theological introduction to Jesus Christ. The story of Jesus is vitally linked to the story of Israel, and his appearance is from Matthew's perspective a climax and fulfillment to that history. The story of Israel that is recapitulated in the genealogy has a clear plot that begins with Abraham, the father of the nation, and follows the rise up to the highpoint of King David. However, that story turns tragically toward disaster, beginning with David himself and follows the list of kings that ultimately end with the exile of Israel in the deportation to Babylon. The story finally turns once again upward from that devastating event toward the completion and climax of Israel's history in the son of David, Jesus the Christ.

The genealogy in Matthew is therefore a theological interpretation of Israel's history, that recapitulates Israel's history through a teleological and narratological genealogy that introduces the story of Jesus in the Gospel of Matthew. The genealogy functions as a compressed retelling and recapitulation of Israel's history. The teleological format of the genealogy also serves a "reverse-legitimating" function, as Israel's history is retold because it is precisely that story that needs repeating and it is that story which is properly concluded in the coming of the Messiah, the goal of Israel's history. Matthew's introduction retells and recapitulates the story of Israel because the story of Jesus cannot be understood without it, nor for Matthew can Israel's story be understood without Jesus. Each will now need to be read in light of one another. For understanding Matthew's Gospel, the two are forever intertwined, enmeshed into one single story of God's people. Matthew's genealogy and the subsequent narrative serve as an affirmation and proclamation of this theological recapitulation of Israel's history. Affirming the importance of Israel's history for Matthew's Gospel, particularly as it is given special prominence appearing at the very beginning of the Gospel, should help toward redressing an imbalance in some studies of Matthew that have overemphasized the negative in regard to Matthew's portrayal of both Israel's past and present history.

The next section of Matthew's Gospel examined was 2:1–23, where it was argued that Jesus passively recapitulates Israel's history. Through repeating and reliving Israel's history in his early movements as a child, with the exodus period of Israel's history as especially prominent, it was determined that Jesus' passive recapitulation of Israel adequately encapsulates the focus of Matthew 2. The background that the exodus contributes to Matthew 2, particularly in terms of plot, characterization, verbal allusions, and themes, as adapted and utilized by Matthew for retelling Jesus' story, was the primary focus of the chapter. The argument centered upon how

Jesus recapitulates Israel's exodus history in Matthew 2, a passive recapitulation of Israel in that Jesus is moved according to the actions of others. Past scholarship on Matthew 2 was shown to have concluded that geography and the fulfillment quotations are the key elements of the chapter.
Both of these elements play a significant role in how Jesus is portrayed as
recapitulating Israel's history.

Broadly, it was observed that Jesus recapitulates the whole of Israel's
scriptural history: the exodus, kingship, and exile. All of these were fundamental events in Israel's history, and they can rightly be observed as almost spanning the entire scriptural history of Israel. This has already been
summarized in a similar manner in 1:17. Jesus passively experiences and
repeats the movement, providence, and tragedy of Israel's history, but he is
dramatically preserved as the deliverer, with both Mosaic and Davidic
overtones, who emerges to redeem an Israel still in exile (1:17, 21).

The strongest motif that dominates the entire narrative of Matthew 2
however is the exodus motif, and the bulk of the chapter was given to examining this viewpoint. This began with detailed attention to the flow and
impact of the entire narrative. To enter the narrative's portrayal and recapitulation of the exodus, it was important to elucidate how the chapter itself unfolds as a narrative. Based on this conception of the entire narrative,
the ways that Matthew 2 utilizes the exodus was discussed and outlined in
five subsections that follow the sequential flow of the narrative. Close
analysis of the text was necessary to observe the use of exodus. Throughout each of the subsections, the exodus motif, particularly how the exodus
is passively recapitulated by Jesus, was dealt with broadly as a background
motif. This was demonstrated in the characterization and plot of the narrative that encompasses the whole of chapter two, and given full attention in
each of the five subsections.

The first section sought to illuminate the exodus background of the narrative, particularly how the plot is set in motion and advanced, as well as
highlighting the unique characterization that is achieved. Herod receives
an ominous signal from two sources, first from the magi, and then from the
chief priests and scribes of the people, which serves to drive the action of
the chapter forward through what becomes a conflict between two kings.
Prophetic warning was demonstrated as a useful characterization of this
material as portrayed in Matthew. Help from the book of Exodus as well as
other Jewish sources, particularly Josephus' *Jewish Antiquities* and the
Targum Pseudo-Jonathan on Exodus, which evidence traditions utilized
during the first century, also aided the search for better understanding this
chapter as a recapitulation of the exodus. Herod is portrayed much like
Pharaoh is his response to an ominous threat to his kingship.

The second section continued to follow the narrative, where divine
warning through a revelatory dream was received by Joseph to flee the

harm Herod intended, and thus their flight to safety was narrated. The portrayal of this event was shown to parallel both Israel's early history and Moses' early life. Like the Pharaoh of Exodus, Herod seeks to eliminate a threat, and like exodus, God preserves both Israel at large and especially Moses in particular. This unique exodus portrayal is best understood as a passive recapitulation by Jesus of the history and geographical movements of both Israel and Moses.

The third section looked closely at the curious way that Egypt is employed in the narrative, and the distinctive characterization and subtle reversal thereby achieved when Judea under Herod resembles Israel's experience in Egypt under Pharaoh. Placement of the Hosea quotation was decisive in observing this subtle metaphorical reversal in geographical orientation. Again, a recapitulation can be observed, albeit in a rather surprising manner that was examined in detail. In addition, further discussion as to the use and meaning of this specific fulfillment quotation was undertaken. It was determined that Matthew's use of this Old Testament quotation is flexible and complex, and this opened up the possibility of reevaluating the other fulfillment quotations from this perspective. Overly literal and restrictive understandings of Matthew's use of the Old Testament were shown to be inadequate interpretations of this Gospel that have too often proceeded upon the exegetical task with assumptions about Matthew's fulfillment quotations that do not match what appears in the text itself, therefore leading to interpretations that fail to adequately exegete the text. Further extensive research into this flexibility is sorely needed.

The fourth section examined the role of the Rachel lament within the overall narrative. Its placement and role was demonstrated to well serve the exodus recapitulation of the entire narrative. Again, the astounding geographic reversal was observed, in that within the land of Israel oppression and murder resembling the exodus period occurred, and a recapitulation of that period is narrated within the early life of Jesus. The exilic event that provoked the Rachel lament as depicted in Jeremiah parallels the oppressive period of Israel in Egypt. This time of lamentation is again repeated with the murder of the Bethlehem boys under a tyrannical Herod, who clearly resembles Pharaoh. Jesus therefore passively recapitulates Israel's history in his geographic movements as a child, experiencing the oppression as well as the deliverance and preservation that Moses had experienced as a child.

Finally, in the fifth section the return to the land of Israel was examined. Again, Jesus passively recapitulates the exodus. He recapitulates Israel's geographic exodus movement out of Egypt and back to the land of Israel. Jesus also recapitulates the life of Moses who returned to Egypt to take up his vocation in leading God's people out of Egypt after the death of the Pharaoh that had sought his life. Herod's death corresponds and recapitu-

lates this event. Jesus' return to the land of Israel, having passively recapitulated Israel's history and the providential preservation as their deliverer now sets up the remaining story of his deliverance of his people (cf.
1:21).

The outcome of the chapter's focus on Matthew 2 determined that the
exodus motif dominates, and Jesus is portrayed as recapitulating the exodus. Because Jesus is a child in this narrative, his movements are the result
of other characters' actions, primarily Joseph's. Therefore, Jesus can be
observed as passively recapitulating Israel in this chapter, by recapitulating
Israel's exodus period as well as recapitulating aspects of Moses' life.

The final section of Matthew's narrative examined was 3:1–4:11, where
it was determined and argued that Jesus actively recapitulates the history
of Israel, through repeating, re-living and embodying that history in this
section of Matthew. Jesus now begins his ministry by first accepting baptism in obedience to God's call through his prophet John. In response to
his baptism, he is divinely approved by God as the Son, and he is then led
out into the wilderness by the Spirit to be tested as the Son. In the portrayal of Jesus in the overall narrative it was demonstrated how Jesus is the
representative embodiment of Israel in his active recapitulation of Israel's
history. To ascertain Jesus as the recapitulation of Israel in this section,
there was close attention to all the Jesus/Israel connections, through the
way the narrative unfolds, chronological aspects, and especially the use of
scriptural texts, key words, titles, and themes.

The narratival and theological unity of 1:1–4:11 was the first area of focus where an extensive list of eleven various connections and parallels between Matthew chapters 1–2 and 3–4:11 evidence this unified perspective,
helping the reader continue to observe Jesus as Israel recapitulated. It was
shown that there is a continued metaphorical usage of Judea as a place of
threat and danger, which is a perspective that continues from chapter 2.
The metaphorical interpretation of Judea as 'Egypt' that was discussed in
the second chapter of this study helps toward a recognition of the overall
narrative context in which Jesus' entrance is set. Jesus accepts John's baptism, which recapitulates Israel's exodus. He does so as the one who will
redeem his people, already programmatically expressed at 1:21 (cf. 20:28),
but also, and this is fundamental for understanding 3:13–4:11, as an obedient Israelite, fulfilling a role that demands all righteousness (3:15). The
narrative focuses attention solely upon Jesus by narrowing down to him
alone, one who recapitulates in himself Israel's history. The metaphorical
aspects of the text helped toward recognizing this, but these narratival aspects also lead toward better recognizing this characterization of Jesus recapitulating Israel.

To understand the overall presentation of 3:1–4:11 it was necessary to
examine the unity of the baptism narrative and the testing narrative, and

this was demonstrated through a detailed list of thirteen connections that evidence an overall unity to the narrative. This unity is exhibited literarily, geographically, structurally, and theologically. Therefore, the fundamental unity that is observed then principally aids toward allowing the testing narrative to color one's reading of the baptism narrative. The detailed list evidencing the unity of 3:1–4:11 adequately demonstrates the suitability of viewing the baptism and testing as connected events, with the entire section seen as a narrative to be read and interpreted as a whole. In addition, as the unity of 3:1–4:11 is recognized, a fuller understanding of Jesus as the recapitulation of Israel is demonstrated because the analysis of unity in the narrative has helped toward observing Jesus as Israel recapitulated; a point that continued to be discussed as the baptism narrative and testing narrative was examined in detail. What the chapter sought to explicate is that it would appear that one should read the wilderness testing of Jesus as the Son, which comes prior to his ministry that begins at 4:12ff, as closely related to Israel's history in the exodus and wilderness events. The connections that Jesus' testing has with Israel's testing in the wilderness are obvious and widely recognized, but because within Israel's scriptural history the exodus and wilderness events are chronologically and sequentially related, one should also observe Jesus' baptism and testing as mirroring this aspect of Israel's history. Israel crosses through the sea and then is tested, prior to their task of taking the land. Jesus is baptized and then he is tested prior to his ministry in the land of Israel.

Having observed the unity of 3:1–4:11 and the assistance this supplies toward observing Jesus recapitulating Israel's history at a broader level, it was then necessary to examine much more closely the baptism narrative and how Jesus is presented as the recapitulation of Israel. The setting in the wilderness supplies a literary and theological motif that is further evidenced in the quotation from Isaiah 40, which provides an exodus perspective upon John's baptism at the Jordan River. The baptism narrative narrows its focus from the crowds down to the leaders and down further to Jesus alone. The narrative depicts the crowds from Jerusalem, all Judea, and all the surrounding area, coming for John to baptize them, which he does. Then many Pharisees and Sadducees come to the area of John's baptism. However, it was argued that they do not come for his baptism, and they receive a sharp rebuke from John for their failure to exhibit obedience to God. Finally, Jesus obediently comes for the purpose of being baptized by John and receives a divine response of approval to his baptism. The way this narrative unfolds and the successive groups that come to John indicate a narrowing, from "all" the people of Jerusalem, Judea and the surrounding area, to the religious leaders, down to Jesus alone. The primary goal of the narrative therefore narrows through these successive groups to focus upon Jesus alone, the Son of God, Israel recapitulated. It was important to observe this narrowing unfold because it directly impacts how Jesus alone is presented as the recapitulation of Israel, the embodiment and vicarious representative of Israel.

The overwhelmingly positive response that Jesus receives from God, in contrast to the scathingly negative response the leaders receive, is a dramatic divine approval to his obedience in baptism. Jesus, in solidarity with his people Israel, obeys God's call through his prophet John to be baptized. The divine approval that Jesus receives underscores his representative role as Israel recapitulated by means of three important titles that Israel had also been called: υἱός, ἀγαπητός, εὐδόκησα. Israel as son is a primary title in this regard, as it continues to be so for Jesus as well. The connection in this narrative between Jesus and Israel, specifically in Jesus recapitulating Israel's history, is observable through what is explicitly stated in the text. This viewpoint is maintained through attention to what Jesus is openly called by God in response to his baptism by John, Οὗτός ἐστιν ὁ υἱός μου ὁ ἀγαπητός, ἐν ᾧ εὐδόκησα. The divine response, affirming Jesus' purpose and actions to fulfill all righteousness, is therefore fundamental for observing Jesus' recapitulation of Israel precisely because of the specific, evocative titles he is called. The use of the three special designations has particular relevance to the relationship of God with Israel. Jesus is described utilizing scriptural terms that had been used for Israel, or its representative. In addition, by obediently aligning himself with the ministry of John, a prophet of God, Jesus therefore fully embodies the Israel that John sought to restore. The structure and technique of the narrative in narrowing down upon Jesus further makes it clear that he alone does this as representative, recapitulating in himself Israel's scriptural history. These titles therefore affirm that Jesus alone is 'Israel'.

Thus, the baptism narrative is shown to narrow down the focus to Jesus alone: from the crowds, down to the leaders, who were rejected, down finally to Jesus alone, who is fully commended and approved by God. Jesus' acceptance of John's baptism was done to fulfill all righteousness, where he fully identifies himself with his people as an Israelite obedient to God's call through his prophet John. John's baptism was shown to have resemblance to the exodus, and the divine response that Jesus receives fully identifies him as the Son, which is what Israel had been called in the Exodus. Jesus recapitulates Israel's exodus and then, like Israel, he is led out into the wilderness to be tested.

Jesus is led into the wilderness by the Spirit to be tested by the devil, and he is alone in the wilderness to be tested as the Son, following sequentially from the preceding narrative that is fundamentally linked to the testing narrative. Jesus' test as Son, alone in the wilderness, is a test that recapitulates Israel's wilderness testing. This testing event is a divinely orchestrated test of the Son, which Israel, God's son, also had experienced.

Through the utilization of three texts from Deuteronomy, it is more fully understood that Jesus' experience in the wilderness matches Israel's experience because the contexts of these Deuteronomy passages allude to Israel's tests as described in the book of Exodus. Jesus quotes these Deuteronomy texts in response to the tempter, evidencing his obedient stance as an Israelite submissive to God's word that had been spoken to Israel, as depicted in the text of Deuteronomy.

The focus of the testing narrative centers upon Jesus as the recapitulation of Israel's history, repeating and re-enacting Israel's experience following their exodus from Egypt. The wilderness setting initially directs the reader to observe this recapitulation. Fasting in the wilderness for forty days also clearly parallels Israel's forty-year humbling experience wandering in the wilderness, at various times also facing hunger and deprivation. That forty-year wilderness experience, according to Deuteronomy 8, had an educative and disciplinary purpose, and thus Jesus' use of Deuteronomy 8 in his scriptural response to temptation further reveals the parallel between Israel and Jesus. Like Israel, Jesus faces a test with an educational purpose, divinely orchestrated to prepare him for his ministry to Israel as the Son of God.

In the presentation of the three tests, Matthew follows the order of the book of Exodus, which makes sense as the chronological order experienced by Israel as narrated in the text of Exodus. Each test is linked to a text quoted by Jesus from Deuteronomy, and these texts from Deuteronomy are linked to a failure by Israel as recounted in the book of Exodus. These failures had been assumed background in Deuteronomy, in that the setting of Deuteronomy depicts Moses speaking to Israel at the end of the wilderness period, reminding them of their past failures and therefore challenging them to loyalty and obedience. Highlighting these connections in each of the three tests that Jesus faced proved highly significant for understanding Jesus' recapitulation of Israel. The obedience he exhibits in light of Israel's failures is also made evident in that while he recapitulates Israel's testing experience in the wilderness, he certainly does not repeat the disobedience of Israel. Jesus as Son obediently fulfills God's will where Israel had failed, which is a necessary duty for delivering Israel, according to Matthew's presentation of Jesus' story.

Like the baptism narrative, the testing narrative concludes with a divine response of approval to Jesus' obedience. Continuing to fulfill all righteousness, Jesus now receives what Israel had also received in the wilderness, the provisions that sustain life which he had refused to acquire outside of God's will. Jesus therefore recapitulates Israel's wilderness experience, however remaining obedient where Israel had failed, fulfilling his duty as the one who came to save Israel.

5.2 Main Conclusions

When the three major sections of this work are synthesized, the overall result is a fuller understanding of the use of Israel's history in these beginning chapters of Matthew's Gospel. To set forth the story of Jesus Christ that the Gospel seeks to narrate, the history of Israel is a formative component in the proclamation of Jesus as the Christ. The concept of recapitulation aptly categorizes the use of Israel's history in these chapters, and this has been the highly distinctive feature of this work, filling a lacuna in Matthean studies by delineating the recapitulation of Israel utilizing an eclectic combination of critical approaches. Israel's history is recapitulated in the genealogy to focus upon Jesus as the fulfillment and climax to Israel's story. Jesus is portrayed as passively recapitulating Israel's history as a child, and then he is portrayed as actively recapitulating Israel's history as an adult. The vital connection of Jesus with Israel's story is thereby evidenced and adds further coloring to the fulfillment theme that is especially dominant in Matthew. This work therefore substantiates what many have stated in abbreviated form, as for example Moltmann when he writes,

Matthew tells the story of Jesus, not as an individual history, but as the collective biography of Israel, from the flight into Egypt, the call out of Egypt, the days of temptation in the wilderness, to the story of the passion. Israel's messiah is at the same time Israel's representative.[1]

Combining the entirety of Matthew 1:1–4:11 and the cumulative effect upon the observant reader, what emerges is that there is more than a mere parallel between Jesus and Israel, in that while Jesus clearly recapitulates Israel's history as well as embodies "Israel" as Son, this is a role which he must fulfill (3:15; cf. 1:21). While Jesus recapitulates Israel's history in fundamental ways, he certainly does not recapitulate Israel's failures, nor is he depicted as simply mimicking these aspects of her history. From Matthew's perspective, Jesus is required to exhibit this obedient sonship as the embodiment of Israel, in that his recapitulation serves a salvific purpose for Israel. Jesus is the true Israel, he does everything Israel was to be and do,[2] as a corporate individual, embodying Israel in his recapitulation and representation.

Dodd has summarized these points when he notes how there is a "fusion of the two ideal figures of Messiah and Servant of the Lord" in Jesus as depicted in the baptism and temptation. He argues for the importance of recognizing Jesus as a corporate unity and representative, which is based on the characterization of Jesus in the Gospel reports. He summarizes, "the

---

[1] Moltmann, *The Way of Jesus Christ*, 36; cf. Wright, *The New Testament and the People of God*, 401–402.

[2] Cf. Holwerda, *Jesus and Israel*, 32.

Messiah is not only founder and leader of the Israel-to-be, the new people of God; he is its 'inclusive representative'. In a real sense he *is* the true Israel, carrying through in his own experience the process through which it comes into being."[3] This helpful insight from Dodd is only a small part of his larger general work on Jesus, and a major component of the present work has been to thoroughly investigate the validity of such brief statements within the early chapters of Matthew in a way not undertaken in the book by Dodd. The conclusion of this study has found that they are indeed exegetically defendable statements grounded in the text of Matthew.

Jesus as the recapitulation of Israel and representative of Israel are organically connected within Matthew's overall christology. The programmatic text in Matthew is 1:21, which serves a fundamental purpose in this regard: Jesus is presented as the one who will save his people from their sins (αὐτὸς γὰρ σώσει τὸν λαὸν αὐτοῦ ἀπὸ τῶν ἁμαρτιῶν αὐτῶν).[4] The presentation and proclamation of Jesus in Matthew concerns Jesus' role as Savior (20:28), and the recapitulation he embodies appears to be a significant part of that salvific purpose.[5] This would clearly relate to why Jesus needs to be baptized, which is initially problematic at a theological level. When one combines Jesus' recapitulation of Israel with his representative and vicarious role as Savior of his people, these themes are then integrally related, leading toward a greater understanding of why he must be baptized and later why he must die.[6] The beginning of Matthew's Gospel has brought this christological orientation to the forefront through the genealogy that recapitulates Israel's history and through the following chapters (2:1–4:11) that directly portray Jesus recapitulating Israel's history passively in 2:1–23 and actively in 3:1–4:11.

Numerous further considerations are prompted by Jesus as the recapitulation of Israel. It certainly enriches an understanding of Matthew's christology. The narrative portrayal of Jesus recapitulating Israel's history not only links him to that prior history, especially as seen in the genealogy, but it also provides insight into identifying Jesus' role as the Messiah. Beginning his Gospel account in this way orients the hearer and reader toward realizing the particular means by which their salvation has been undertaken in their Redeemer. While it certainly requires further research, it appears

---

[3] Dodd, *Founder of Christianity*, 105–106. Cf. Gibbs, "Son of God as Torah," 38–39.

[4] The genealogy has already alerted the reader to Israel's failure, resulting finally in the exile. It appears that Matthew intends 1:21 to refer to more than Jesus' salvation from Israel's present sins but reaches back to her history of failure, also evidenced in his active recapitulation of that history. Cf. Witherington, *Matthew*, 46.

[5] Albright and Mann, *Matthew*, LXIII: "Jesus in his obedience is to relive, and reverse, Israel's dallying with temptation in the wilderness."

[6] This certainly deserves further attention than can be offered in this study, incorporating the entirety of Matthew's Gospel.

that given the results of this present study, for the Evangelist, Jesus' recapitulation of Israel's history is a necessity "to save his people from their sins" (1:21).[7] This redeeming role is immediately highlighted when the young Jesus' is severely endangered, one of many dark shadows that recur throughout the Gospel narrative indicating Jesus' horrific execution.

A clue toward identifying Jesus' role in Matthew is by attending to what is recapitulated. Israel's history, a sacred story textually preserved in their scriptures, is what Jesus recapitulates and embodies. The moments he repeats are formative for Israel and they serve as key markers that later generations point back to as evidence of God's work among them. As noted several times before but worthy of reiterating, Jesus as the recapitulation of Israel affirms in a definitive and positive manner these people both past, present, and future. As a corporate body of the past known through their scriptures and traditions, the Matthean Jesus stands in continuity with that history and people. As a people contemporary with Jesus' life, though widely diverse and scattered, the Matthean Jesus stands in the role of Savior. Indeed, Jesus' role as Savior in Matthew's portrayal, while obviously a future-oriented endeavor within the timeframe of the story, is also retrospective.[8] Jesus as Savior, through his recapitulation, extends backward toward those that preceeded him, his people Israel.

While Jesus repeats formative events in Israel's sacred history, many of these scenes involved pain and failure on the part of Israel. Exodus and exile were oppressive times of tremendous suffering. The wilderness period was a time of repeated failures, culminating with the golden calf incident. Jesus' recapitulation of Israel brings him into contact with similar oppressive circumstances (cf. 8:17, 20; 12:1–42; 21:23–46; Passion Narrative). These oppressive circumstances and suffering break forth upon him as a child and they continue throughout his adult life and ending with his agonizing death (27:46).[9] However, his obedience throughout these ordeals is maintained as part of his mission to save his people, which involves his fulfilling all righteousness as a neccessity. The implications therefore indicate that Jesus' role as Savior, which is inextricably interwoven with his recapitulation of Israel, involves a vicarious life of obedience and suffering given for his people and then a vicarious death on behalf of his people as the Servant (20:28). This representative role encompasses the whole of his life and ministry.

---

[7] Cf. Gerhardsson, "Sacrificial Service and Atonement in the Gospel of Matthew," 25–35, who offers some suggestive comments in this regard.

[8] Cf. Torrance, *Space, Time and Resurrection*, 86–87.

[9] Allison, *Studies in Matthew*, 254: "In Matthew's story, Jesus suffers far more than anyone else. The savior is the innocent victim writ large."

5.3 Suggestions for Future Research

The analysis of the recapitulation of Israel in the Gospel of Matthew should certainly continue with the rest of the Gospel text where there are sections that Israel's history is variously utilized. There are several places in particular, among other smaller sections and phrases, which deserve closer attention in this regard: 11:2–15; 12:38–42; 17:1–13; 21:33–43; and 23:29–36. A detailed investigation of recapitulation in these texts, as well as other minor places, should be undertaken and then conclusions as to its overall usage in Matthew could then be proposed and described.[10] In addition, there are other Old Testament persons and institutions that are variously utilized in Matthew that should also be examined. The story of Jesus as narrated in Matthew should prove to yield further uses of Israel's history.[11] Waetjen regards "the whole life of Jesus – from birth to resurrection – is a repetition of the history of Israel. Indeed, for Mt, Jesus is the very embodiment of Israel and it history."[12] Furthermore, Wright thinks Jesus "regarded himself as the one who summed up Israel's vocation and destiny in himself."[13] The insights gleaned from the such investigations would also contribute to understanding the complicated issue of Matthew's interaction with the Judaism contemporary to his time, as well as the larger depiction of Israel's past and present. Also important would be further research into the impact of Matthew's use of Israel's history within the larger focus of the Evangelist upon the gospel going out to the Gentiles (28:19).[14]

The conclusions about the use of Israel's history in the rest of Matthew should then be woven into the overall discussion of Matthew's christology, which rightly continues to be a much-discussed topic, particularly in regard to nuancing and balancing this research away from an overemphasis on the titles in Matthew. Other data such as what this thesis has sought to provide should be utilized to further fill out the understanding of christology in Matthew. To adequately do so will demand utilization of all the critical tools, as well as a methodology that handles all the complexities.

---

[10] See Swartley, *Israel's Scripture Traditions and the Synoptic Gospels*, for an attempt at this.

[11] For example, Van Aarde, "ΙΗΣΟΥΣ" 7, argues that Matthew is "a story that retells the 'history' of how God sent Joshua from Egypt as Moses' successor to save Israel. It narrates a 'history' of how God 'heals' Israel through Jesus, God's son. Jesus is Israel's Davidic Messiah."

[12] Waetjen, *The Transformation of Judaism according to St. Matthew* (Diss. Tübingen, 1958), cited in Hummel, *Die Auseinandersetzung*, 130.

[13] Wright, *Jesus and the Victory of God*, 517; cf. Torrance, *The Mediation of Christ*, 31–32.

[14] Cf. Moltmann, *The Way of Jesus Christ*, 36.

Examination of recapitulation in other texts of the New Testament as well as other early Christian texts should also be undertaken. These texts utilize Israel's history in other various ways that deserve attention. They could be compared and contrasted with Matthew's use of recapitulation. These insights would also serve to deepen the understanding of Christianity's interaction with Judaism in these early centuries of the church. A wider grasp of the characterization of Israel's history in Jewish and other ancient literature would also yield many valuable insights.

This study lends greater support for further refinement in regard to Matthew's use of the Old Testament. It has been shown at various points that a literal prediction-fulfillment understanding of Matthew's use of the Old Testament does not adequately describe what occurs in the text of Matthew. It has been observed that Evangelist's use of the Old Testament in his quotations is more flexible and complex than often assumed, especially in regard to the fulfillment quotations. From Matthew's perspective, the Old Testament is used to understand Christ and Christ is the key to understanding the Old Testament. Each facilitates understanding the other through their mutual interaction.[15] These issues deserve further detailed research because too many discussions of Matthew have begun with inadequate, unsubstantiated assumptions about his use of the Old Testament, which has only perpetuated these mistaken viewpoints. Modern assessment, whether positive or negative, of the flexible exegetical methods exhibited in Matthew must not prejudice careful interpretation of the text.

While this work has remained focused primarily upon interpreting the text of Matthew's Gospel within its first century environment, the results of this work might also provoke further reflection. For those oriented toward theologizing, there are numerous avenues for research, some of which have already been described. Only a few will be mentioned here. Attention to the theological implications of Jesus as the recapitulation of Israel could be undertaken. The relation this has upon views of the incarnation, theories of the atonement, and the relation between the testaments could prove useful. Appropriating these into a descriptive christological enterprise would also be valuable. Discussion of the impact of this work for contemporary dialogue between Jews and Christians might be productive.

The distinctive result of this study has been a greater understanding of Matthew's christology and his use of the Old Testament through ascertaining his utilization of Israel's history. The expression recapitulation has been employed as a suitable term to characterize the use of Israel's history in Matthew 1:1–4:11 in relation to Jesus Christ. This recapitulation in-

---

[15] Cf. Watson, *Text and Truth*, 216–219; Thiselton, *New Horizons in Hermeneutics*, 150–151.

volves the repetition, reliving, and representative embodiment of Israel's history. The details and conclusions of this thesis will hopefully aid further research and stimulate productive work on christology and the use of the Old Testament in the Gospel of Matthew, as well as promote wider contributions to appreciating the rich variety of interpretations of Jesus Christ in the ancient world.

Bibliography

Ackroyd, P. R., *The Chronicler in His Age* (JSOTSup 101; Sheffield: JSOT, 1991).

Albright, W. F., and C. S. Mann, *Matthew* (AB 26; Garden City: Doubleday, 1971).

Alexander, T. D., "From Adam to Judah: The Significance of the Family Tree in Genesis," *EvQ* 61 (1989) 5–19.

– "Genealogies, Seed and the Compositional Unity of Genesis," *TynBul* 44 (1993) 255–70.

– *From Paradise to the Promised Land* (Carlisle: Paternoster Press, 1995).

Allen, W. C., *A Critical and Exegetical Commentary on the Gospel according to St. Matthew* (Edinburgh: T. & T. Clark, 1912).

Allison, D. C., "The Son of God as Israel: A Note on Matthean Christology," *IBS* 9 (1987) 74–81.

– *The New Moses: A Matthean Typology* (Philadelphia: Fortress Press, 1993).

– *The Intertextual Jesus: Scripture in Q* (Harrisburg: Trinity Press International, 2000).

– "Matthew" in *The Oxford Bible Commentary*, eds. J. Barton and J. Muddiman (Oxford: Oxford University Press, 2001).

– *Studies in Matthew* (Grand Rapids: Baker, 2005).

Anderson, F. I. and D. N. Freedman, *Hosea* (AB; Garden City: Doubleday, 1980), Anderson, J. C., *Matthew's Narrative Web: Over, and Over, and Over Again* (JSNTSS 91; Sheffield: Sheffield Academic Press, 1994).

Aune, D. E., *The New Testament in Its Literary Environment* (Philadelphia: Fortress, 1988).

– ed., *Greco-Roman Literature and the New Testament* (Atlanta: Scholars Press, 1988).

– ed., *The Gospel of Matthew in Current Study* (Grand Rapids: Eerdmans, 2001).

Bailey, J. L. and L. D. Vanderbroek, *Literary Forms in the New Testament* (Louisville: Westminster/John Knox, 1992).

Baker, D. L., *Two Testaments, One Bible* (Downers Grove: InterVarsity, 1977).

Balch, D. L., ed., *Social History of the Matthean Community* (Minneapolis: Fortress, 1991).

Barnet, J. A., *Not the Righteous but Sinners: M. M. Bakhtin's Theory of Aesthetics and the Problem of Reader-Character Interaction in Matthew's Gospel* (JSNTSS 246; London: T&T Clark International, 2003).

Barr, J., *Old and New in Interpretation* (London: SCM Press, 1966).

Barrett, C. K., *The Holy Spirit and the Gospel Tradition* (London: SPCK, 1966).

Bauckham, R., "Tamar's Ancestry and Rahab's Marriage: Two Problems in the Matthean Genealogy," *NovT* 37 (1995) 313–329.

– ed., *The Gospel for All Christians* (Grand Rapids: Eerdmans, 1998).

– *Gospel Women* (Grand Rapids: Eerdmans, 2002).

– *Jesus and the Eyewitnesses: The Gospel as Eyewitness Testimony* (Grand Rapids: Eerdmans, 2006).

Bauer, D. R., *The Structure of Matthew's Gospel* (Sheffield: Sheffield Academic Press, 1988).
– "The Kingship of Jesus in the Matthean Infancy Narratives" A Literary Analysis," *CBQ* 57 (1995) 306–323.
Bauer, D. R., and M. A. Powell, eds., *Treasures New and Old* (Atlanta: Scholars Press, 1996).
– "The Literary and Theological Function of the Genealogy in Matthew's Gospel," in *Treasures New and Old: Recent Contributions to Matthean Studies*, eds. D. R. Bauer and M. A. Powell (Atlanta: Scholars Press, 1996) 129–159.
Bauer, W., *A Greek-English Lexicon of the New Testament and Other Early Christian Literature*, ed. F. W. Danker (3rd ed.; Chicago: University of Chicago, 2001).
Beare, F. W., *The Gospel According to Matthew* (San Francisco: Harper & Row, 1981).
Beaton, R., *Isaiah's Christ in Matthew's Gospel* (Cambridge: Cambridge University Press, 2002).
Beattie, D. R. G., *Aramaic Bible: Translation of the Targum of Ruth* (Vol. 19; Edinburgh: T & T Clark, 1994).
Blair, E., *Jesus in the Gospel of Matthew* (Nashville: Abingdon, 1960).
Blass, F. and A. Debrunner, *A Greek Grammar of the New Testament and Other Early Christian Literature*, trans. and rev. by R. W. Funk (Chicago: University of Chicago Press, 1961).
Blomberg, C. "Matthew," in *Commentary on the New Testament Use of the Old Testament*, eds. G. K. Beale and D. A. Carson (Grand Rapids: Baker, 2007).
Bonnard, P., *L'Évangile selon Saint Matthieu* (Geneva: Labor et Fides, 2002).
Borgen, P., "Response to Lindars," *NTS* 23 (1977) 67–75.
Boring, M. E., K. Berger, and C. Colpe, *Hellenistic Commentary to the New Testament* (Nashville: Abingdon, 1995).
– "Matthew," *New Interpreters Bible* (Vol. 8; Nashville: Abingdon Press, 1995).
Bornkamm, G., G. Barth, and H. J. Held, *Tradition and Interpretation in Matthew* (Philadelphia: Westminster, 1963).
Bourke, M., "The Literary Genius of Matthew 1–2," *CBQ* 22 (1960) 160–175.
Braun, R., *1 Chronicles* (WBC; Dallas: Word Books, 1986).
Brooks, J. A., and C. L. Winbery, *Syntax of New Testament Greek* (Lanham: University Press of America, 1979).
Brotzman, E. R., *Old Testament Textual Criticism* (Grand Rapids: Baker, 1994).
Brown, R. E., *The Birth of the Messiah* (Garden City: Doubleday, 1993).
Bruce, A. B. *The Expositor's Greek Testament: Synoptic Gospels* (Grand Rapids: Eerdmans, 1965).
Bultmann, C., "Deuteronomy," in *The Oxford Bible Commentary*, eds. J. Barton and J. Muddiman (Oxford: Oxford University Press, 2001).
Bultmann, R., *Theology of the New Testament* (trans. K. Grobel; New York: Charles Scribner's, 1951).
– *The History of the Synoptic Tradition*. (2nd ed.; trans. J. Marsh; New York: Harper & Row, 1968).
Burger, C., *Jesus als Davidssohn* (FRLANT 98; Göttingen: Vandenhoeck & Ruprecht, 1970).
Burridge, R. A., *What are the Gospels? A Comparison with Greco-Roman Biography* (SNTSMS 70; Cambridge: Cambridge University Press, 1992).
Bush, F., *Ruth, Esther* (WBC; Dallas: Word, 1996).
Calvin, J., *A Harmony of Matthew, Mark, and Luke* (Vol. 1; Grand Rapids: Eerdmans, 1972).

Campbell, E. F., *Ruth* (Garden City: Doubleday, 1975).

Capes, D. B., "Intertextual Echoes in the Matthean Baptism Narrative," *BBR* 9 (1999) 37–49.

Carson, D. A., *Matthew 1–12* (EBC; Grand Rapids: Zondervan, 1995).

Carter, W., *Matthew: Storyteller, Interpreter, Evangelist* (Peabody: Hendrickson, 1996).

– *Matthew and the Margins: A Sociopolitical and Religious Reading* (Maryknoll: Orbis, 2000).

Cartlidge, D. R., and D. L. Dungan, *Documents for the Study of the Gospels* (Minneapolis: Fortress Press, 1994).

Cassuto, U., *A Commentary on the Book of Genesis: Part I* (trans. I. Abrahams; Jerusalem: Magnes Press, 1961).

Childs, B. S., *The Book of Exodus* (OTL; Louisville: Westminster Press, 1974).

– *Introduction to the Old Testament as Scripture* (Philadelphia: Fortress, 1979).

– *The New Testament as Canon: An Introduction* (Philadelphia: Fortress, 1984).

Chilton, B., and J. Neusner, *Judaism in the New Testament* (London: Routledge, 1995).

Clarke, H., *The Gospel of Matthew and Its Readers* (Bloomington: Indiana University Press, 2003).

Coats, G., *Genesis with an Introduction to Narrative Literature* (FOTL Vol. 1; Grand Rapids: Eerdmans, 1983).

Cope, O. L., *Matthew: A Scribe Trained for the Kingdom of Heaven* (CBQMS 5; Washington, D.C.: The Catholic Biblical Association of America, 1976).

Crossan, J. D., "From Moses to Jesus: Parallel Themes," BR 2 (1986) 18–27.

Danker, F. W., "Matthew: A Patriot's Gospel," in *The Gospels and the Scriptures of Israel*, eds. C. A. Evans and W. R. Stegner (JSNTSS104; Sheffield: Sheffield Academic Press, 1994) 94–115.

Daube, D., *The New Testament and Rabbinic Judaism* (London: Athlone Press, 1956).

Davies, M., *Matthew: Readings, a New Biblical Commentary* (Sheffield: JSOT Press, 1992).

Davies, W. D., *The Setting of the Sermon on the Mount* (Cambridge: Cambridge University, 1966).

– "The Jewish Sources of Matthew's Messianism," in *The Messiah: Developments in Earliest Judaism and Christianity*, ed. J. H. Charlesworth (Minneapolis: Fortress, 1992).

Davies, W. D. and D. C. Allison, *A Critical and Exegetical Commentary on the Gospel according to Saint Matthew* (ICC; 3 vols.; Edinburgh: T. & T. Clark, 1988, 1991, 1997).

Deines, R., *Die Gerechtigkeit der Tora im Reich des Messias: Mt 5,13–20 als Schlüsseltext der matthäischen Theologie* (WUNT 177; Tübingen: Mohr Siebeck, 2004).

– "Not the Law but the Messiah: Law and Righteousness in the Gospel of Matthew – An Ongoing Debate," in *Built Upon the Rock: Studies in the Gospel of Matthew*, eds. D. M. Gurtner and J. Nolland (Grand Rapids: Eerdmans, 2008) 53–84.

Deutsch, C. M., *Lady Wisdom, Jesus, and the Sages: Metaphor and Social Context in Matthew's Gospel* (Valley Forge: Trinity Press International, 1996).

Dibelius, M., *From Tradition to Gospel* (New York: Scribner's, 1935).

Didier, M., ed., *L'Évangile selon Matthieu: Rédaction et théologie* (BETL 29; Gembloux: Duculot, 1972).

Dillard, R. B., *2 Chronicles* (Waco, TX: Word, 1987).

Dodd, C. H., *According to the Scriptures: The Sub-Structure of New Testament Theology* (London: Nisbet & Co., 1952).

– *The Founder of Christianity* (London: Collins, 1971).

Donaldson, T. L., *Jesus on the Mountain: A Study in Matthean Theology* (JSNTSup 8; Sheffield: JSOT, 1985).

Duke, R. P., *The Persuasive Appeal of the Chronicler: A Rhetorical Analysis* (JSOTSup 88; Sheffield: Almond, 1990).

Duling, D. C., "The Therapeutic Son of David: An Element in Matthew's Christology," *NTS* 24 (1978) 392–410.

Dungan, D. L., *A History of the Synoptic Problem* (New York: Doubleday, 1999).

Dunn, J. D. G., *Christology in the Making* (Philadelphia: Westminster Press, 1980).

– *Jesus Remembered* (Grand Rapids: Eerdmans, 2003).

Dupont, J., "L'Arriere-Fond Biblique Du Recit Des Tentations De Jesus," *NTS* 53 (1956–57) 287–304.

Dyck, J. E., *The Theocratic Ideology of the Chronicler* (BIS 33; Leiden: Brill, 1998).

Edgar, S. L., "Respect for Context in Quotations from the Old Testament," *NTS* 9 (1962–1963).

Eichrodt, W., "Is Typological Exegesis an Appropriate Method?," in *Essays on Old Testament Interpretation*, ed. C. Westermann (London: SCM Press, 1963).

Eissfeldt, O., *The Old Testament: An Introduction* (trans. P. R. Ackroyd; Oxford: Basil Blackwell, 1965).

– "Πληρῶσαι πᾶσαν δικαιοσύνην in Matthäus 3,15," *ZNW* 61 (1970) 209–215.

Elliott, J. K., *The Apocryphal New Testament* (Oxford: Oxford University Press, 1993).

Ellis, E. E., *Prophecy and Hermeneutic in Early Christianity* (Tübingen: J. C B. Mohr, 1978).

– *The Old Testament Canon in Early Christianity* (Grand Rapids: Baker, 1991).

– *The Making of the New Testament Documents* (Leiden: Brill, 1999).

Eloff, M., "Exile, Restoration and Matthew's Genealogy of Jesus Ὁ ΧΡΙΣΤΟΣ," *Neot* 38 (2004) 75–87.

– " Ἀπό ... ἕως and Salvation History in Matthew's Gospel," in *Built Upon the Rock: Studies in Matthew's Gospel*, eds. D. M. Gurtner and J. Nolland (Grand Rapids: Eerdmans, 2008) 85–107.

Eusebius, *The History of the Church* (trans. G. A. Williamson; New York: Penguin, 1989).

Evans, C. A., *Noncanonical Writings and New Testament Interpretation* (Peabody: Hendrickson, 1995)

– "Aspects of Exile and Restoration", in *Jesus in Context: Temple, Purity, and Restoration*, eds. B. Chilton and C. A. Evans (Leiden: Brill, 1997).

– "The Old Testament in the New," in *The Face of New Testament Studies*, eds. S. McKnight and G. R. Osborne (Grand Rapids: Baker Academic, 2004).

Farmer, W. R., *The Synoptic Problem* (Dillsboro: Western North Carolina Press, 1976).

Feldman, L. H., *Flavius Josephus: Translation and Commentary*, ed. S. Mason, *Vol. 3: Judean Antiquities 1–4* (Leiden: Brill, 2000).

Filson, F. V., *A Commentary on the Gospel according to St. Matthew* (BNTC; London: A. & C. Black, 1960).

Fishbane, M., *Text and Texture* (New York: Schocken Books, 1979).

Fitzmyer, J., *Essays on the Semitic Background of the New Testament* (2nd ed.; Studies in Biblical in Biblical Theology 5; Missoula: Scholars Press, 1974).

Foster, P., *Community, Law and Mission in Matthew's Gospel* (WUNT 177; Tübingen: Mohr Siebeck, 2004).

France, R. T., *Jesus and the Old Testament* (London: Tyndale Press, 1971).

– "The Formula-Quotations of Matthew 2 and the Problem of Communication," *NTS* 27 (1980–81) 233–251.
– *Matthew* (TNTC; Grand Rapids: Eerdmans, 1985).
– *Matthew: Evangelist and Teacher* (Downers Grove: InterVarsity Press, 1989).
– *The Gospel of Matthew* (NICNT; Grand Rapids: Eerdmans, 2007).
Frankemölle, H., *Matthäus: Kommentar 1* (Düsseldorf: Patmos, 1994).
Freed, E. D., *The Stories of Jesus' Birth: A Critical Introduction* (Sheffield: Sheffield Academic Press, 2001).
Fretheim, T. E., *Exodus* (Louisville: John Knox, 1991).
– "Genesis," in *New Interpreter's Bible* (Vol. 1; Nashville: Abingdon, 1994).
Gaechter, P., *Das Matthäus-Evangelium* (Innsbruck: Tyrolia, 1963).
Garbe, G., *Der Hirte Israels: Eine Untersuchung zur Israeltheologie des Matthäusevangeliums* (Neukirchener Verlag, 2005).
Gardner, B. K., *The Genesis Calendar: The Synchronistic Tradition in Genesis 1–11* (Lanham, Maryland: University Press of America, 2001).
Garland, D. E., *Reading Matthew: A Literary and Theological Commentary on the First Gospel* (Macon: Smyth & Helwys Publishing, 2001).
Gärtner, B., "The Habakkuk Commentary (DSH) and the Gospel of Matthew," *ST* 8 (1954) 1–24.
Gaston, L., "The Messiah of Israel as Teacher of the Gentiles," in *Interpreting the Gospels*, ed. J. L. Mays (Philadelphia: Fortress, 1981), 78–96.
Gerhardsson, B., *The Testing of God's Son* (Lund: Gleerup, 1966).
– "Sacrificial Service and Atonement in the Gospel of Matthew," in *Reconciliation and Hope*, ed. R. Banks (Grand Rapids: Eerdmans, 1974) 25–35.
Gibbs, J. A., "Israel Standing with Israel: The Baptism of Jesus in Matthew's Gospel," *CBQ* 64 (2002) 511–526.
Gibbs, J. M., "The Son of God as the Torah Incarnate in Matthew," *Studia Evangelica* Vol. 4, ed. F. L. Cross (Berlin: Akademie Verlag, 1968) 38–59.
– "Purpose and Pattern in Matthew's Use of the Title 'Son of David'," *NTS* 10 (1964) 446–464.
Gibson, J. B., "Testing and Trial in Secular Greek Thought," in *Dictionary of New Testament Background* (Downers Grove: InterVarsity Press, 2000) 1207–1210.
Gnilka, J., *Das Matthäusevangelium* (HTKNT 2 vols.; Freiburg: Herder, 1986, 1988).
Goldingay, J., *Approaches to Old Testament Interpretation* (Leicester: InterVarsity, 1981).
– "Old Testament and Christian Faith," *Themelios* 8.1 (Sept 1982).
Goodacre, M., *The Synoptic Problem: A Way through the Maze* (London: Sheffield Academic Press, 2001).
– *The Case Against Q* (Harrisburg, PA: Trinity Press International, 2002).
Goppelt, L., *Theology of the New Testament* (Vol. 1; Grand Rapids: Eerdmans, 1981).
– *Theology of the New Testament* (Vol. 2; Grand Rapids: Eerdmans, 1982).
– *Typos: The Theological Interpretation of the Old Testament in the New* (Grand Rapids: Eerdmans, 1982).
Goulder, M. D., *Midrash and Lection* (London: SPCK, 1974).
Gundry, R. H., *The Use of the Old Testament in St. Matthew's Gospel* (NovTSup 18; Leiden: Brill, 1967).
– *Matthew: A Commentary on His Handbook for a Mixed Church under Persecution* (2nd ed.; Grand Rapids: Eerdmans, 1994).
Gurtner, D. M., "Matthew's Theology of the Temple and the 'Parting of the Ways': Christian Origins and the First Gospel," in *Built Upon the Rock: Studies in the Gospel*

of Matthew, eds. D. M. Gurtner and J. Nolland (Grand Rapids: Eerdmans, 2008) 128–153.

– *Built Upon the Rock: Studies in the Gospel of Matthew* (Grand Rapids: Eerdmans, 2008).

Hagner, D. A., *Matthew 1–13* (WBC 33a; Dallas: Word Books, 1993).

– "Matthew: Apostate, Reformer, Revolutionary?" *NTS* 49 (2003) 193–209.

Hanna, R., *A Grammatical Aid to the Greek New Testament* (Grand Rapids: Baker, 1983).

Hare, D. R. A., *The Theme of Jewish Persecution of Christians in the Gospel according to St. Matthew* (SNTSMS 6; Cambridge: Cambridge University Press, 1967).

Harrington, D. J., *The Gospel of Matthew* (SacPag; Collegeville Liturgical, 1991).

Hartman, L., "Scriptural Exegesis in the Gospel of St. Matthew," in *L'Évangile selon Matthieu: Rédaction et théologie*, ed. M. Didier (BETL 29; Gembloux: Duculot, 1972).

Heckl, R., "Der biblische Begrundungsrahmen fur die Jungfrauengeburt bei Matthaüs," *ZNW* 95 (2004) 161–180.

Head, P. M., *Christology and the Synoptic Problem* (Cambridge: Cambridge University Press, 1997).

Hendrickx, H., *The Infancy Narratives* (London: Geoffrey Chapman, 1984).

Hengel, M., and H. Merkel, "Die Magier aus dem Osten und die Flucht nach Ägypten (Mt 2) im Rahmen der anitiken Religionsgeschichte und der Theologie des Matthaüs," in *Orientierung an Jesus*, ed. P. Hoffmann (Freiburg: Herder, 1973).

Hengel, M., *The Zealots* (Edinburgh: T. & T. Clark, 1989).

– *Judaism and Hellenism: Studies in Their Encounter in Palestine During the Early Hellenistic Period*, trans. J. Bowden (Philadelphia: Fortress, 1991).

– "Aufgaben der neutestamentlichen Wissenschaft," *NTS* 40 (1994) 321–357.

– "Tasks of New Testament Scholarship," *BBR* 6 (1996) 67–86.

– *The Four Gospels and the One Gospel of Jesus Christ* (Harrisburg: Trinity Press International, 2000).

Hill, D., *The Gospel of Matthew* (NCB; London: Marshall, Morgan, and Scott, 1972).

– "Son and Servant: An Essay on Matthean Christology," *JSNT* 6 (1980) 2–16.

– "The Figure of Jesus in Matthew's Story: A Response to Professor Kingsbury's Literary-Critical Probe," *JSNT* 21 (1984) 37–52.

Holmgren, F. C., *The Old Testament and the Significance of Jesus* (Grand Rapids: Eerdmans, 1999).

Holwerda, D. E., *Jesus and Israel* (Grand Rapids: Eerdmans, 1995).

Hooker, M. D., *Jesus and the Servant* (London: SPCK, 1959).

– *Beginnings: Keys That Open the Gospels* (London: SCM Press, 1997).

Hornblower, S. and A. Spawforth, eds., *The Oxford Classical Dictionary* (3rd ed. rev.; New York: Oxford, 2003).

Horsley, R. A., *The Liberation of Christmas* (New York: Crossroad, 1989).

Horst, P. W. van der, *Jews and Christians in Their Graeco-Roman Context* (WUNT 196; Tübingen: Mohr Siebeck, 2006).

Howard, T. L., "The Use of Hosea 11:1 in Matthew 2:15: An Alternative Solution," *BSac* 143 (1986) 314–328.

Howell, D. B., *Matthew's Inclusive Story: A Study in the Narrative Rhetoric of the First Gospel* (JSNTSup 42; Sheffield: JSOT, 1990).

Hummel, R., *Die Auseinandersetzung zwischen Kirche and Judentum im Matthäusevangelium* 2nd ed. (BevT 33: Munich: Kaiser, 1966).

Hurtado, L. W., *Lord Jesus Christ* (Grand Rapids: Eerdmans, 2003).

Hutchison, J. C., "Women, Gentiles, and the Messianic Mission in Matthew's Gospel," *BSac* 158 (2001),152–64.

Instone-Brewer, D. "Balaam-Laban as the Key to the Old Testament Quotations in Matthew 2," in *Built Upon the Rock: Studies in the Gospel of Matthew*, eds. D. M. Gurtner and J. Nolland (Grand Rapids: Eerdmans, 2008), 207-227.

Irenaeus, "Against Heresies," in *The Ante-Nicene Fathers Vol. 1*, eds. A. R. Roberts and J. Donaldson Grand Rapids: Eerdmans, 1985).

Japhet, S., *I and II Chronicles* (OTL; Louisville: Westminster/John Knox, 1993).

– *The Ideology of the Book of Chronicles and Its Place in Biblical Thought* 2nd ed. (BEATAJ 9; Frankfurt am Main: Lang, 1997).

Jeremias, J., *Jerusalem in the Time of Jesus* (London: SCM Press, 1969).

– *New Testament Theology* (New York: Charles Scribner's Sons, 1971).

Johnson, M. D., "Reflections on a Wisdom Approach to Matthew's Christology," *CBQ* 36 (1974) 44–64.

– *The Purpose of Biblical Genealogies* 2nd ed. (Cambridge: Cambridge University Press, 1988).

Johnson, S. E., "The Biblical Quotations in Matthew," *HTR* 36 (1943) 135–153.

Jones, I., "Matthew," in *Early Christian Thought in its Jewish Context*, eds. J. Barclay and J. Sweet (Cambridge: Cambridge University Press, 1996) 59–69.

Jonge, M. de., *Christology in Context* (Philadelphia: Westminster, 1988).

Juel, D., *Messianic Exegesis* (Philadelphia: Fortress Press, 1988).

Kealy, S. P., *Matthew's Gospel and the History of Biblical Interpretation* 2 vols. (Mellen Biblical Press Series 55; Lewiston/Queenston: Edwin Mellon, 1997).

Keck, L. E., "The Spirit and the Dove," *NTS* 17 (1970) 41–67.

– "Toward the Renewal of New Testament Christology," *NTS* 32 (1986) 362–377.

Keener, C., *A Commentary on the Gospel of Matthew* (Grand Rapids: Eerdmans, 1999).

Kilpatrick, G. D., *The Origins of the Gospel according to Matthew* (Oxford: Oxford University Press, 1946).

Kingsbury, J. D., *Matthew: Structure, Christology, Kingdom* (Philadelphia: Fortress, 1975).

– "The Title 'Son of David' in Matthew's Gospel," *JBL* 95 (1976) 591–602.

– *Matthew as Story* (2nd ed.; Philadelphia: Fortress, 1988).

Kittel, G. and G. Friedrich, eds., *Theological Dictionary of the New Testament* (trans. G. W. Bromiley; Grand Rapids: Eerdmans, 1964–1976).

Knoppers, G. N., "Intermarriage, Social Complexity, and Ethnic Diversity in the Genealogy of Judah," *JBL* 120 (2001) 15–20.

– *1 Chronicles 1–9* (AB; Garden City, NY: Doubleday, 2003).

Knowles, M., *Jeremiah in Matthew's Gospel* (Sheffield: JSOT Sheffield Academic Press, 1993).

Koester, H., *Introduction to the New Testament: History and Literature of Early Christianity* Vol. 2 (Philadelphia: Fortress, 1982).

Kotze, P. P. A., "The Structure of Matthew One," *Neot* 11 (1977) 1–9.

Kümmel, W. G., *Introduction to the New Testament* (trans. H.C. Kee; Nashville: Abingdon, 1975).

Kupp, D., *Matthew's Emmanuel: Divine Presence and God's People in the First Gospel* (SNTSMS 90; Cambridge: Cambridge University Press, 1996).

Kynes, W. L., *A Christology of Solidarity: Jesus as the Representative of His People in Matthew* (Lanham: University Press of America, 1991).

Lampe, G. W. H., "Typological Exegesis," *Th* 56 (1953).

238   *Bibliography*

Lampe, G. W. H., and K. J. Woollcombe, *Essays on Typology* (London: SCM Press, 1957).
Lane, W. L., *The Gospel According to Mark* (Grand Rapids: Eerdmans, 1974).
Larkin, K. J. A., *Ruth and Esther* (Sheffield: Sheffield Academic Press, 1986).
LeD'eaut, R., *The Message of the New Testament and the Aramaic Bible* (Rome: Biblical Institute Press, 1982).
Lee, S., *Mission to the Jews and the Gentiles in the Gospel of Matthew* (Unpublished Ph.D. Thesis: University of Aberdeen, 2002).
Levine, A., *The Social and Ethnic Dimension of Matthean Salvation History* (Lampeter: Edwin Mellon Press, 1988).
Levinsohn, S. H., *Discourse Features of New Testament Greek* (Dallas: SIL, 2002).
Lindars, B., *New Testament Apologetic* (London: SCM, 1961).
– "The Place of the Old Testament in the Formation of New Testament Theology," *NTS* 23 (1977).
Lohmeyer, E., *Das Evangelium des Matthäus* (4th ed.; Göttingen: Vandenhoeck & Ruprecht, 1967).
Longenecker, R. N., *The Christology of Early Jewish Christianity* (Grand Rapids: Baker, 1981).
– *Biblical Exegesis in the Apostolic Period* (2nd ed.; Grand Rapids: Eerdmans, 1999).
Loubser, J. A., "Invoking the Ancestors: Some Socio-Rhetorical Aspects of the Genealogies in the Gospels of Matthew and Luke," *Neot* 39 (2005) 127–140.
Louw, J. P., and E. A. Nida, *Greek-English Lexicon of the New Testament Based on Semantic Domains* Vol. 1 (New York: United Bible Societies, 1988).
Luomanen, P., *Entering the Kingdom of Heaven: A Study on the Structure of Matthew's View of Salvation* (WUNT 2.101; Tübingen; Mohr Siebeck, 1998).
Luz, U., *Matthew 1–7: A Commentary* (trans. W. C. Linss; Minneapolis: Augsburg, 1989).
– "Eine thetische Skizze der matthäischen Christologie," in *Anfänge der Christologie*, ed. C. Breytenbach and H. Paulsen (Göttingen: Vandenhoeck & Ruprecht, 1991) 221–236.
– "The Son of Man in Matthew: Heavenly Judge or Human Christ," *JSNT* 48 (1992) 3–21.
– *Matthew in History* (Minneapolis: Fortress, 1994).
– *The Theology of the Gospel of Matthew* (Cambridge: Cambridge University Press, 1995).
– *Matthew 21–28* (Hermeneia; Minneapolis: Fortress, 2005)
– *Studies in Matthew* (Grand Rapids: Eerdmans, 2005).
– *Matthew 1–7* (Hermeneia; Minneapolis: Fortress, 2007).
Manson, W., *Jesus the Messiah* (London: Hodder & Stoughton, 1943).
Massaux, E., *Influence de l'évangile de saint Matthien sur la littérature chrétienne avant saint Irénée* (BETL 75; Louvain: Presses universitaires de Louvain, 1986). ET: *The Influence of the Gospel of Saint Matthew on Christian Literature before Saint Irenaeus* (trans. N. J. Belval and S. Hecht; ed. A. J. Bellinzoni; New Gospel Studies 5; Macon, GA: Mercer University Press, 1990, 1993; 3 vols.).
Mayordomo-Marín, M., *Den Anfang hören: Leserorientierte Evangelienexegese am Beispiel von Matthaüs 1–2* (Gottingen: Vandenhoeck & Ruprecht, 1998).
Maher, M., *Targum Neofiti Exodus, The Aramaic Bible* (Vol. 2; Edinburgh: T&T Clark, 1994).
Malina, B. J. and J. H. Neyrey, *Calling Jesus Names* (Sonoma, CA: Polebridge, 1988).

Malina, B. J., and R. L. Rohrbaugh, *Social-Science Commentary on the Synoptic Gospels* (Minneapolis: Fortress, 1992).

Marshall, I. H., "Son of God or Servant of Yahweh?," *NTS* 15 (1969) 326–336.

Matera, F. J., "The Plot of Matthew's Gospel," *CBQ* 49 (1987) 233–253.

– *New Testament Christology* (Louisville, KY: Westminster John Knox, 1999).

McCartney, D., and P. Enns, "Matthew and Hosea: A Response to J. Sailhamer," *WTJ* 63 (2001).

McCasland, S. V., "Matthew Twists the Scriptures," *JBL* 80 (1961) 143–148.

McConnell, R. S., *Law and Prophecy in Matthew's Gospel* (Basel: Reinhardt, 1969).

McKnight, S., "Matthew," in *Dictionary of Jesus and the Gospels*, ed. J. B. Green and S. McKnight (Downers Grove: InterVarsity Press, 1992), 527–541.

– "A Loyal Critic: Matthew's Polemic with Judaism in Theological Perspective," in *Anti-Semitism and the New Testament: Issues of Faith and Polemic*, ed. C. A. Evans and D. A. Hagner (Minneapolis: Fortress, 1993) 55–79.

McNeile, A. H., *The Gospel According to St. Matthew* (London: Macmillan, 1961).

Mead, R. T., "A Dissenting Opinion About Respect for Context in Old Testament Quotations," *NTS* 10 (1963–1964).

Meier, J. P., "Salvation-History in Matthew: In Search of a Starting Point," *CBQ* 37 (1975) 203–215.

– *The Vision of Matthew: Christ, Church and Morality in the First Gospel* (New York: Paulist, 1979).

– *Matthew* (NT Message 3; Wilmington, DE: Glazier, 1980).

– *A Marginal Jew* (Vol. 1; New York: Doubleday, 1991).

– "Matthew," in *Anchor Bible Dictionary*, ed. D. N. Freedman (Vol. 4; New York: Doubleday, 1992) 622–641.

Menken, M. J. J., *Matthew's Bible: The Old Testament Text of the Evangelist* (Leuven: Leuven University Press, 2004).

– "Deuteronomy in Matthew's Gospel," in *Deuternonomy in the New Testament*, ed. S. Moyise and M. J. J. Menken (NY: T&T Clark International, 2007) 42–62.

Menninger, R. E., *Israel and the Church in the Gospel of Matthew* (New York: Peter Lang, 1994).

Metzger, B. M., *A Textual Commentary on the Greek New Testament* (New York: United Bible Societies, 1971).

Metzner, R. "Der Rückzug Jesu im Matthäusevangelium: Ein literarisches Déjà-vu-Erlebnis," *ZNW* 94 (2003) 258-268.

Meyer, H. A. W., *Critical and Exegetical Handbook to the Gospel of Matthew* (New York: Funk & Wagnalls, 1884).

Milton, D. H., "The Structure of the Prologue to St. Matthew's Gospel," JBL 81 (1962) 175–81.

Moberly, R. W. L., *The Bible, Theology, and Faith: A Study of Abraham and Jesus* (Cambridge: Cambridge University Press, 2000).

Moltmann, J., *The Way of Jesus Christ: Christology in Messianic Dimensions* (New York: HarperCollins, 1990).

Moore, S. D., *Literary Criticism and the Gospels* (New Haven: Yale University Press, 1989).

Moreton, M. J., 'Genealogy of Jesus," *SE* 2 [TU 87] (1964) 219–24.

Morris, L., *The Gospel according to Matthew* (Grand Rapids: Eerdmans, 1992).

Moule, C. F. D., "Fulfillment-Words in the New Testament : Use and Abuse," *NTS* 14 (1967–68) 293–320.

– *The Birth of the New Testament* (3rd ed.; London: Adam & Charles Black, 1981).

Müller, M., "The Theological Interpretation of the Figure of Jesus in the Gospel of Matthew: Some Principle Features in Matthean Christology," *NTS* 45 (1999) 157–73.

Mussies, G., "Parallels to Matthew's Version of the Pedigree of Jesus," *NovT* 28 (1986) 32–47.

Nellessen, E., *Das Kind und seine Mutter* (Stuttgart: Katholisches Bibelwerk, 1969).

Nelson, R. D., *Deuteronomy: A Commentary* (Louisville: Westminster John Knox, 2002).

Nepper-Christensen, P., *Das Matthäusevangelium: Ein judenchristliches Evangelium?* (Aarhus: Universitetsforlaget, 1954).

Neusner, J., *Judaism in the Matrix of Christianity* (Philadelphia: Fortress Press, 1986).

– *Rabbinic Literature and the New Testament: What We Cannot Show, We Do Not Know* (Valley Forge: Trinity Press International, 1994).

Neyrey, J., *Honor and Shame in the Gospel of Matthew* (Louisville: Westminster John Knox, 1998).

Nielsen, K., *Ruth: A Commentary* (London: SCM Press, 1997).

Nolan, B. M., *The Royal Son of God: The Christology of Matthew 1–2 in the Setting of the Gospel.* OBO 23 (Göttingen: Vandenhoeck & Ruprecht, 1979).

Nolland, J., "The Four (Five) Women and Other Annotations in Matthew's Genealogy," *NTS* 43 (1997) 527–539.

– "Jechoniah and His Brothers (Matthew 1:11)," *BBR* 7 (1997) 169–178.

– *The Gospel of Matthew* (Grand Rapids: Eerdmans, 2005).

– "Matthew and Anti-Semitism," in *Built Upon the Rock: Studies in the Gospel of Matthew*, eds. D. M. Gurtner and J. Nolland (Grand Rapids: Eerdmans, 2008) 154–169.

North, R. G., "Theology of the Chronicler," *JBL* 82 (1963), 369–381.

O'Leary, A. M., *Matthew's Judaization of Mark* (LNTS 323; NY: T&TClark/Continuum, 2006).

Ostmeyer, K., "Der Stammbaum des Verheissenen: Theologische Implikationen der Namen und Zahlen in Mt 1.1–17," NTS 46 (2000) 175–192.

Overman, J. A., *Matthew's Gospel and Formative Judaism* (Minneapolis: Fortress, 1990).

– *Church and Community in Crisis* (Valley Forge: Trinity Press International, 1996).

Patte, D., *Early Jewish Hermeneutic in Palestine* (SBLDS 22; Missoula: Scholars Press, 1973).

– *The Gospel according to Matthew: A Structural Commentary on Matthew's Faith* (Philadelphia: Fortress, 1987).

Pesch, R., "Der Gottessohn im matthäischen Evangelienprolog (Mt 1–2). Beobachtungen zu den Zitationsformeln der Reflexionszitate," *Bib* 48 (1967) 395–420.

– "He Will Be Called A Nazorean: Messianic Exegesis in Matthew 1–2," in *The Gospels and the Scriptures of Israel*, eds. C. A. Evans and W. R. Stegner (JSNTSS 104; Sheffield: Sheffield Academic Press, 1994)

Plummer, A., *An Exegetical Commentary on the Gospel according to St. Matthew* (London: Stock, 1909).

Pokorny, P., "The Temptation Stories and Their Intention," *NTS* 20 (1974) 115–127.

Porter, S. E., "The Use of the Old Testament in the New Testament: A Brief Comment on Method and Terminology," in *Early Christian Interpretation of the Scriptures of Israel*, eds. C. A. Evans and J. A. Sanders (JSNTSuppS 148; Sheffield: Sheffield Academic Press, 1997)

Powell, M. A., "The Plot and Subplots of Matthew's Gospel," *NTS* 38 (1992), 187–204.

– "Matthew," in *HarperCollins Bible Commentary*, ed. J. L. Mays (New York: HarperCollins, 2000) 868–900.

– "The Magi as Wise Men: Re-examining a Basic Supposition," *NTS* 46 (2000), 1–20.

Powery, E. B., *Jesus Reads Scripture: The Function of Jesus' Use of Scripture in the Synoptic Gospels* (Leiden: Brill, 2003).

Prabhu, G. M. S., *The Formula Quotations in the Infancy Narrative of Matthew* (Analecta Biblica 63; Rome: Biblical Institute Press, 1976).

Pratt, R. L., *1 and 2 Chronicles* (Ross-shire: Christian Focus Publications, 1998).

Przybylski, B., "The Role of Matthew 3:13–4:11 in the Structure and Theology of the Gospel of Matthew," *BTB* 4 (1974) 222–235.

– "The Setting of Matthean Anti-Judaism," in *Anti-Judaism in Early Christianity*: *Paul and the Gospels*, ed. P. Richardson with D. Granskou, (Vol. 1; Waterloo: Wilfrid Laurier University, 1986) 181–200.

Rad, G. von, 'Typological Interpretation of the Old Testament," in *Essays on Old Testament Interpretation*, ed. C. Westermann (London: SCM Press, 1963).

– *Old Testament Theology* (Vol. 2; Edinburgh & London: Oliver & Boyd, 1965).

Rasco, E., "Matthew I–II: Structure, Meaning, Reality," *SE* 4 (TU 102) (1968) 214–230.

Renan, E., Les Évangiles et la seconde génération Chrétienne (Paris: Calmann Lévy, 1877).

Repschinski, B., "For He Will Save His People From Their Sins (1:21) Christology for Christian Jews," *CBQ* 68 (2006) 248–267.

Riches, J., Matthew (Sheffield: Sheffield Academic Press, 1996).

Riches, J. and D. C. Sim, eds., *The Gospel of Matthew in its Roman Imperial Context* (JSNTSS 276; New York: T & T Clark International, 2005).

Ridderbos, H. N., *Matthew* (Grand Rapids: 1987).

Robertson, A. T. *A Grammar of the Greek New Testament in the Light of Historical Research* 2nd ed. (New York: Hodder & Stoughton, 1914).

Robinson, R. B., "Literary Functions of the Genealogies of Genesis," *CBQ* 48 (1986) 595–608.

Rohde, J., *Rediscovering the Teaching of the Evangelists* (Philadelphia: Westminster, 1968).

Rothfuchs, W., *Die Erfüllungszitate des Matthäus-Evangeliums* (BWANT 88; Stuttgart: Kohlhammer, 1969).

Sabourin, L., *The Gospel according to St. Matthew* (Vol. 1; Bombay: St. Paul, 1982).

Sailhamer, J., *The Pentateuch as Narrative* (Grand Rapids: Zondervan, 1992).

– "Hosea 11:1 and Matthew 2:15," *WTJ* 63 (2001) 87–105.

Saldarini, A. J., *Matthew Christian-Jewish Community* (Chicago: University of Chicago Press, 1994).

– "Reading Matthew without Anti-Semitism," in *The Gospel of Matthew in Current Study*, ed. D. E. Aune (Grand Rapid: Eerdmans, 2001) 166–184.

– "Matthew," in *Eerdman's Commentary on the Bible*, eds. J. D. G. Dunn and J. W. Rogerson (Grand Rapids: Eerdmans, 2003).

Sand, A., *Das Evangelium nach Matthäus* (Regensburger Neues Testament; Regensburg: Friedrich Pustet, 1986).

Sanders, E. P. and M. Davies, *Studying the Synoptic Gospels* (London: SCM Press, 1989).

Sanders, J. A., "The Gospels and the Canonical Process," *The Relationships Among the Gospels*, ed. W. O. Walker (San Antonio: Trinity Press, 1978) 219–236.

Sarna, N. M., *The JPS Torah Commentary: Exodus* (Philadelphia: JPS, 1991).

Sasson, J. M., "A Genealogical Convention in Biblical Chronography," *ZAW* 90 (1978) 171–185.

– *Ruth* (Sheffield: Sheffield Academic Press, 1989).

Schaberg, J., *The Illegitimacy of Jesus* (Sheffield: Sheffield Academic Press, 1995).

Schlatter, A., *Der Evangelist Matthäus* (2ⁿᵈ ed.; Stuttgart: Calwer, 1933).

Schmidt, K., *Der Rahmen der Geschichte Jesu* (Berlin: Trowitzsch & Sohn, 1919).

Schnabel, E. J., *Early Christian Mission: Paul and the Early Church* (Downers Grove: InterVarsity, 2004).

Schnackenburg, R., *The Gospel of Matthew* (trans. R. R. Barr; Grand Rapids: Eerdmans, 2002).

– *Jesus in the Gospels* (trans. O. C. Dean; Louisville: Westminster John Knox, 1995).

Schneemelcher, W., *New Testament Apocrypha* (trans. R. McL. Wilson; Vol. 1; Philadelphia: Westminster, 1963).

Schnelle, U., *The History and Theology of the New Testament Writings*, (trans. M. E. Boring; Minneapolis: Fortress Press, 1998).

Schniewind, J., *Das Evangelium nach Matthäus* (Göttingen: Vandenhoeck & Ruprecht, 1950).

Schöllig, H., "Die Zählung der Generationen im matthäischen Stammbaum," *ZNW* 59 (1968).

Schweizer, E., *The Good News according to Matthew* (London: SPCK, 1975).

Scott, B. B., "The Birth of the Reader," *Semeia* 52 (1990) 83–102.

Segbroeck, F. van, "Les citations d'accomplissement dans l'Évangile selon saint Matthieu d'après trios ouvrages récents," in *L'Évangile selon Matthieu: Rédaction et théologie*, ed. M. Didier (BETL 29; Gembloux: Duculot, 1972) 107–130.

Selman, M. J., *1 Chronicles* (TOTC; Leicester: InterVarsity, 1994).

Senior, D., *What Are They Saying About Matthew?* (New York: Paulist Press, 1996).

Shuler, P. L., *A Genre for the Gospels* (Philadelphia: Fortress, 1982).

Silberman, L. H., "Haben Sua Fata Libelli: The Role of Wandering Themes," in *The Relationships Among the Gospels*, ed. W. O. Walker (San Antonio: Trinity University Press, 1978).

Sim, D. C., *The Gospel of Matthew and Christian Judaism* (SNTW; Edinburgh: T. & T. Clark, 1998).

Simonetti, M., *Matthew 1–13* (ACCS; Downers Grove: InterVarsity Press, 2001).

– *Matthew 14–28* (ACCS; Downers Grove: InterVarsity Press, 2002).

Smith, D. M., "The Use of the Old Testament in the New," in *The Use of the Old Testament in the New and Other Essays*, ed. J. M. Efird (Durham: Duke, 1972).

Smith, R. H., *Matthew* (Minneapolis: Augsburg, 1989).

Solomon, A. M., "The Structure of the Chronicler's History," *Semeia* 46 (1989).

Sparks, K. L., *Ancient Texts for the Study of the Hebrew Bible* (Peabody: Hendrickson, 2005).

Stanton, G., *Jesus of Nazareth in New Testament Preaching* (SNTSMS 27; Cambridge: Cambridge University Press, 1974)

– ed., *The Interpretation of Matthew* (Philadelphia: Fortress, 1983).

– *A Gospel for a New People* (Louisville: Westminster/John Knox Press, 1993).

Stegemann, W., "Die Versuchung Jesu im Matthäusevangelium: Mt 4,1–11," *EvT* 45 (1985) 29–44.

Stein, R. H., *Studying the Synoptic Gospels* (2ⁿᵈ ed.; Grand Rapids: Baker, 2001).

Stendahl, K., *The School of St. Matthew and Its Use of the Old Testament* (Philadelphia: Fortress, 1968).

– "Quis et Unde," in *The Interpretation of Matthew*, ed. G. Stanton (Philadelphia: Fortress, 1983) 69–80.

Sternberg, M., *Poetics of Biblical Language* (Bloomington: Indiana University Press, 1985).

Sternberg, N., "The Genealogical Framework of the Family Stories in Genesis," *Semeia* 46 (1989).
- *Kinship and Marriage in Genesis* (Minneapolis: Fortress Press, 1993).
Strecker, G., *Der Weg der Gerichtigkeit* (Göttingen: Vandenhoeck & Ruprecht, 1962).
- *Theology of the New Testament* (trans. M. E. Boring; Louisville: Westminster John Knox, 2000).
Streeter, B. H., *The Four Gospels* (London: Macmillan, 1924).
Stuhlmueller, C., "Psalms," in *HarperCollins Bible Commentary*, ed. J. L. Mays (New York: HarperCollins, 2000) 394–446.
Suggs, M. J. *Wisdom, Christology and Law in Matthew's Gospel* (Cambridge, MA: Harvard, 1970).
Suhl, A., "Der Davidssohn im Matthäusevangelium," *ZNW* 59 (1968) 67–81.
Swartley, W. M., *Israel's Scripture Traditions and the Synoptic Gospels: Story Shaping Story* (Peabody: Hendrickson, 1994).
Talbert, C. H., *What is a Gospel? The Genre of the Canonical Gospels* (Philadelphia: Fortress, 1977).
Tasker, R. V. G., *The Gospel according to St. Matthew* (TNTC; London: Tyndale, 1961).
Taylor, Jr., A. B., "Decision in the Desert," *Int* 14 (1960).
Teeple, H. M., *The Mosaic Eschatological Prophet* (Philadelphia: Society of Biblical Literature, 1957).
Theissen, G., *The Gospels in Context: Social and Political History in the Synoptic Tradition* (Minneapolis: Fortress, 1991).
Thiselton, A. C., *New Horizons in Hermeneutics* (Grand Rapids: Zondervan, 1992).
Thompson, G. H. P., "Called-Proved-Obedient," *JTS* 11 (1960) 1–12.
Thompson, T. L., *The Origin Tradition of Ancient Israel* (Sheffield: Sheffield Academic Press, 1987).
Tigay, J. H., *The JPS Torah Commentary: Deuteronomy* (Philadelphia: JPS, 1996).
Torrance, T. F., *The Mediation of Christ* (Grand Rapids: Eerdmans, 1984).
- *Divine Meaning: Studies in Patristic Hermeneutics* (Edinburgh: T&T Clark, 1995).
- *Space, Time and Resurrection* (Edinburgh: T&T Clark, 1998).
Trilling, W., *Das wahre Israel: Studien zur Theologie des Matthäusevangeliums* (3rd ed.; Leipzig: St. Benno, 1975).
Tuckett, C., *Christology and the New Testament* (Louisville: WJKP, 2001).
Turner, D. L., *Matthew* (BECNT; Grand Rapids: Baker Academic, 2008).
Turner, H. E. W., *Jesus, Master and Lord* (London: Mowbray, 1970).
Van Aarde, A. G., "ΙΗΣΟΥΣ, The Davidic Messiah, As Political Saviour in Matthew's History," in *Salvation in the New Testament*, ed. J. G. van der Watt (Boston: Brill, 2005) 7–31.
Van Elderen, B., "The Significance of Structure of Matthew 1," in *Chronos, Kairos, Christos*. FS J. Finegan, eds. J. Vardaman and E. M. Yamauchi (Winona Lake, IN: Eisenbrauns, 1989).
VanGemeren, W. A., "Psalms," in *The Expositor's Bible Commentary* (Vol. 5; Grand Rapids: Zondervan, 1991).
- ed., *New International Dictionary of Old Testament Theology and Exegesis* (Vol. 4; Grand Rapids: Zondervan, 1997).
Van Voorst, R. E., *Jesus Outside the New Testament* (Grand Rapids: Eerdmans, 2000).
Verseput, D., *The Rejection of the Humble Messianic King: A Study of the Composition of Matthew 11–12* (European University Studies 291: Frankfurt am Main: Peter Lang, 1986).

Via, D. A., "Narrative World and Ethical Response: The Marvelous and Righteousness in Matthew 1–2," *Semeia* 10 (1978).

Viviano, B. T., "The Genres of Matthew 1–2: Light from 1 Timothy 1:4" *RB* 97 (1990) 31–53.

Vögtle, A., "Die matthaische Kindheitsgeschichte," in *L'Evangile selon Matthieu: Redaction et theologie*, ed. M. Didier (Gembloux: Duculot, 1972) 153–183.

Waetjen, H. C., "The Genealogy as the Key to the Gospel according to Matthew," *JBL* 95 (1976).

Wainwright, E., "The Gospel of Matthew," in *Searching the Scriptures Vol. 2: A Feminist Commentary*, ed. E. S. Fiorenza (London: SCM Press,1994).

Walker, R., *Die Heilsgeschichte im ersten Evangelium* (FRLANT 91; Göttingen: Vandenhoeck & Ruprecht, 1984).

Wallace, D. B., *Greek Grammar Beyond the Basics* (Grand Rapids: Zondervan, 1996).

Watson, F., *Text and Truth* (Grand Rapids: Eerdmans, 1997).

Watts, R., *Isaiah's New Exodus in Mark* (Grand Rapids: Baker, 2000).

Weaver, D. J., *Matthew's Missionary Discourse: A Literary Critical Analysis* (JSNTSS 38; Sheffield: JSOT, 1990).

– "Rewriting the Messianic Script: Matthew's Account of the Birth of Jesus," *Int* 54 (2000) 376–385.

Weinfeld, M., *Deuteronomy 1–11* (AB; New York: Doubleday, 1991).

Wenham, G., *Genesis 1–15* (WBC; Dallas: Word, 1987).

Weren, W., "The History and Social Setting of the Matthean Community," in *Matthew and the Didache*, ed. H. vande Sandt (Minneapolis: Fortress, 2005).

Westermann, C., *Genesis 37–50* (trans. J. J. Scullion; London: SPCK, 1987).

– *Genesis: An Introduction* (trans. J. J. Scullion; Minneapolis: Fortress, 1992).

– "Genealogies," in *The Oxford Companion to Bible*, eds. B. M. Metzger and M. D. Coogan (New York: Oxford University Press, 1993) 243–245.

Wilk, F., *Jesus und die Völker in der Sicht der Synoptiker* (New York: De Gruyter, 2002).

Wilkens, W., "Die Versuchung Jesu Nach Matthäus," *NTS* 28 (1982) 479–489.

Williamson, H. G. M., *Israel in the Books of Chronicles* (Cambridge: Cambridge University Press, 1977).

– *1 and 2 Chronicles*. NCB (Grand Rapids: Eerdmans, 1982).

Willitts, J., *Matthew's Messianic Shepherd-King* (Berlin: de Gruyter, 2007).

Wilson, R. R., *Genealogy and History in the Biblical World* (New Haven: Yale University Press, 1977).

– "Genealogies," in *Anchor Bible Dictionary*, ed. D. N. Freedman (Vol. 2; New York: Doubleday, 1992) 929–932.

Witherington, B., "Birth of Jesus," in *Dictionary of Jesus and the Gospels*, eds. J. B. Green and S. McKnight (Downers Grove: InterVarsity Press, 1992) 60–74.

– *The Many Faces of the Christ* (New York: Crossroad, 1998).

– *Matthew* (Macon: Smyth & Helwys, 2006).

Wright, A. G., "The Literary Genre Midrash," *CBQ* 28 (1966) 417–475.

Wright, G. E., *God Who Acts: Biblical Theology as Recital* (London: SCM Press, 1952).

Wright, N. T., *The New Testament and the People of God* (Minneapolis: Fortress, 1992).

– *Jesus and the Victory of God* (Minneapolis: Fortress, 1996).

Yeiven, S., *The Israelite Conquest of Canaan* (Istanbul Nederlands Historisch-Archaelogisch Instituut in het Natsije Oosten, 1971).

Zahn, T. B., *Introduction to the New Testament* (3 vols; Edinburgh: T.& T. Clark, 1909).

Index of Ancient Sources

1. Old Testament

2. Old Testament Apocrypha

3. Pseudepigrapha

4. Qumran Writings

5. Philo

6. Josephus

7. New Testament

8. Greco-Roman Writings

9. Rabbinic Writings

10. Early Christian Writings

Index of Modern Authors

Index of Subjects and Key Terms

Wissenschaftliche Untersuchungen zum Neuen Testament

Alphabetical Index of the First and Second Series

Betz, Otto: Jesus, der Messias Israels. 1987. *Vol. 42.*
– Jesus, der Herr der Kirche. 1990. *Vol. 52.*
Beyschlag, Karlmann: Simon Magus und die christliche Gnosis. 1974. *Vol. 16.*
Bieringer, Reimund: see *Koester, Craig.*
Bittner, Wolfgang J.: Jesu Zeichen im Johannesevangelium. 1987. *Vol. II/26.*
Bjerkelund, Carl J.: Tauta Egeneto. 1987. *Vol. 40.*
Blackburn, Barry Lee: Theios Aner and the Markan Miracle Traditions. 1991. *Vol. II/40.*
Blanton IV, Thomas R.: Constructing a New Covenant. 2007. *Vol. II/233.*
Bock, Darrell L.: Blasphemy and Exaltation in Judaism and the Final Examination of Jesus. 1998. *Vol. II/106.*
Bockmuehl, Markus N.A.: Revelation and Mystery in Ancient Judaism and Pauline Christianity. 1990. *Vol. II/36.*
Bøe, Sverre: Gog and Magog. 2001. *Vol. II/135.*
Böhlig, Alexander: Gnosis und Synkretismus. Vol. 1 1989. *Vol. 47* – Vol. 2 1989. *Vol. 48.*
Böhm, Martina: Samarien und die Samaritai bei Lukas. 1999. *Vol. II/111.*
Böttrich, Christfried: Weltweisheit – Menschheitsethik – Urkult. 1992. *Vol. II/50.*
– and *Herzer, Jens* (Ed.): Josephus und das Neue Testament. 2007. *Vol. 209.*
Bolyki, János: Jesu Tischgemeinschaften. 1997. *Vol. II/96.*
Bosman, Philip: Conscience in Philo and Paul. 2003. *Vol. II/166.*
Bovon, François: Studies in Early Christianity. 2003. *Vol. 161.*
Brändl, Martin: Der Agon bei Paulus. 2006. *Vol. II/222.*
Breytenbach, Cilliers: see *Frey, Jörg.*
Brocke, Christoph vom: Thessaloniki – Stadt des Kassander und Gemeinde des Paulus. 2001. *Vol. II/125.*
Brunson, Andrew: Psalm 118 in the Gospel of John. 2003. *Vol. II/158.*
Büchli, Jörg: Der Poimandres – ein paganisiertes Evangelium. 1987. *Vol. II/27.*
Bühner, Jan A.: Der Gesandte und sein Weg im 4. Evangelium. 1977. *Vol. II/2.*
Burchard, Christoph: Untersuchungen zu Joseph und Aseneth. 1965. *Vol. 8.*
– Studien zur Theologie, Sprache und Umwelt des Neuen Testaments. Ed. by D. Sänger. 1998. *Vol. 107.*
Burnett, Richard: Karl Barth's Theological Exegesis. 2001. *Vol. II/145.*
Byron, John: Slavery Metaphors in Early Judaism and Pauline Christianity. 2003. *Vol. II/162.*

Byrskog, Samuel: Story as History – History as Story. 2000. *Vol. 123.*
Cancik, Hubert (Ed.): Markus-Philologie. 1984. *Vol. 33.*
Capes, David B.: Old Testament Yaweh Texts in Paul's Christology. 1992. *Vol. II/47.*
Caragounis, Chrys C.: The Development of Greek and the New Testament. 2004. *Vol. 167.*
– The Son of Man. 1986. *Vol. 38.*
– see *Fridrichsen, Anton.*
Carleton Paget, James: The Epistle of Barnabas. 1994. *Vol. II/64.*
Carson, D.A., O'Brien, Peter T. and *Mark Seifrid* (Ed.): Justification and Variegated Nomism.
Vol. 1: The Complexities of Second Temple Judaism. 2001. *Vol. II/140.*
Vol. 2: The Paradoxes of Paul. 2004. *Vol. II/181.*
Chae, Young Sam: Jesus as the Eschatological Davidic Shepherd. 2006. *Vol. II/216.*
Chapman, David W.: Ancient Jewish and Christian Perceptions of Crucifixion. 2008. *Vol. II/244.*
Chester, Andrew: Messiah and Exaltation. 2007. *Vol. 207.*
Chibici-Revneanu, Nicole: Die Herrlichkeit des Verherrlichten. 2007. *Vol. II/231.*
Ciampa, Roy E.: The Presence and Function of Scripture in Galatians 1 and 2. 1998. *Vol. II/102.*
Classen, Carl Joachim: Rhetorical Criticsm of the New Testament. 2000. *Vol. 128.*
Colpe, Carsten: Griechen – Byzantiner – Semiten – Muslime. 2008. *Vol. 221.*
– Iranier – Aramäer – Hebräer – Hellenen. 2003. *Vol. 154.*
Crump, David: Jesus the Intercessor. 1992. *Vol. II/49.*
Dahl, Nils Alstrup: Studies in Ephesians. 2000. *Vol. 131.*
Daise, Michael A.: Feasts in John. 2007. *Vol. II/229.*
Deines, Roland: Die Gerechtigkeit der Tora im Reich des Messias. 2004. *Vol. 177.*
– Jüdische Steingefäße und pharisäische Frömmigkeit. 1993. *Vol. II/52.*
– Die Pharisäer. 1997. *Vol. 101.*
Deines, Roland and *Karl-Wilhelm Niebuhr* (Ed.): Philo und das Neue Testament. 2004. *Vol. 172.*
Dennis, John A.: Jesus' Death and the Gathering of True Israel. 2006. *Vol. 217.*
Dettwiler, Andreas and *Jean Zumstein* (Ed.): Kreuzestheologie im Neuen Testament. 2002. *Vol. 151.*

Dickson, John P.: Mission-Commitment in Ancient Judaism and in the Pauline Communities. 2003. *Vol. II/159.*

Dietzfelbinger, Christian: Der Abschied des Kommenden. 1997. *Vol. 95.*

Dimitrov, Ivan Z., James D.G. Dunn, Ulrich Luz and *Karl-Wilhelm Niebuhr* (Ed.): Das Alte Testament als christliche Bibel in orthodoxer und westlicher Sicht. 2004. *Vol. 174.*

Dobbeler, Axel von: Glaube als Teilhabe. 1987. *Vol. II/22.*

Downs, David J.: The Offering of the Gentiles. 2008. *Vol. II/248.*

Dryden, J. de Waal: Theology and Ethics in 1 Peter. 2006. *Vol. II/209.*

Dübbers, Michael: Christologie und Existenz im Kolosserbrief. 2005. *Vol. II/191.*

Dunn, James D.G.: The New Perspective on Paul. 2005. *Vol. 185.*

Dunn, James D.G. (Ed.): Jews and Christians. 1992. *Vol. 66.*

– Paul and the Mosaic Law. 1996. *Vol. 89.*

– see *Dimitrov, Ivan Z.*

–, *Hans Klein, Ulrich Luz,* and *Vasile Mihoc* (Ed.): Auslegung der Bibel in orthodoxer und westlicher Perspektive. 2000. *Vol. 130.*

Ebel, Eva: Die Attraktivität früher christlicher Gemeinden. 2004. *Vol. II/178.*

Ebertz, Michael N.: Das Charisma des Gekreuzigten. 1987. *Vol. 45.*

Eckstein, Hans-Joachim: Der Begriff Syneidesis bei Paulus. 1983. *Vol. II/10.*

– Verheißung und Gesetz. 1996. *Vol. 86.*

Ego, Beate: Im Himmel wie auf Erden. 1989. *Vol. II/34.*

Ego, Beate, Armin Lange and *Peter Pilhofer* (Ed.): Gemeinde ohne Tempel – Community without Temple. 1999. *Vol. 118.*

– and *Helmut Merkel* (Ed.): Religiöses Lernen in der biblischen, frühjüdischen und frühchristlichen Überlieferung. 2005. *Vol. 180.*

Eisen, Ute E.: see *Paulsen, Henning.*

Elledge, C.D.: Life after Death in Early Judaism. 2006. *Vol. II/208.*

Ellis, E. Earle: Prophecy and Hermeneutic in Early Christianity. 1978. *Vol. 18.*

– The Old Testament in Early Christianity. 1991. *Vol. 54.*

Endo, Masanobu: Creation and Christology. 2002. *Vol. 149.*

Ennulat, Andreas: Die 'Minor Agreements'. 1994. *Vol. II/62.*

Ensor, Peter W.: Jesus and His 'Works'. 1996. *Vol. II/85.*

Eskola, Timo: Messiah and the Throne. 2001. *Vol. II/142.*

– Theodicy and Predestination in Pauline Soteriology. 1998. *Vol. II/100.*

Fatehi, Mehrdad: The Spirit's Relation to the Risen Lord in Paul. 2000. *Vol. II/128.*

Feldmeier, Reinhard: Die Krisis des Gottessohnes. 1987. *Vol. II/21.*

– Die Christen als Fremde. 1992. *Vol. 64.*

Feldmeier, Reinhard and *Ulrich Heckel* (Ed.): Die Heiden. 1994. *Vol. 70.*

Fletcher-Louis, Crispin H.T.: Luke-Acts: Angels, Christology and Soteriology. 1997. *Vol. II/94.*

Förster, Niclas: Marcus Magus. 1999. *Vol. 114.*

Forbes, Christopher Brian: Prophecy and Inspired Speech in Early Christianity and its Hellenistic Environment. 1995. *Vol. II/75.*

Fornberg, Tord: see *Fridrichsen, Anton.*

Fossum, Jarl E.: The Name of God and the Angel of the Lord. 1985. *Vol. 36.*

Foster, Paul: Community, Law and Mission in Matthew's Gospel. *Vol. II/177.*

Fotopoulos, John: Food Offered to Idols in Roman Corinth. 2003. *Vol. II/151.*

Frenschkowski, Marco: Offenbarung und Epiphanie. Vol. 1 1995. *Vol. II/79* – Vol. 2 1997. *Vol. II/80.*

Frey, Jörg: Eugen Drewermann und die biblische Exegese. 1995. *Vol. II/71.*

– Die johanneische Eschatologie. Vol. I. 1997. *Vol. 96.* – Vol. II. 1998. *Vol. 110.* – Vol. III. 2000. *Vol. 117.*

Frey, Jörg and *Cilliers Breytenbach* (Ed.): Aufgabe und Durchführung einer Theologie des Neuen Testaments. 2007. *Vol. 205.*

– and *Udo Schnelle (Ed.):* Kontexte des Johannesevangeliums. 2004. *Vol. 175.*

– and *Jens Schröter* (Ed.): Deutungen des Todes Jesu im Neuen Testament. 2005. *Vol. 181.*

–, *Jan G. van der Watt,* and *Ruben Zimmermann* (Ed.): Imagery in the Gospel of John. 2006. *Vol. 200.*

Freyne, Sean: Galilee and Gospel. 2000. *Vol. 125.*

Fridrichsen, Anton: Exegetical Writings. Edited by C.C. Caragounis and T. Fornberg. 1994. *Vol. 76.*

Gäbel, Georg: Die Kulttheologie des Hebräerbriefes. 2006. *Vol. II/212.*

Gäckle, Volker: Die Starken und die Schwachen in Korinth und in Rom. 2005. *Vol. 200.*

Garlington, Don B.: 'The Obedience of Faith'. 1991. *Vol. II/38.*

– Faith, Obedience, and Perseverance. 1994. *Vol. 79.*

Garnet, Paul: Salvation and Atonement in the Qumran Scrolls. 1977. *Vol. II/3.*

Gemünden, Petra von (Ed.): see *Weissenrieder, Annette.*

Gese, Michael: Das Vermächtnis des Apostels. 1997. *Vol. II/99.*

Gheorghita, Radu: The Role of the Septuagint in Hebrews. 2003. *Vol. II/160.*

Gordley, Matthew E.: The Colossian Hymn in Context. 2007. *Vol. II/228.*

Gräbe, Petrus J.: The Power of God in Paul's Letters. 2000, ²2008. *Vol. II/123.*

Gräßer, Erich: Der Alte Bund im Neuen. 1985. *Vol. 35.*

– Forschungen zur Apostelgeschichte. 2001. *Vol. 137.*

Grappe, Christian (Ed.): Le Repas de Dieu / Das Mahl Gottes. 2004. *Vol. 169.*

Gray, Timothy C.: The Temple in the Gospel of Mark. 2008. *Vol. II/242.*

Green, Joel B.: The Death of Jesus. 1988. *Vol. II/33.*

Gregg, Brian Han: The Historical Jesus and the Final Judgment Sayings in Q. 2005. *Vol. II/207.*

Gregory, Andrew: The Reception of Luke and Acts in the Period before Irenaeus. 2003. *Vol. II/169.*

Grindheim, Sigurd: The Crux of Election. 2005. *Vol. II/202.*

Gundry, Robert H.: The Old is Better. 2005. *Vol. 178.*

Gundry Volf, Judith M.: Paul and Perseverance. 1990. *Vol. II/37.*

Häußer, Detlef: Christusbekenntnis und Jesusüberlieferung bei Paulus. 2006. *Vol. 210.*

Hafemann, Scott J.: Suffering and the Spirit. 1986. *Vol. II/19.*

– Paul, Moses, and the History of Israel. 1995. *Vol. 81.*

Hahn, Ferdinand: Studien zum Neuen Testament.
Vol. I: Grundsatzfragen, Jesusforschung, Evangelien. 2006. *Vol. 191.*
Vol. II: Bekenntnisbildung und Theologie in urchristlicher Zeit. 2006. *Vol. 192.*

Hahn, Johannes (Ed.): Zerstörungen des Jerusalemer Tempels. 2002. *Vol. 147.*

Hamid-Khani, Saeed: Relevation and Concealment of Christ. 2000. *Vol. II/120.*

Hannah, Darrel D.: Michael and Christ. 1999. *Vol. II/109.*

Hardin, Justin K.: Galatians and the Imperial Cult? 2007. *Vol. II /237.*

Harrison; James R.: Paul's Language of Grace in Its Graeco-Roman Context. 2003. *Vol. II/172.*

Hartman, Lars: Text-Centered New Testament Studies. Ed. von D. Hellholm. 1997. *Vol. 102.*

Hartog, Paul: Polycarp and the New Testament. 2001. *Vol. II/134.*

Heckel, Theo K.: Der Innere Mensch. 1993. *Vol. II/53.*

– Vom Evangelium des Markus zum viergestaltigen Evangelium. 1999. *Vol. 120.*

Heckel, Ulrich: Kraft in Schwachheit. 1993. *Vol. II/56.*

– Der Segen im Neuen Testament. 2002. *Vol. 150.*

– see *Feldmeier, Reinhard.*

– see *Hengel, Martin.*

Heiligenthal, Roman: Werke als Zeichen. 1983. *Vol. II/9.*

Heliso, Desta: Pistis and the Righteous One. 2007. *Vol. II/235.*

Hellholm, D.: see *Hartman, Lars.*

Hemer, Colin J.: The Book of Acts in the Setting of Hellenistic History. 1989. *Vol. 49.*

Hengel, Martin: Jesus und die Evangelien. Kleine Schriften V. 2007. *Vol. 211.*

– Die johanneische Frage. 1993. *Vol. 67.*

– Judaica et Hellenistica. Kleine Schriften I. 1996. *Vol. 90.*

– Judaica, Hellenistica et Christiana. Kleine Schriften II. 1999. *Vol. 109.*

– Judentum und Hellenismus. 1969, ³1988. *Vol. 10.*

– Paulus und Jakobus. Kleine Schriften III. 2002. *Vol. 141.*

– Studien zur Christologie. Kleine Schriften IV. 2006. *Vol. 201.*

– Studien zum Urchristentum. Kleine Schriften VI. 2008. *Vol. 234.*

– and *Anna Maria Schwemer:* Paulus zwischen Damaskus und Antiochien. 1998. *Vol. 108.*

– Der messianische Anspruch Jesu und die Anfänge der Christologie. 2001. *Vol. 138.*

– Die vier Evangelien und das eine Evangelium von Jesus Christus. 2008. *Vol. 224.*

Hengel, Martin and *Ulrich Heckel* (Ed.): Paulus und das antike Judentum. 1991. *Vol. 58.*

– and *Hermut Löhr* (Ed.): Schriftauslegung im antiken Judentum und im Urchristentum. 1994. *Vol. 73.*

– and *Anna Maria Schwemer* (Ed.): Königsherrschaft Gottes und himmlischer Kult. 1991. *Vol. 55.*

– Die Septuaginta. 1994. *Vol. 72.*

–, *Siegfried Mittmann* and *Anna Maria Schwemer* (Ed.): La Cité de Dieu / Die Stadt Gottes. 2000. *Vol. 129.*

Hentschel, Anni: Diakonia im Neuen Testament. 2007. *Vol. 226.*

Hernández Jr., Juan: Scribal Habits and Theological Influence in the Apocalypse. 2006. *Vol. II/218.*

Herrenbrück, Fritz: Jesus und die Zöllner. 1990. *Vol. II/41.*

Herzer, Jens: Paulus oder Petrus? 1998.
Vol. 103.
– see *Böttrich, Christfried.*
Hill, Charles E.: From the Lost Teaching of Polycarp. 2005. *Vol. 186.*
Hoegen-Rohls, Christina: Der nachösterliche Johannes. 1996. *Vol. II/84.*
Hoffmann, Matthias Reinhard: The Destroyer and the Lamb. 2005. *Vol. II/203.*
Hofius, Otfried: Katapausis. 1970. *Vol. 11.*
– Der Vorhang vor dem Thron Gottes. 1972. *Vol. 14.*
– Der Christushymnus Philipper 2,6–11. 1976, ²1991. *Vol. 17.*
– Paulusstudien. 1989, ²1994. *Vol. 51.*
– Neutestamentliche Studien. 2000. *Vol. 132.*
– Paulusstudien II. 2002. *Vol. 143.*
– Exegetische Studien. 2008. *Vol. 223.*
– and *Hans-Christian Kammler:* Johannesstudien. 1996. *Vol. 88.*
Holmberg, Bengt (Ed.): Exploring Early Christian Identity. 2008. *Vol. 226.*
– and *Mikael Winninge* (Ed.): Identity Formation in the New Testament. 2008. *Vol. 227.*
Holtz, Traugott: Geschichte und Theologie des Urchristentums. 1991. *Vol. 57.*
Hommel, Hildebrecht: Sebasmata.
Vol. 1 1983. *Vol. 31.*
Vol. 2 1984. *Vol. 32.*
Horbury, William: Herodian Judaism and New Testament Study. 2006. *Vol. 193.*
Horst, Pieter W. van der: Jews and Christians in Their Graeco-Roman Context. 2006. *Vol. 196.*
Hvalvik, Reidar: The Struggle for Scripture and Covenant. 1996. *Vol. II/82.*
Jauhiainen, Marko: The Use of Zechariah in Revelation. 2005. *Vol. II/199.*
Jensen, Morten H.: Herod Antipas in Galilee. 2006. *Vol. II/215.*
Johns, Loren L.: The Lamb Christology of the Apocalypse of John. 2003. *Vol. II/167.*
Jossa, Giorgio: Jews or Christians? 2006. *Vol. 202.*
Joubert, Stephan: Paul as Benefactor. 2000. *Vol. II/124.*
Judge, E. A.: The First Christians in the Roman World. 2008. *Vol. 229.*
Jungbauer, Harry: „Ehre Vater und Mutter". 2002. *Vol. II/146.*
Kähler, Christoph: Jesu Gleichnisse als Poesie und Therapie. 1995. *Vol. 78.*
Kamlah, Ehrhard: Die Form der katalogischen Paränese im Neuen Testament. 1964. *Vol. 7.*
Kammler, Hans-Christian: Christologie und Eschatologie. 2000. *Vol. 126.*
– Kreuz und Weisheit. 2003. *Vol. 159.*

– see *Hofius, Otfried.*
Karakolis, Christos: see *Alexeev, Anatoly A.*
Karrer, Martin und *Wolfgang Kraus* (Ed.): Die Septuaginta – Texte, Kontexte, Lebenswelten. 2008. *Vol. 219.*
Kelhoffer, James A.: The Diet of John the Baptist. 2005. *Vol. 176.*
– Miracle and Mission. 1999. *Vol. II/112.*
Kelley, Nicole: Knowledge and Religious Authority in the Pseudo-Clementines. 2006. *Vol. II/213.*
Kennedy, Joel: The Recapitulation of Israel. 2008. *Vol. II/257.*
Kieffer, René and *Jan Bergman (Ed.)*: La Main de Dieu / Die Hand Gottes. 1997. *Vol. 94.*
Kierspel, Lars: The Jews and the World in the Fourth Gospel. 2006. *Vol. 220.*
Kim, Seyoon: The Origin of Paul's Gospel. 1981, ²1984. *Vol. II/4.*
– Paul and the New Perspective. 2002. *Vol. 140.*
– "The 'Son of Man'" as the Son of God. 1983. *Vol. 30.*
Klauck, Hans-Josef: Religion und Gesellschaft im frühen Christentum. 2003. *Vol. 152.*
Klein, Hans: see *Dunn, James D.G.*
Kleinknecht, Karl Th.: Der leidende Gerechtfertigte. 1984, ²1988. *Vol. II/13.*
Klinghardt, Matthias: Gesetz und Volk Gottes. 1988. *Vol. II/32.*
Kloppenborg, John S.: The Tenants in the Vineyard. 2006. *Vol. 195.*
Koch, Michael: Drachenkampf und Sonnenfrau. 2004. *Vol. II/184.*
Koch, Stefan: Rechtliche Regelung von Konflikten im frühen Christentum. 2004. *Vol. II/174.*
Köhler, Wolf-Dietrich: Rezeption des Matthäusevangeliums in der Zeit vor Irenäus. 1987. *Vol. II/24.*
Köhn, Andreas: Der Neutestamentler Ernst Lohmeyer. 2004. *Vol. II/180.*
Koester, Craig and *Reimund Bieringer* (Ed.): The Resurrection of Jesus in the Gospel of John. 2008. *Vol. 222.*
Konradt, Matthias: Israel, Kirche und die Völker im Matthäusevangelium. 2007. *Vol. 215.*
Kooten, George H. van: Cosmic Christology in Paul and the Pauline School. 2003. *Vol. II/171.*
– Paul's Anthropology in Context. 2008. *Vol. 232.*
Korn, Manfred: Die Geschichte Jesu in veränderter Zeit. 1993. *Vol. II/51.*
Koskenniemi, Erkki: Apollonios von Tyana in der neutestamentlichen Exegese. 1994. *Vol. II/61.*

– The Old Testament Miracle-Workers in Early Judaism. 2005. *Vol. II/206.*
Kraus, Thomas J.: Sprache, Stil und historischer Ort des zweiten Petrusbriefes. 2001. *Vol. II/136.*
Kraus, Wolfgang: Das Volk Gottes. 1996. *Vol. 85.*
– see *Karrer, Martin.*
– see *Walter, Nikolaus.*
– and *Karl-Wilhelm Niebuhr* (Ed.): Frühjudentum und Neues Testament im Horizont Biblischer Theologie. 2003. *Vol. 162.*
Kreplin, Matthias: Das Selbstverständnis Jesu. 2001. *Vol. II/141.*
Kuhn, Karl G.: Achtzehngebet und Vaterunser und der Reim. 1950. *Vol. 1.*
Kvalbein, Hans: see *Ådna, Jostein.*
Kwon, Yon-Gyong: Eschatology in Galatians. 2004. *Vol. II/183.*
Laansma, Jon: I Will Give You Rest. 1997. *Vol. II/98.*
Labahn, Michael: Offenbarung in Zeichen und Wort. 2000. *Vol. II/117.*
Lambers-Petry, Doris: see *Tomson, Peter J.*
Lange, Armin: see *Ego, Beate.*
Lampe, Peter: Die stadtrömischen Christen in den ersten beiden Jahrhunderten. 1987, ²1989. *Vol. II/18.*
Landmesser, Christof: Wahrheit als Grundbegriff neutestamentlicher Wissenschaft. 1999. *Vol. 113.*
– Jüngerberufung und Zuwendung zu Gott. 2000. *Vol. 133.*
Lau, Andrew: Manifest in Flesh. 1996. *Vol. II/86.*
Lawrence, Louise: An Ethnography of the Gospel of Matthew. 2003. *Vol. II/165.*
Lee, Aquila H.I.: From Messiah to Preexistent Son. 2005. *Vol. II/192.*
Lee, Pilchan: The New Jerusalem in the Book of Relevation. 2000. *Vol. II/129.*
Lichtenberger, Hermann: Das Ich Adams und das Ich der Menschheit. 2004. *Vol. 164.*
– see *Avemarie, Friedrich.*
Lierman, John: The New Testament Moses. 2004. *Vol. II/173.*
– (Ed.): Challenging Perspectives on the Gospel of John. 2006. *Vol. II/219.*
Lieu, Samuel N.C.: Manichaeism in the Later Roman Empire and Medieval China. ²1992. *Vol. 63.*
Lindgård, Fredrik: Paul's Line of Thought in 2 Corinthians 4:16–5:10. 2004. *Vol. II/189.*
Loader, William R.G.: Jesus' Attitude Towards the Law. 1997. *Vol. II/97.*
Löhr, Gebhard: Verherrlichung Gottes durch Philosophie. 1997. *Vol. 97.*

Löhr, Hermut: Studien zum frühchristlichen und frühjüdischen Gebet. 2003. *Vol. 160.*
– see *Hengel, Martin.*
Löhr, Winrich Alfried: Basilides und seine Schule. 1995. *Vol. 83.*
Lorenzen, Stefanie: Das paulinische Eikon-Konzept. 2008. *Vol. II/250.*
Luomanen, Petri: Entering the Kingdom of Heaven. 1998. *Vol. II/101.*
Luz, Ulrich: see *Alexeev, Anatoly A.*
– see *Dunn, James D.G.*
Mackay, Ian D.: John's Raltionship with Mark. 2004. *Vol. II/182.*
Mackie, Scott D.: Eschatology and Exhortation in the Epistle to the Hebrews. 2006. *Vol. II/223.*
Maier, Gerhard: Mensch und freier Wille. 1971. *Vol. 12.*
– Die Johannesoffenbarung und die Kirche. 1981. *Vol. 25.*
Markschies, Christoph: Valentinus Gnosticus? 1992. *Vol. 65.*
Marshall, Peter: Enmity in Corinth: Social Conventions in Paul's Relations with the Corinthians. 1987. *Vol. II/23.*
Martin, Dale B.: see *Zangenberg, Jürgen.*
Mayer, Annemarie: Sprache der Einheit im Epheserbrief und in der Ökumene. 2002. *Vol. II/150.*
Mayordomo, Moisés: Argumentiert Paulus logisch? 2005. *Vol. 188.*
McDonough, Sean M.: YHWH at Patmos: Rev. 1:4 in its Hellenistic and Early Jewish Setting. 1999. *Vol. II/107.*
McDowell, Markus: Prayers of Jewish Women. 2006. *Vol. II/211.*
McGlynn, Moyna: Divine Judgement and Divine Benevolence in the Book of Wisdom. 2001. *Vol. II/139.*
Meade, David G.: Pseudonymity and Canon. 1986. *Vol. 39.*
Meadors, Edward P.: Jesus the Messianic Herald of Salvation. 1995. *Vol. II/72.*
Meißner, Stefan: Die Heimholung des Ketzers. 1996. *Vol. II/87.*
Mell, Ulrich: Die „anderen" Winzer. 1994. *Vol. 77.*
– see *Sänger, Dieter.*
Mengel, Berthold: Studien zum Philipperbrief. 1982. *Vol. II/8.*
Merkel, Helmut: Die Widersprüche zwischen den Evangelien. 1971. *Vol. 13.*
– see *Ego, Beate.*
Merklein, Helmut: Studien zu Jesus und Paulus. Vol. 1 1987. *Vol. 43.* – Vol. 2 1998. *Vol. 105.*
Metzdorf, Christina: Die Tempelaktion Jesu. 2003. *Vol. II/168.*

Metzler, Karin: Der griechische Begriff des Verzeihens. 1991. *Vol. II/44.*

Metzner, Rainer: Die Rezeption des Matthäusevangeliums im 1. Petrusbrief. 1995. *Vol. II/74.*

– Das Verständnis der Sünde im Johannesevangelium. 2000. *Vol. 122.*

Mihoc, Vasile: see *Dunn, James D.G..*

Mineshige, Kiyoshi: Besitzverzicht und Almosen bei Lukas. 2003. *Vol. II/163.*

Mittmann, Siegfried: see *Hengel, Martin.*

Mittmann-Richert, Ulrike: Magnifikat und Benediktus. *1996. Vol. II/90.*

– Der Sühnetod des Gottesknechts. 2008. *Vol. 220.*

Miura, Yuzuru: David in Luke-Acts. 2007. *Vol. II/232.*

Mournet, Terence C.: Oral Tradition and Literary Dependency. 2005. *Vol. II/195.*

Mußner, Franz: Jesus von Nazareth im Umfeld Israels und der Urkirche. Ed. von M. Theobald. 1998. *Vol. 111.*

Mutschler, Bernhard: Das Corpus Johanneum bei Irenäus von Lyon. 2005. *Vol. 189.*

Nguyen, V. Henry T.: Christian Identity in Corinth. 2008. *Vol. II/243.*

Niebuhr, Karl-Wilhelm: Gesetz und Paränese. 1987. *Vol. II/28.*

– Heidenapostel aus Israel. 1992. *Vol. 62.*

– see *Deines, Roland*

– see *Dimitrov, Ivan Z.*

– see *Kraus, Wolfgang*

Nielsen, Anders E.: "Until it is Fullfilled". 2000. *Vol. II/126.*

Nissen, Andreas: Gott und der Nächste im antiken Judentum. 1974. *Vol. 15.*

Noack, Christian: Gottesbewußtsein. 2000. *Vol. II/116.*

Noormann, Rolf: Irenäus als Paulusinterpret. 1994. *Vol. II/66.*

Novakovic, Lidija: Messiah, the Healer of the Sick. 2003. *Vol. II/170.*

Obermann, Andreas: Die christologische Erfüllung der Schrift im Johannesevangelium. 1996. *Vol. II/83.*

Öhler, Markus: Barnabas. 2003. *Vol. 156.*

– see *Becker, Michael.*

Okure, Teresa: The Johannine Approach to Mission. 1988. *Vol. II/31.*

Onuki, Takashi: Heil und Erlösung. 2004. *Vol. 165.*

Oropeza, B. J.: Paul and Apostasy. 2000. *Vol. II/115.*

Ostmeyer, Karl-Heinrich: Kommunikation mit Gott und Christus. 2006. *Vol. 197.*

– Taufe und Typos. 2000. *Vol. II/118.*

Paulsen, Henning: Studien zur Literatur und Geschichte des frühen Christentums. Ed. von Ute E. Eisen. 1997. *Vol. 99.*

Pao, David W.: Acts and the Isaianic New Exodus. 2000. *Vol. II/130.*

Park, Eung Chun: The Mission Discourse in Matthew's Interpretation. 1995. *Vol. II/81.*

Park, Joseph S.: Conceptions of Afterlife in Jewish Insriptions. 2000. *Vol. II/121.*

Pate, C. Marvin: The Reverse of the Curse. 2000. *Vol. II/114.*

Pearce, Sarah J.K.: The Land of the Body. 2007. *Vol. 208.*

Peres, Imre: Griechische Grabinschriften und neutestamentliche Eschatologie. 2003. *Vol. 157.*

Philip, Finny: The Origins of Pauline Pneumatology. 2005. *Vol. II/194.*

Philonenko, Marc (Ed.): Le Trône de Dieu. 1993. *Vol. 69.*

Pilhofer, Peter: Presbyteron Kreitton. 1990. *Vol. II/39.*

– Philippi. Vol. 1 1995. *Vol. 87.* – Vol. 2 2000. *Vol. 119.*

– Die frühen Christen und ihre Welt. 2002. *Vol. 145.*

– see *Becker, Eve-Marie.*

– see *Ego, Beate.*

Pitre, Brant: Jesus, the Tribulation, and the End of the Exile. 2005. *Vol. II/204.*

Plümacher, Eckhard: Geschichte und Geschichten. 2004. *Vol. 170.*

Pöhlmann, Wolfgang: Der Verlorene Sohn und das Haus. 1993. *Vol. 68.*

Pokorný, Petr and *Josef B. Souček:* Bibelauslegung als Theologie. 1997. *Vol. 100.*

– and *Jan Roskovec* (Ed.): Philosophical Hermeneutics and Biblical Exegesis. 2002. *Vol. 153.*

Popkes, Enno Edzard: Das Menschenbild des Thomasevangeliums. 2007. *Vol. 206.*

– Die Theologie der Liebe Gottes in den johanneischen Schriften. 2005. *Vol. II/197.*

Porter, Stanley E.: The Paul of Acts. 1999. *Vol. 115.*

Prieur, Alexander: Die Verkündigung der Gottesherrschaft. 1996. *Vol. II/89.*

Probst, Hermann: Paulus und der Brief. 1991. *Vol. II/45.*

Räisänen, Heikki: Paul and the Law. 1983, ²1987. *Vol. 29.*

Rehkopf, Friedrich: Die lukanische Sonderquelle. 1959. *Vol. 5.*

Rein, Matthias: Die Heilung des Blindgeborenen (Joh 9). 1995. *Vol. II/73.*

Reinmuth, Eckart: Pseudo-Philo und Lukas. 1994. *Vol. 74.*

Reiser, Marius: Bibelkritik und Auslegung der Heiligen Schrift. 2007. *Vol. 217.*
– Syntax und Stil des Markusevangeliums. 1984. *Vol. II/11.*
Reynolds, Benjamin E.: The Apocalyptic Son of Man in the Gospel of John. 2008. *Vol. II/249.*
Rhodes, James N.: The Epistle of Barnabas and the Deuteronomic Tradition. 2004. *Vol. II/188.*
Richards, E. Randolph: The Secretary in the Letters of Paul. 1991. *Vol. II/42.*
Riesner, Rainer: Jesus als Lehrer. 1981, ³1988. *Vol. II/7.*
– Die Frühzeit des Apostels Paulus. 1994. *Vol. 71.*
Rissi, Mathias: Die Theologie des Hebräerbriefs. 1987. *Vol. 41.*
Roskovec, Jan: see *Pokorný, Petr.*
Röhser, Günter: Metaphorik und Personifikation der Sünde. 1987. *Vol. II/25.*
Rose, Christian: Theologie als Erzählung im Markusevangelium. 2007. *Vol. II/236.*
– Die Wolke der Zeugen. 1994. *Vol. II/60.*
Rothschild, Clare K.: Baptist Traditions and Q. 2005. *Vol. 190.*
– Luke Acts and the Rhetoric of History. 2004. *Vol. II/175.*
Rüegger, Hans-Ulrich: Verstehen, was Markus erzählt. 2002. *Vol. II/155.*
Rüger, Hans Peter: Die Weisheitsschrift aus der Kairoer Geniza. 1991. *Vol. 53.*
Sänger, Dieter: Antikes Judentum und die Mysterien. 1980. *Vol. II/5.*
– Die Verkündigung des Gekreuzigten und Israel. 1994. *Vol. 75.*
– see *Burchard, Christoph*
– and *Ulrich Mell* (Ed.): Paulus und Johannes. 2006. *Vol. 198.*
Salier, Willis Hedley: The Rhetorical Impact of the Semeia in the Gospel of John. 2004. *Vol. II/186.*
Salzmann, Jorg Christian: Lehren und Ermahnen. 1994. *Vol. II/59.*
Sandnes, Karl Olav: Paul – One of the Prophets? 1991. *Vol. II/43.*
Sato, Migaku: Q und Prophetie. 1988. *Vol. II/29.*
Schäfer, Ruth: Paulus bis zum Apostelkonzil. 2004. *Vol. II/179.*
Schaper, Joachim: Eschatology in the Greek Psalter. 1995. *Vol. II/76.*
Schimanowski, Gottfried: Die himmlische Liturgie in der Apokalypse des Johannes. 2002. *Vol. II/154.*
– Weisheit und Messias. 1985. *Vol. II/17.*
Schlichting, Günter: Ein jüdisches Leben Jesu. 1982. *Vol. 24.*
Schließer, Benjamin: Abraham's Faith in Romans 4. 2007. *Vol. II/224.*

Schnabel, Eckhard J.: Law and Wisdom from Ben Sira to Paul. 1985. *Vol. II/16.*
Schnelle, Udo: see *Frey, Jörg.*
Schröter, Jens: Von Jesus zum Neuen Testament. 2007. *Vol. 204.*
– see *Frey, Jörg.*
Schutter, William L.: Hermeneutic and Composition in I Peter. 1989. *Vol. II/30.*
Schwartz, Daniel R.: Studies in the Jewish Background of Christianity. 1992. *Vol. 60.*
Schwemer, Anna Maria: see *Hengel, Martin*
Scott, Ian W.: Implicit Epistemology in the Letters of Paul. 2005. *Vol. II/205.*
Scott, James M.: Adoption as Sons of God. 1992. *Vol. II/48.*
– Paul and the Nations. 1995. *Vol. 84.*
Shi, Wenhua: Paul's Message of the Cross as Body Language. 2008. *Vol. II/254.*
Shum, Shiu-Lun: Paul's Use of Isaiah in Romans. 2002. *Vol. II/156.*
Siegert, Folker: Drei hellenistisch-jüdische Predigten. Teil I 1980. *Vol. 20* – Teil II 1992. *Vol. 61.*
– Nag-Hammadi-Register. 1982. *Vol. 26.*
– Argumentation bei Paulus. 1985. *Vol. 34.*
– Philon von Alexandrien. 1988. *Vol. 46.*
Simon, Marcel: Le christianisme antique et son contexte religieux I/II. 1981. *Vol. 23.*
Smit, Peter-Ben: Fellowship and Food in the Kingdom. 2008. *Vol. II/234.*
Snodgrass, Klyne: The Parable of the Wicked Tenants. 1983. *Vol. 27.*
Söding, Thomas: Das Wort vom Kreuz. 1997. *Vol. 93.*
– see *Thüsing, Wilhelm.*
Sommer, Urs: Die Passionsgeschichte des Markusevangeliums. 1993. *Vol. II/58.*
Sorensen, Eric: Possession and Exorcism in the New Testament and Early Christianity. 2002. *Vol. II/157.*
Souček, Josef B.: see *Pokorný, Petr.*
Southall, David J.: Rediscovering Righteousness in Romans. 2008. *Vol. 240.*
Spangenberg, Volker: Herrlichkeit des Neuen Bundes. 1993. *Vol. II/55.*
Spanje, T.E. van: Inconsistency in Paul? 1999. *Vol. II/110.*
Speyer, Wolfgang: Frühes Christentum im antiken Strahlungsfeld. Vol. I: 1989. *Vol. 50.*
– Vol. II: 1999. *Vol. 116.*
– Vol. III: 2007. *Vol. 213.*
Spittler, Janet E.: Animals in the Apocryphal Acts of the Apostles. 2008. *Vol. II/247.*
Sprinkle, Preston: Law and Life. 2008. *Vol. II/241.*
Stadelmann, Helge: Ben Sira als Schriftgelehrter. 1980. *Vol. II/6.*
Stein, Hans Joachim: Frühchristliche Mahlfeiern. 2008. *Vol. II/255.*

Stenschke, Christoph W.: Luke's Portrait of Gentiles Prior to Their Coming to Faith. *Vol. II/108.*

Sterck-Degueldre, Jean-Pierre: Eine Frau namens Lydia. 2004. *Vol. II/176.*

Stettler, Christian: Der Kolosserhymnus. 2000. *Vol. II/131.*

Stettler, Hanna: Die Christologie der Pastoralbriefe. 1998. *Vol. II/105.*

Stökl Ben Ezra, Daniel: The Impact of Yom Kippur on Early Christianity. 2003. *Vol. 163.*

Strobel, August: Die Stunde der Wahrheit. 1980. *Vol. 21.*

Stroumsa, Guy G.: Barbarian Philosophy. 1999. *Vol. 112.*

Stuckenbruck, Loren T.: Angel Veneration and Christology. 1995. *Vol. II/70.*

–, *Stephen C. Barton* and *Benjamin G. Wold* (Ed.): Memory in the Bible and Antiquity. 2007. *Vol. 212.*

Stuhlmacher, Peter (Ed.): Das Evangelium und die Evangelien. 1983. *Vol. 28.*

– Biblische Theologie und Evangelium. 2002. *Vol. 146.*

Sung, Chong-Hyon: Vergebung der Sünden. 1993. *Vol. II/57.*

Tajra, Harry W.: The Trial of St. Paul. 1989. *Vol. II/35.*

– The Martyrdom of St.Paul. 1994. *Vol. II/67.*

Theißen, Gerd: Studien zur Soziologie des Urchristentums. 1979, ³1989. *Vol. 19.*

Theobald, Michael: Studien zum Römerbrief. 2001. *Vol. 136.*

Theobald, Michael: see *Mußner, Franz.*

Thornton, Claus-Jürgen: Der Zeuge des Zeugen. 1991. *Vol. 56.*

Thüsing, Wilhelm: Studien zur neutestamentlichen Theologie. Ed. von Thomas Söding. 1995. *Vol. 82.*

Thurén, Lauri: Derhethorizing Paul. 2000. *Vol. 124.*

Thyen, Hartwig: Studien zum Corpus Iohanneum. 2007. *Vol. 214.*

Tibbs, Clint: Religious Experience of the Pneuma. 2007. *Vol. II/230.*

Toit, David S. du: Theios Anthropos. 1997. *Vol. II/91.*

Tolmie, D. Francois: Persuading the Galatians. 2005. *Vol. II/190.*

Tomson, Peter J. and *Doris Lambers-Petry* (Ed.): The Image of the Judaeo-Christians in Ancient Jewish and Christian Literature. 2003. *Vol. 158.*

Toney, Carl N.: Paul's Inclusive Ethic. 2008. *Vol. II/252.*

Trebilco, Paul: The Early Christians in Ephesus from Paul to Ignatius. 2004. *Vol. 166.*

Treloar, Geoffrey R.: Lightfoot the Historian. 1998. *Vol. II/103.*

Tsuji, Manabu: Glaube zwischen Vollkommenheit und Verweltlichung. 1997. *Vol. II/93.*

Twelftree, Graham H.: Jesus the Exorcist. 1993. *Vol. II/54.*

Ulrichs, Karl Friedrich: Christusglaube. 2007. *Vol. II/227.*

Urban, Christina: Das Menschenbild nach dem Johannesevangelium. 2001. *Vol. II/137.*

Vahrenhorst, Martin: Kultische Sprache in den Paulusbriefen. 2008. *Vol. 230.*

Vegge, Ivar: 2 Corinthians – a Letter about Reconciliation. 2008. *Vol. II/239.*

Visotzky, Burton L.: Fathers of the World. 1995. *Vol. 80.*

Vollenweider, Samuel: Horizonte neutestamentlicher Christologie. 2002. *Vol. 144.*

Vos, Johan S.: Die Kunst der Argumentation bei Paulus. 2002. *Vol. 149.*

Waaler, Erik: The *Shema* and The First Commandment in First Corinthians. 2008. *Vol. II/253.*

Wagener, Ulrike: Die Ordnung des „Hauses Gottes". 1994. *Vol. II/65.*

Wahlen, Clinton: Jesus and the Impurity of Spirits in the Synoptic Gospels. 2004. *Vol. II/185.*

Walker, Donald D.: Paul's Offer of Leniency (2 Cor 10:1). 2002. *Vol. II/152.*

Walter, Nikolaus: Praeparatio Evangelica. Ed. von Wolfgang Kraus und Florian Wilk. 1997. *Vol. 98.*

Wander, Bernd: Gottesfürchtige und Sympathisanten. 1998. *Vol. 104.*

Wasserman, Emma: The Death of the Soul in Romans 7. 2008. *Vol. 256.*

Waters, Guy: The End of Deuteronomy in the Epistles of Paul. 2006. *Vol. 221.*

Watt, Jan G. van der: see *Frey, Jörg.*

Watts, Rikki: Isaiah's New Exodus and Mark. 1997. *Vol. II/88.*

Wedderburn, A.J.M.: Baptism and Resurrection. 1987. *Vol. 44.*

Wegner, Uwe: Der Hauptmann von Kafarnaum. 1985. *Vol. II/14.*

Weiß, Hans-Friedrich: Frühes Christentum und Gnosis. 2008. *Vol. 225.*

Weissenrieder, Annette: Images of Illness in the Gospel of Luke. 2003. *Vol. II/164.*

–, *Friederike Wendt* and *Petra von Gemünden* (Ed.): Picturing the New Testament. 2005. *Vol. II/193.*

Welck, Christian: Erzählte ‚Zeichen'. 1994. *Vol. II/69.*

Wendt, Friederike (Ed.): see *Weissenrieder, Annette.*

Wiarda, Timothy: Peter in the Gospels. 2000. *Vol. II/127.*

Wifstrand, Albert: Epochs and Styles. 2005. *Vol. 179.*

Wilk, Florian: see *Walter, Nikolaus.*

Williams, Catrin H.: I am He. 2000. *Vol. II/113.*

Wilson, Todd A.: The Curse of the Law and the Crisis in Galatia. 2007. *Vol. II/225.*

Wilson, Walter T.: Love without Pretense. 1991. *Vol. II/46.*

Winn, Adam: The Purpose of Mark's Gospel. 2008. *Vol. II/245.*

Winninge, Mikael: see *Holmberg, Bengt.*

Wischmeyer, Oda: Von Ben Sira zu Paulus. 2004. *Vol. 173.*

Wisdom, Jeffrey: Blessing for the Nations and the Curse of the Law. 2001. *Vol. II/133.*

Witmer, Stephen E.: Divine Instruction in Early Christianity. 2008. *Vol. II/246.*

Wold, Benjamin G.: Women, Men, and Angels. 2005. *Vol. II/2001.*

– see *Stuckenbruck, Loren T.*

Wright, Archie T.: The Origin of Evil Spirits. 2005. *Vol. II/198.*

Wucherpfennig, Ansgar: Heracleon Philologus. 2002. *Vol. 142.*

Yates, John W.: The Spirit and Creation in Paul. 2008. *Vol. II/251.*

Yeung, Maureen: Faith in Jesus and Paul. 2002. *Vol. II/147.*

Zangenberg, Jürgen, Harold W. Attridge and *Dale B. Martin* (Ed.): Religion, Ethnicity and Identity in Ancient Galilee. 2007. *Vol. 210.*

Zimmermann, Alfred E.: Die urchristlichen Lehrer. 1984, ²1988. *Vol. II/12.*

Zimmermann, Johannes: Messianische Texte aus Qumran. 1998. *Vol. II/104.*

Zimmermann, Ruben: Christologie der Bilder im Johannesevangelium. 2004. *Vol. 171.*

– Geschlechtermetaphorik und Gottesverhältnis. 2001. *Vol. II/122.*

– (Ed.): Hermeneutik der Gleichnisse Jesu. 2008. *Vol. 231.*

– see *Frey, Jörg*

Zumstein, Jean: see *Dettwiler, Andreas*

Zwiep, Arie W.: Judas and the Choice of Matthias. 2004. *Vol. II/187.*

For a complete catalogue please write to the publisher
Mohr Siebeck • P.O. Box 2030 • D–72010 Tübingen/Germany
Up-to-date information on the internet at www.mohr.de